2

KÖNIGLICHE FAMILIE LEHRER

Higasa Akai

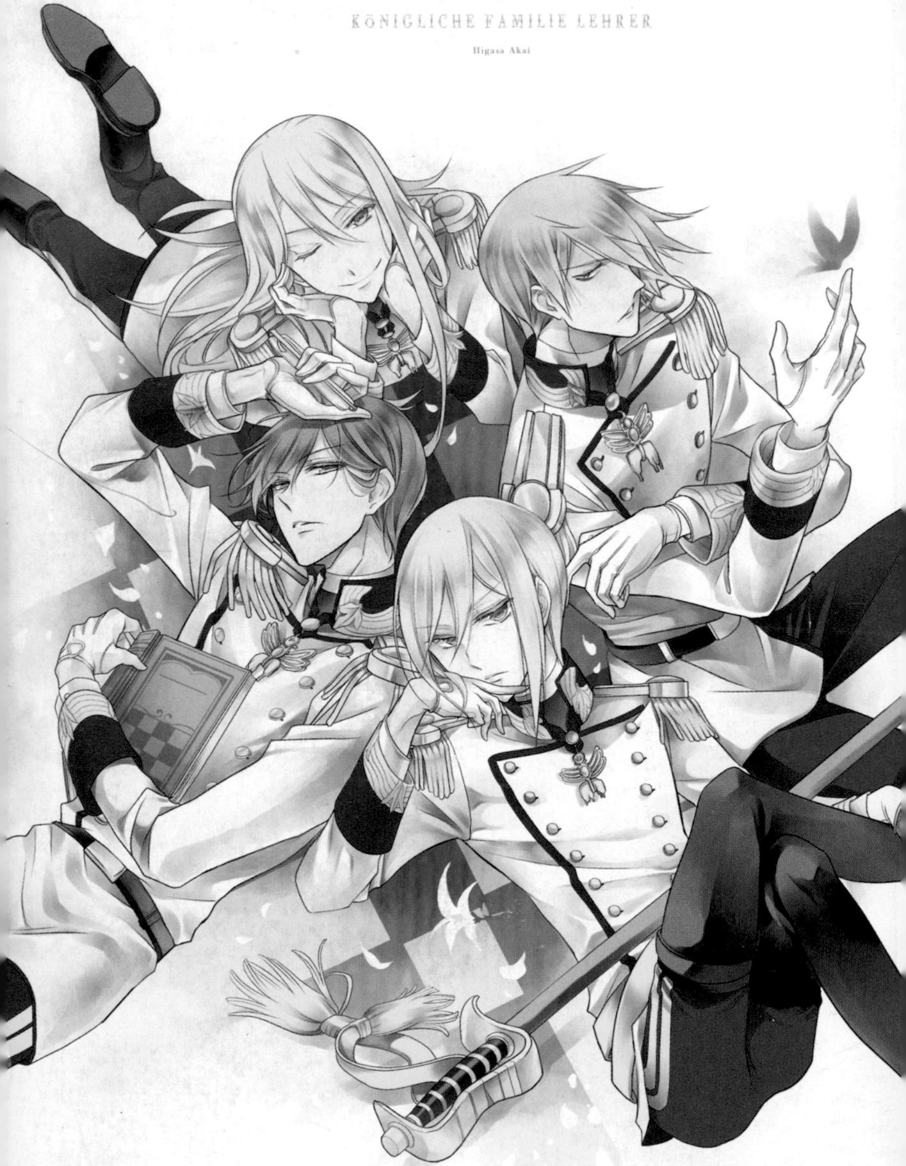

CONTENTS

KÖNIGLICHE TAGEBÜCHER

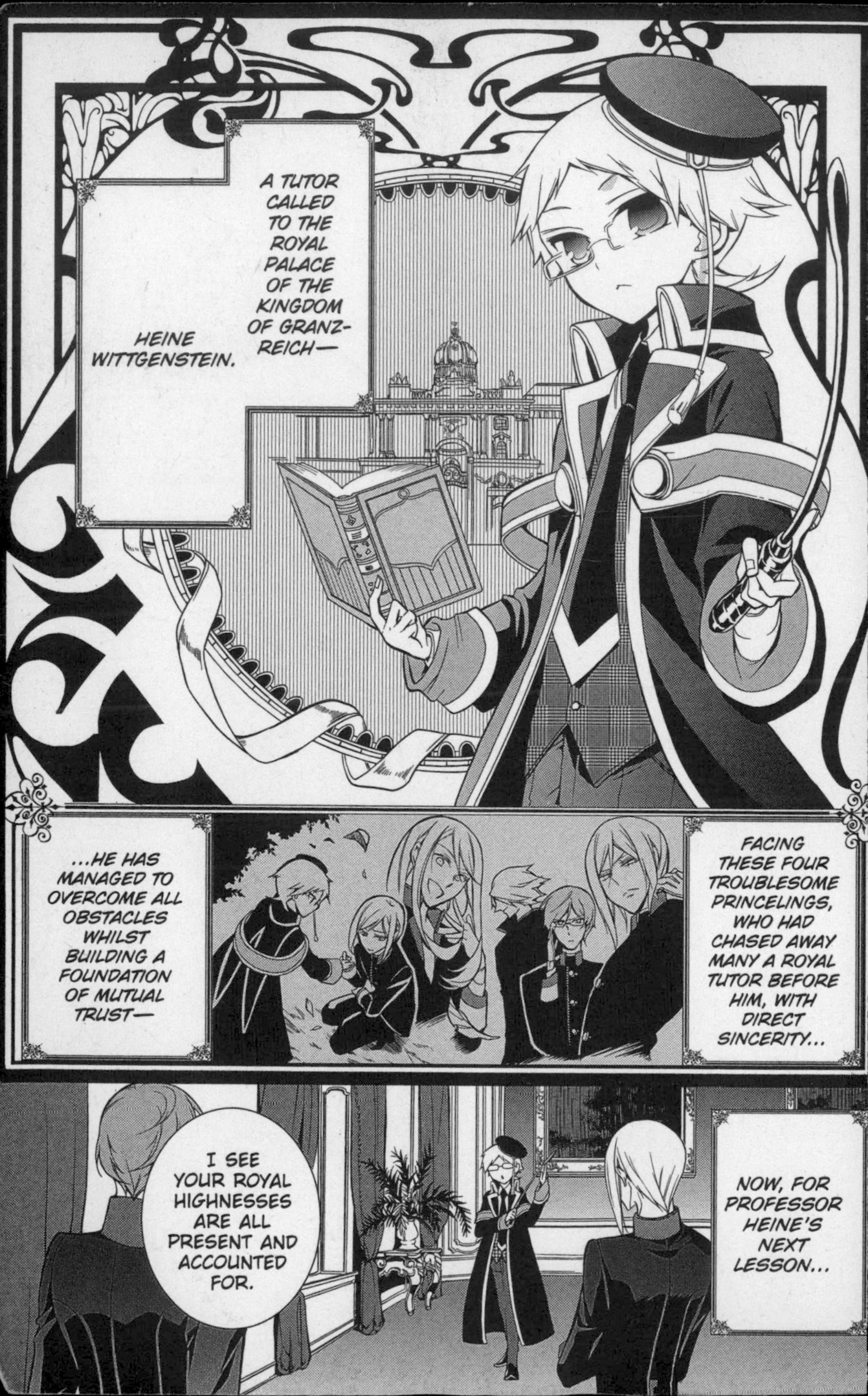
A TUTOR CALLED TO THE ROYAL PALACE OF THE KINGDOM OF GRANZ-REICH—
HEINE WITTGENSTEIN.
FACING THESE FOUR TROUBLESOME PRINCELINGS, WHO HAD CHASED AWAY MANY A ROYAL TUTOR BEFORE HIM, WITH DIRECT SINCERITY...
...HE HAS MANAGED TO OVERCOME ALL OBSTACLES WHILST BUILDING A FOUNDATION OF MUTUAL TRUST—
NOW, FOR PROFESSOR HEINE'S NEXT LESSON...
I SEE YOUR ROYAL HIGHNESSES ARE ALL PRESENT AND ACCOUNTED FOR.

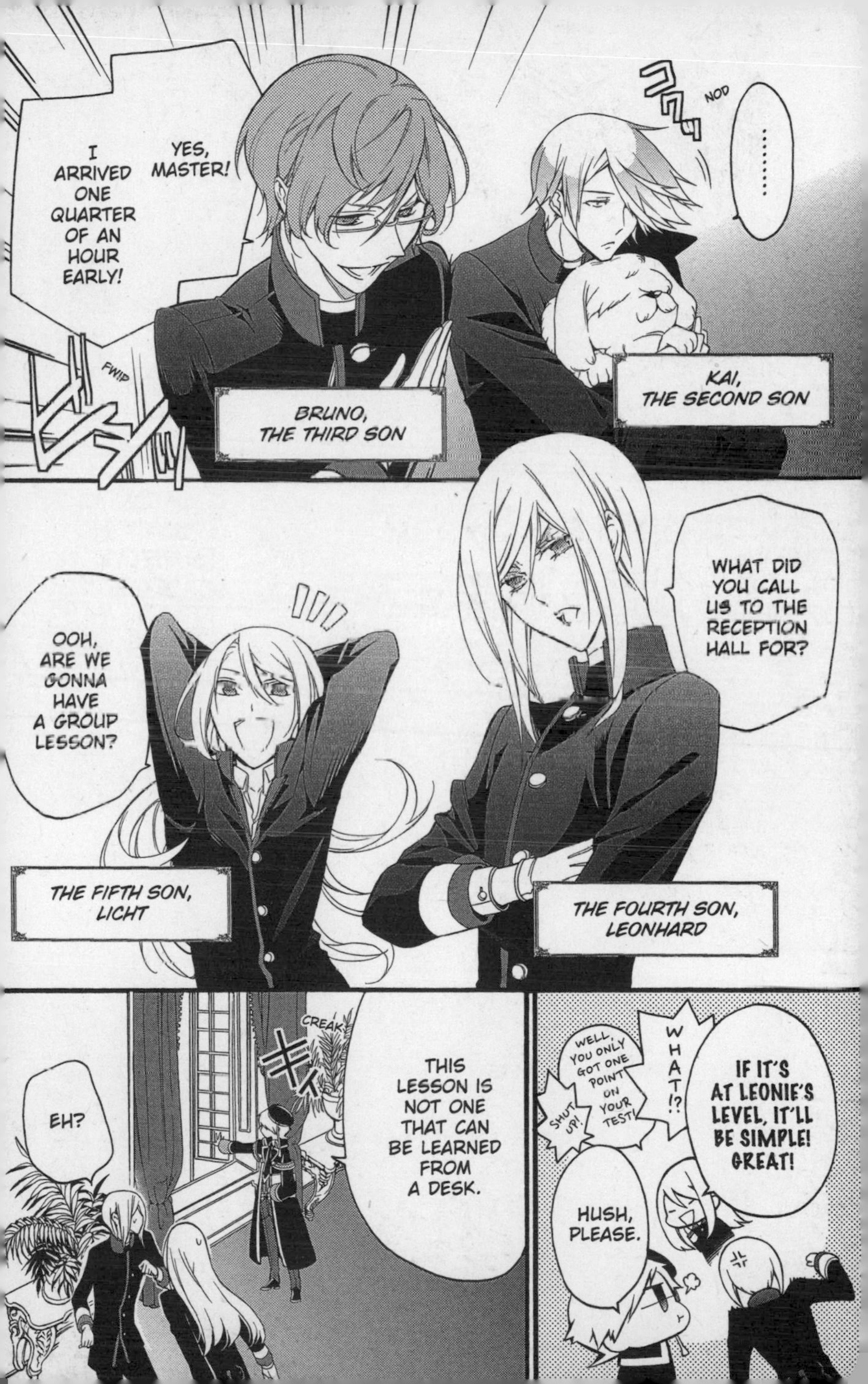

......
NOD
YES, MASTER!
I ARRIVED ONE QUARTER OF AN HOUR EARLY!
KAI, THE SECOND SON
BRUNO, THE THIRD SON
FWIP
WHAT DID YOU CALL US TO THE RECEPTION HALL FOR?
THE FOURTH SON, LEONHARD
OOH, ARE WE GONNA HAVE A GROUP LESSON?
THE FIFTH SON, LICHT
IF IT'S AT LEONIE'S LEVEL, IT'LL BE SIMPLE! GREAT!
WHAT!?
WELL, YOU ONLY GOT ONE POINT ON YOUR TEST!
SHUT UP!
HUSH, PLEASE.
CREAK
THIS LESSON IS NOT ONE THAT CAN BE LEARNED FROM A DESK.
EH?

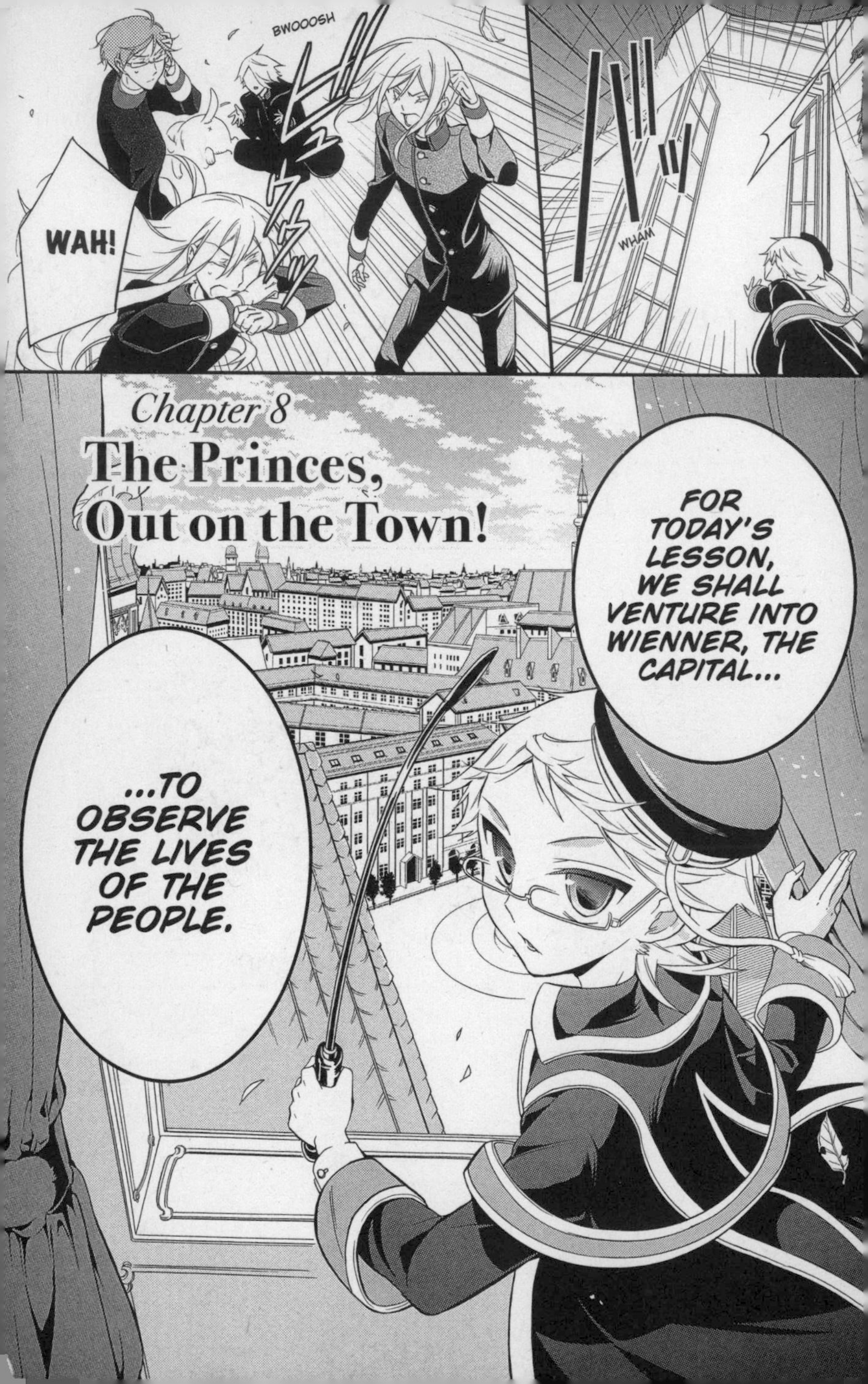
WHAM
BWOOOSH
WAH!
Chapter 8
The Princes, Out on the Town!
FOR TODAY'S LESSON, WE SHALL VENTURE INTO WIENNER, THE CAPITAL...
...TO OBSERVE THE LIVES OF THE PEOPLE.

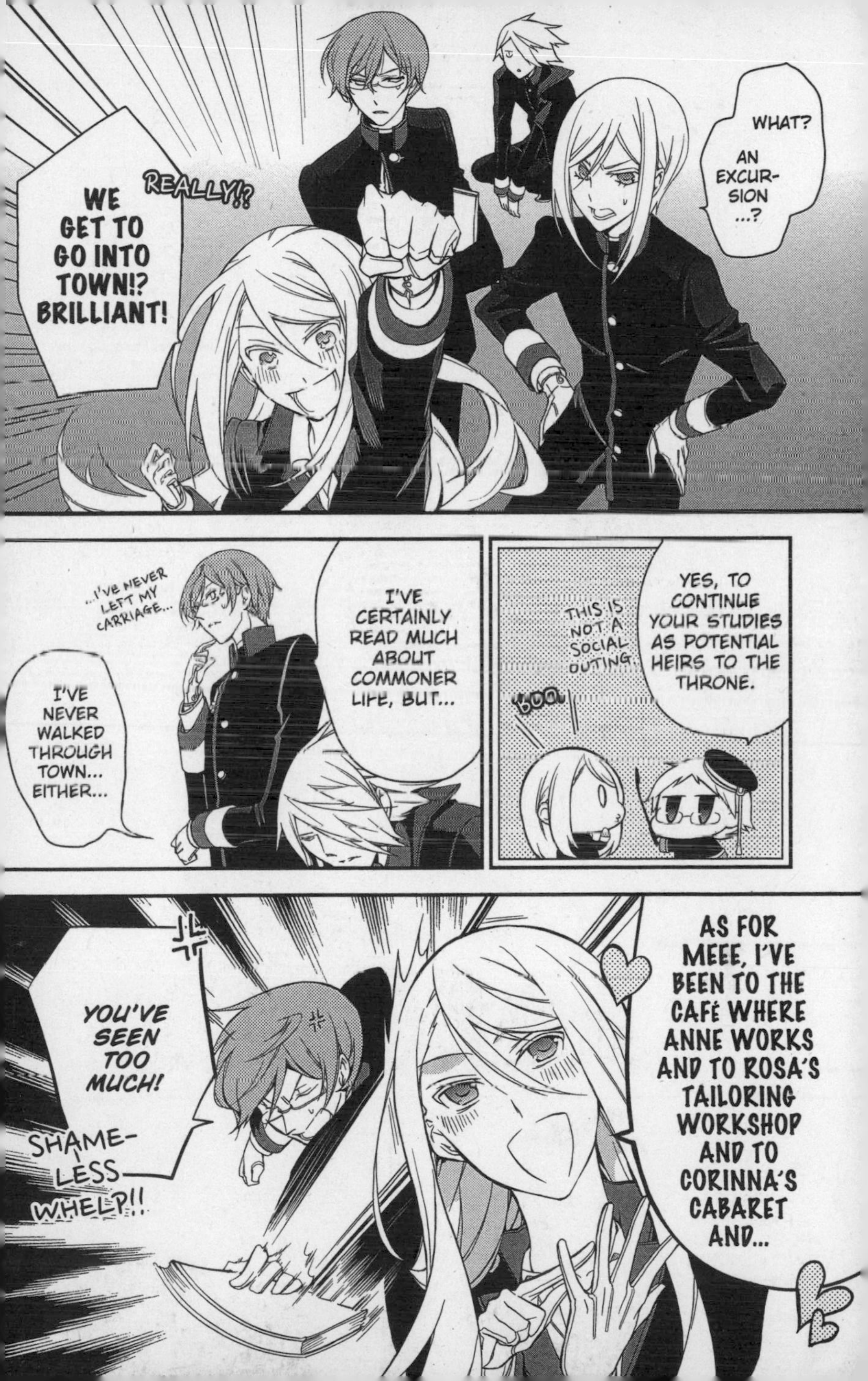
WHAT? AN EXCURSION...?
REALLY!?
WE GET TO GO INTO TOWN!? BRILLIANT!
YES, TO CONTINUE YOUR STUDIES AS POTENTIAL HEIRS TO THE THRONE.
THIS IS NOT A SOCIAL OUTING.
BOO!
I'VE CERTAINLY READ MUCH ABOUT COMMONER LIFE, BUT...
...I'VE NEVER LEFT MY CARRIAGE...
I'VE NEVER WALKED THROUGH TOWN... EITHER...
AS FOR MEEE, I'VE BEEN TO THE CAFÉ WHERE ANNE WORKS AND TO ROSA'S TAILORING WORKSHOP AND TO CORINNA'S CABARET AND...
YOU'VE SEEN TOO MUCH!
SHAME-LESS WHELP!!

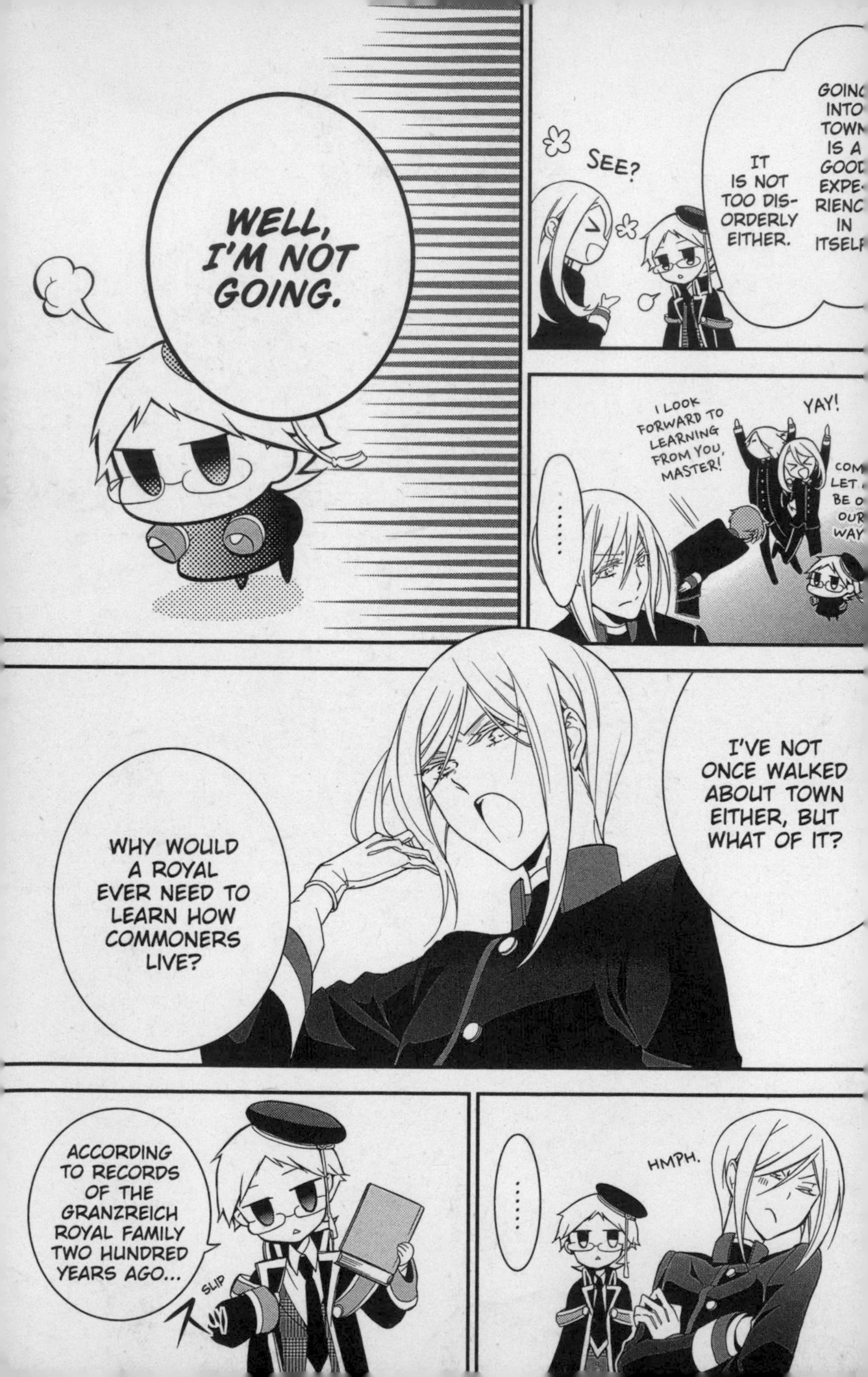
GOIN INTO TOW IS A GOO EXPE- RIEN IN ITSEL
IT IS NOT TOO DIS-ORDERLY EITHER.
SEE?
YAY!
COM LET BE O OUR WAY
I LOOK FORWARD TO LEARNING FROM YOU, MASTER!
……
WELL, I'M NOT GOING.
I'VE NOT ONCE WALKED ABOUT TOWN EITHER, BUT WHAT OF IT?
WHY WOULD A ROYAL EVER NEED TO LEARN HOW COMMONERS LIVE?
HMPH.
……
ACCORDING TO RECORDS OF THE GRANZREICH ROYAL FAMILY TWO HUNDRED YEARS AGO...
SLIP

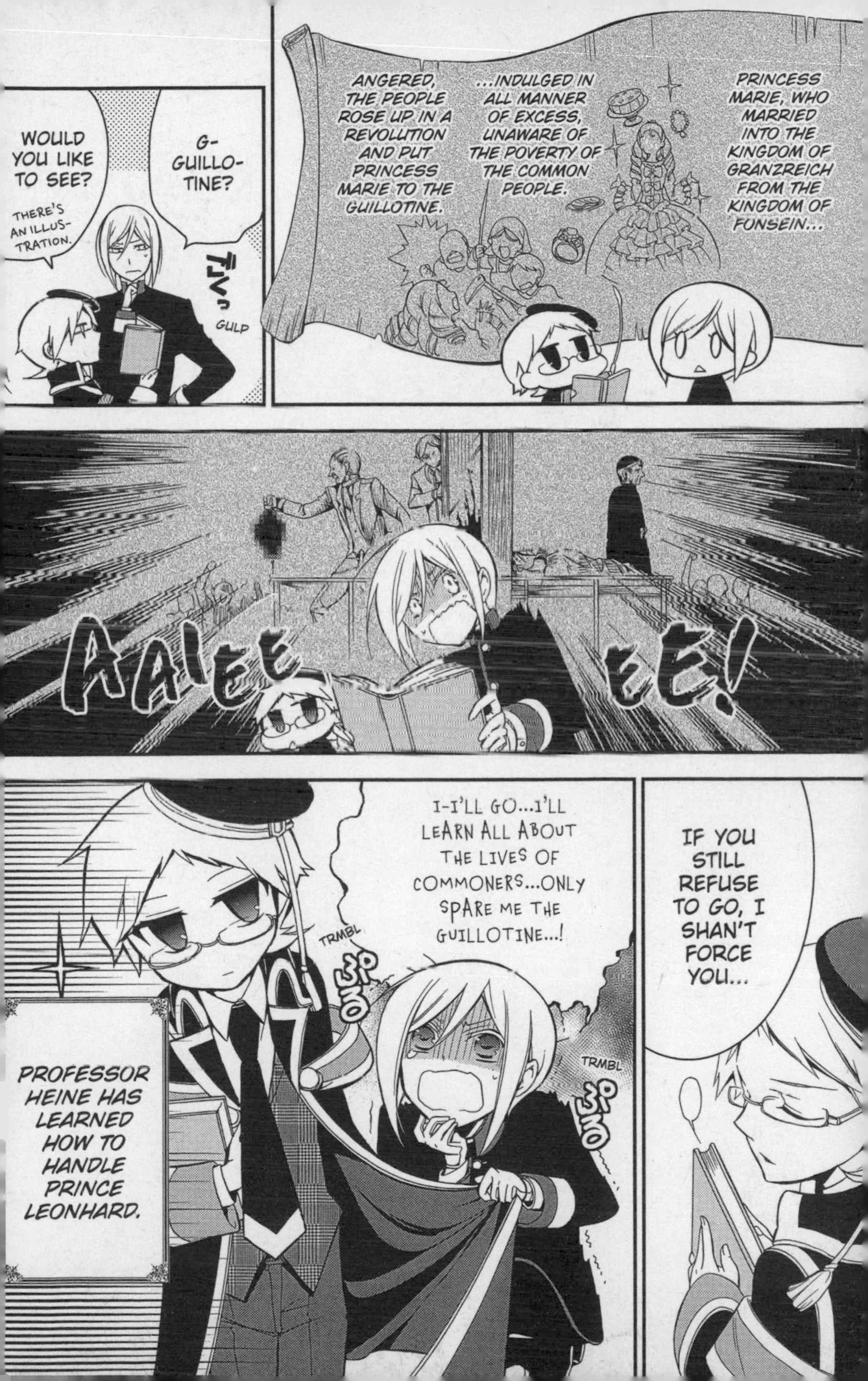
PRINCESS MARIE, WHO MARRIED INTO THE KINGDOM OF GRANZREICH FROM THE KINGDOM OF FONSEIN...
...INDULGED IN ALL MANNER OF EXCESS, UNAWARE OF THE POVERTY OF THE COMMON PEOPLE.
ANGERED, THE PEOPLE ROSE UP IN A REVOLUTION AND PUT PRINCESS MARIE TO THE GUILLOTINE.
G-GUILLOTINE?
WOULD YOU LIKE TO SEE?
THERE'S AN ILLUSTRATION.
GULP
AAIEE
EE!
IF YOU STILL REFUSE TO GO, I SHAN'T FORCE YOU...
I-I'LL GO...I'LL LEARN ALL ABOUT THE LIVES OF COMMONERS...ONLY SPARE ME THE GUILLOTINE...!
TRMBL
TRMBL
PROFESSOR HEINE HAS LEARNED HOW TO HANDLE PRINCE LEONHARD.

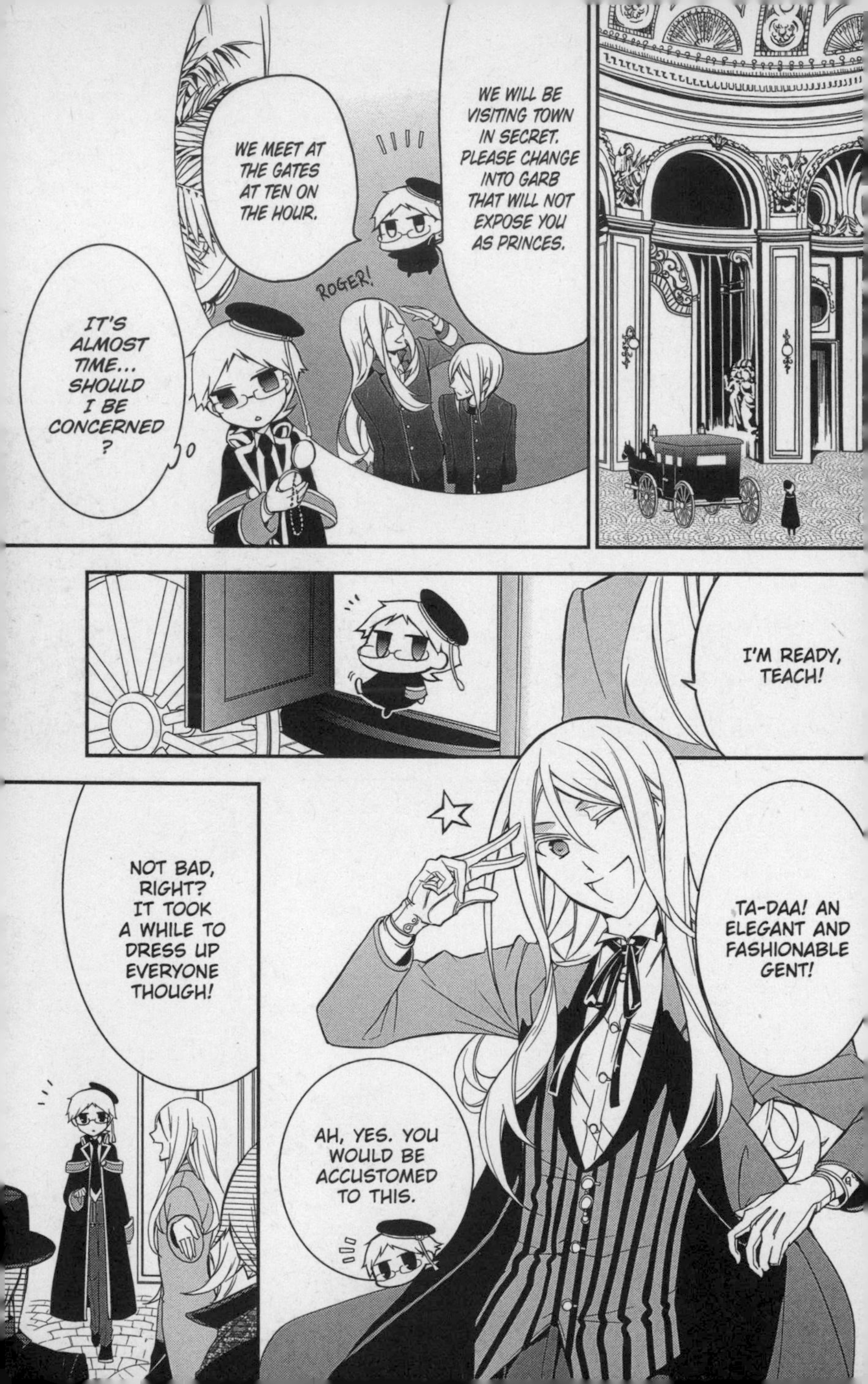
WE WILL BE VISITING TOWN IN SECRET. PLEASE CHANGE INTO GARB THAT WILL NOT EXPOSE YOU AS PRINCES.
WE MEET AT THE GATES AT TEN ON THE HOUR.
ROGER!
IT'S ALMOST TIME... SHOULD I BE CONCERNED?
I'M READY, TEACH!
TA-DAA! AN ELEGANT AND FASHIONABLE GENT!
AH, YES. YOU WOULD BE ACCUSTOMED TO THIS.
NOT BAD, RIGHT? IT TOOK A WHILE TO DRESS UP EVERYONE THOUGH!

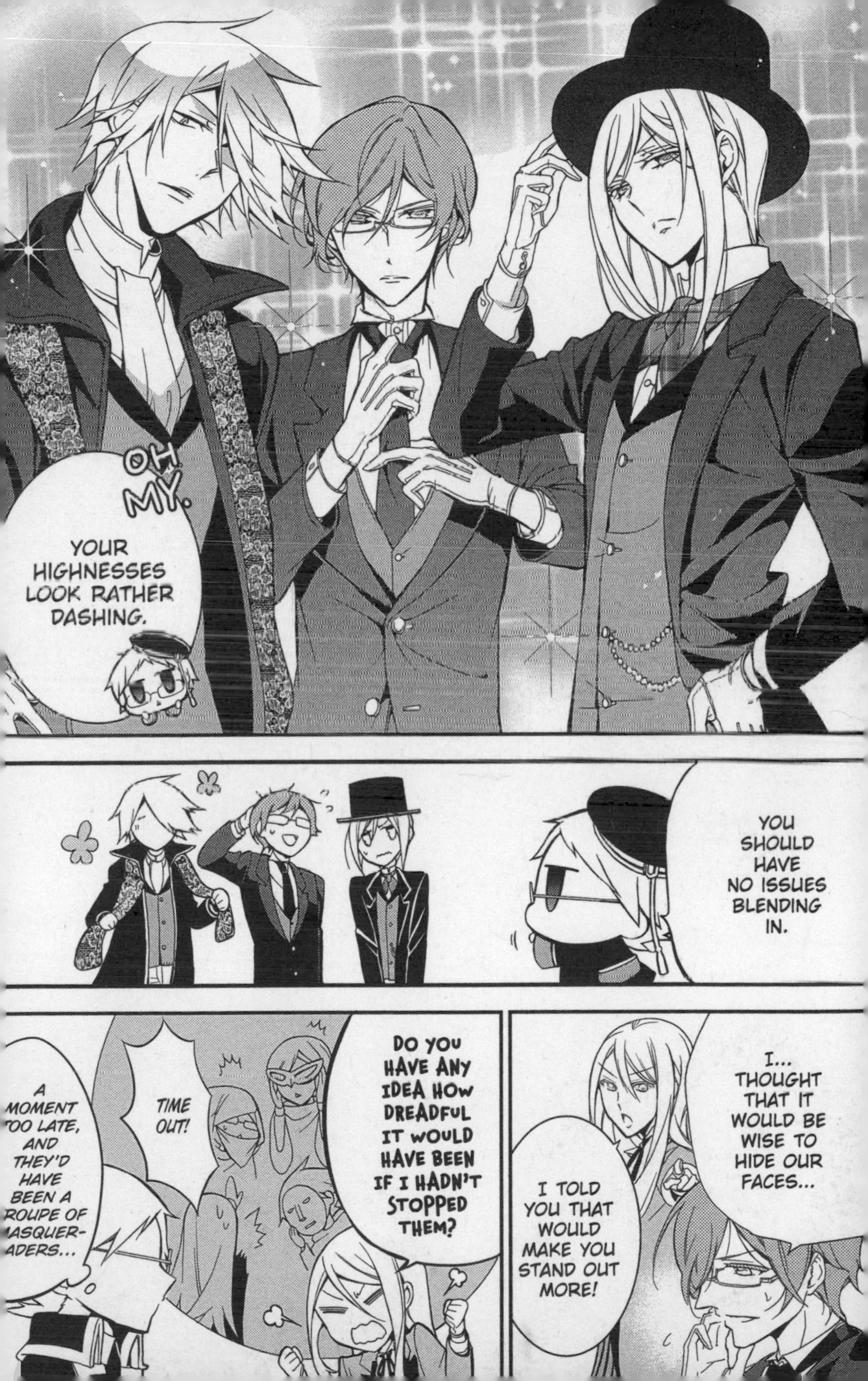
OH MY.
YOUR HIGHNESSES LOOK RATHER DASHING.
YOU SHOULD HAVE NO ISSUES BLENDING IN.
I... THOUGHT THAT IT WOULD BE WISE TO HIDE OUR FACES...
I TOLD YOU THAT WOULD MAKE YOU STAND OUT MORE!
DO YOU HAVE ANY IDEA HOW DREADFUL IT WOULD HAVE BEEN IF I HADN'T STOPPED THEM?
TIME OUT!
A MOMENT OO LATE, AND THEY'D HAVE BEEN A ROUPE OF ASQUER- ADERS...

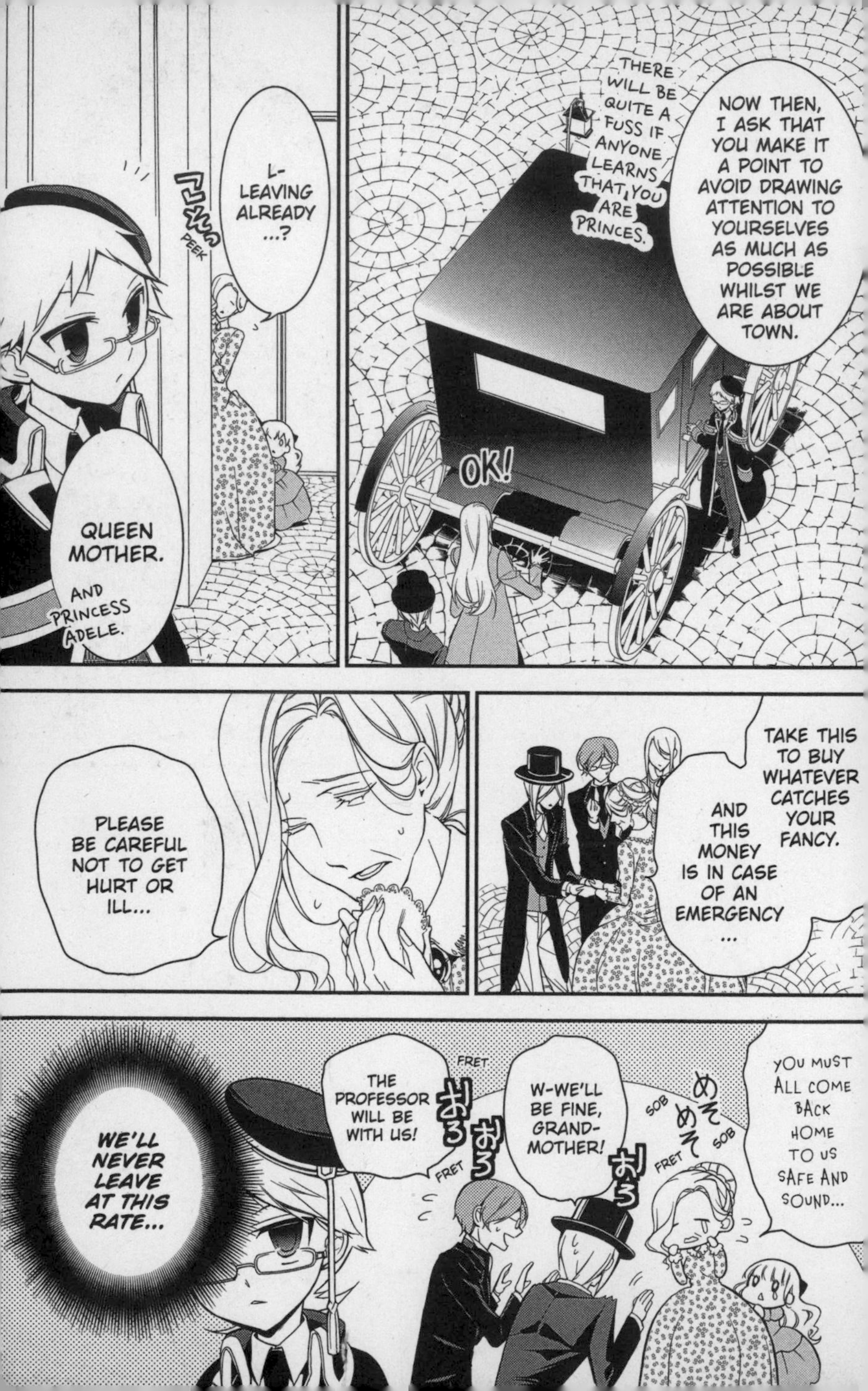
NOW THEN, I ASK THAT YOU MAKE IT A POINT TO AVOID DRAWING ATTENTION TO YOURSELVES AS MUCH AS POSSIBLE WHILST WE ARE ABOUT TOWN.
THERE WILL BE QUITE A FUSS IF ANYONE LEARNS THAT YOU ARE PRINCES.
OK!
L-LEAVING ALREADY ...?
こそっ
PEEK
QUEEN MOTHER.
AND PRINCESS ADELE.
TAKE THIS TO BUY WHATEVER CATCHES YOUR FANCY.
AND THIS MONEY IS IN CASE OF AN EMERGENCY ...
PLEASE BE CAREFUL NOT TO GET HURT OR ILL...
YOU MUST ALL COME BACK HOME TO US SAFE AND SOUND...
めそめそ
SOB SOB
おろ
FRET
W-WE'LL BE FINE, GRANDMOTHER!
おろおろ
FRET FRET
THE PROFESSOR WILL BE WITH US!
WE'LL NEVER LEAVE AT THIS RATE...

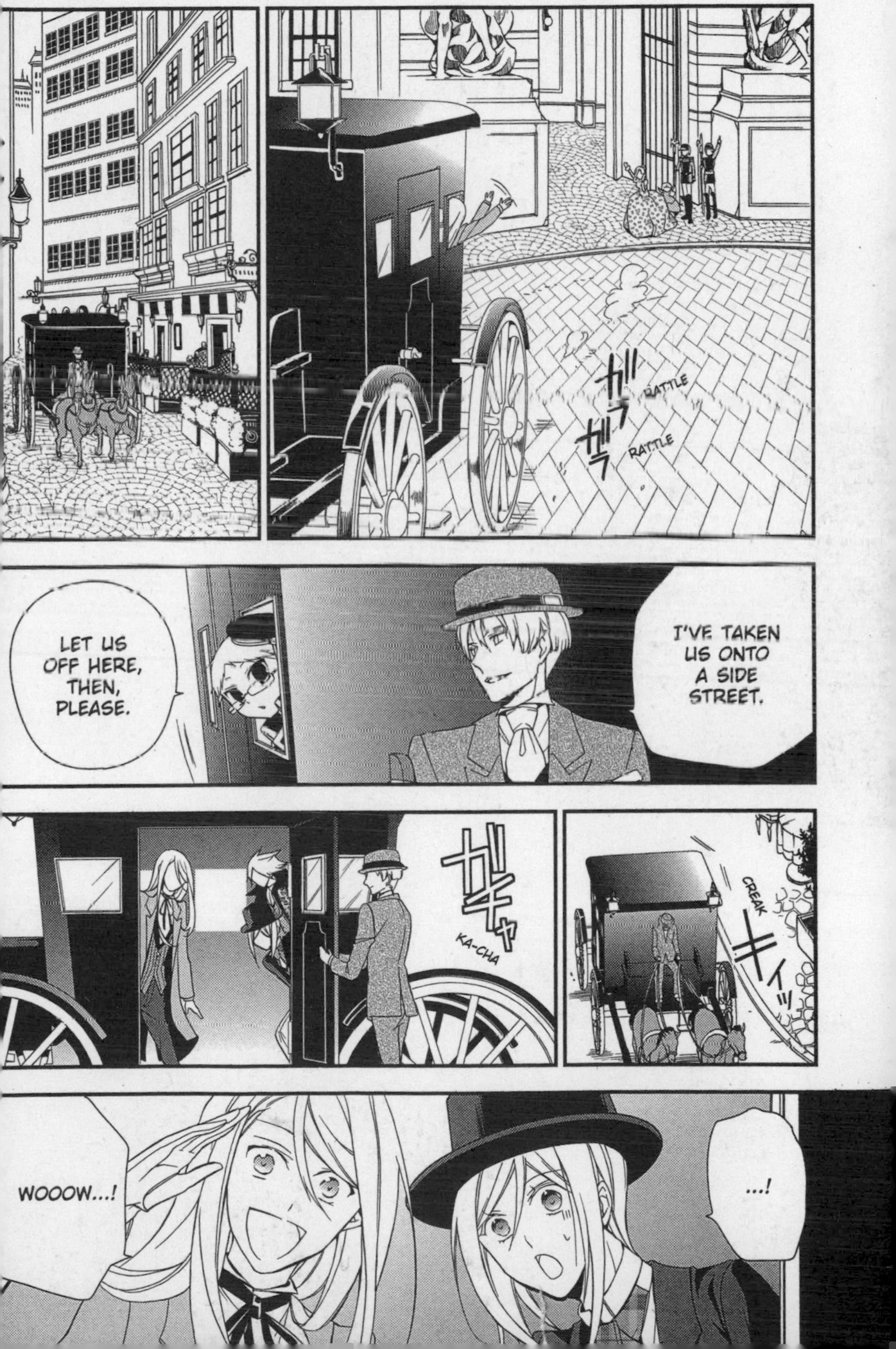
RATTLE
RATTLE
I'VE TAKEN US ONTO A SIDE STREET.
LET US OFF HERE, THEN, PLEASE.
CREAK
キイッ
ガチャ
KA-CHA
...!
WOOOW...!

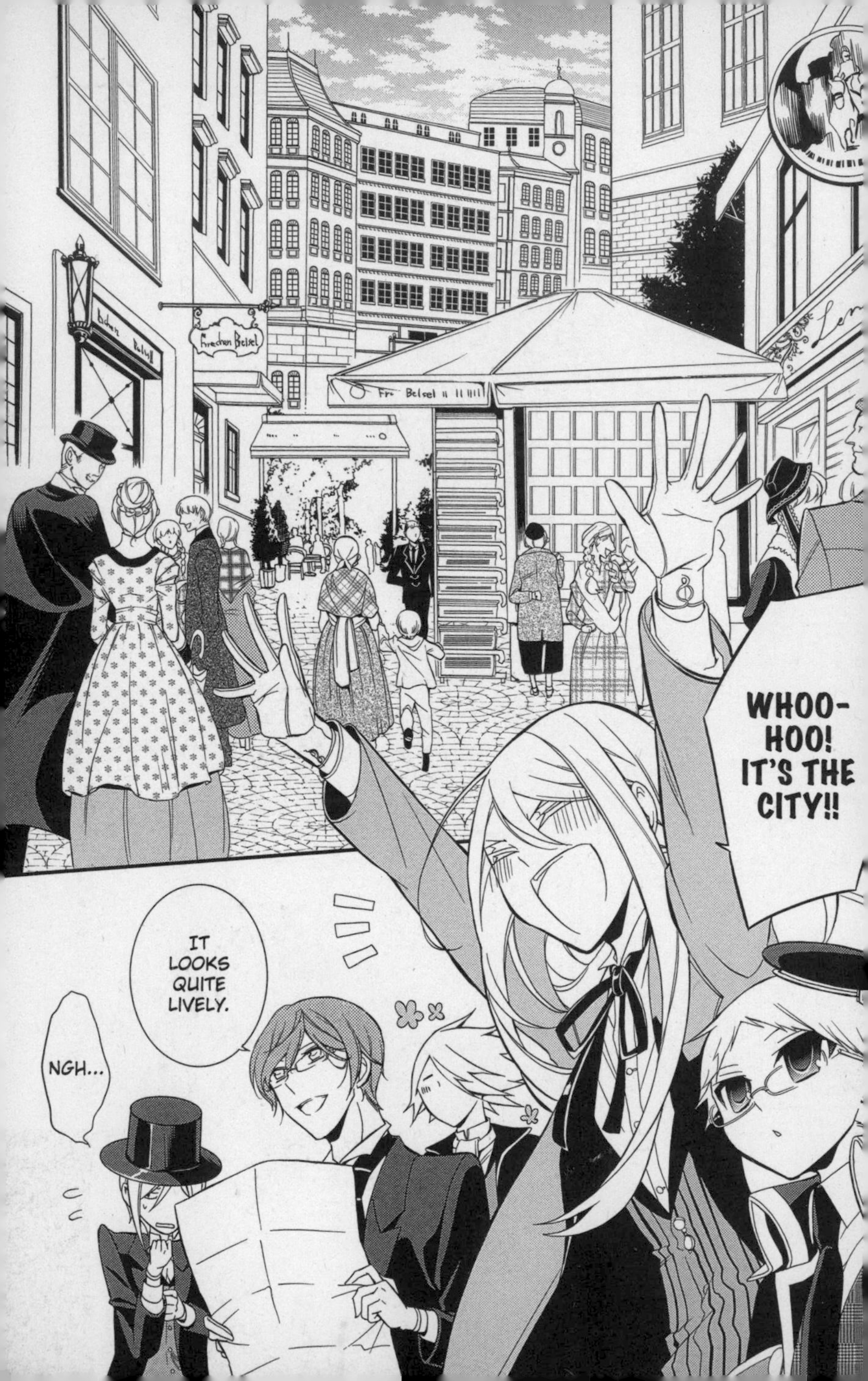
WHOO-HOO! IT'S THE CITY!!
IT LOOKS QUITE LIVELY.
NGH...

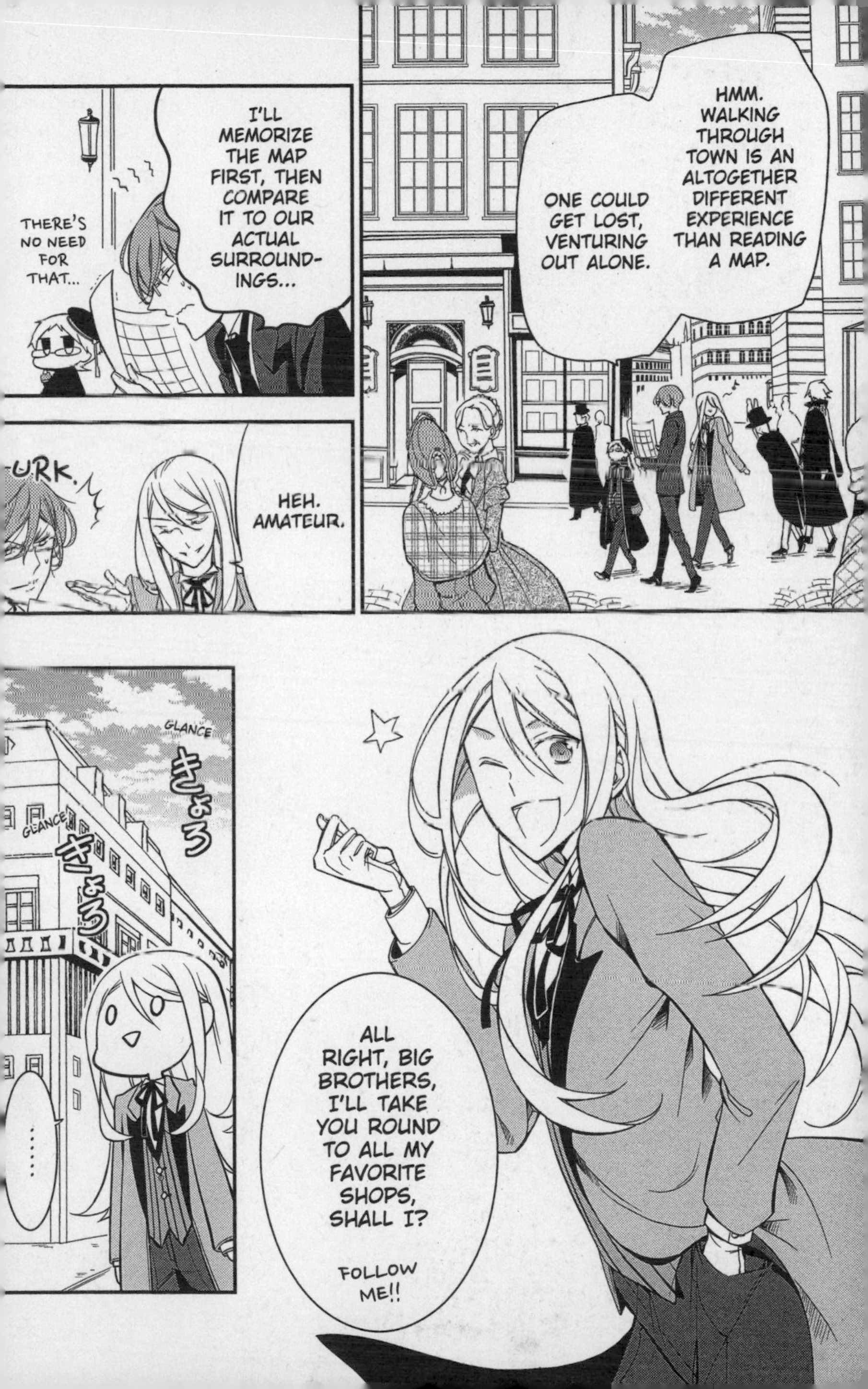
HMM. WALKING THROUGH TOWN IS AN ALTOGETHER DIFFERENT EXPERIENCE THAN READING A MAP.
ONE COULD GET LOST, VENTURING OUT ALONE.
I'LL MEMORIZE THE MAP FIRST, THEN COMPARE IT TO OUR ACTUAL SURROUNDINGS...
THERE'S NO NEED FOR THAT...
HEH. AMATEUR.
URK.
ALL RIGHT, BIG BROTHERS, I'LL TAKE YOU ROUND TO ALL MY FAVORITE SHOPS, SHALL I?
FOLLOW ME!!
GLANCE
きょろ
GLANCE
きょろ
......

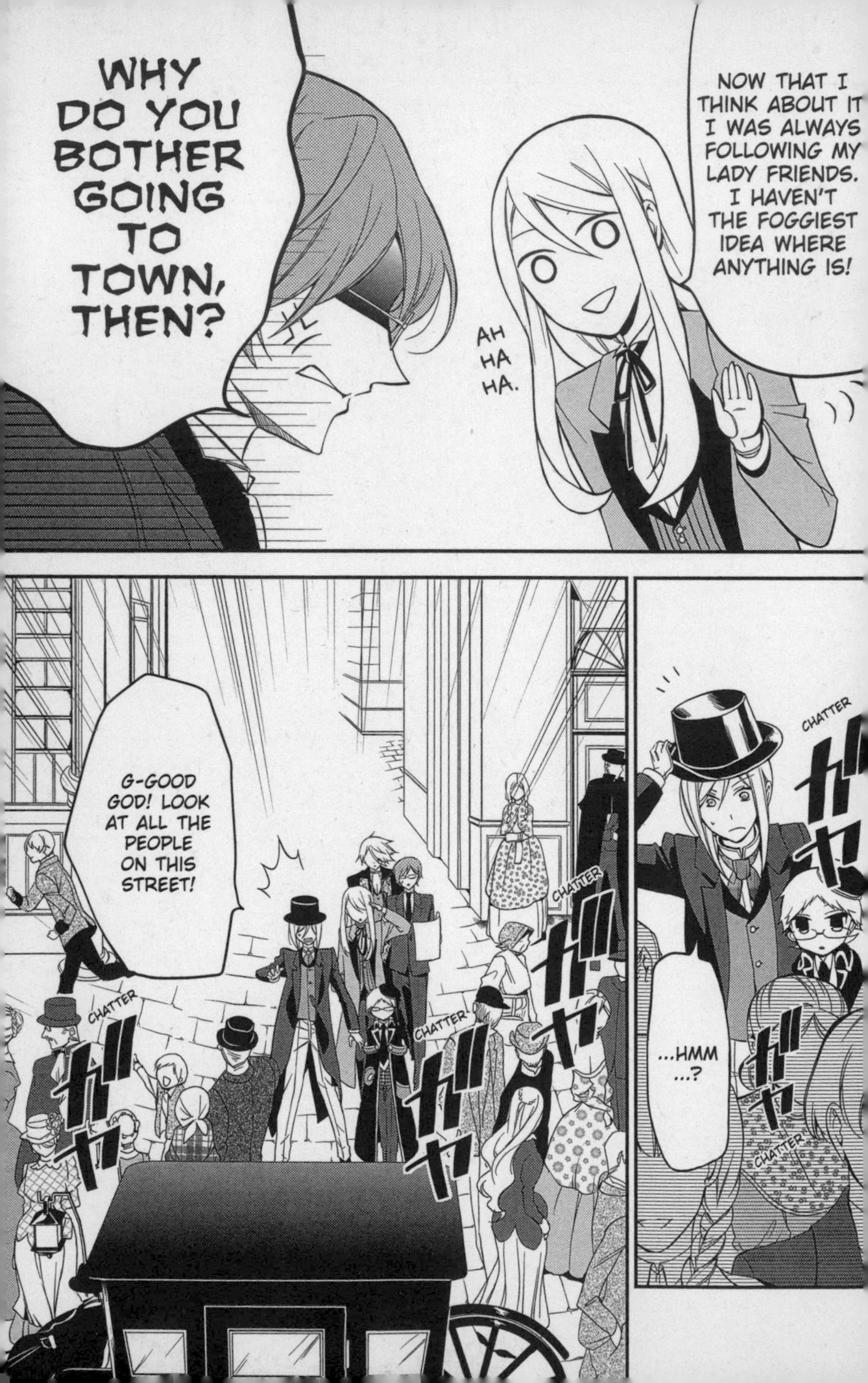
NOW THAT I THINK ABOUT IT I WAS ALWAYS FOLLOWING MY LADY FRIENDS. I HAVEN'T THE FOGGIEST IDEA WHERE ANYTHING IS!
AH HA HA.
WHY DO YOU BOTHER GOING TO TOWN, THEN?
CHATTER
...HMM ...?
CHATTER
G-GOOD GOD! LOOK AT ALL THE PEOPLE ON THIS STREET!
CHATTER
CHATTER
CHATTER

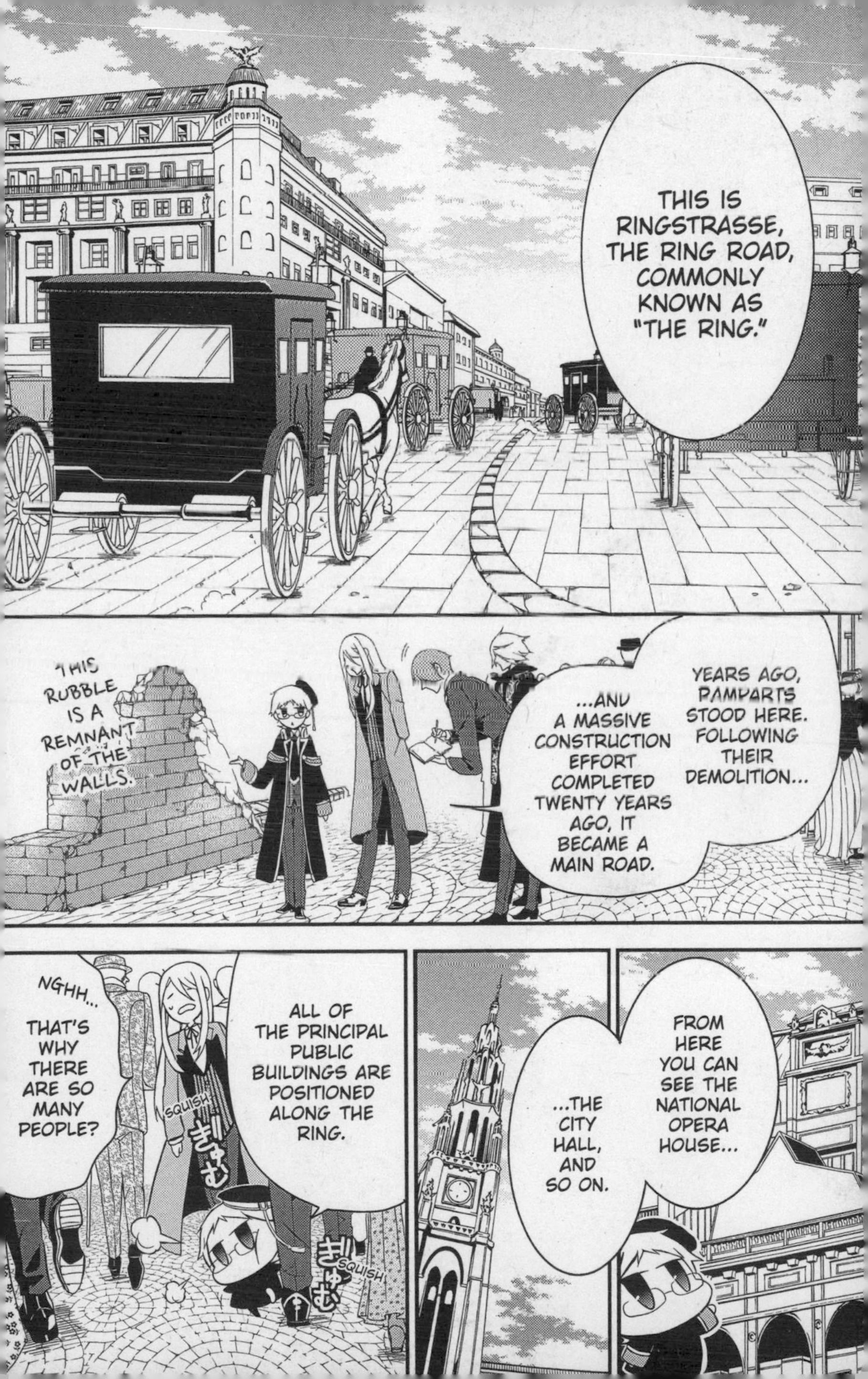
THIS IS RINGSTRASSE, THE RING ROAD, COMMONLY KNOWN AS "THE RING."
YEARS AGO, RAMPARTS STOOD HERE. FOLLOWING THEIR DEMOLITION...
...AND A MASSIVE CONSTRUCTION EFFORT COMPLETED TWENTY YEARS AGO, IT BECAME A MAIN ROAD.
THIS RUBBLE IS A REMNANT OF THE WALLS.
FROM HERE YOU CAN SEE THE NATIONAL OPERA HOUSE...
...THE CITY HALL, AND SO ON.
ALL OF THE PRINCIPAL PUBLIC BUILDINGS ARE POSITIONED ALONG THE RING.
きゅむ SQUISH
きゅむ SQUISH
NGHH...
THAT'S WHY THERE ARE SO MANY PEOPLE?

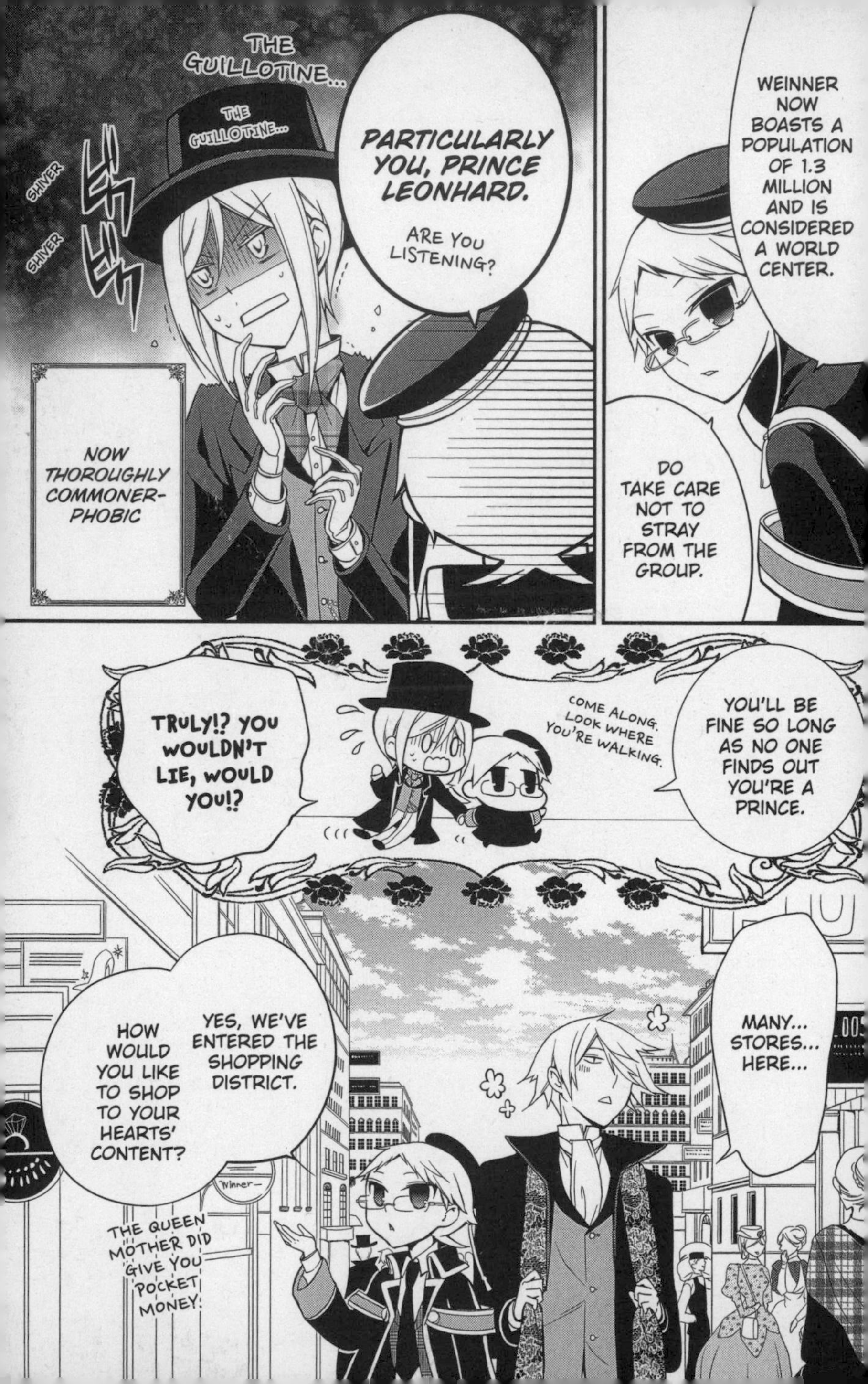
WEINNER NOW BOASTS A POPULATION OF 1.3 MILLION AND IS CONSIDERED A WORLD CENTER.
DO TAKE CARE NOT TO STRAY FROM THE GROUP.
PARTICULARLY YOU, PRINCE LEONHARD.
ARE YOU LISTENING?
THE GUILLOTINE...
THE GUILLOTINE...
SHIVER
SHIVER
NOW THOROUGHLY COMMONER-PHOBIC
YOU'LL BE FINE SO LONG AS NO ONE FINDS OUT YOU'RE A PRINCE.
COME ALONG. LOOK WHERE YOU'RE WALKING.
TRULY!? YOU WOULDN'T LIE, WOULD YOU!?
MANY... STORES... HERE...
YES, WE'VE ENTERED THE SHOPPING DISTRICT.
HOW WOULD YOU LIKE TO SHOP TO YOUR HEARTS' CONTENT?
THE QUEEN MOTHER DID GIVE YOU POCKET MONEY!
Winner

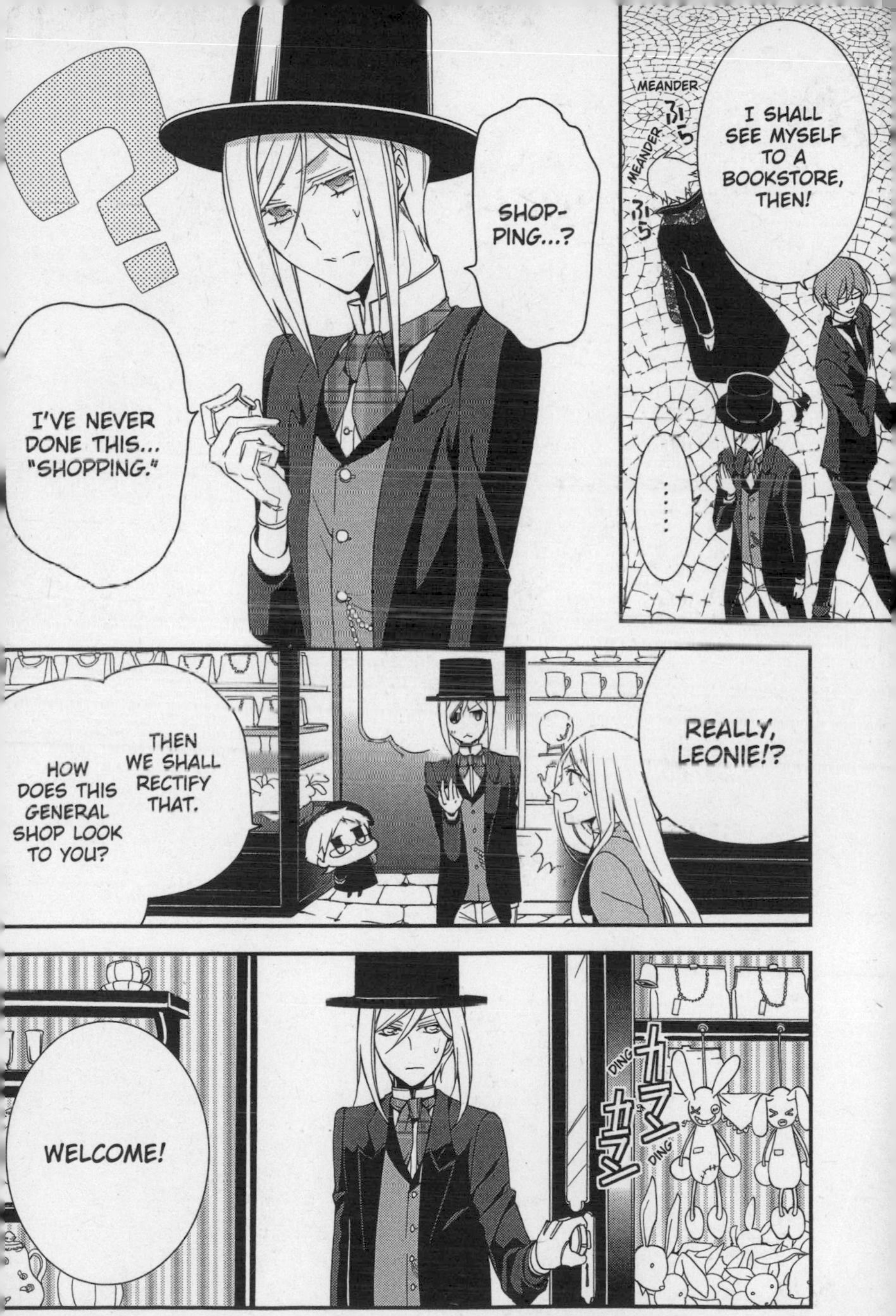
MEANDER
MEANDER
I SHALL SEE MYSELF TO A BOOKSTORE, THEN!
......
SHOP-PING...?
I'VE NEVER DONE THIS... "SHOPPING."
REALLY, LEONIE!?
THEN WE SHALL RECTIFY THAT.
HOW DOES THIS GENERAL SHOP LOOK TO YOU?
DING
DING
WELCOME!

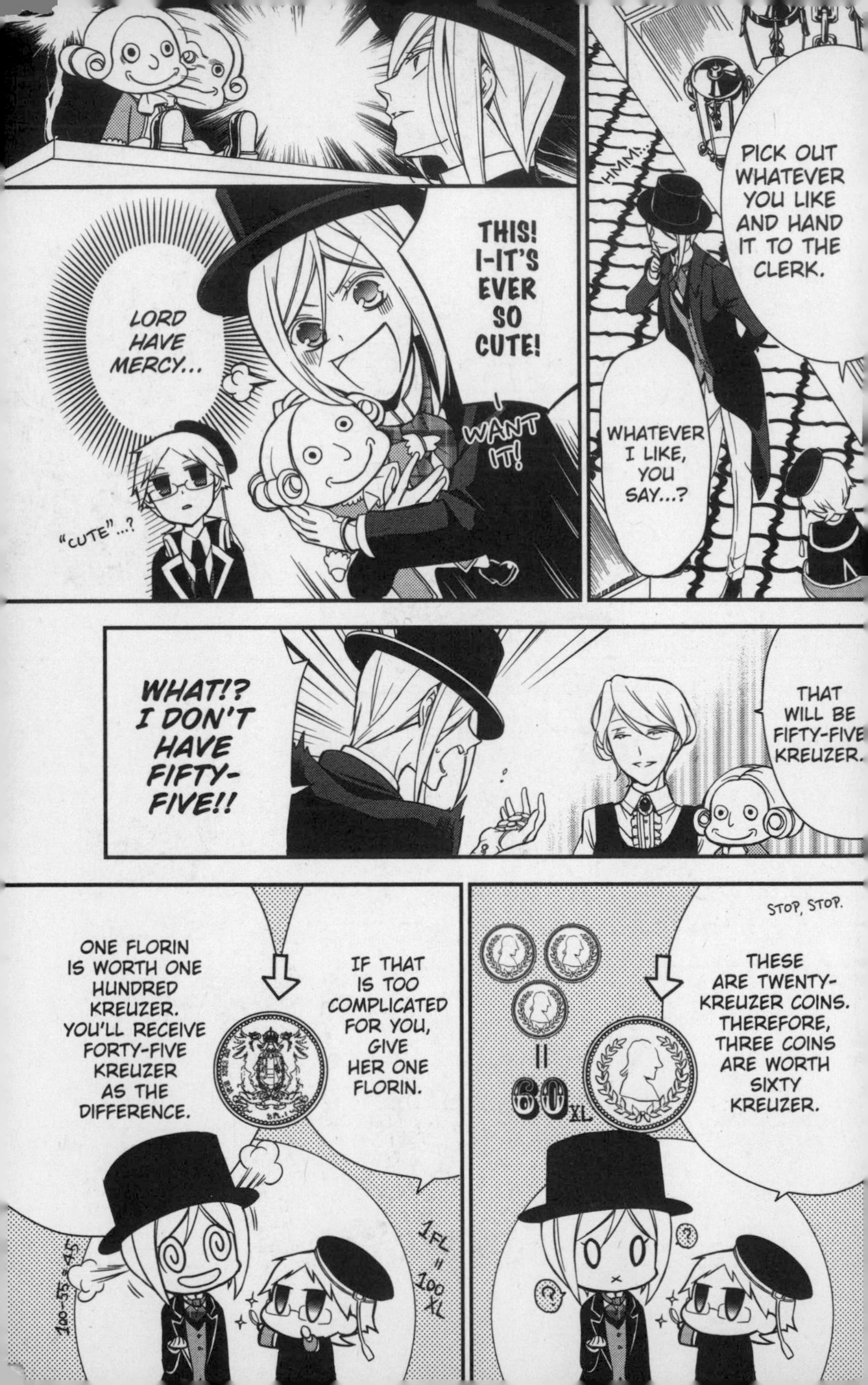
PICK OUT WHATEVER YOU LIKE AND HAND IT TO THE CLERK.
HMM...
WHATEVER I LIKE, YOU SAY...?
THIS! I-IT'S EVER SO CUTE!
I WANT IT!
LORD HAVE MERCY...
"CUTE"...?
THAT WILL BE FIFTY-FIVE KREUZER.
WHAT!? I DON'T HAVE FIFTY-FIVE!!
STOP, STOP.
THESE ARE TWENTY-KREUZER COINS. THEREFORE, THREE COINS ARE WORTH SIXTY KREUZER.
= 60 XL
IF THAT IS TOO COMPLICATED FOR YOU, GIVE HER ONE FLORIN.
ONE FLORIN IS WORTH ONE HUNDRED KREUZER. YOU'LL RECEIVE FORTY-FIVE KREUZER AS THE DIFFERENCE.
1FL = 100 XL
100-55=45

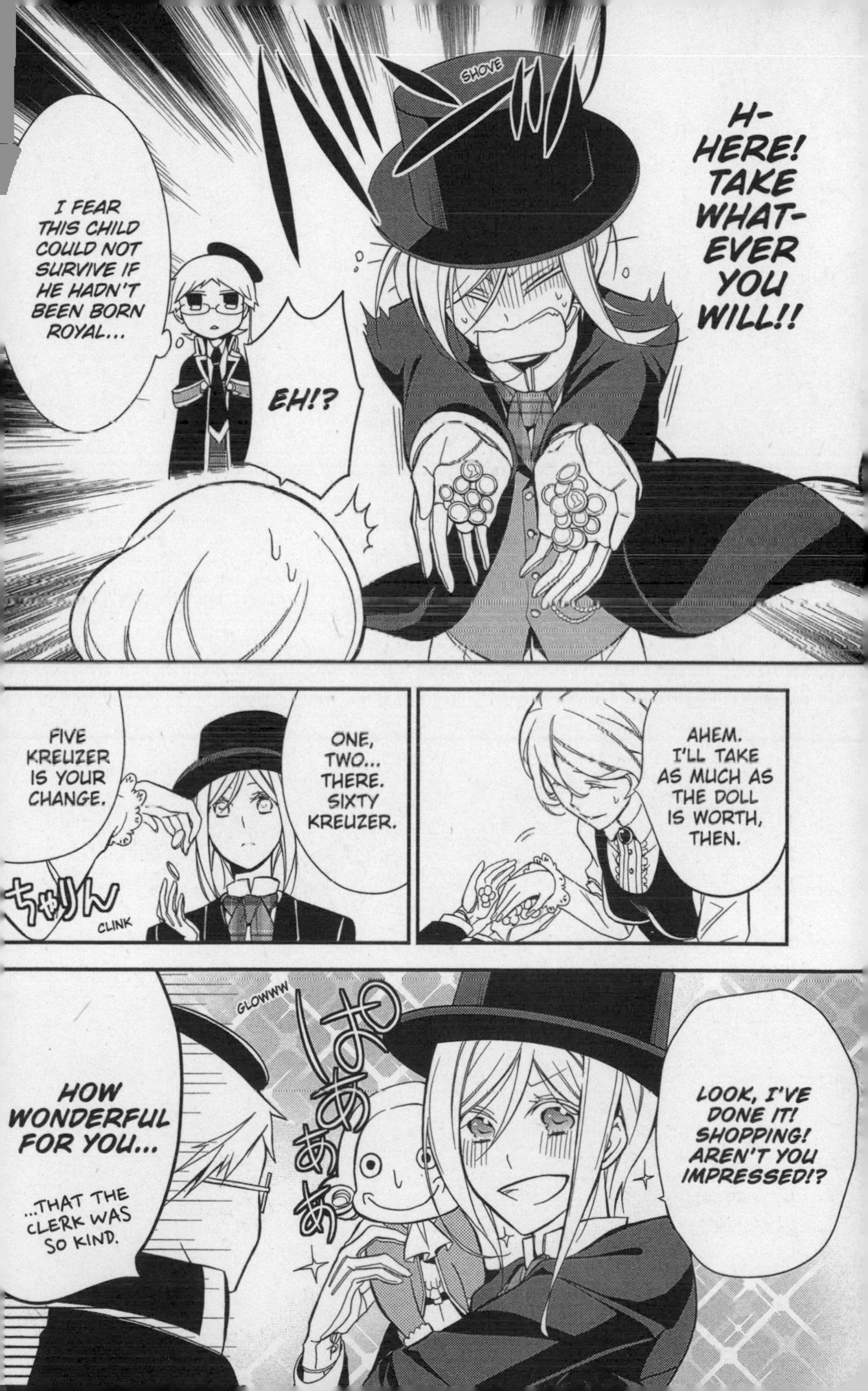
H-HERE! TAKE WHATEVER YOU WILL!!
SHOVE
EH!?
I FEAR THIS CHILD COULD NOT SURVIVE IF HE HADN'T BEEN BORN ROYAL...
AHEM. I'LL TAKE AS MUCH AS THE DOLL IS WORTH, THEN.
ONE, TWO... THERE. SIXTY KREUZER.
FIVE KREUZER IS YOUR CHANGE.
ちゃりん
CLINK
LOOK, I'VE DONE IT! SHOPPING! AREN'T YOU IMPRESSED!?
おーあああ
GLOWWW
HOW WONDERFUL FOR YOU...
...THAT THE CLERK WAS SO KIND.

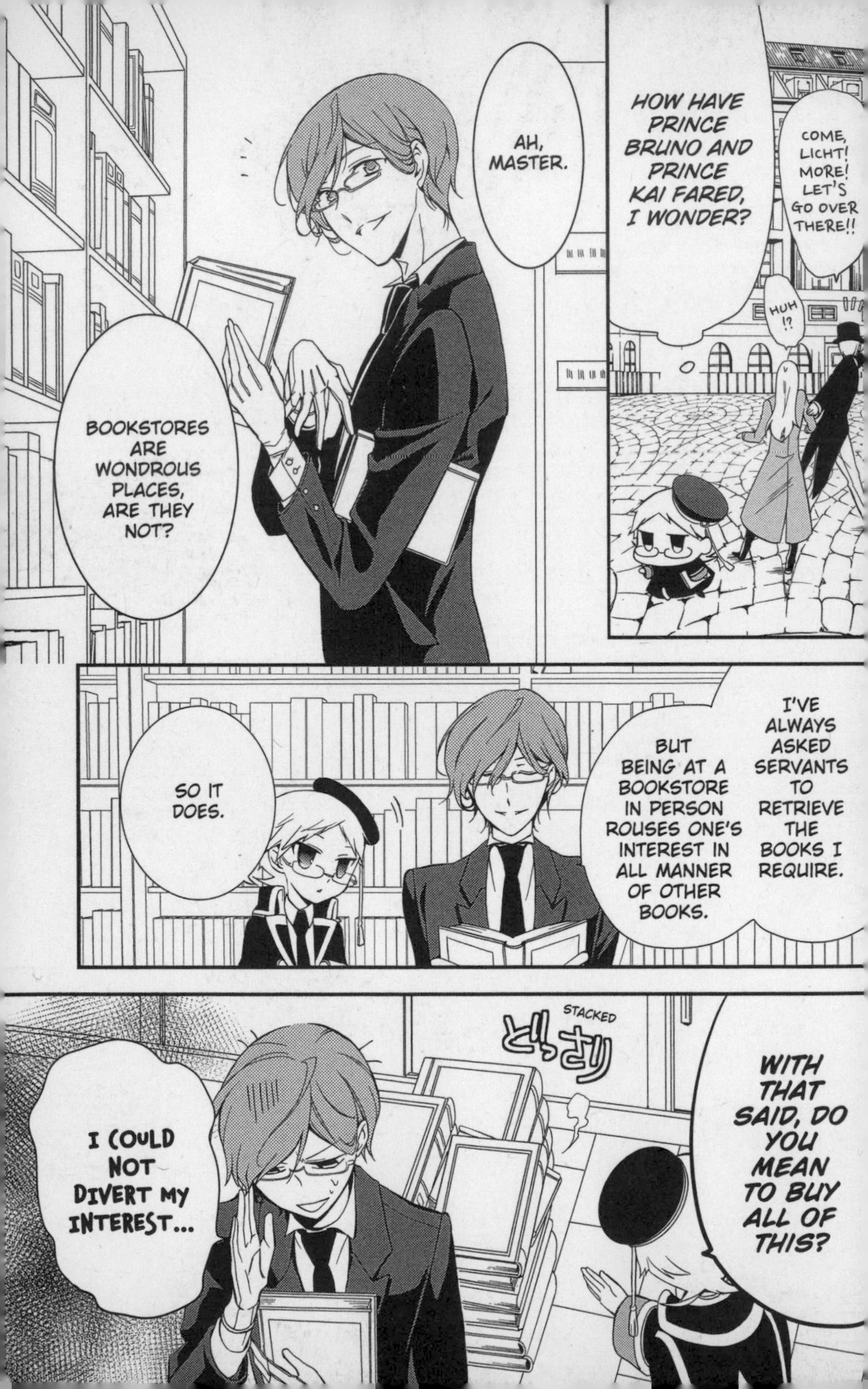
COME, LICHT! MORE! LET'S GO OVER THERE!!
HUH!?
HOW HAVE PRINCE BRUNO AND PRINCE KAI FARED, I WONDER?
AH, MASTER.
BOOKSTORES ARE WONDROUS PLACES, ARE THEY NOT?
I'VE ALWAYS ASKED SERVANTS TO RETRIEVE THE BOOKS I REQUIRE.
BUT BEING AT A BOOKSTORE IN PERSON ROUSES ONE'S INTEREST IN ALL MANNER OF OTHER BOOKS.
SO IT DOES.
WITH THAT SAID, DO YOU MEAN TO BUY ALL OF THIS?
どっさり
STACKED
I COULD NOT DIVERT MY INTEREST...

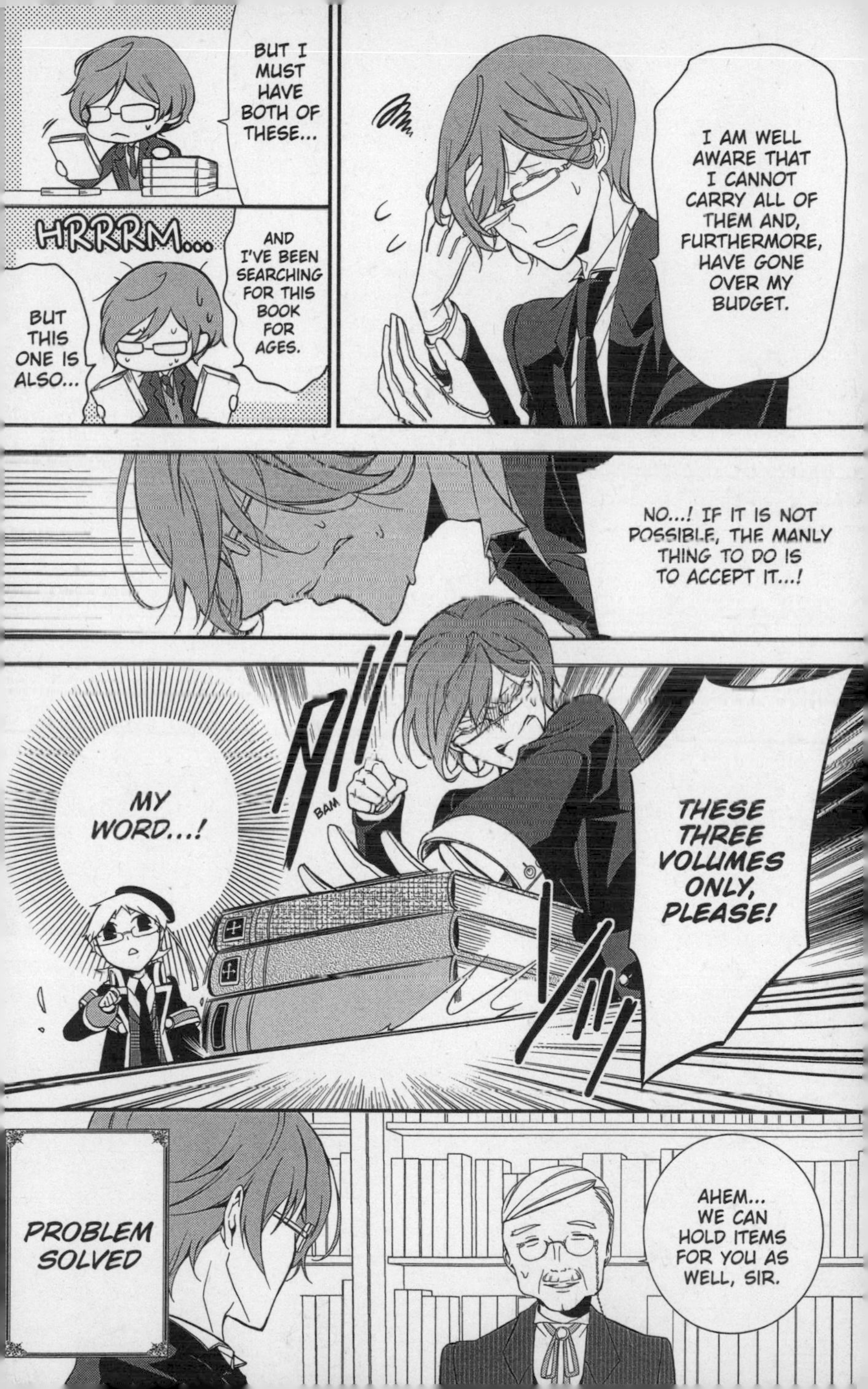
I AM WELL AWARE THAT I CANNOT CARRY ALL OF THEM AND, FURTHERMORE, HAVE GONE OVER MY BUDGET.
BUT I MUST HAVE BOTH OF THESE...
AND I'VE BEEN SEARCHING FOR THIS BOOK FOR AGES.
HRRRM...
BUT THIS ONE IS ALSO...
NO...! IF IT IS NOT POSSIBLE, THE MANLY THING TO DO IS TO ACCEPT IT...!
THESE THREE VOLUMES ONLY, PLEASE!
BAM
MY WORD...!
AHEM... WE CAN HOLD ITEMS FOR YOU AS WELL, SIR.
PROBLEM SOLVED

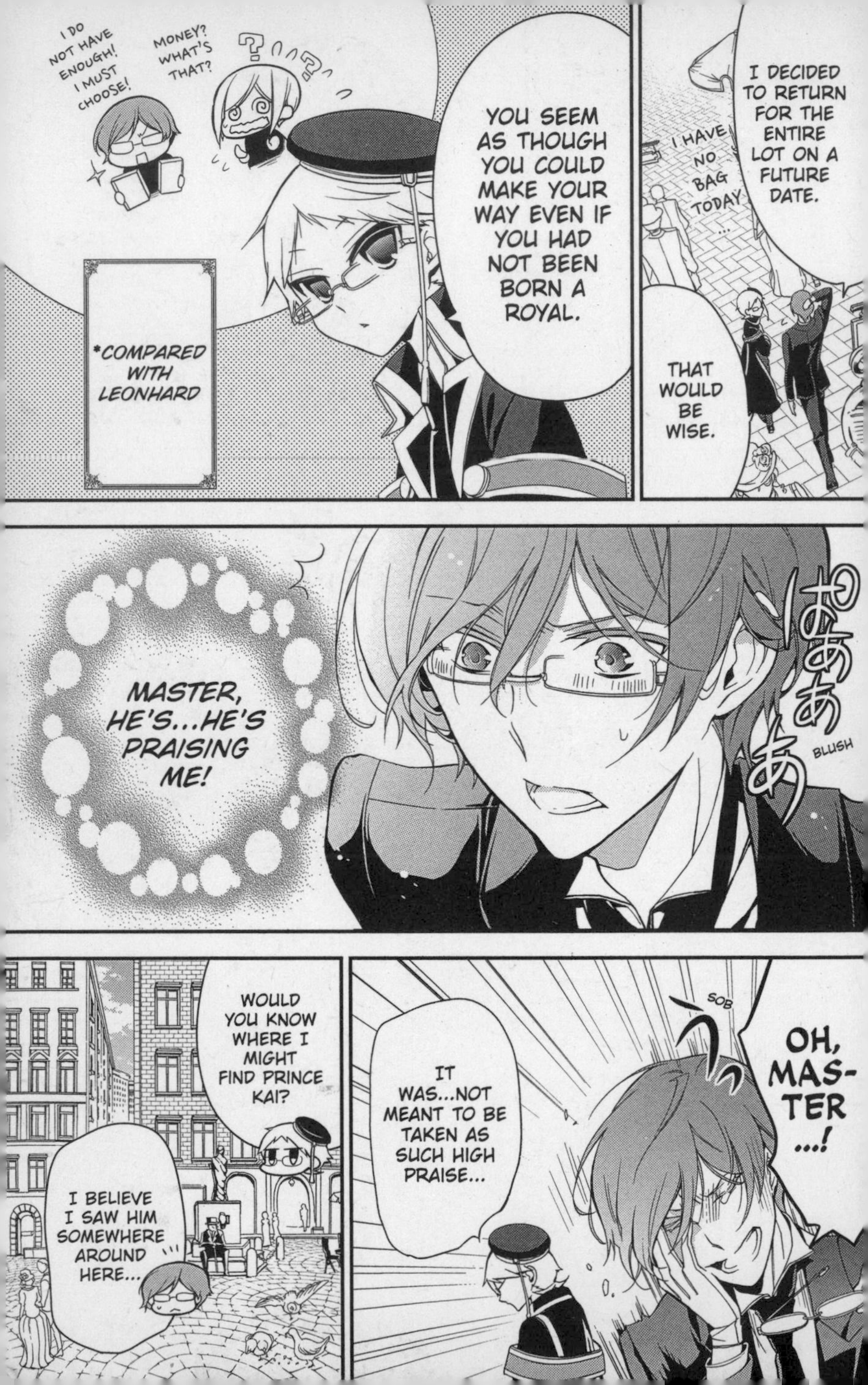
I DECIDED TO RETURN FOR THE ENTIRE LOT ON A FUTURE DATE.
I HAVE NO BAG TODAY ...
THAT WOULD BE WISE.
YOU SEEM AS THOUGH YOU COULD MAKE YOUR WAY EVEN IF YOU HAD NOT BEEN BORN A ROYAL.
MONEY? WHAT'S THAT?
I DO NOT HAVE ENOUGH! I MUST CHOOSE!
*COMPARED WITH LEONHARD
ぽあああ
BLUSH
MASTER, HE'S...HE'S PRAISING ME!
OH, MAS-TER ...!
SOB
IT WAS...NOT MEANT TO BE TAKEN AS SUCH HIGH PRAISE...
WOULD YOU KNOW WHERE I MIGHT FIND PRINCE KAI?
I BELIEVE I SAW HIM SOMEWHERE AROUND HERE...

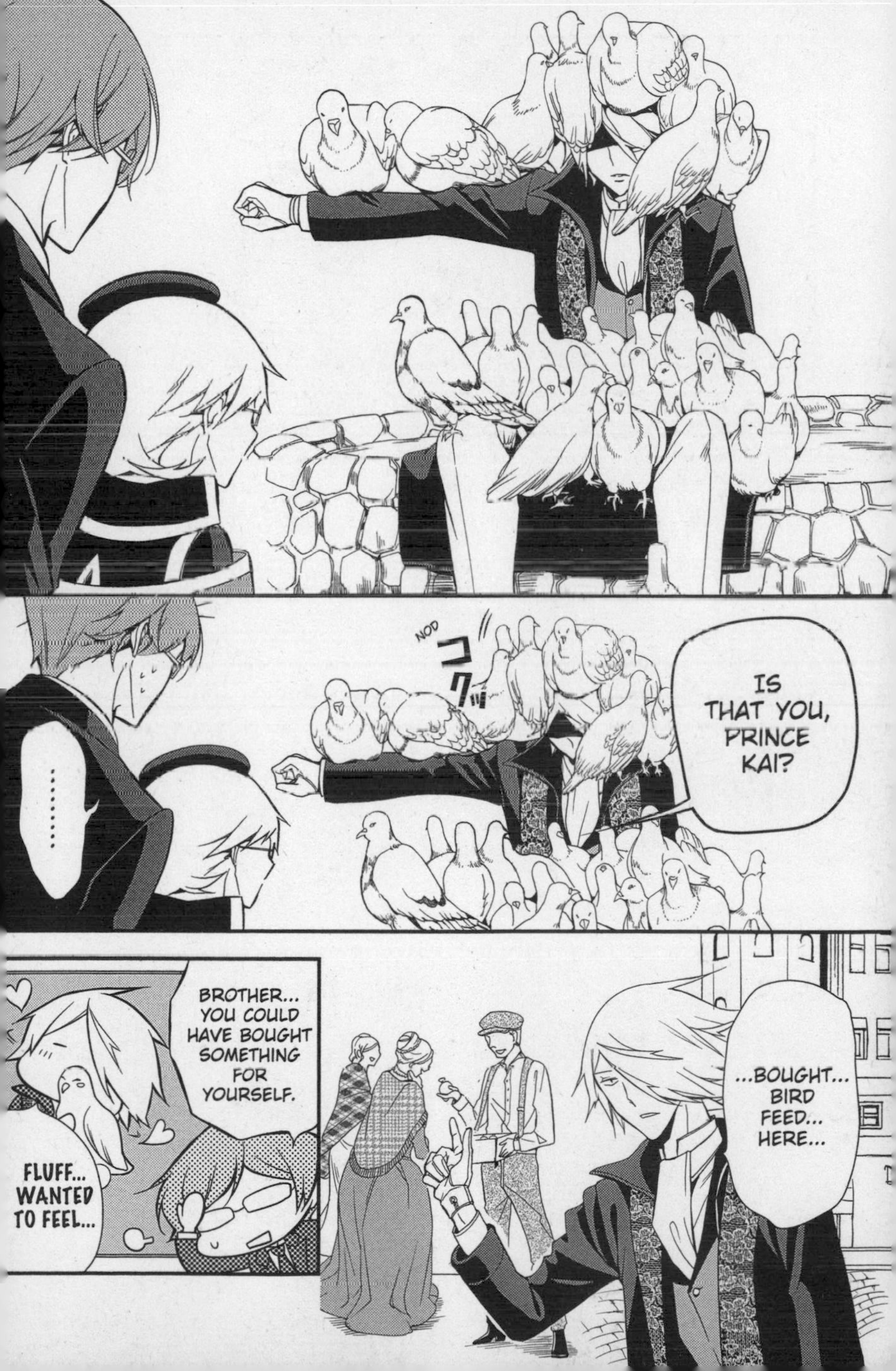
IS THAT YOU, PRINCE KAI?
NOD
コクッ
......
...BOUGHT... BIRD FEED... HERE...
BROTHER... YOU COULD HAVE BOUGHT SOMETHING FOR YOURSELF.
FLUFF... WANTED TO FEEL...

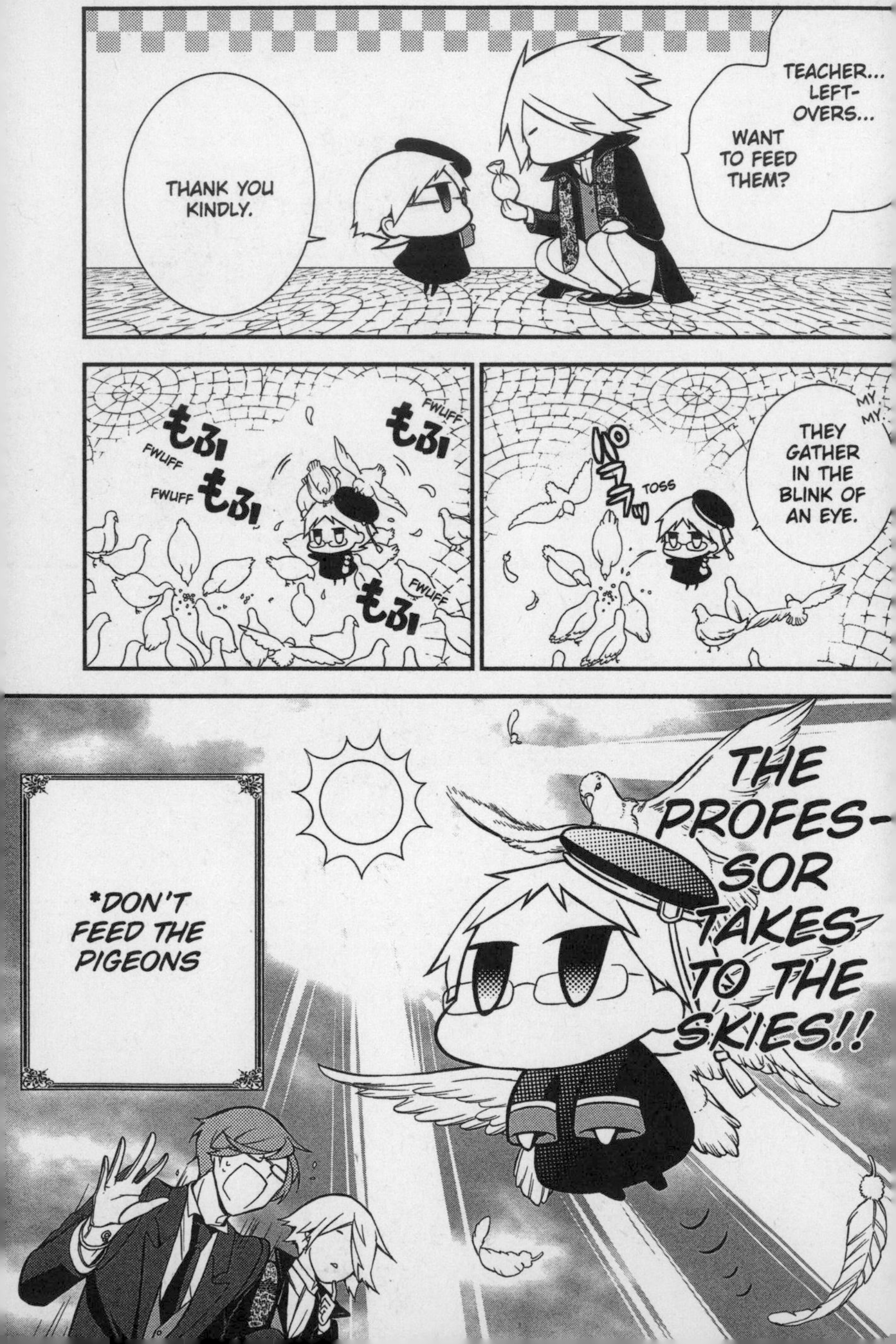
TEACHER... LEFT-OVERS...
WANT TO FEED THEM?
THANK YOU KINDLY.
MY, MY.
THEY GATHER IN THE BLINK OF AN EYE.
TOSS
もふ
FWUFF
もふ
FWUFF
もふ
FWUFF
もふ
FWUFF
THE PROFES-SOR TAKES TO THE SKIES!!
*DON'T FEED THE PIGEONS

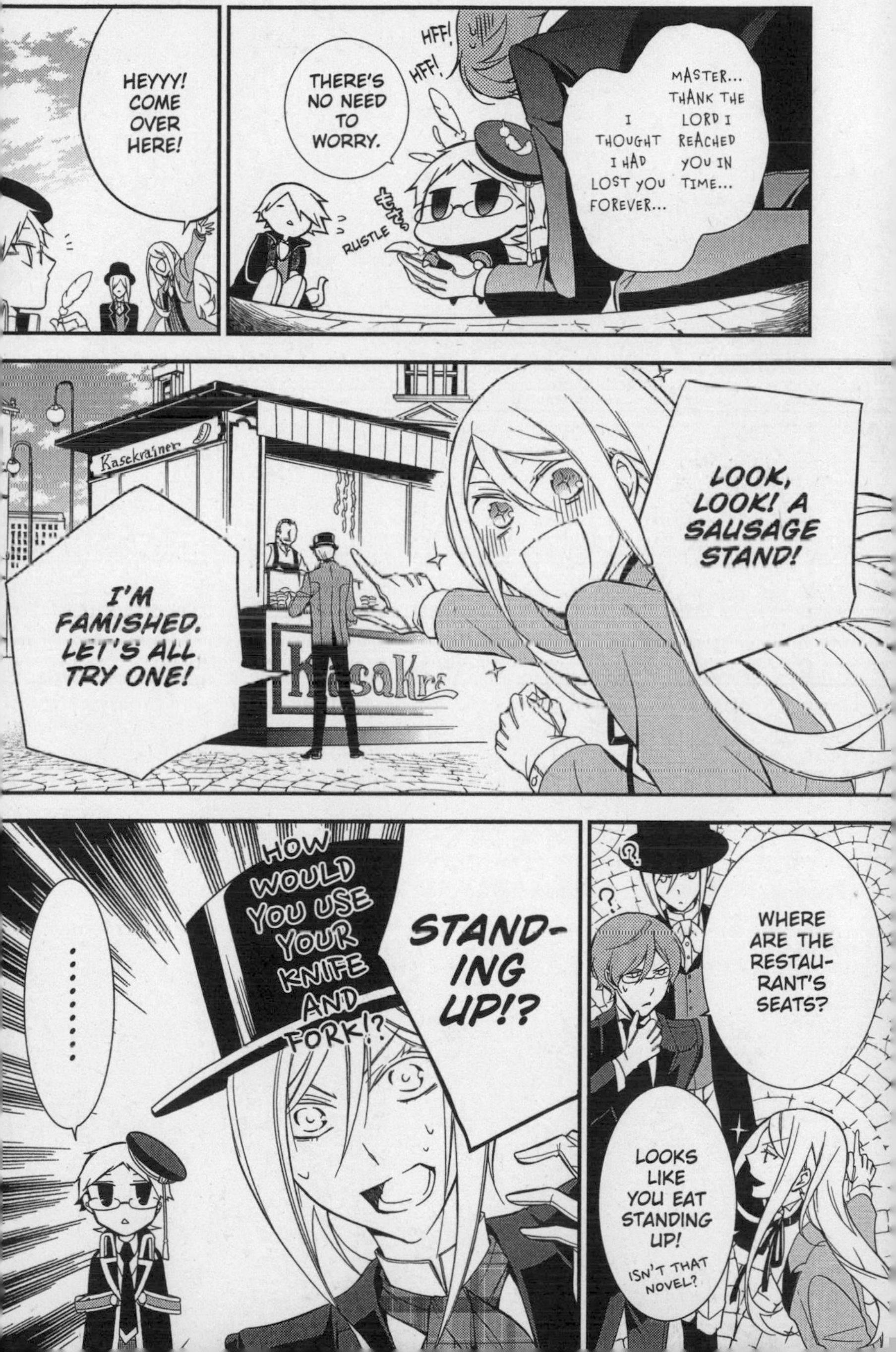
MASTER... THANK THE LORD I REACHED YOU IN TIME...
I THOUGHT I HAD LOST YOU FOREVER...
HFF! HFF!
THERE'S NO NEED TO WORRY.
RUSTLE
HEYYY! COME OVER HERE!
Kasekrainer
LOOK, LOOK! A SAUSAGE STAND!
I'M FAMISHED. LET'S ALL TRY ONE!
WHERE ARE THE RESTAU-RANT'S SEATS?
LOOKS LIKE YOU EAT STANDING UP!
ISN'T THAT NOVEL?
STAND-ING UP!?
HOW WOULD YOU USE YOUR KNIFE AND FORK!?
....

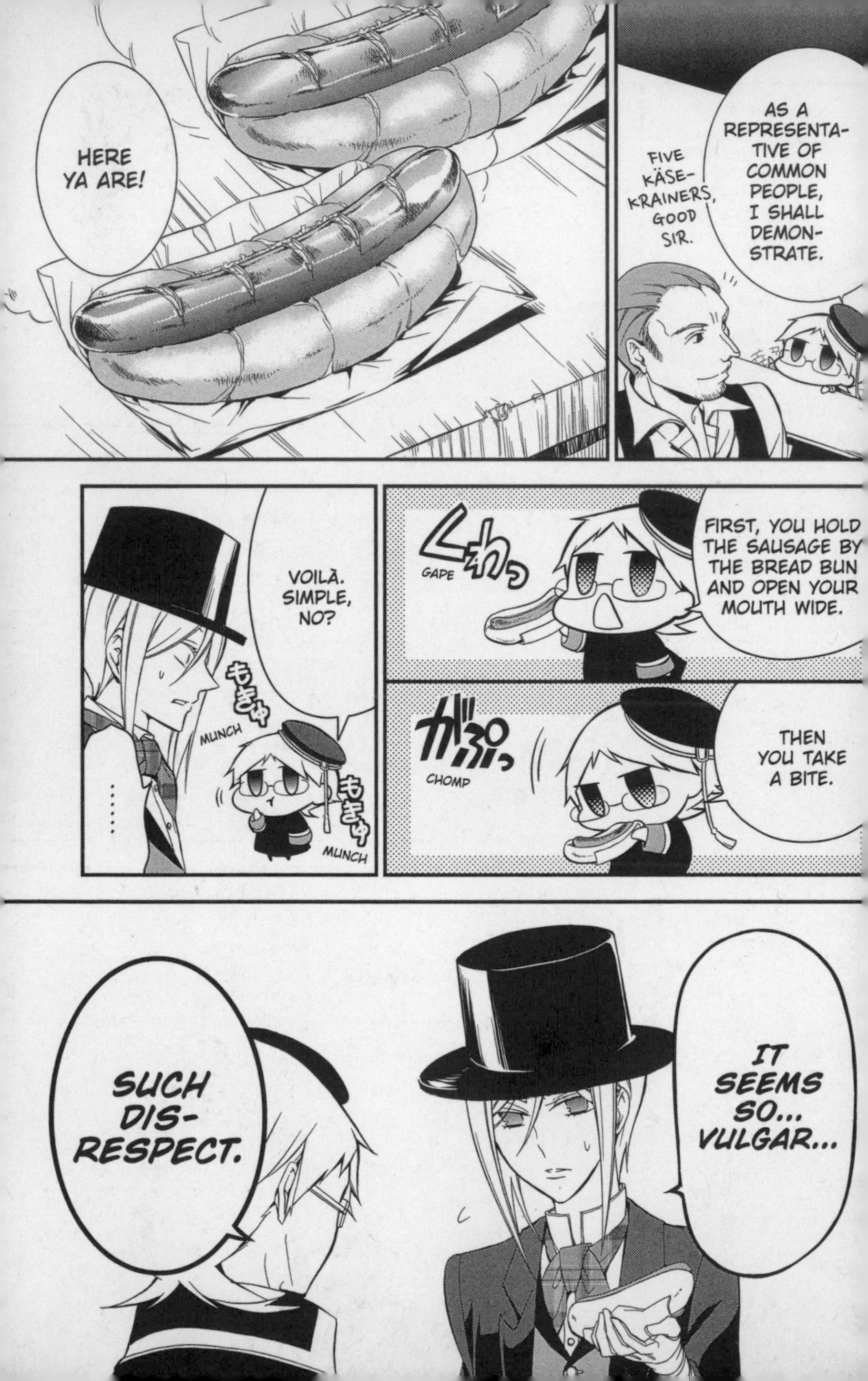
AS A REPRESENTA-TIVE OF COMMON PEOPLE, I SHALL DEMON-STRATE.
FIVE KÄSE-KRAINERS, GOOD SIR.
HERE YA ARE!
FIRST, YOU HOLD THE SAUSAGE BY THE BREAD BUN AND OPEN YOUR MOUTH WIDE.
くわっ
GAPE
THEN YOU TAKE A BITE.
がぶっ
CHOMP
VOILÀ. SIMPLE, NO?
もきゅ
MUNCH
もきゅ
MUNCH
......
IT SEEMS SO... VULGAR...
SUCH DIS-RESPECT.

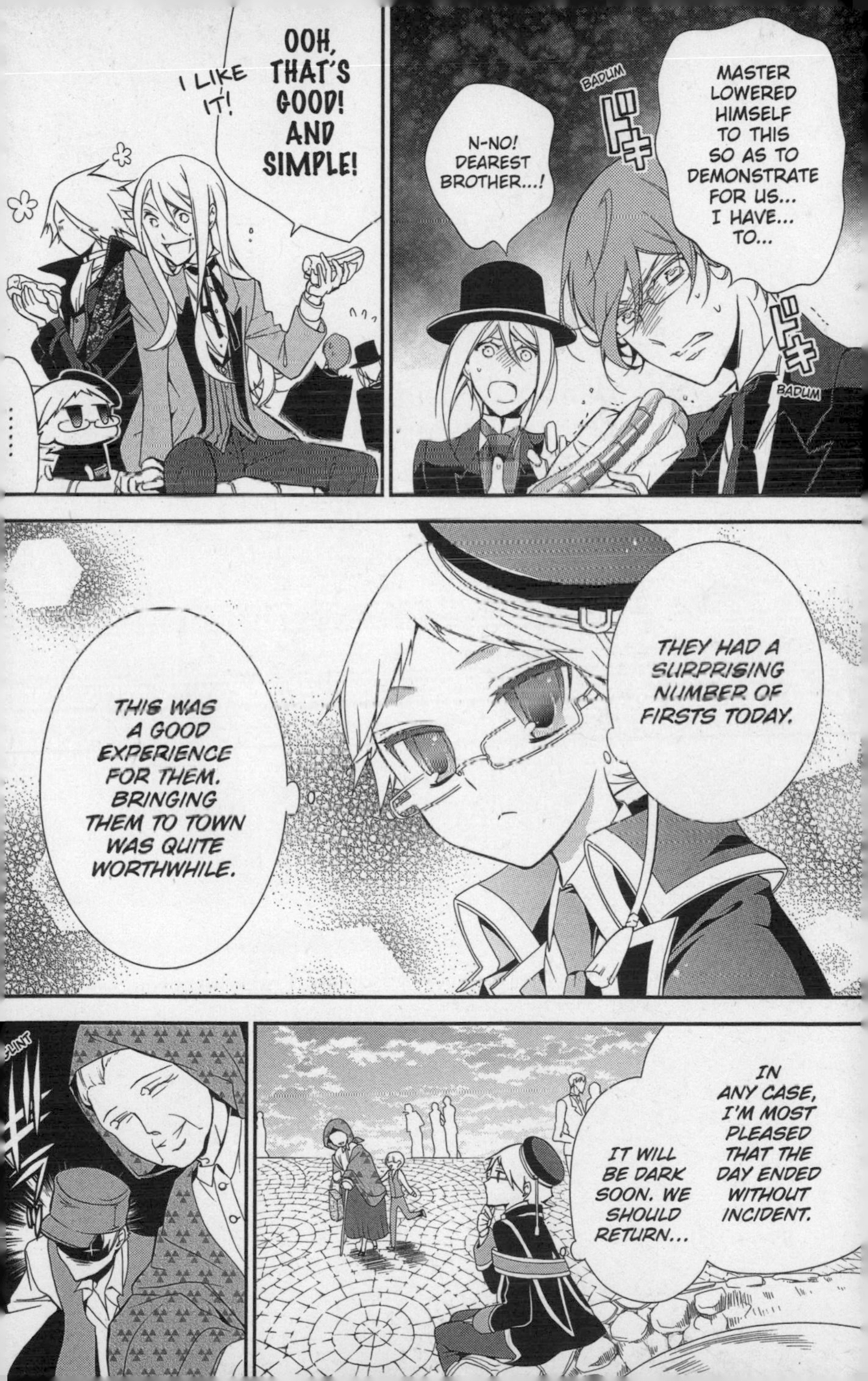
MASTER LOWERED HIMSELF TO THIS SO AS TO DEMONSTRATE FOR US... I HAVE... TO...
BADUM
N-NO! DEAREST BROTHER...!
BADUM
OOH, THAT'S GOOD! AND SIMPLE!
I LIKE IT!
THEY HAD A SURPRISING NUMBER OF FIRSTS TODAY.
THIS WAS A GOOD EXPERIENCE FOR THEM. BRINGING THEM TO TOWN WAS QUITE WORTHWHILE.
IN ANY CASE, I'M MOST PLEASED THAT THE DAY ENDED WITHOUT INCIDENT.
IT WILL BE DARK SOON. WE SHOULD RETURN...

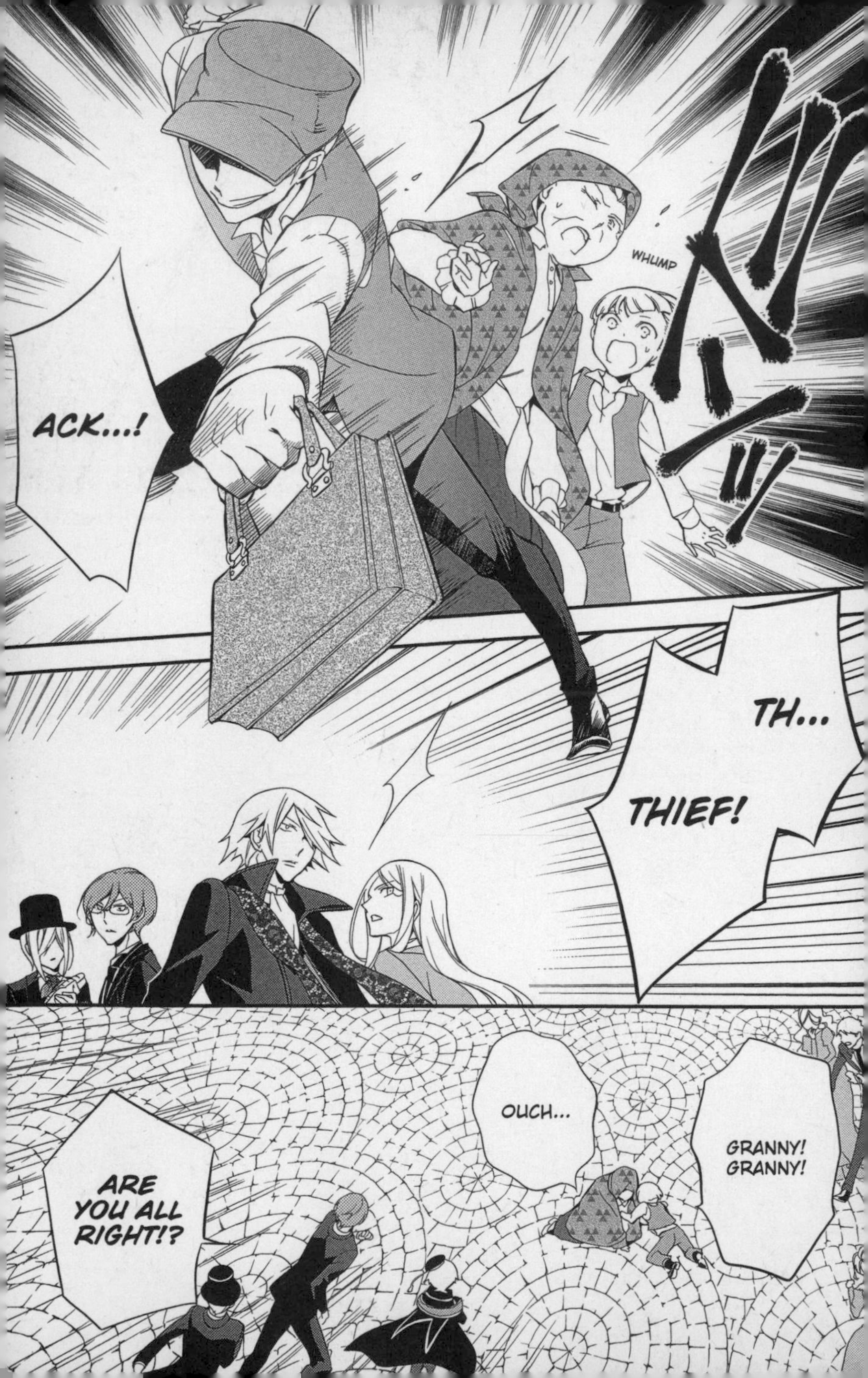
WHUMP
ACK...!
TH...
THIEF!
GRANNY! GRANNY!
OUCH...
ARE YOU ALL RIGHT!?

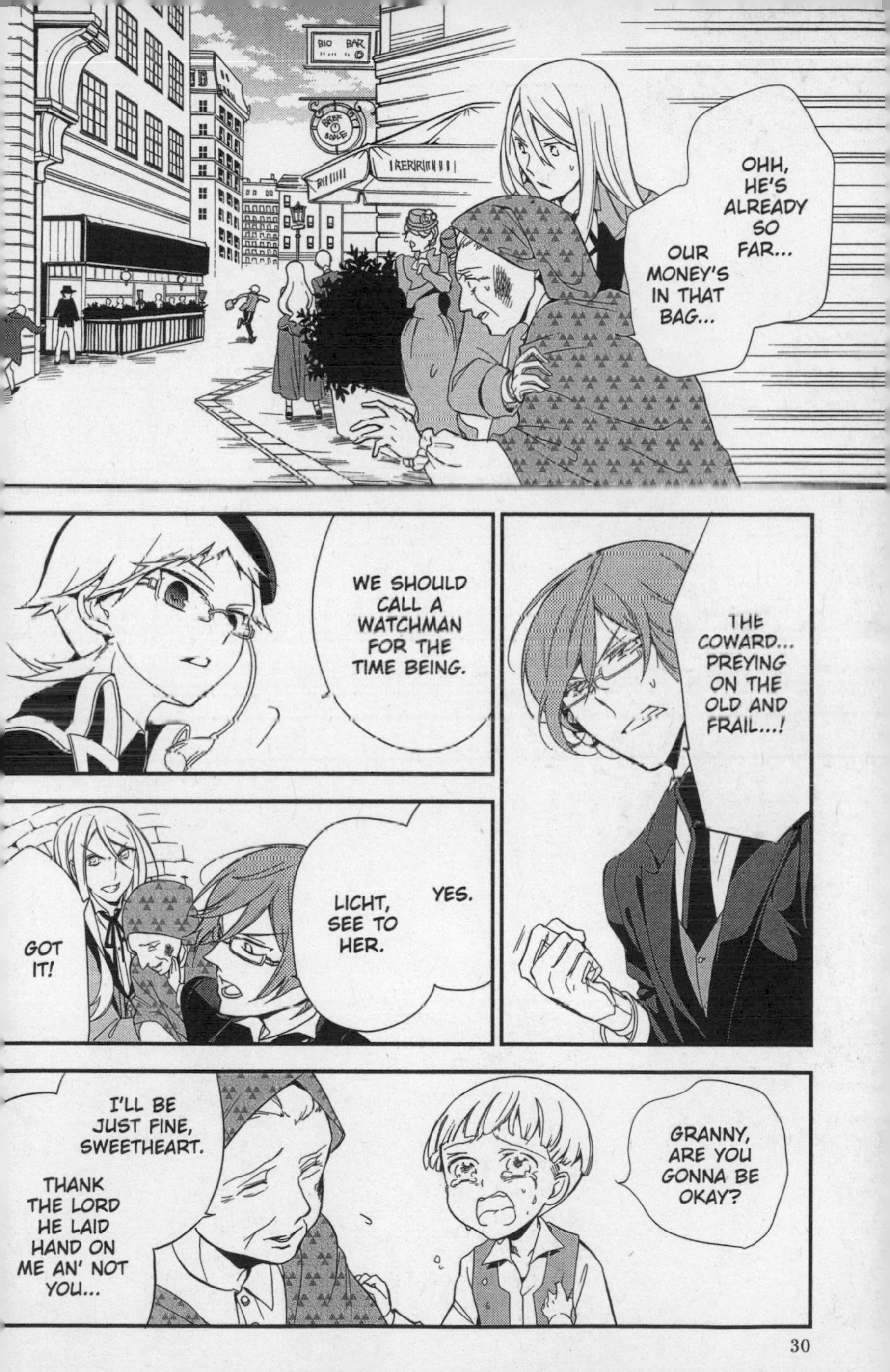
BIO BAR
OHH, HE'S ALREADY SO FAR...
OUR MONEY'S IN THAT BAG...
THE COWARD... PREYING ON THE OLD AND FRAIL...!
WE SHOULD CALL A WATCHMAN FOR THE TIME BEING.
YES.
LICHT, SEE TO HER.
GOT IT!
GRANNY, ARE YOU GONNA BE OKAY?
I'LL BE JUST FINE, SWEETHEART.
THANK THE LORD HE LAID HAND ON ME AN' NOT YOU...

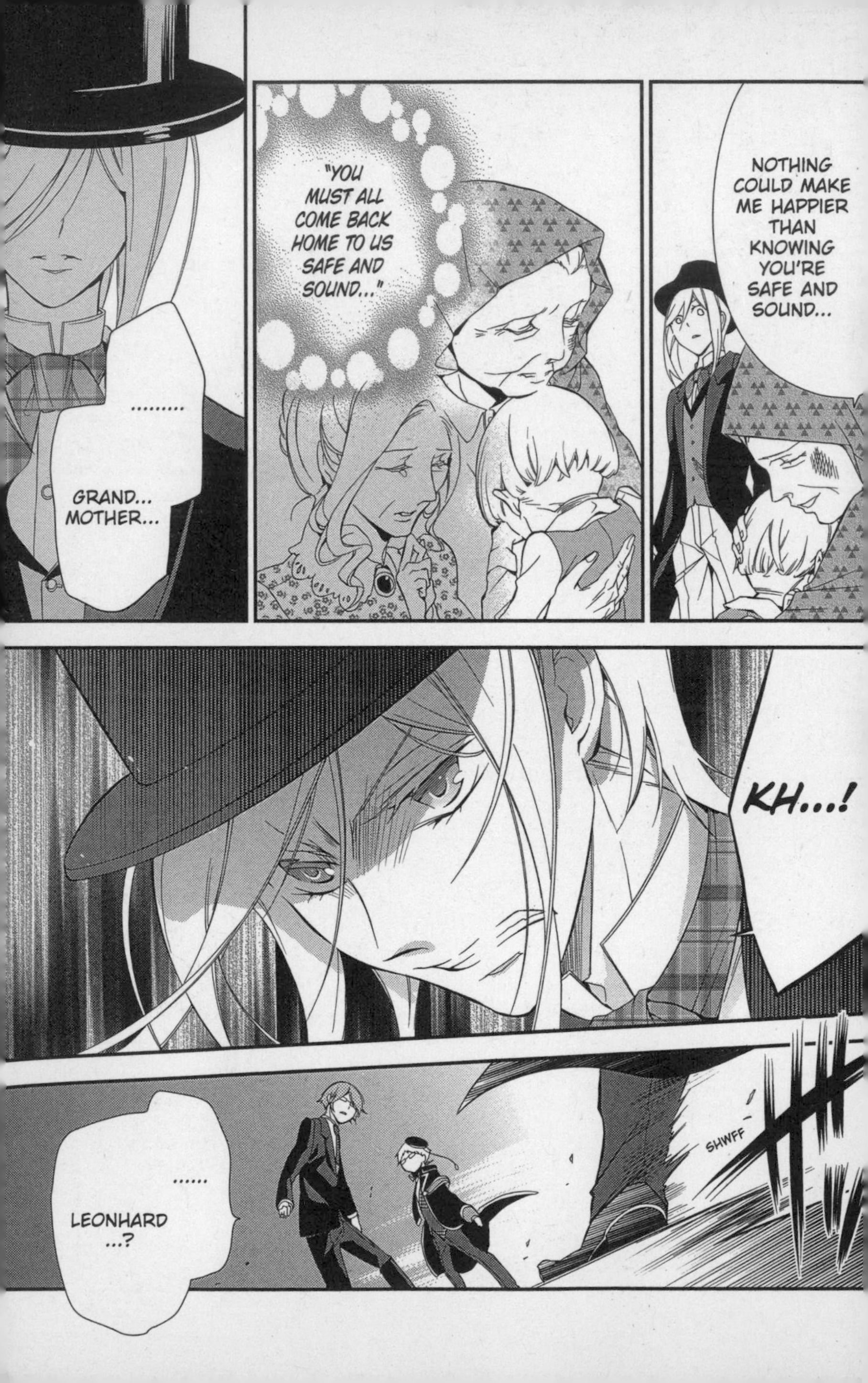
NOTHING COULD MAKE ME HAPPIER THAN KNOWING YOU'RE SAFE AND SOUND...
"YOU MUST ALL COME BACK HOME TO US SAFE AND SOUND..."
....
GRAND... MOTHER...
KH...!
SHWFF
......
LEONHARD ...?

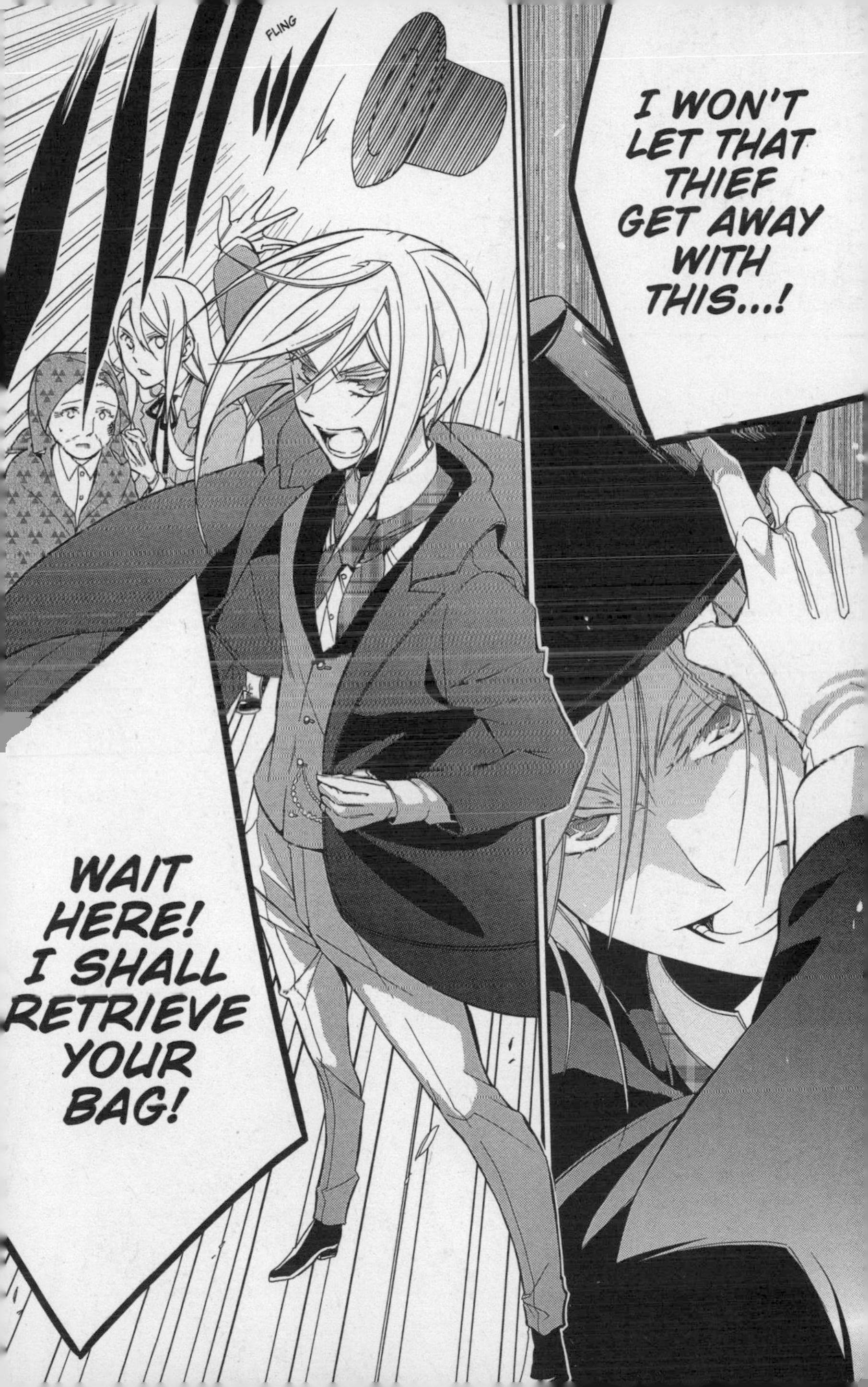

I WON'T LET THAT THIEF GET AWAY WITH THIS...!
FLING
WAIT HERE! I SHALL RETRIEVE YOUR BAG!

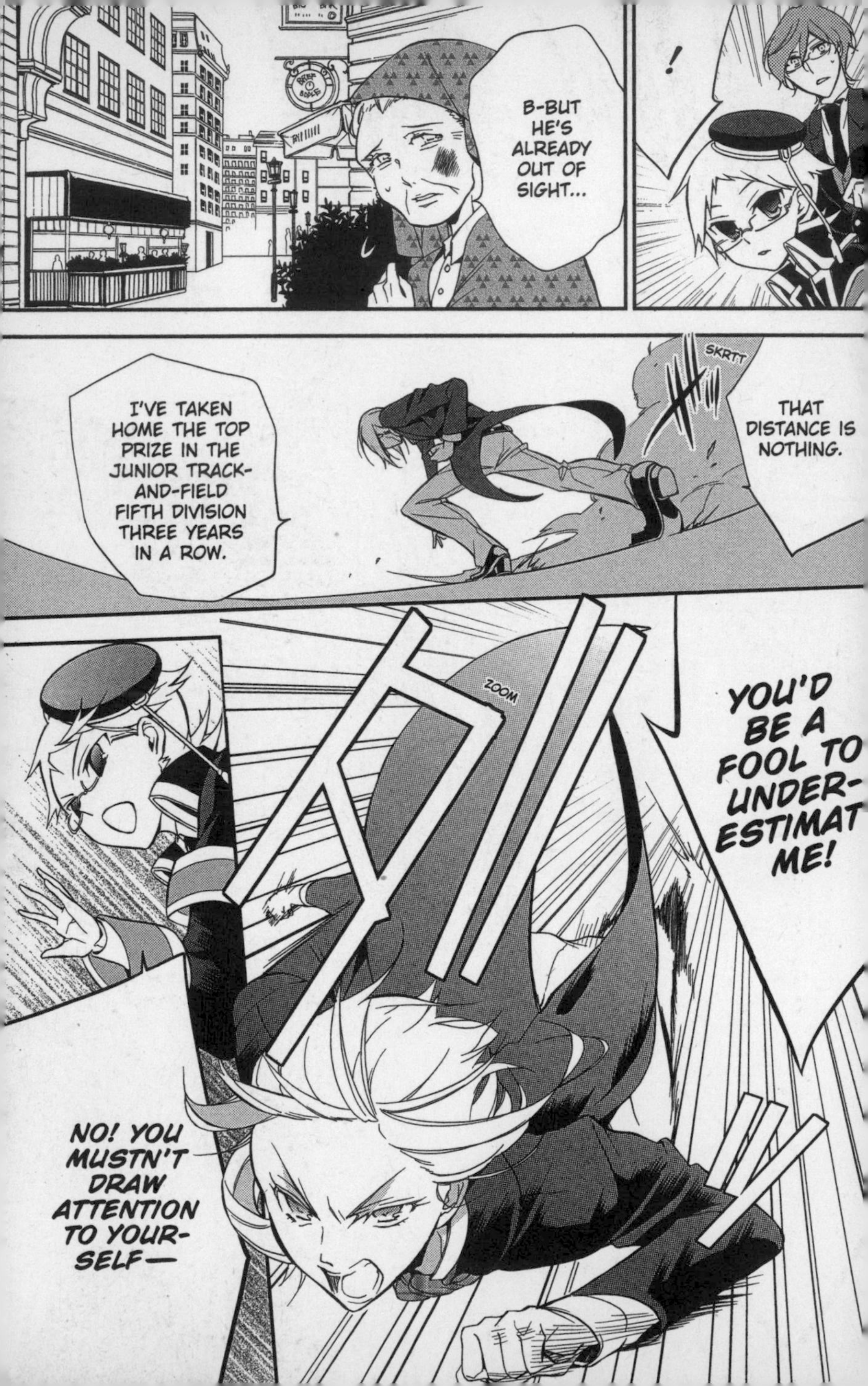
!
B-BUT HE'S ALREADY OUT OF SIGHT...
THAT DISTANCE IS NOTHING.
SKRTT
I'VE TAKEN HOME THE TOP PRIZE IN THE JUNIOR TRACK-AND-FIELD FIFTH DIVISION THREE YEARS IN A ROW.
YOU'D BE A FOOL TO UNDER-ESTIMAT ME!
ZOOM
NO! YOU MUSTN'T DRAW ATTENTION TO YOUR-SELF—

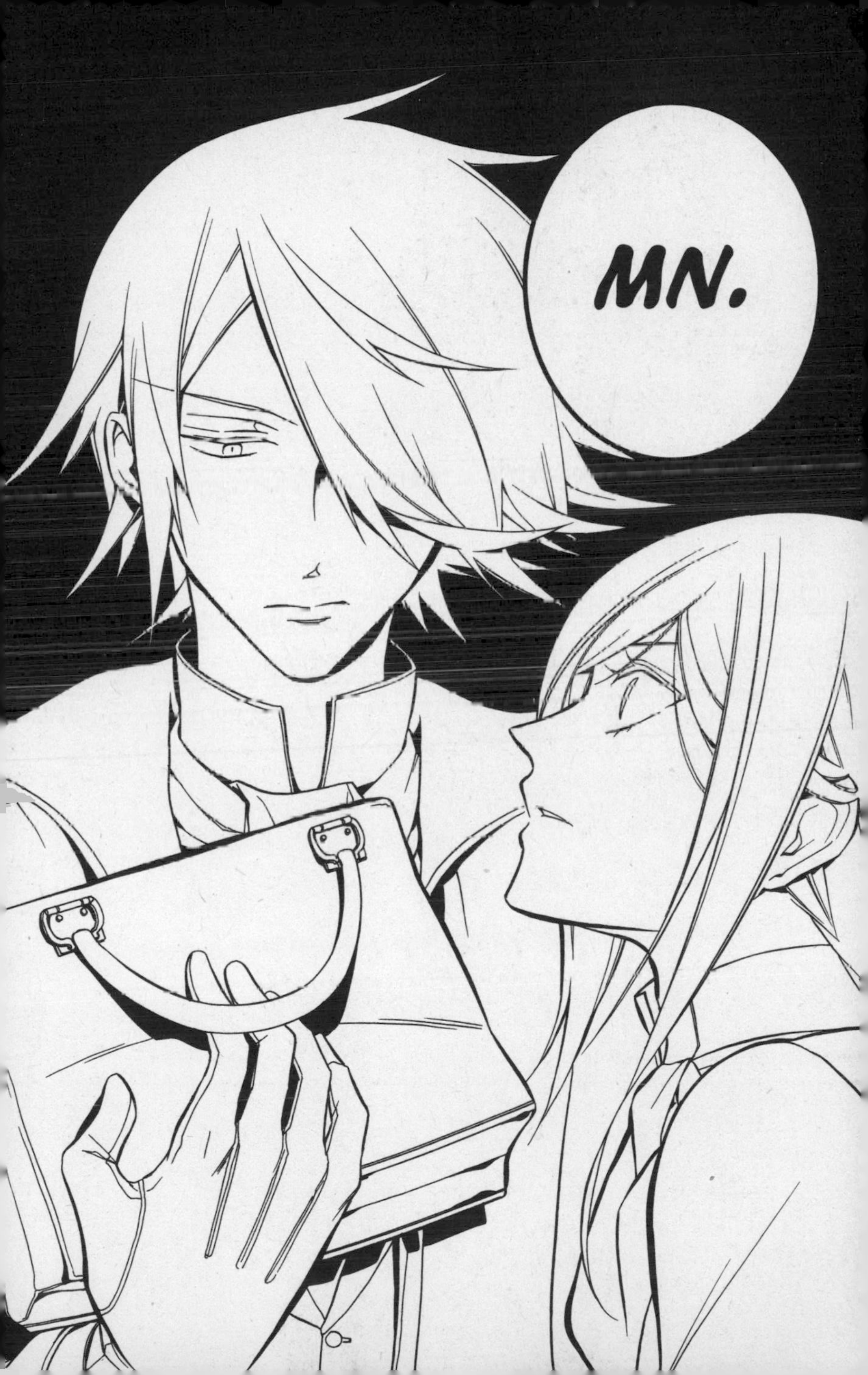
MN.

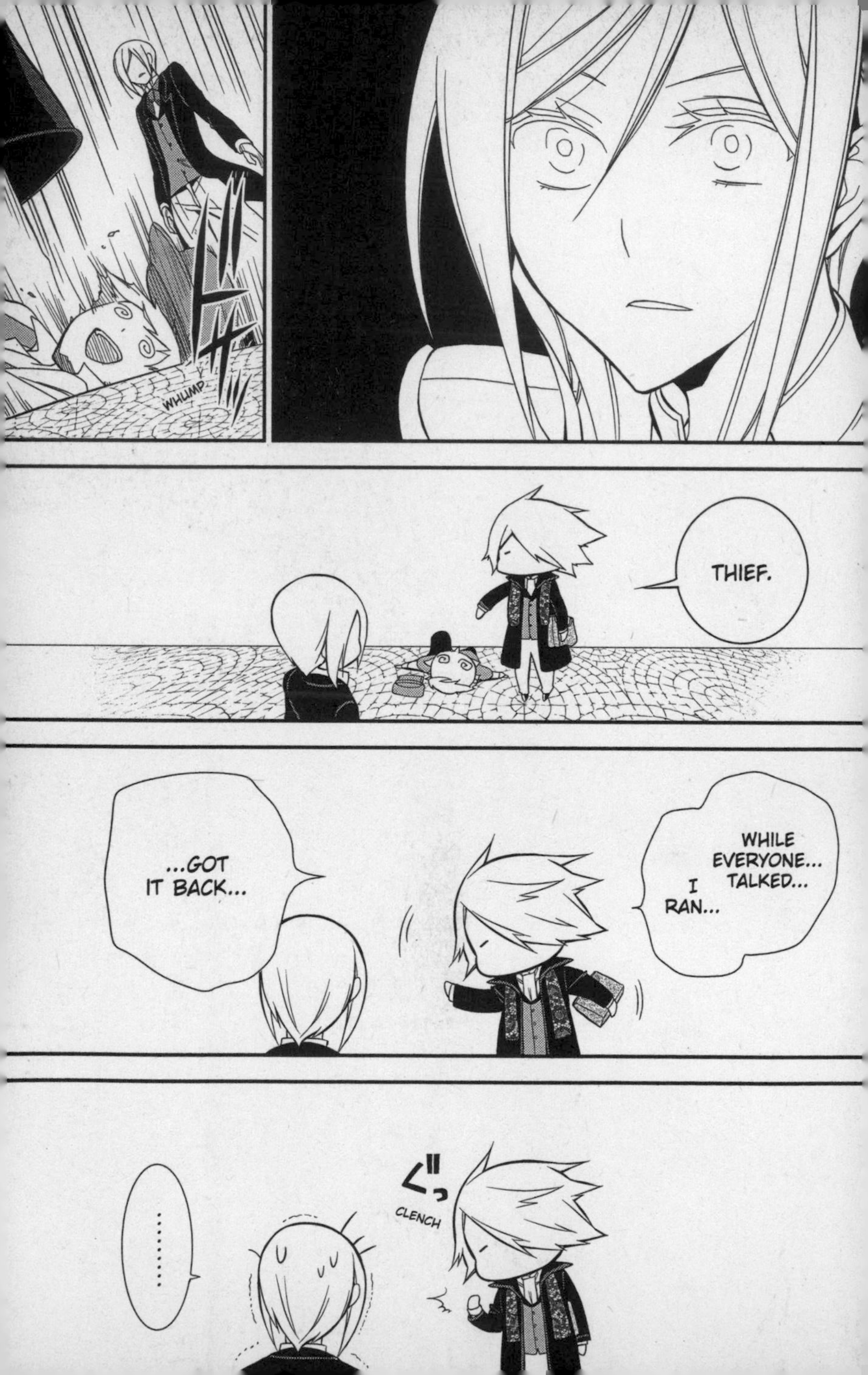
WHUMP
THIEF.
WHILE EVERYONE... TALKED... I RAN...
...GOT IT BACK...
ぐっ
CLENCH
......

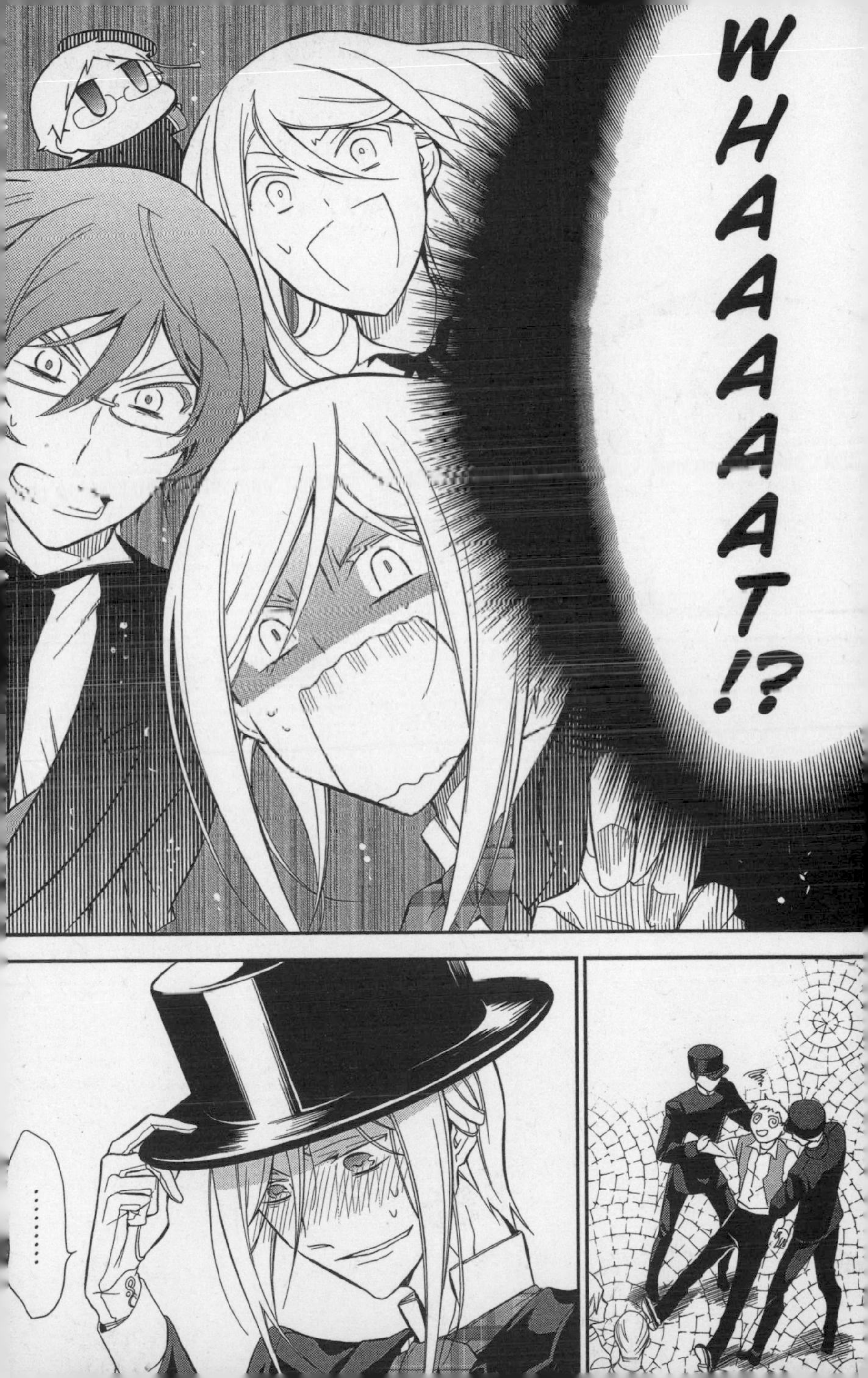
WHAAAAAT!?
......

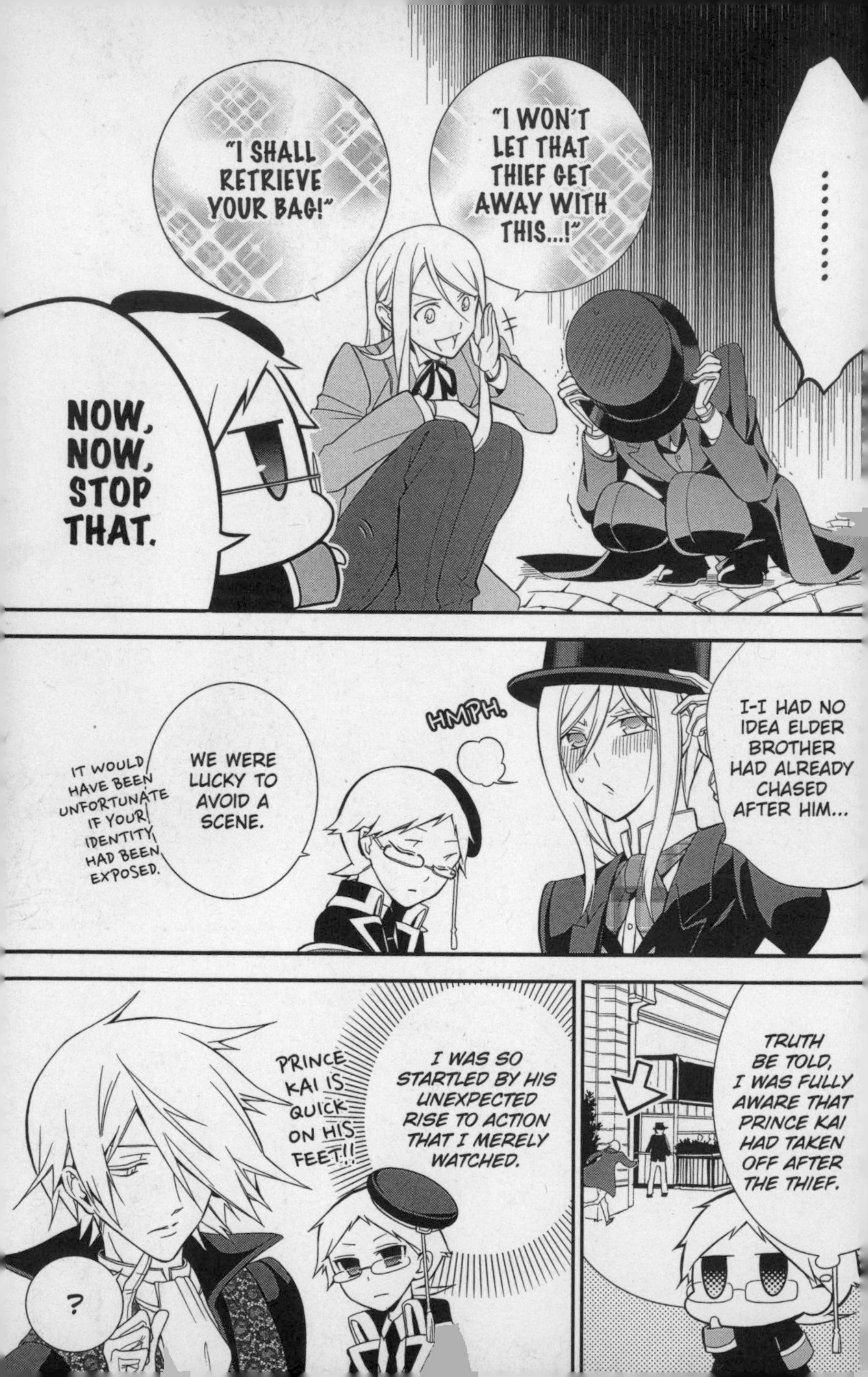
......
"I WON'T LET THAT THIEF GET AWAY WITH THIS...!"
"I SHALL RETRIEVE YOUR BAG!"
NOW, NOW, STOP THAT.
I-I HAD NO IDEA ELDER BROTHER HAD ALREADY CHASED AFTER HIM...
HMPH.
WE WERE LUCKY TO AVOID A SCENE.
IT WOULD HAVE BEEN UNFORTUNATE IF YOUR IDENTITY HAD BEEN EXPOSED.
TRUTH BE TOLD, I WAS FULLY AWARE THAT PRINCE KAI HAD TAKEN OFF AFTER THE THIEF.
I WAS SO STARTLED BY HIS UNEXPECTED RISE TO ACTION THAT I MERELY WATCHED.
PRINCE KAI IS QUICK ON HIS FEET!!
?

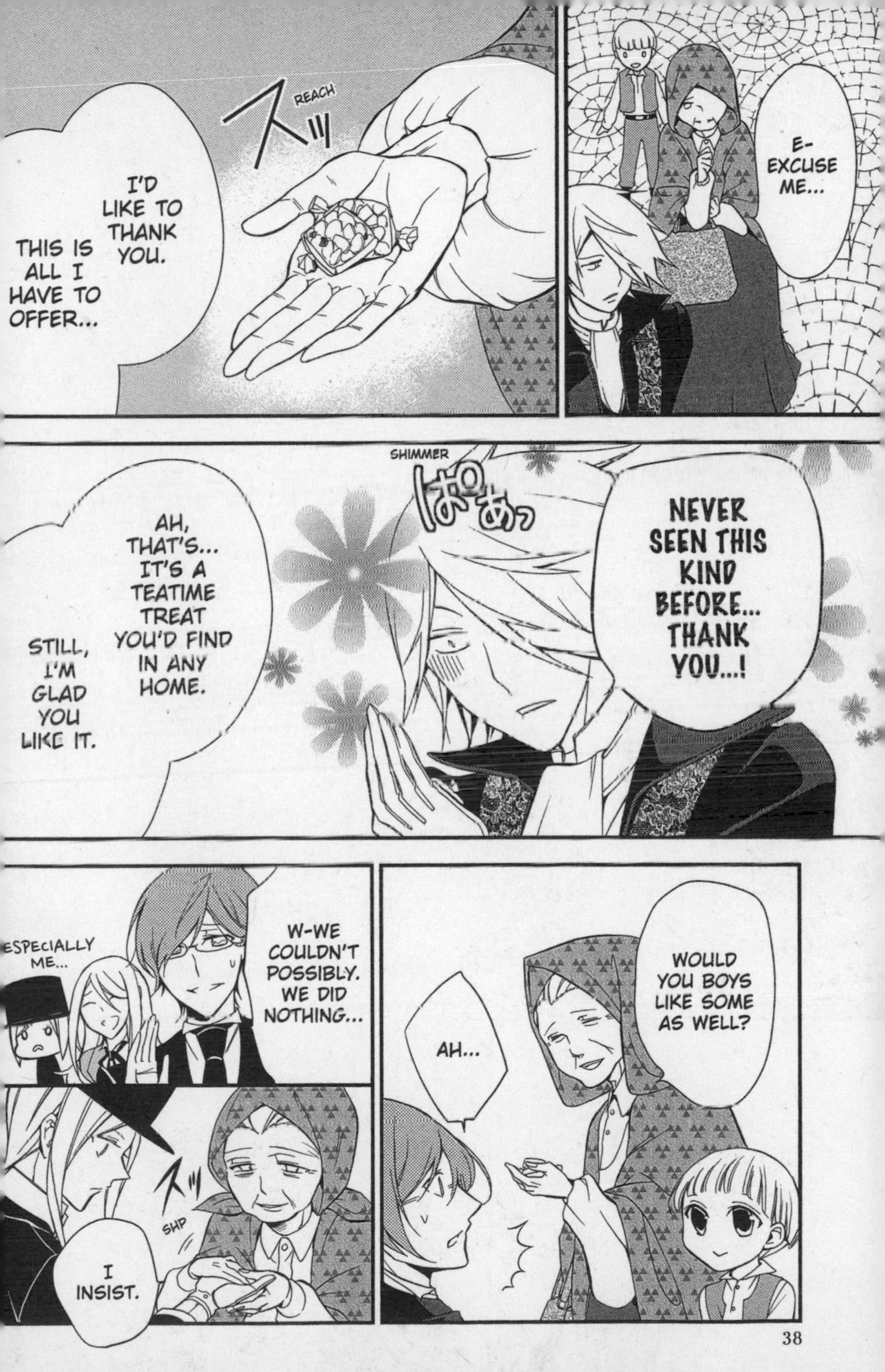
E-EXCUSE ME...
REACH
I'D LIKE TO THANK YOU.
THIS IS ALL I HAVE TO OFFER...
SHIMMER
NEVER SEEN THIS KIND BEFORE... THANK YOU...!
AH, THAT'S... IT'S A TEATIME TREAT YOU'D FIND IN ANY HOME.
STILL, I'M GLAD YOU LIKE IT.
WOULD YOU BOYS LIKE SOME AS WELL?
AH...
W-WE COULDN'T POSSIBLY. WE DID NOTHING...
ESPECIALLY ME...
SHP
I INSIST.

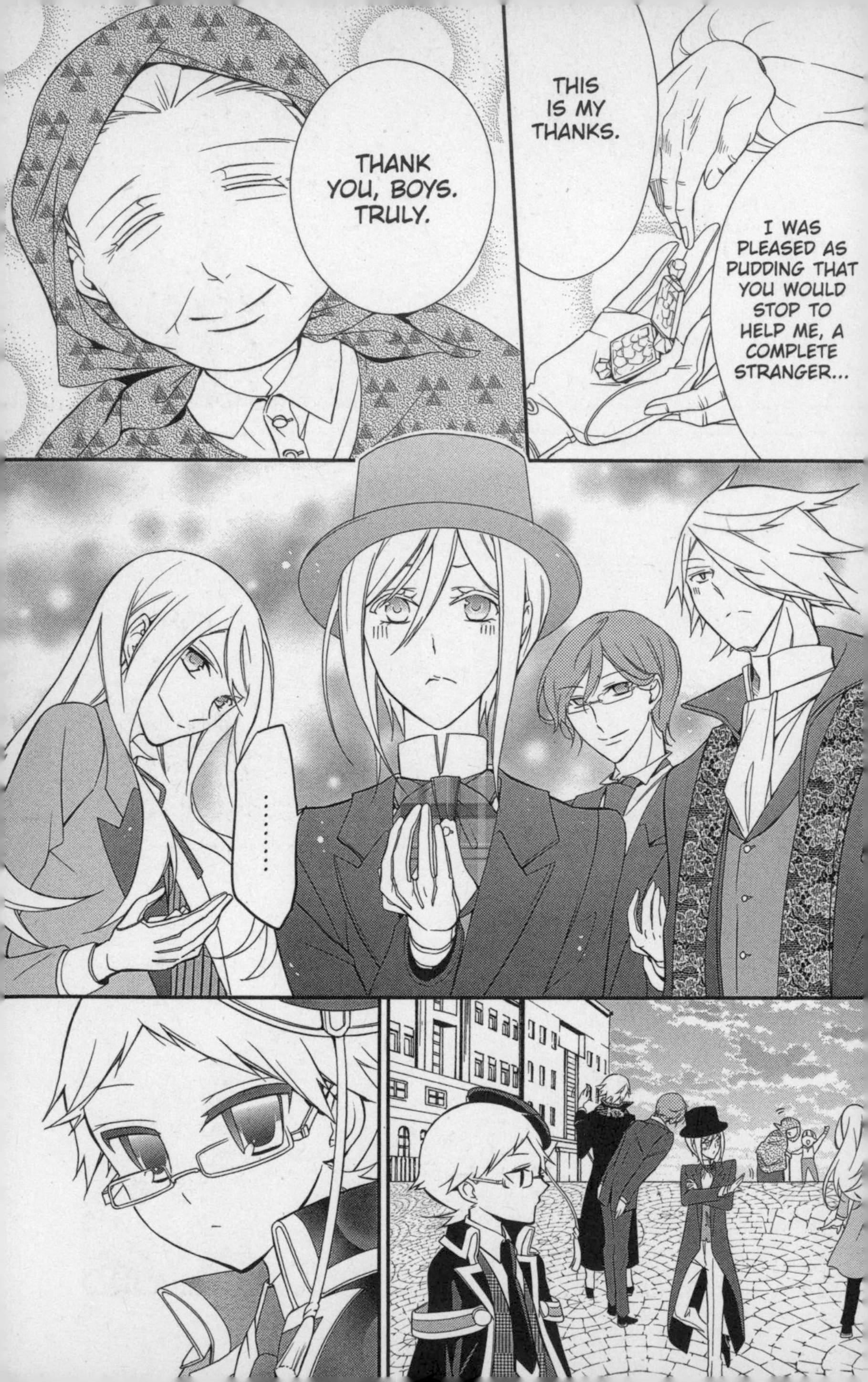
I WAS PLEASED AS PUDDING THAT YOU WOULD STOP TO HELP ME, A COMPLETE STRANGER...
THIS IS MY THANKS.
THANK YOU, BOYS. TRULY.
......

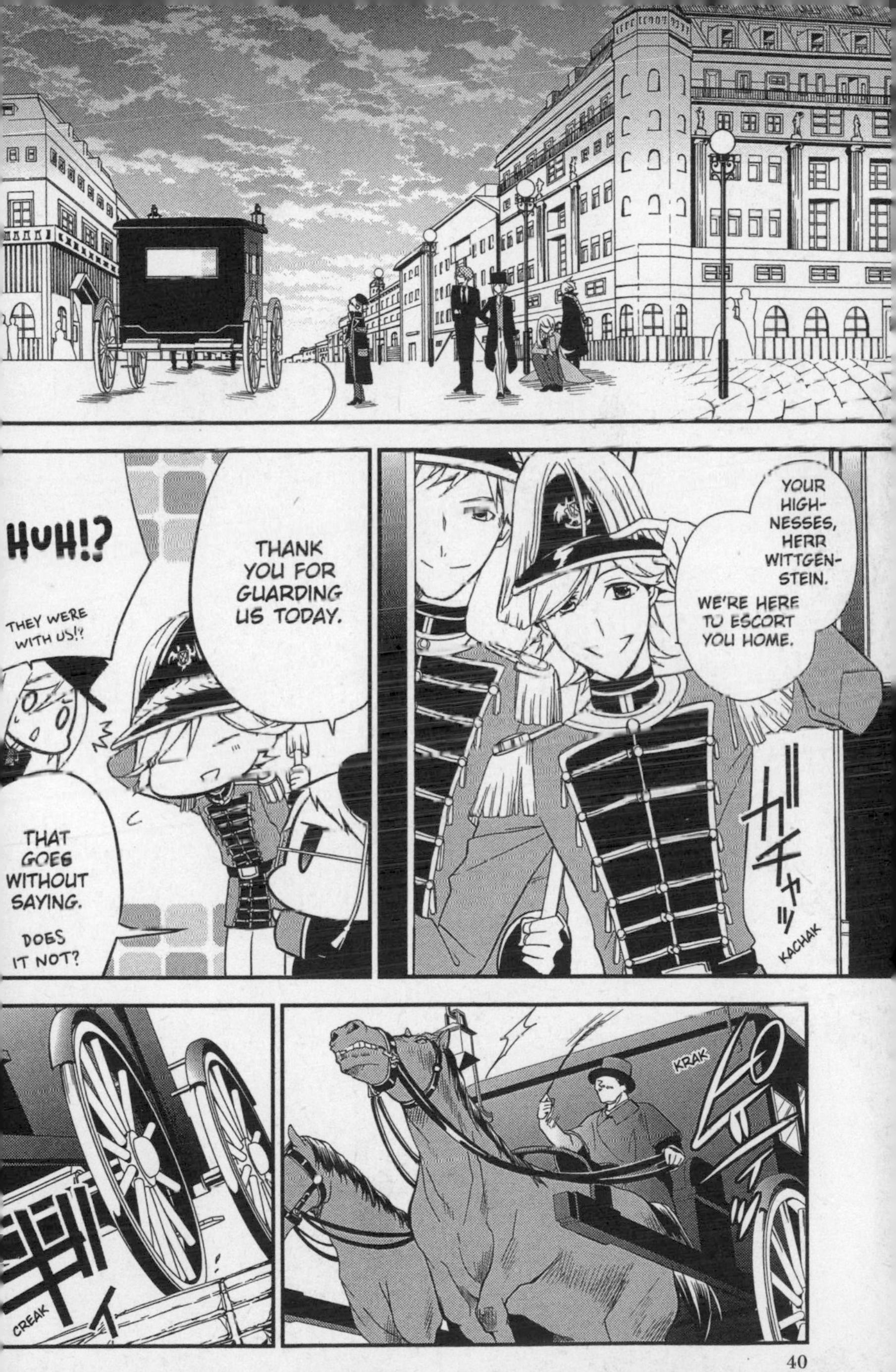
YOUR HIGH-NESSES, HERR WITTGEN-STEIN.
WE'RE HERE TO ESCORT YOU HOME.
ガチャッ
KACHAK
THANK YOU FOR GUARDING US TODAY.
HUH!?
THEY WERE WITH US!?
THAT GOES WITHOUT SAYING.
DOES IT NOT?
KRAK
CREAK

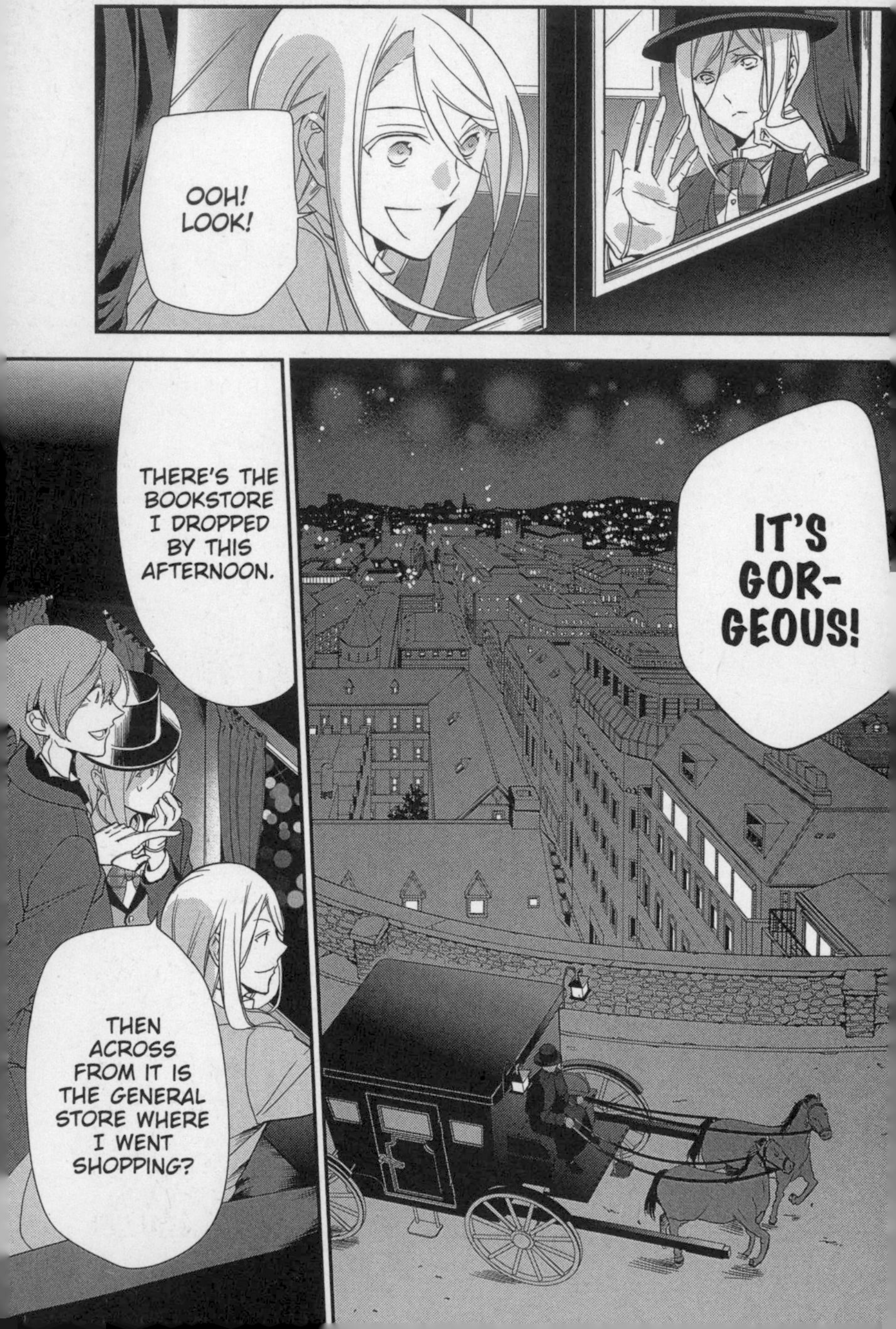
OOH! LOOK!
IT'S GOR-GEOUS!
THERE'S THE BOOKSTORE I DROPPED BY THIS AFTERNOON.
THEN ACROSS FROM IT IS THE GENERAL STORE WHERE I WENT SHOPPING?

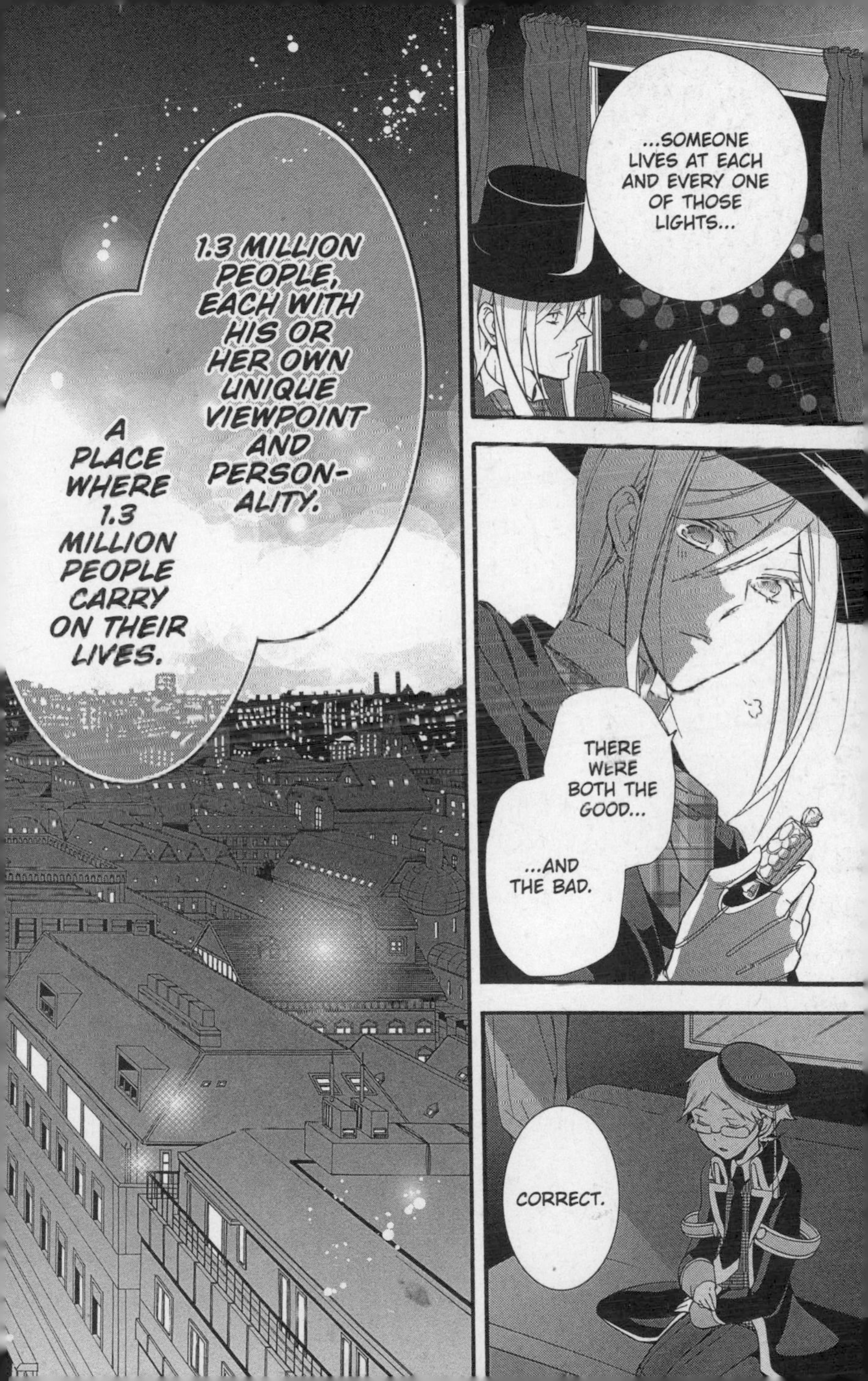
...SOMEONE LIVES AT EACH AND EVERY ONE OF THOSE LIGHTS...
THERE WERE BOTH THE GOOD...
...AND THE BAD.
CORRECT.
1.3 MILLION PEOPLE, EACH WITH HIS OR HER OWN UNIQUE VIEWPOINT AND PERSON-ALITY.
A PLACE WHERE 1.3 MILLION PEOPLE CARRY ON THEIR LIVES.

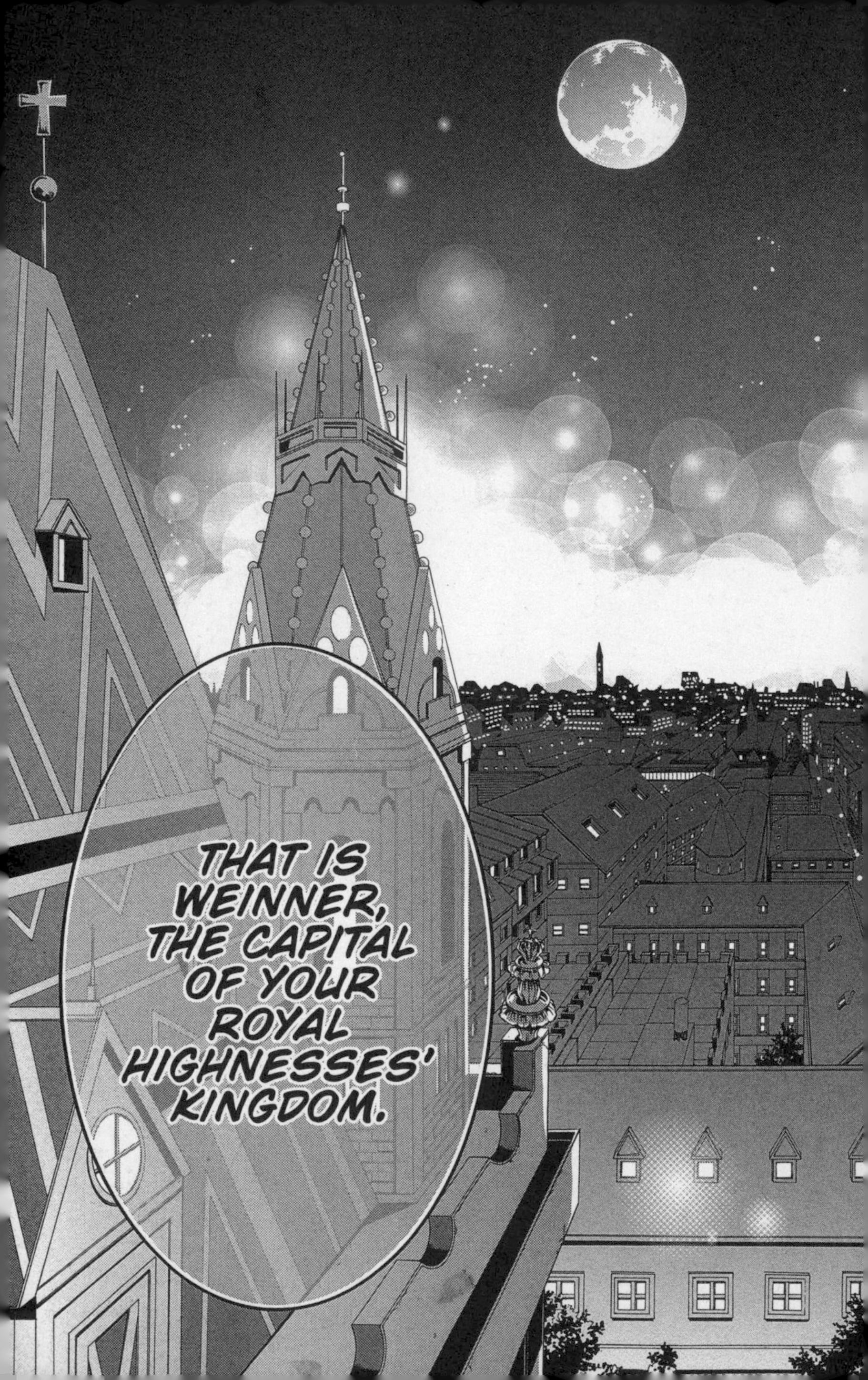
THAT IS WEINNER, THE CAPITAL OF YOUR ROYAL HIGHNESSES' KINGDOM.

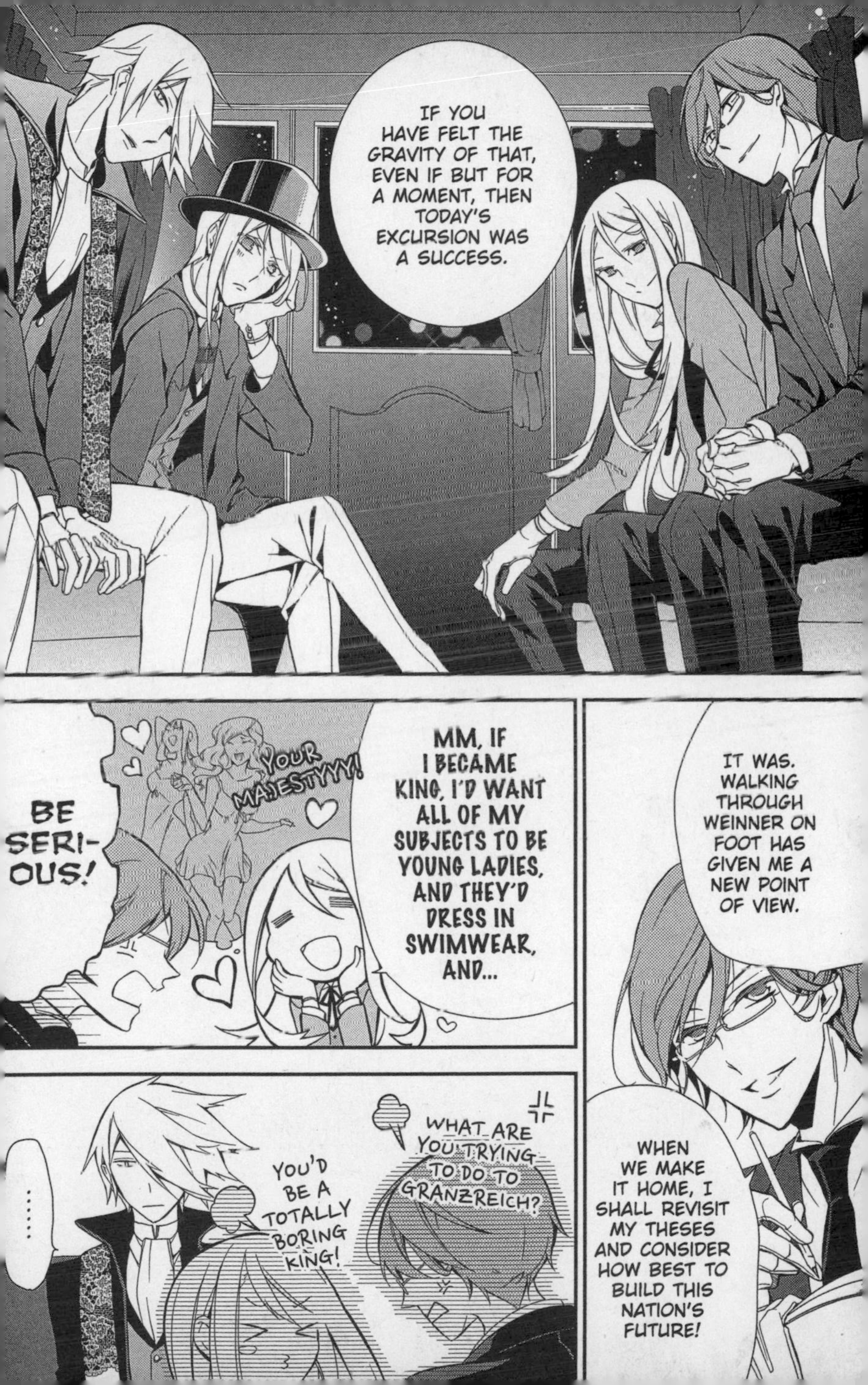
IF YOU HAVE FELT THE GRAVITY OF THAT, EVEN IF BUT FOR A MOMENT, THEN TODAY'S EXCURSION WAS A SUCCESS.
IT WAS. WALKING THROUGH WEINNER ON FOOT HAS GIVEN ME A NEW POINT OF VIEW.
WHEN WE MAKE IT HOME, I SHALL REVISIT MY THESES AND CONSIDER HOW BEST TO BUILD THIS NATION'S FUTURE!
MM, IF I BECAME KING, I'D WANT ALL OF MY SUBJECTS TO BE YOUNG LADIES, AND THEY'D DRESS IN SWIMWEAR, AND...
YOUR MAJESTYYY!
BE SERI-OUS!
WHAT ARE YOU TRYING TO DO TO GRANZREICH?
YOU'D BE A TOTALLY BORING KING!
......

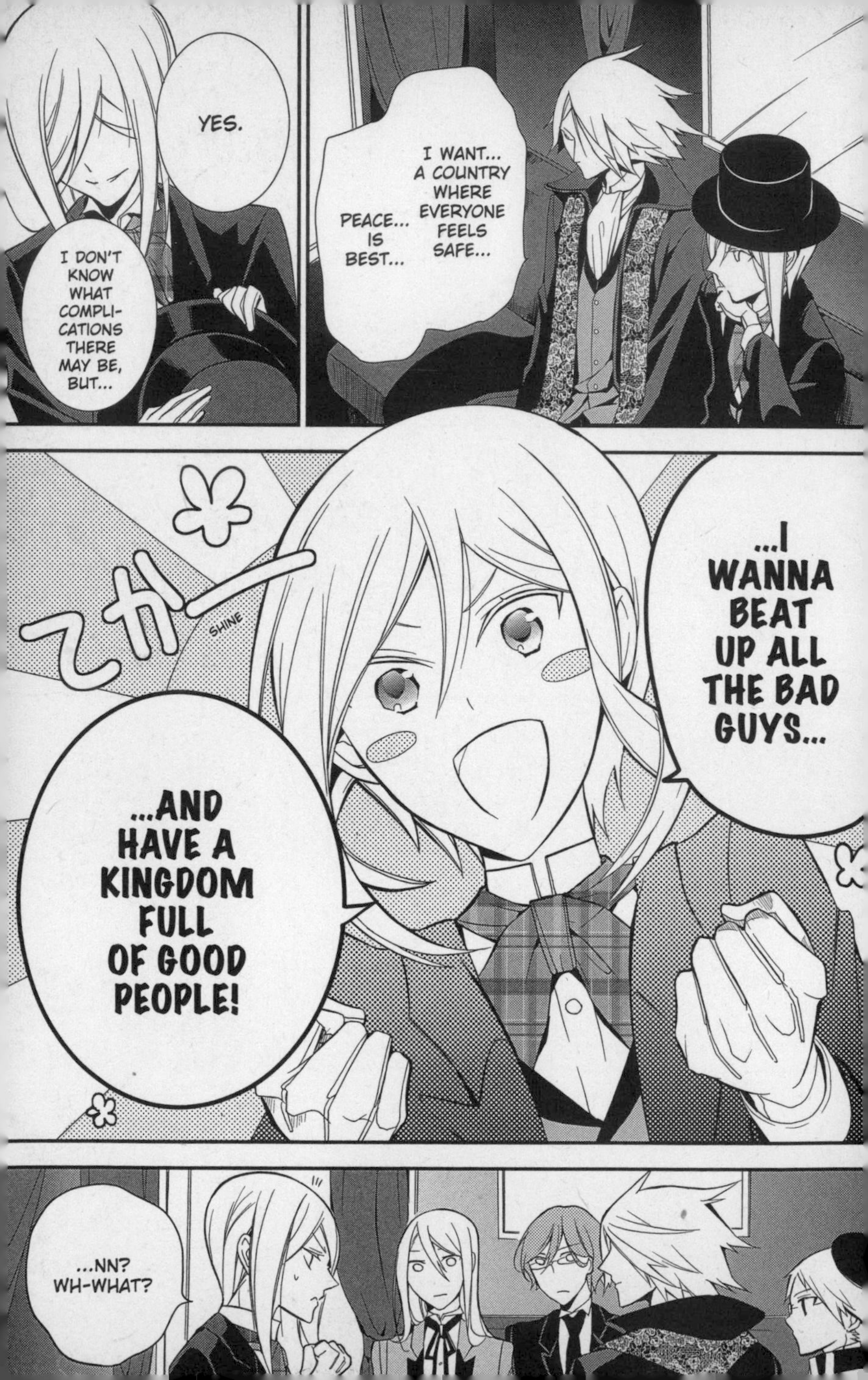
I WANT... A COUNTRY WHERE EVERYONE FEELS SAFE...
PEACE... IS BEST...
YES.
I DON'T KNOW WHAT COMPLI-CATIONS THERE MAY BE, BUT...
...I WANNA BEAT UP ALL THE BAD GUYS...
SHINE
...AND HAVE A KINGDOM FULL OF GOOD PEOPLE!
...NN? WH-WHAT?

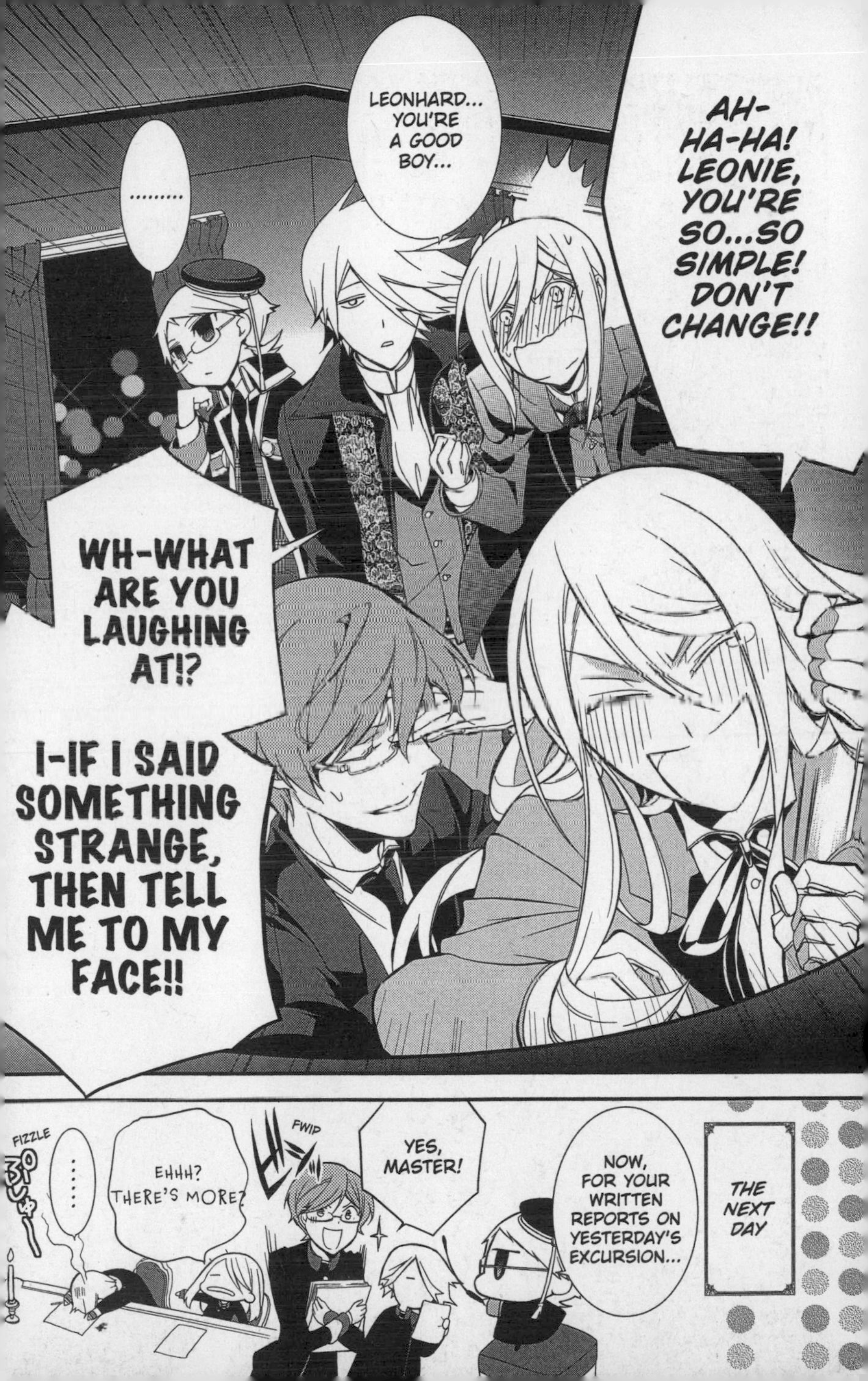
AH-HA-HA! LEONIE, YOU'RE SO...SO SIMPLE! DON'T CHANGE!!
LEONHARD... YOU'RE A GOOD BOY...
....
WH-WHAT ARE YOU LAUGHING AT!?
I-IF I SAID SOMETHING STRANGE, THEN TELL ME TO MY FACE!!
THE NEXT DAY
NOW, FOR YOUR WRITTEN REPORTS ON YESTERDAY'S EXCURSION...
YES, MASTER!
FWIP
EHHH? THERE'S MORE?
......
FIZZLE

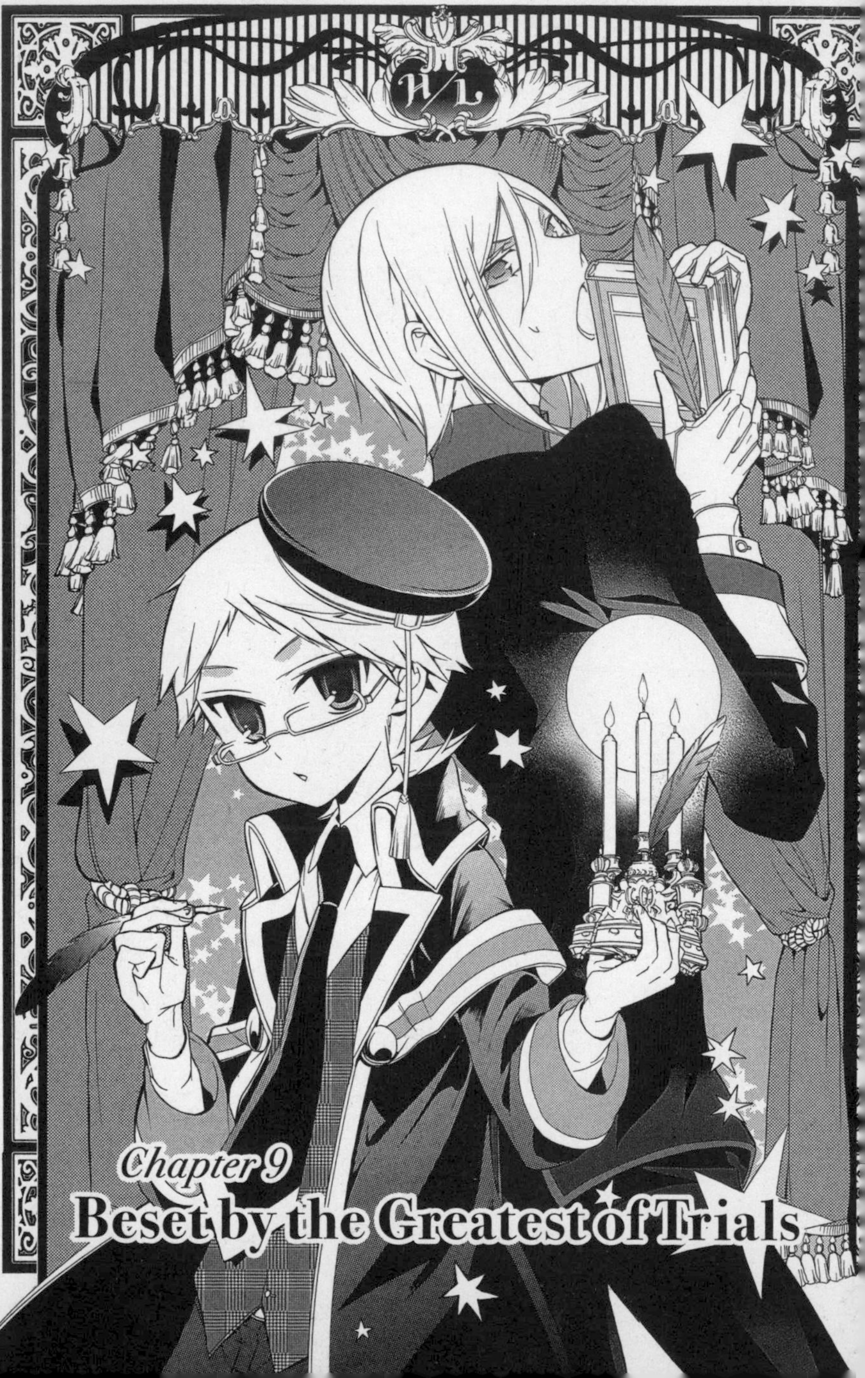
H/L
Chapter 9
Beset by the Greatest of Trials

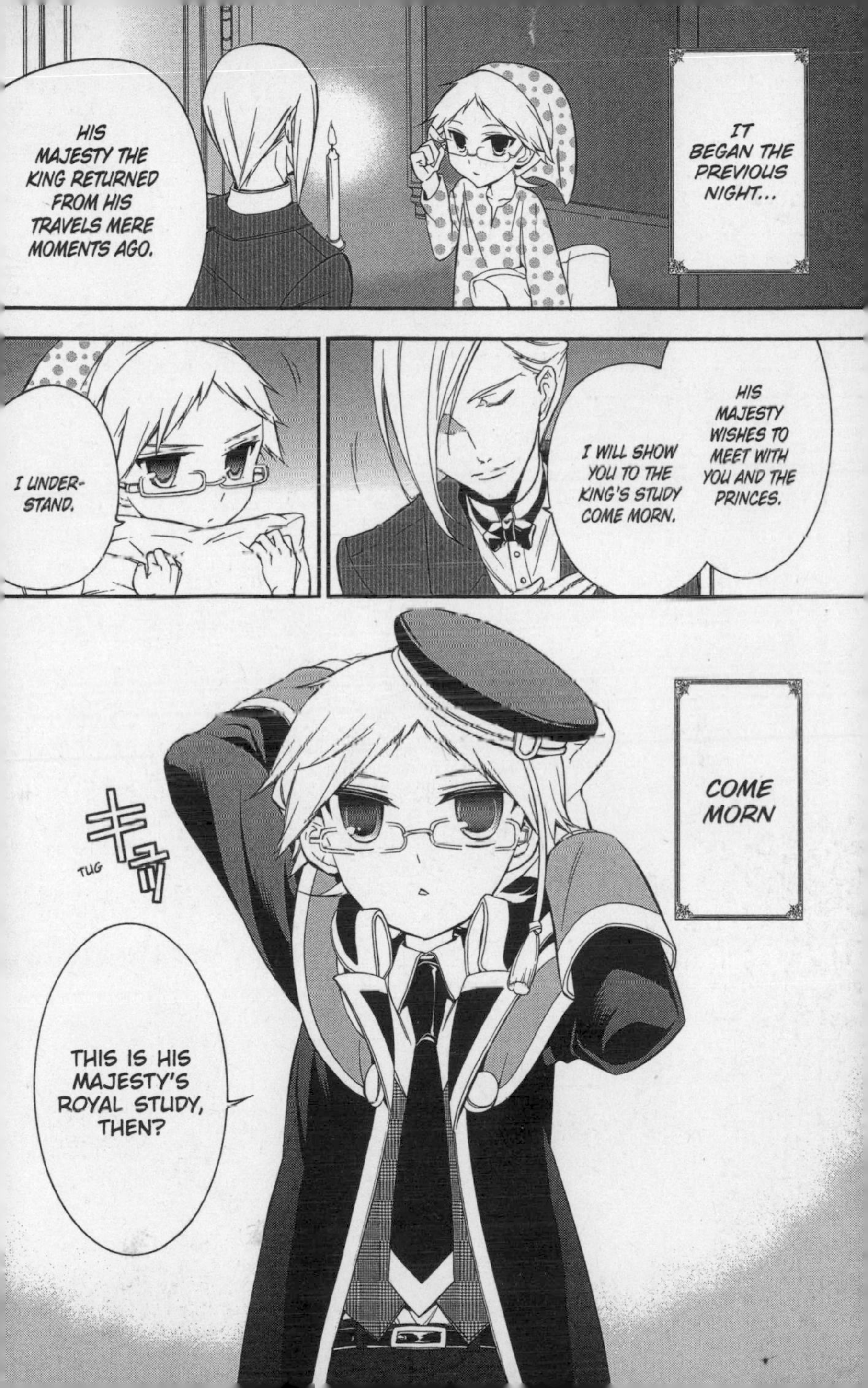
IT BEGAN THE PREVIOUS NIGHT...
HIS MAJESTY THE KING RETURNED FROM HIS TRAVELS MERE MOMENTS AGO.
HIS MAJESTY WISHES TO MEET WITH YOU AND THE PRINCES.
I WILL SHOW YOU TO THE KING'S STUDY COME MORN.
I UNDER-STAND.
COME MORN
TUG
THIS IS HIS MAJESTY'S ROYAL STUDY, THEN?

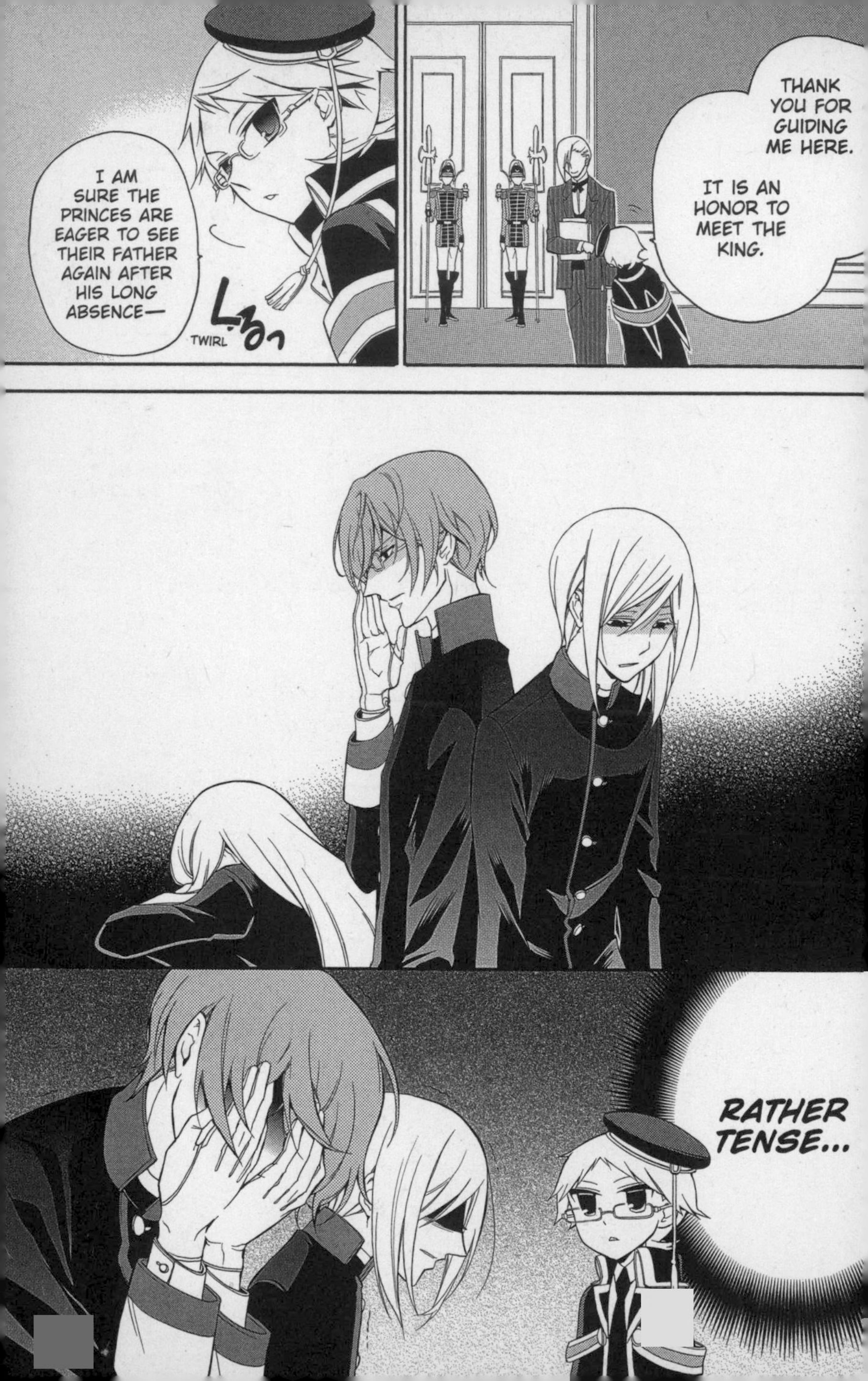
THANK YOU FOR GUIDING ME HERE.
IT IS AN HONOR TO MEET THE KING.
I AM SURE THE PRINCES ARE EAGER TO SEE THEIR FATHER AGAIN AFTER HIS LONG ABSENCE—
TWIRL
RATHER TENSE...

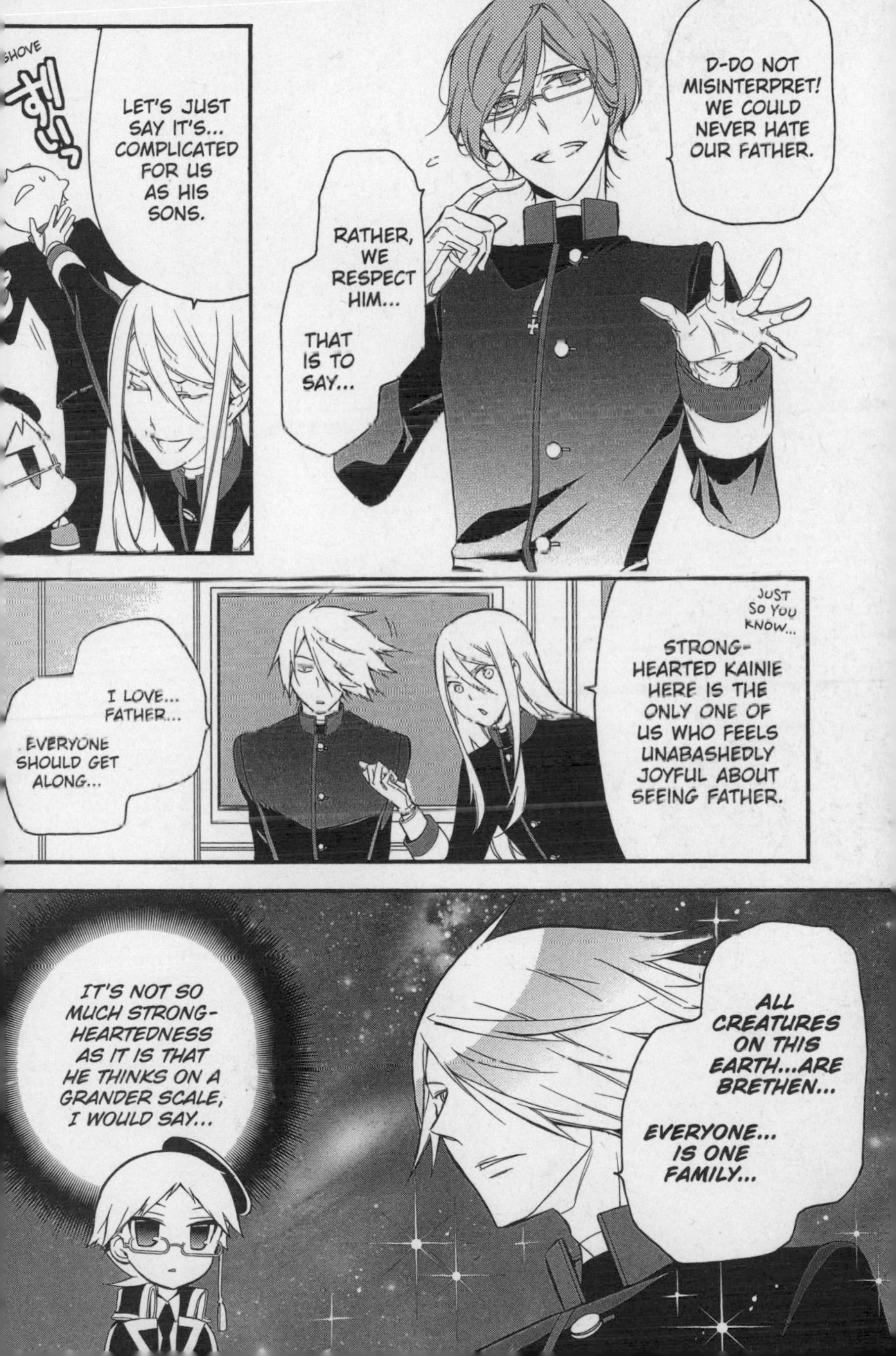
D-DO NOT MISINTERPRET! WE COULD NEVER HATE OUR FATHER.
RATHER, WE RESPECT HIM...
THAT IS TO SAY...
SHOVE
LET'S JUST SAY IT'S... COMPLICATED FOR US AS HIS SONS.
JUST SO YOU KNOW...
STRONG-HEARTED KAINIE HERE IS THE ONLY ONE OF US WHO FEELS UNABASHEDLY JOYFUL ABOUT SEEING FATHER.
I LOVE... FATHER...
EVERYONE SHOULD GET ALONG...
ALL CREATURES ON THIS EARTH...ARE BRETHEN...
EVERYONE... IS ONE FAMILY...
IT'S NOT SO MUCH STRONG-HEARTEDNESS AS IT IS THAT HE THINKS ON A GRANDER SCALE, I WOULD SAY...

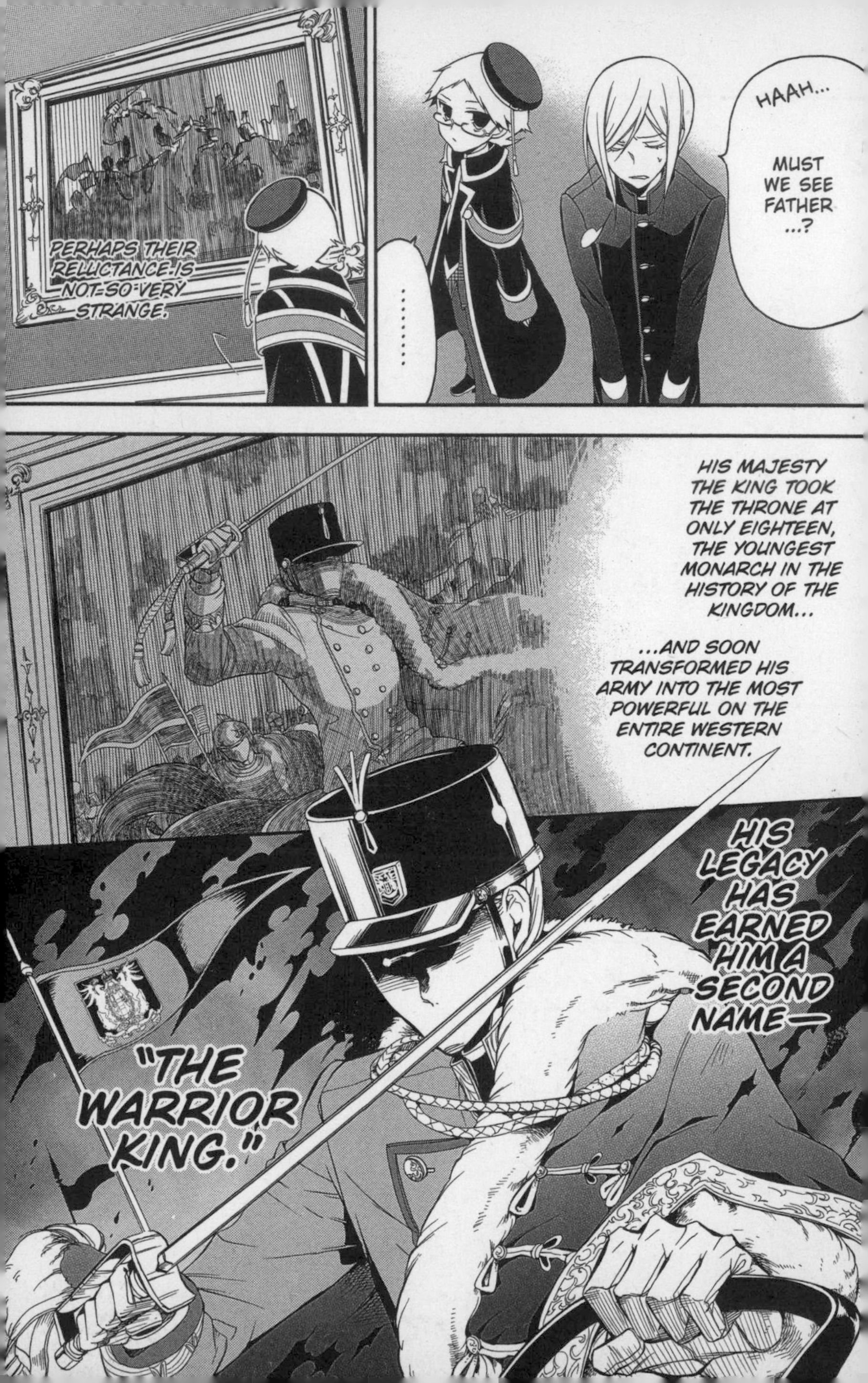
HAAH...
MUST WE SEE FATHER ...?
......
PERHAPS THEIR RELUCTANCE IS NOT SO VERY STRANGE.
HIS MAJESTY THE KING TOOK THE THRONE AT ONLY EIGHTEEN, THE YOUNGEST MONARCH IN THE HISTORY OF THE KINGDOM...
...AND SOON TRANSFORMED HIS ARMY INTO THE MOST POWERFUL ON THE ENTIRE WESTERN CONTINENT.
HIS LEGACY HAS EARNED HIM A SECOND NAME—
"THE WARRIOR KING."

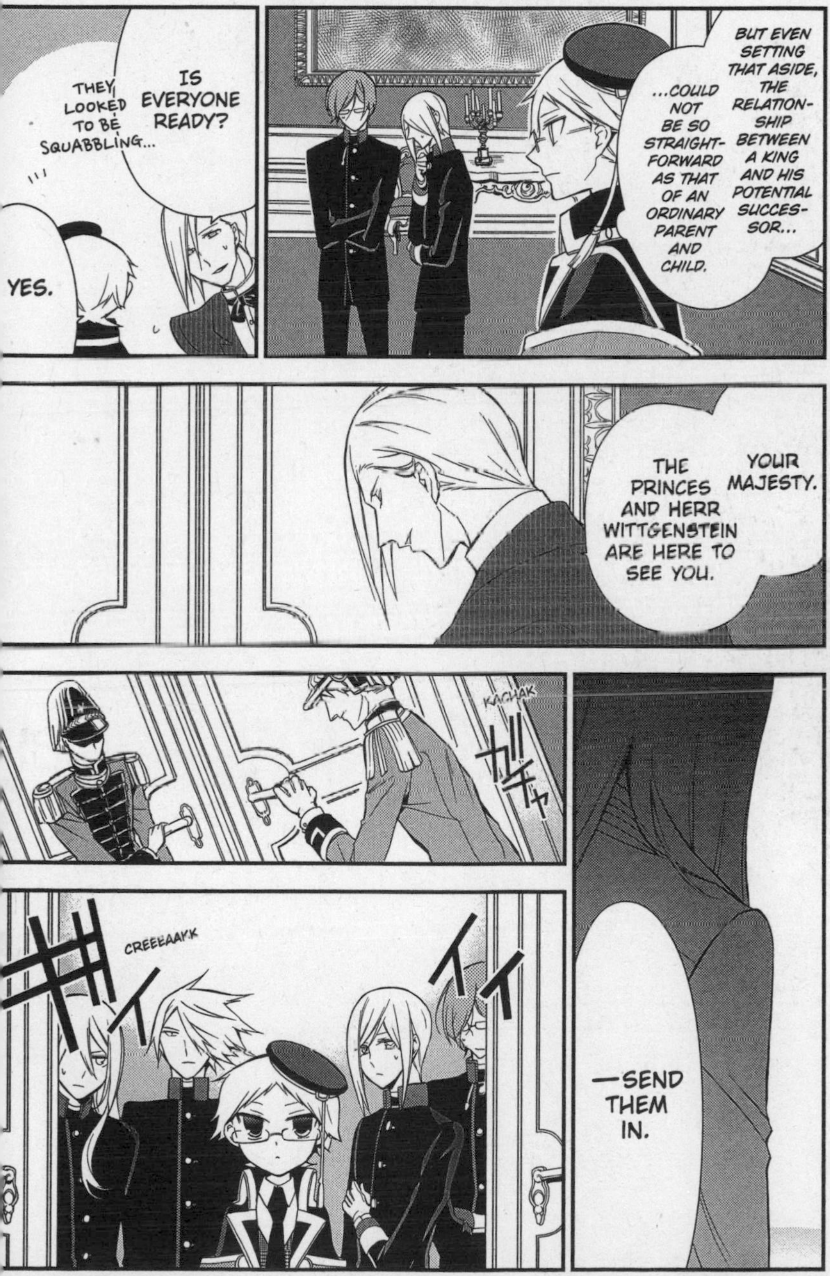
BUT EVEN SETTING THAT ASIDE, THE RELATION-SHIP BETWEEN A KING AND HIS POTENTIAL SUCCES-SOR...
...COULD NOT BE SO STRAIGHT-FORWARD AS THAT OF AN ORDINARY PARENT AND CHILD.
IS EVERYONE READY?
THEY LOOKED TO BE SQUABBLING...
YES.
YOUR MAJESTY.
THE PRINCES AND HERR WITTGENSTEIN ARE HERE TO SEE YOU.
—SEND THEM IN.
KACHAK
CREEEAAKK

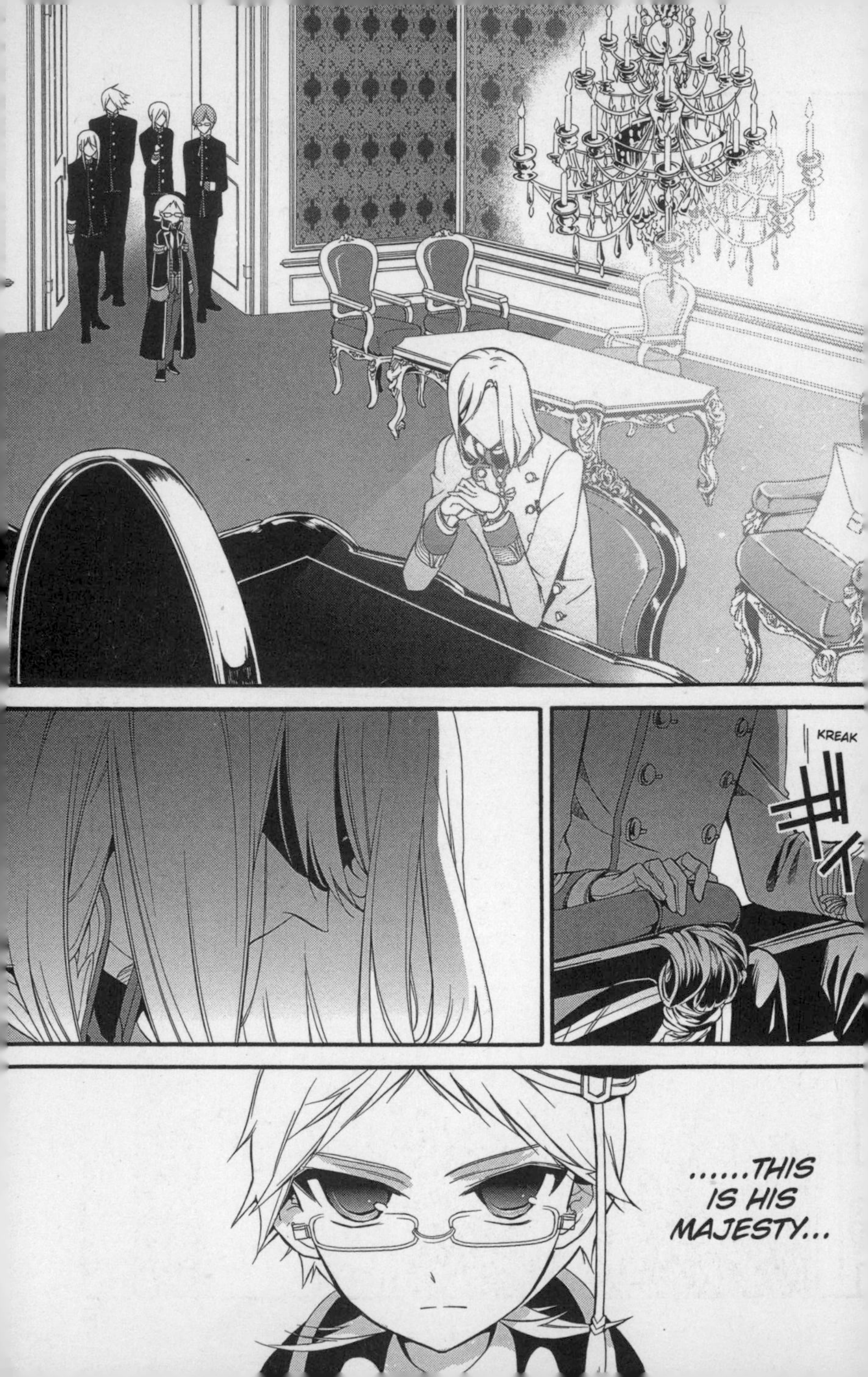
KREAK
ギィ
......THIS IS HIS MAJESTY...

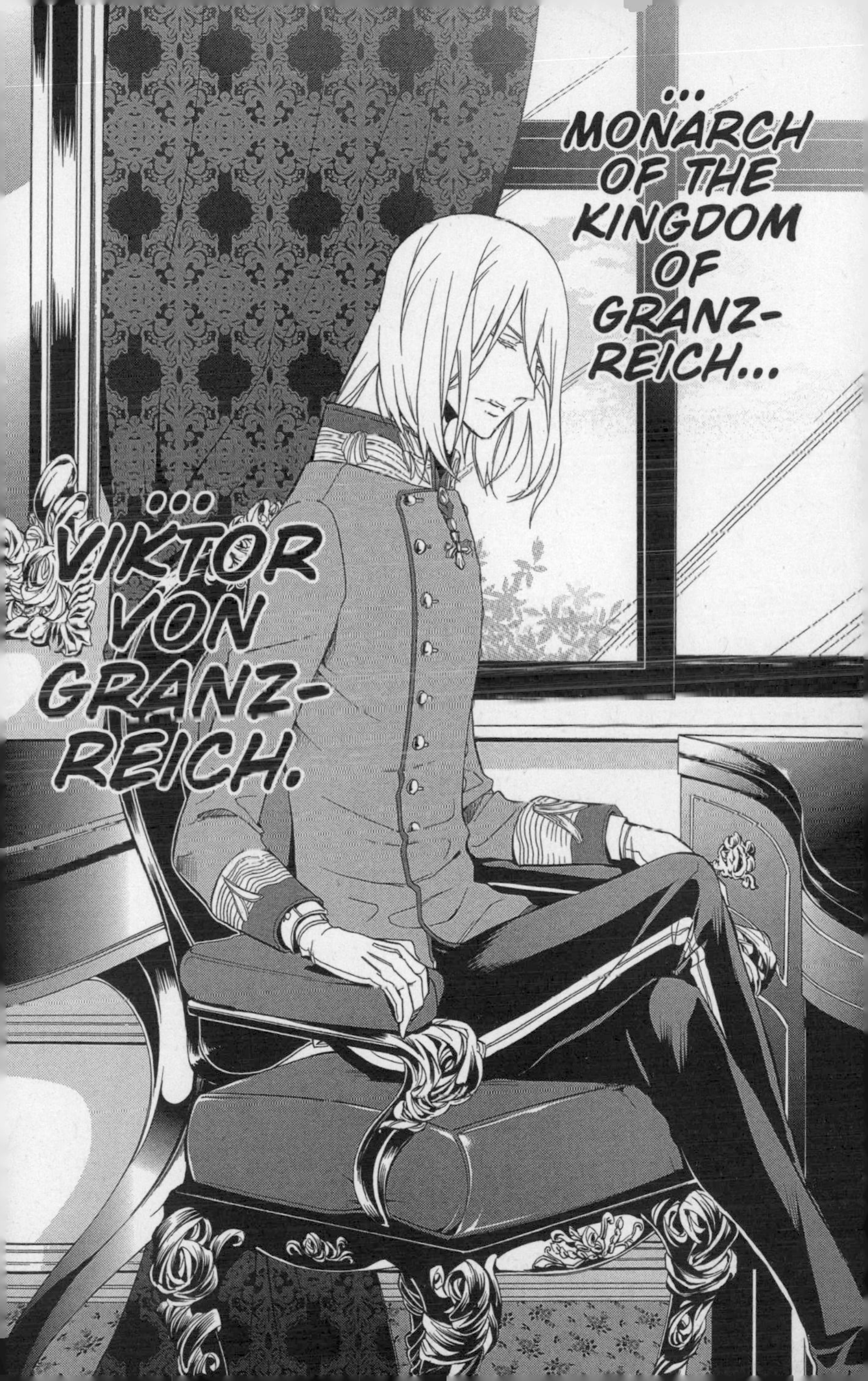
...MONÄRCH OF THE KINGDOM OF GRANZ-REICH...
...VIKTOR VON GRANZ-REICH.

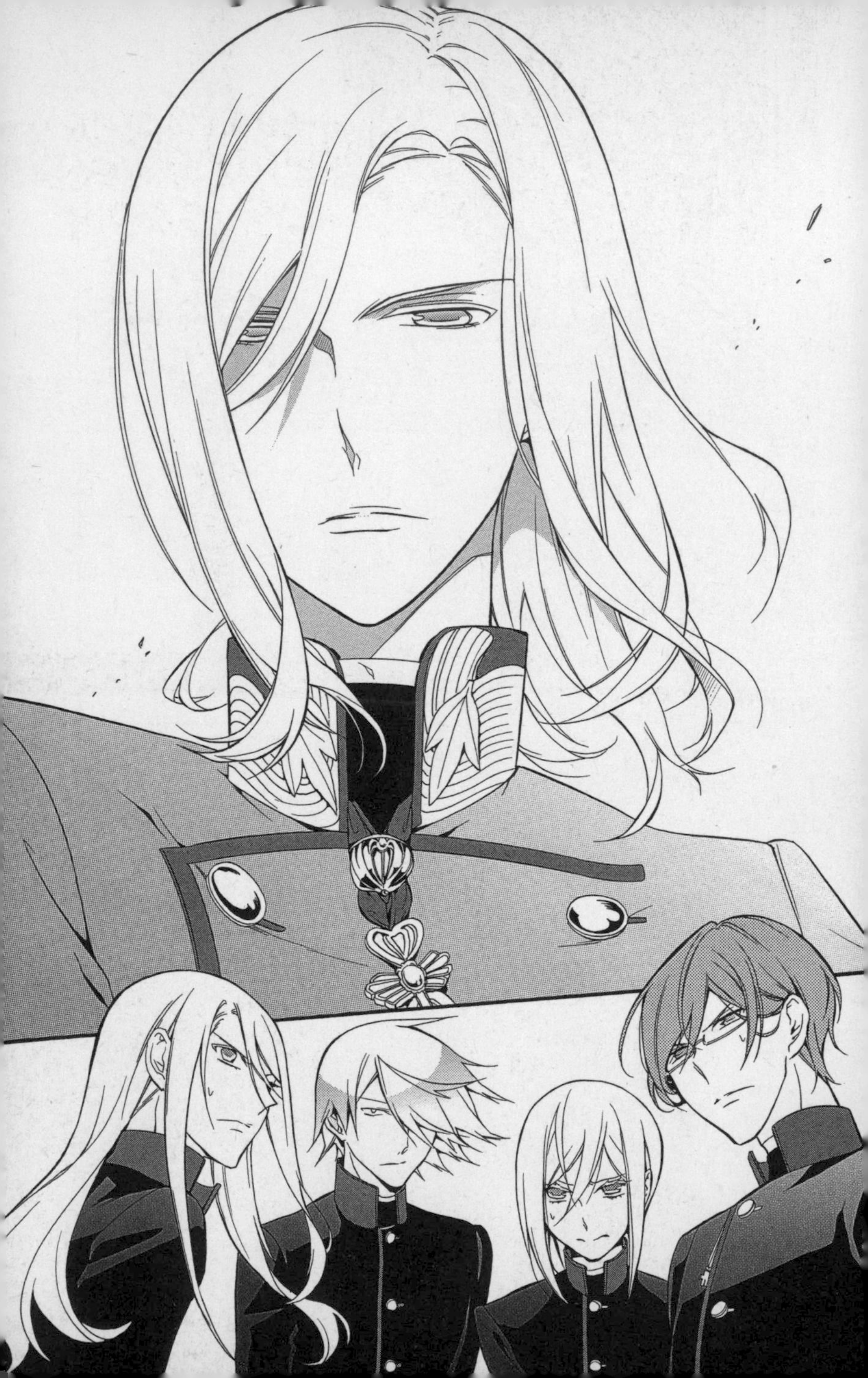

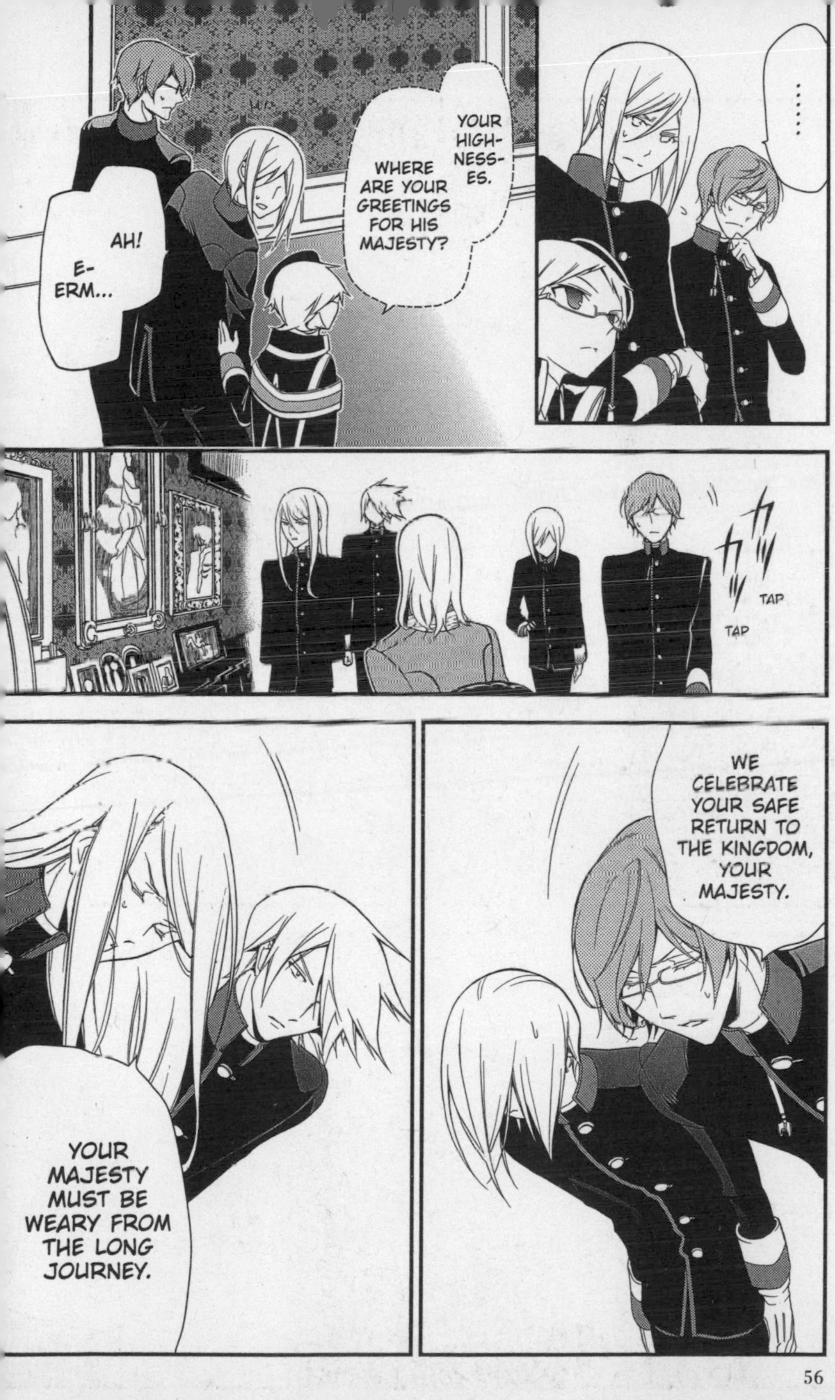
......
YOUR HIGHNESSES.
WHERE ARE YOUR GREETINGS FOR HIS MAJESTY?
AH! E-ERM...
TAP
TAP
WE CELEBRATE YOUR SAFE RETURN TO THE KINGDOM, YOUR MAJESTY.
YOUR MAJESTY MUST BE WEARY FROM THE LONG JOURNEY.

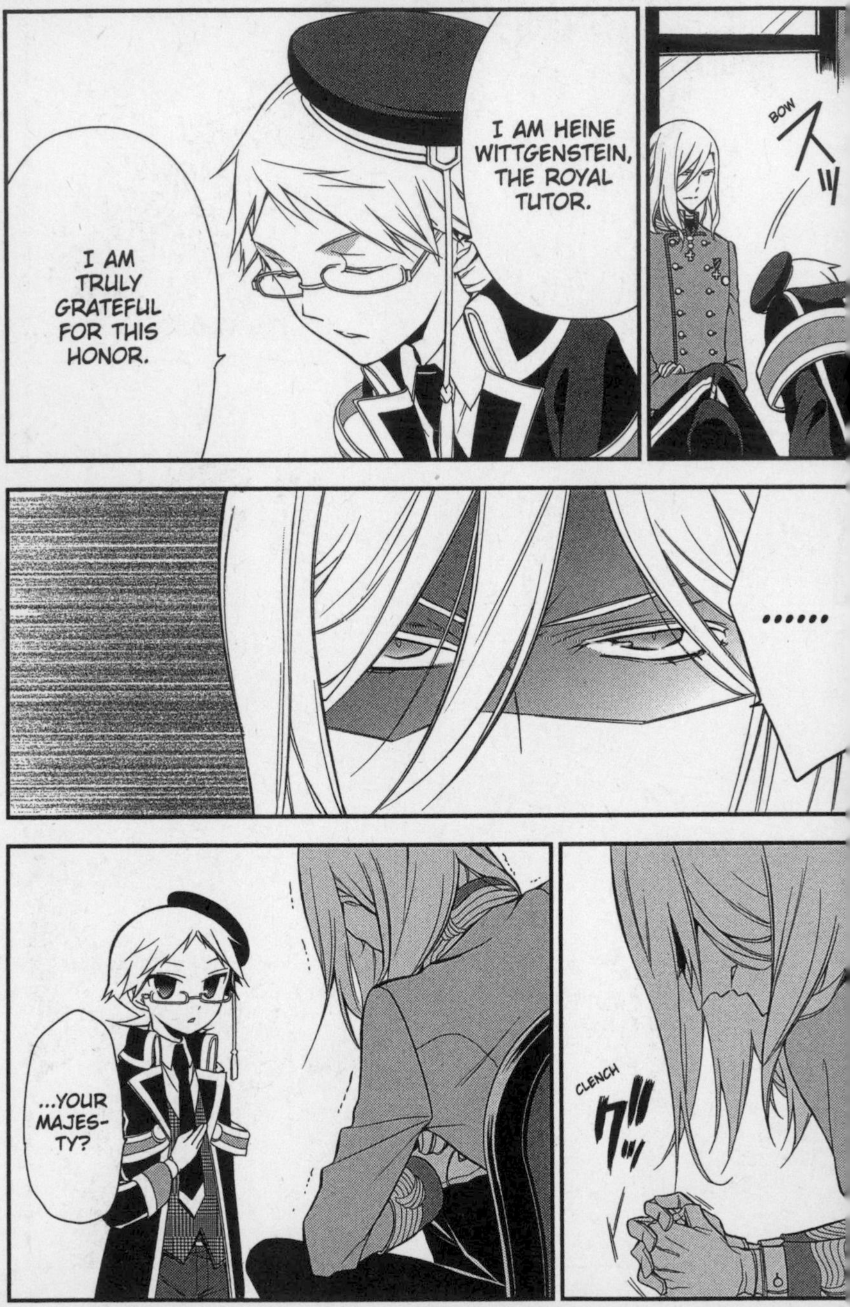
BOW
スッ
I AM HEINE WITTGENSTEIN, THE ROYAL TUTOR.
I AM TRULY GRATEFUL FOR THIS HONOR.
......
CLENCH
グッ
...YOUR MAJES-TY?

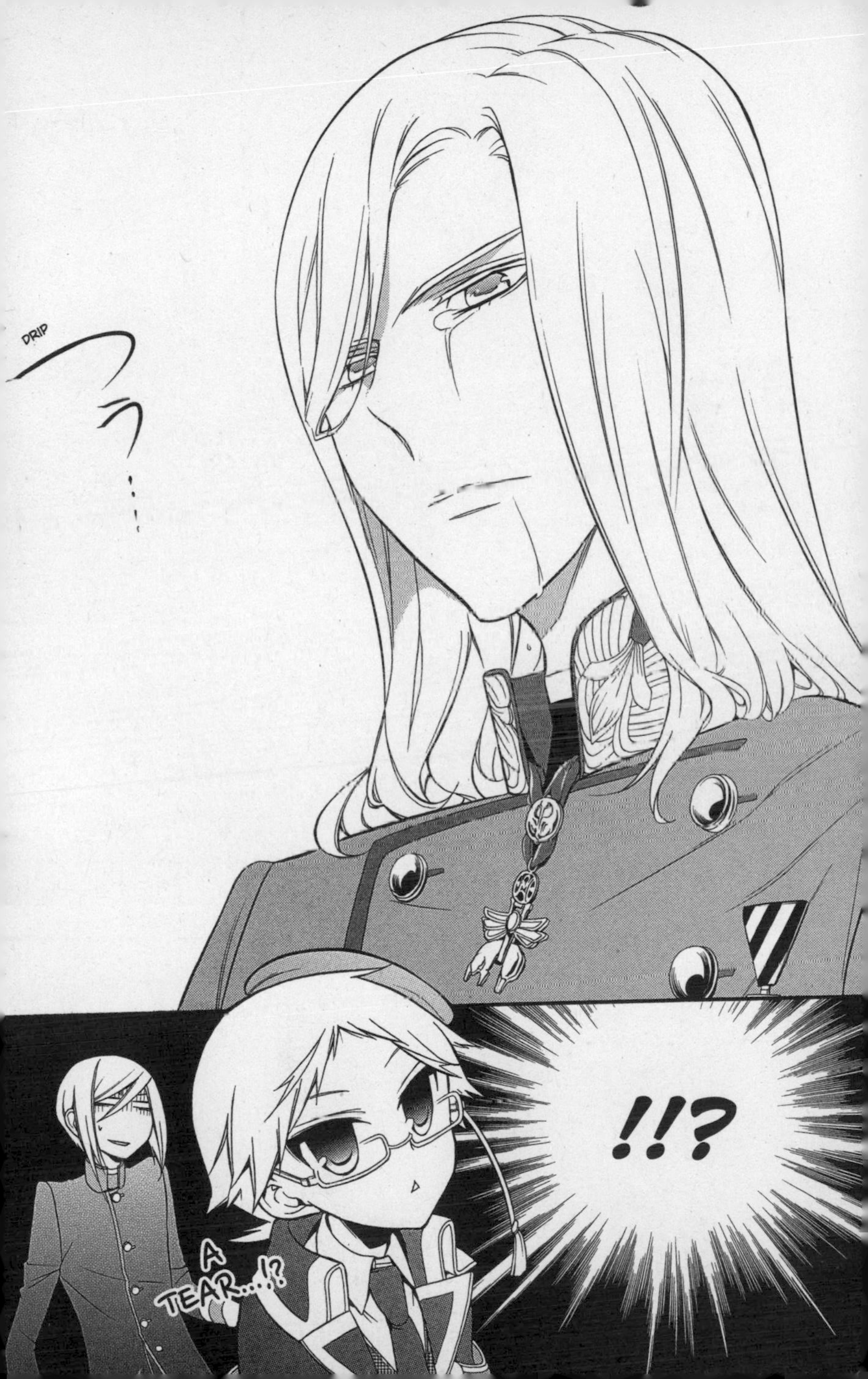
DRIP
...
!!?
A TEAR...!?

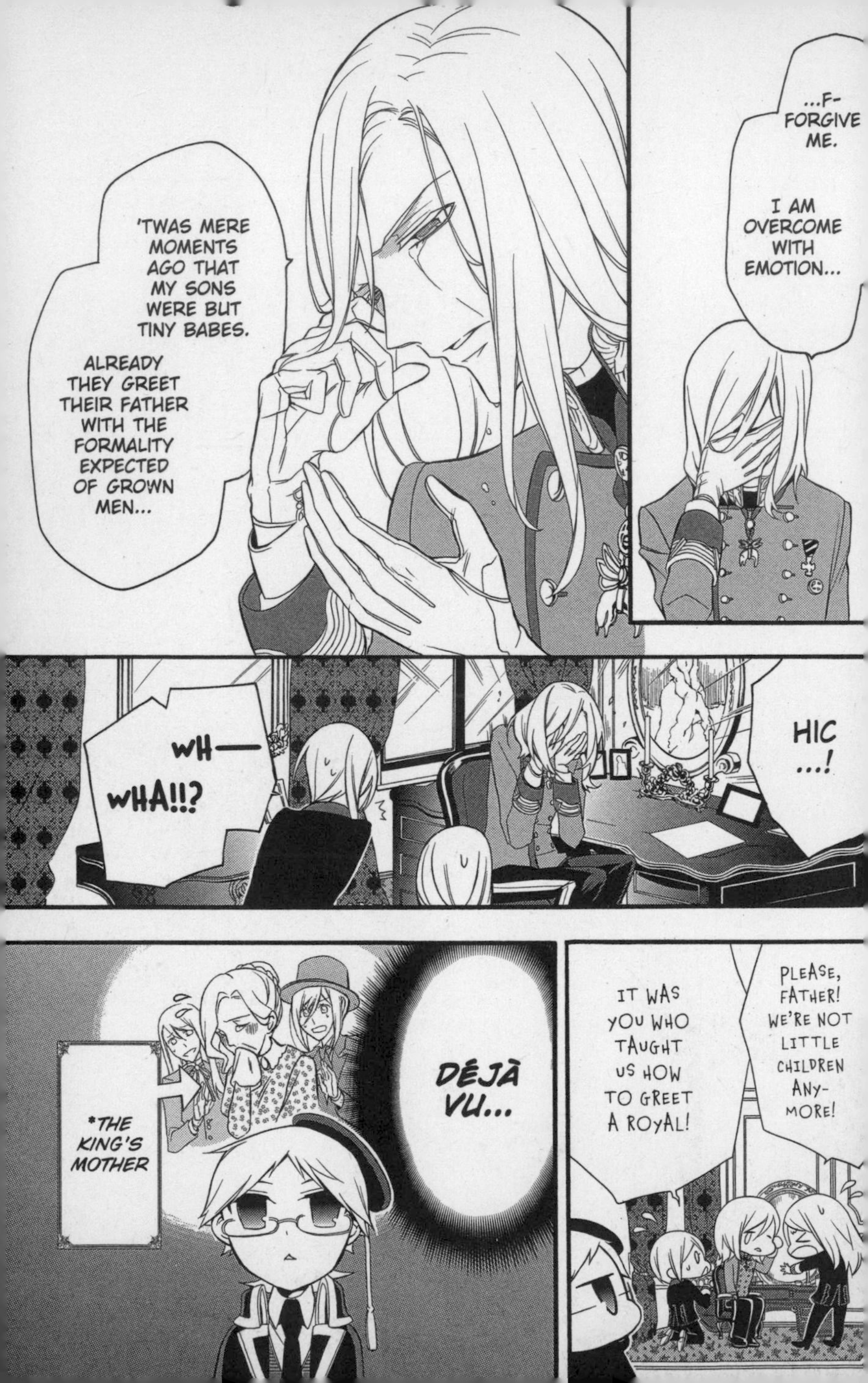
...F-FORGIVE ME.
I AM OVERCOME WITH EMOTION...
'TWAS MERE MOMENTS AGO THAT MY SONS WERE BUT TINY BABES.
ALREADY THEY GREET THEIR FATHER WITH THE FORMALITY EXPECTED OF GROWN MEN...
HIC ...!
WH— WHA!!?
PLEASE, FATHER! WE'RE NOT LITTLE CHILDREN ANYMORE!
IT WAS YOU WHO TAUGHT US HOW TO GREET A ROYAL!
DÉJÀ VU...
*THE KING'S MOTHER

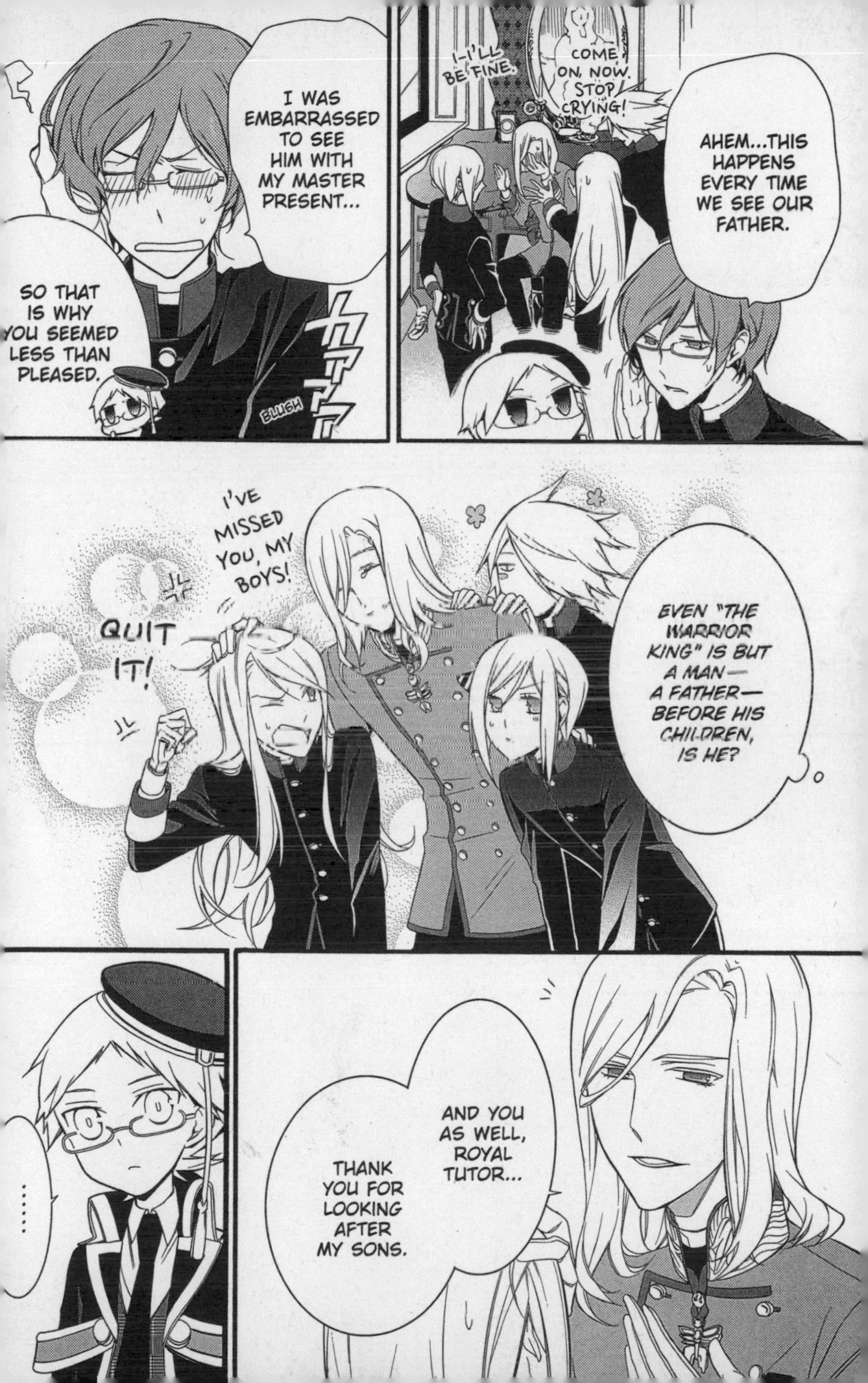
AHEM...THIS HAPPENS EVERY TIME WE SEE OUR FATHER.
COME ON, NOW. STOP CRYING!
I-I'LL BE FINE.
I WAS EMBARRASSED TO SEE HIM WITH MY MASTER PRESENT...
SO THAT IS WHY YOU SEEMED LESS THAN PLEASED.
BLUSH
EVEN "THE WARRIOR KING" IS BUT A MAN—A FATHER—BEFORE HIS CHILDREN, IS HE?
I'VE MISSED YOU, MY BOYS!
QUIT IT!
AND YOU AS WELL, ROYAL TUTOR...
THANK YOU FOR LOOKING AFTER MY SONS.
......

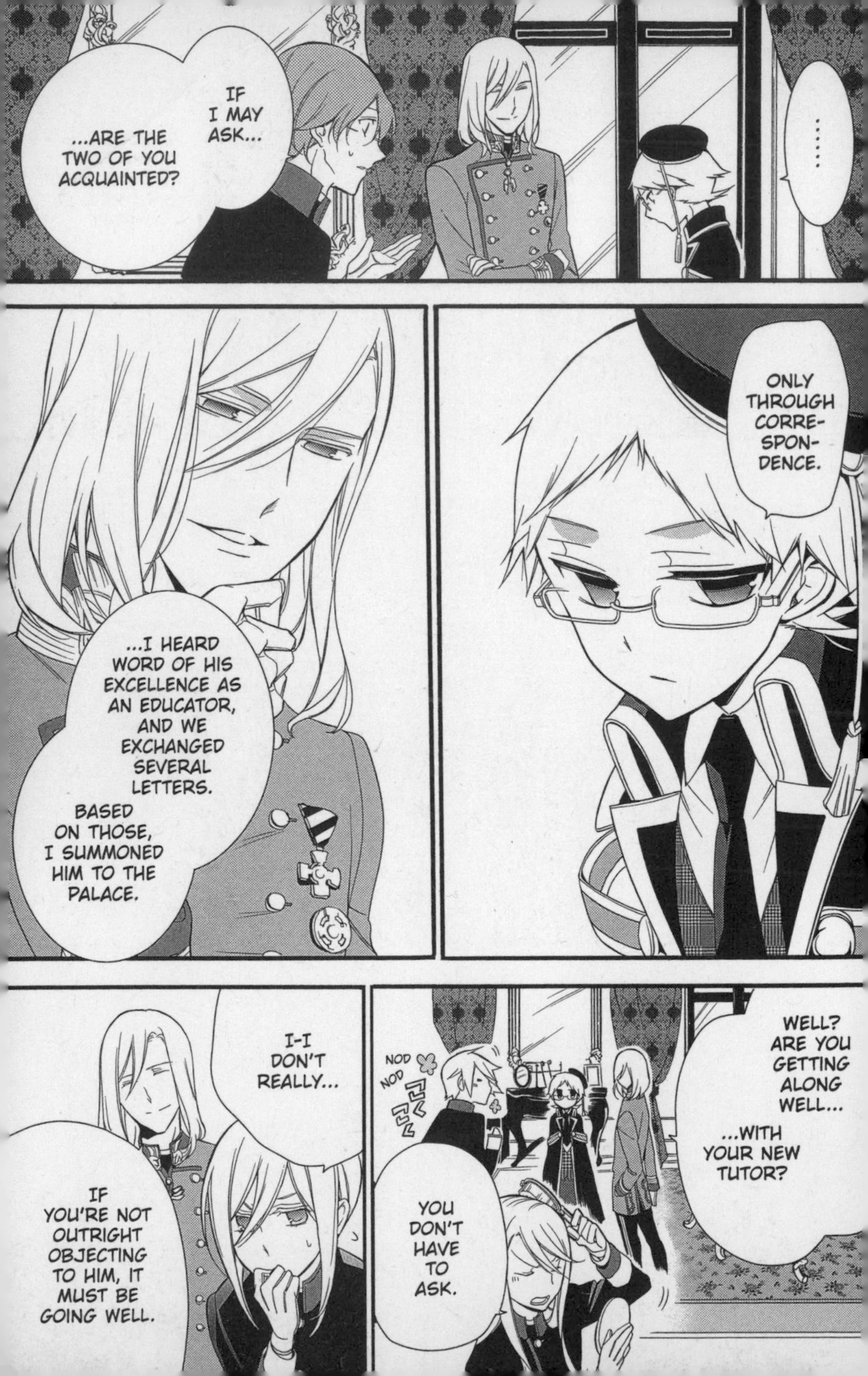
......
IF I MAY ASK...
...ARE THE TWO OF YOU ACQUAINTED?
ONLY THROUGH CORRE-SPON-DENCE.
...I HEARD WORD OF HIS EXCELLENCE AS AN EDUCATOR, AND WE EXCHANGED SEVERAL LETTERS.
BASED ON THOSE, I SUMMONED HIM TO THE PALACE.
WELL? ARE YOU GETTING ALONG WELL...
...WITH YOUR NEW TUTOR?
NOD NOD
YOU DON'T HAVE TO ASK.
I-I DON'T REALLY...
IF YOU'RE NOT OUTRIGHT OBJECTING TO HIM, IT MUST BE GOING WELL.

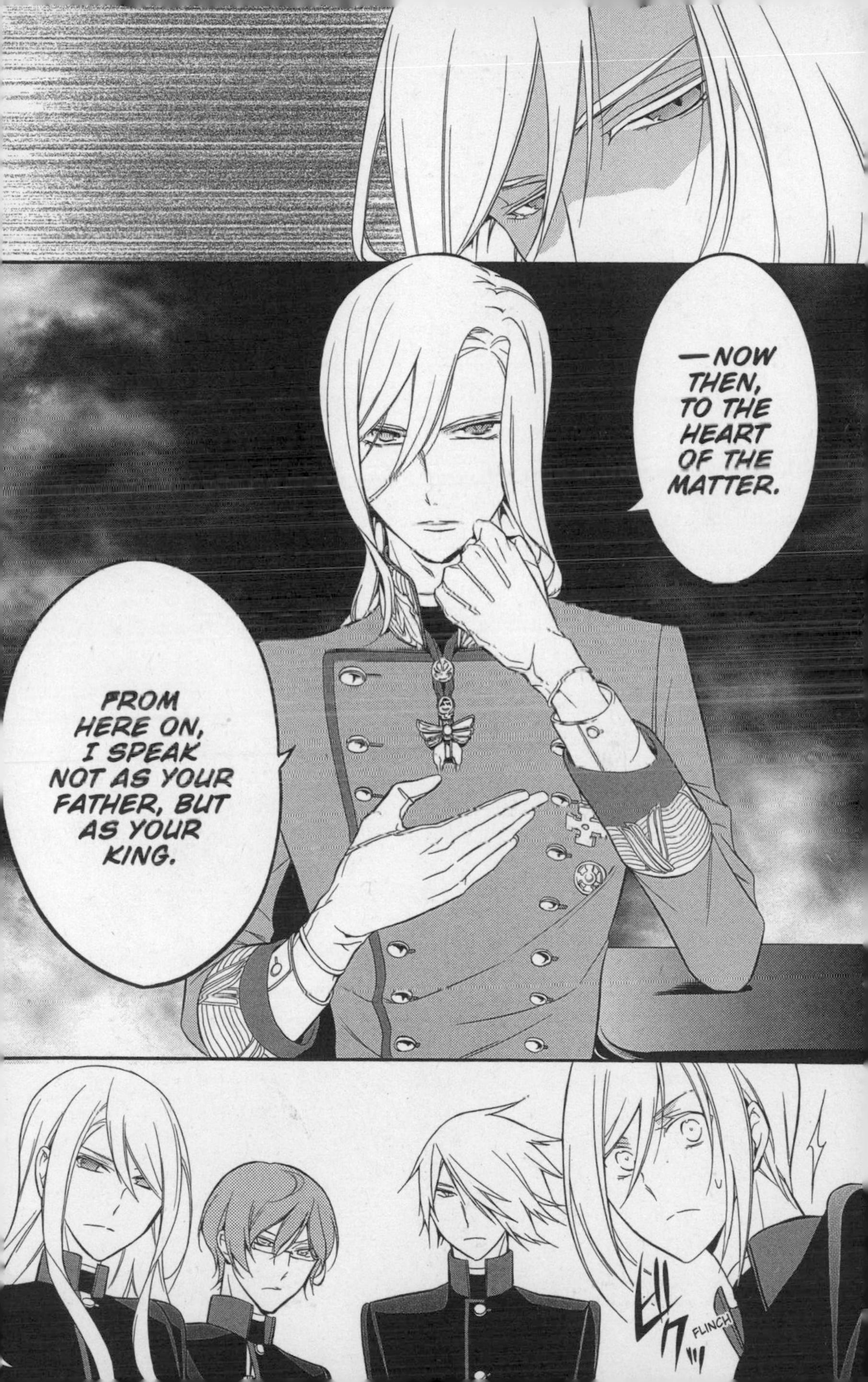
—NOW THEN, TO THE HEART OF THE MATTER.
FROM HERE ON, I SPEAK NOT AS YOUR FATHER, BUT AS YOUR KING.
FLINCH

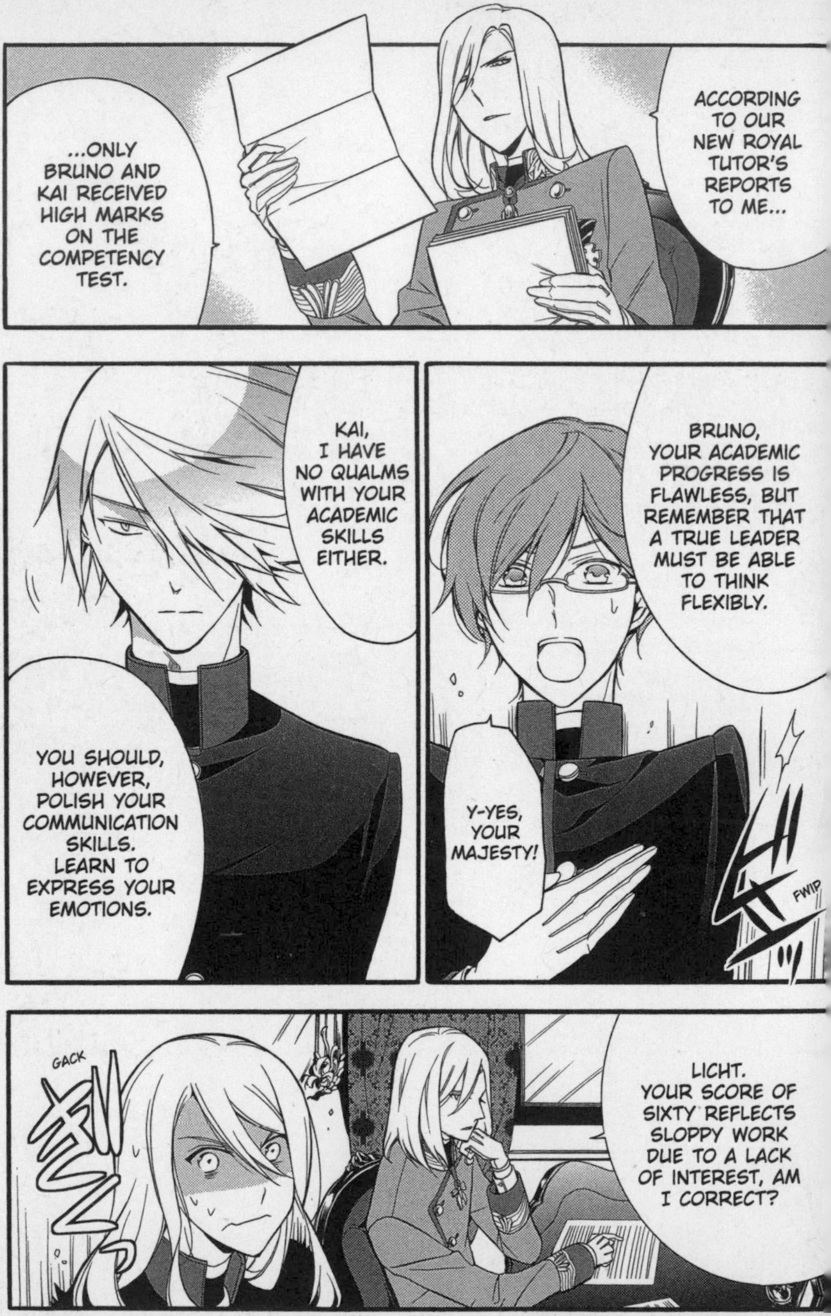
ACCORDING TO OUR NEW ROYAL TUTOR'S REPORTS TO ME...
...ONLY BRUNO AND KAI RECEIVED HIGH MARKS ON THE COMPETENCY TEST.
BRUNO, YOUR ACADEMIC PROGRESS IS FLAWLESS, BUT REMEMBER THAT A TRUE LEADER MUST BE ABLE TO THINK FLEXIBLY.
Y-YES, YOUR MAJESTY!
FWIP
KAI, I HAVE NO QUALMS WITH YOUR ACADEMIC SKILLS EITHER.
YOU SHOULD, HOWEVER, POLISH YOUR COMMUNICATION SKILLS. LEARN TO EXPRESS YOUR EMOTIONS.
LICHT. YOUR SCORE OF SIXTY REFLECTS SLOPPY WORK DUE TO A LACK OF INTEREST, AM I CORRECT?
GACK

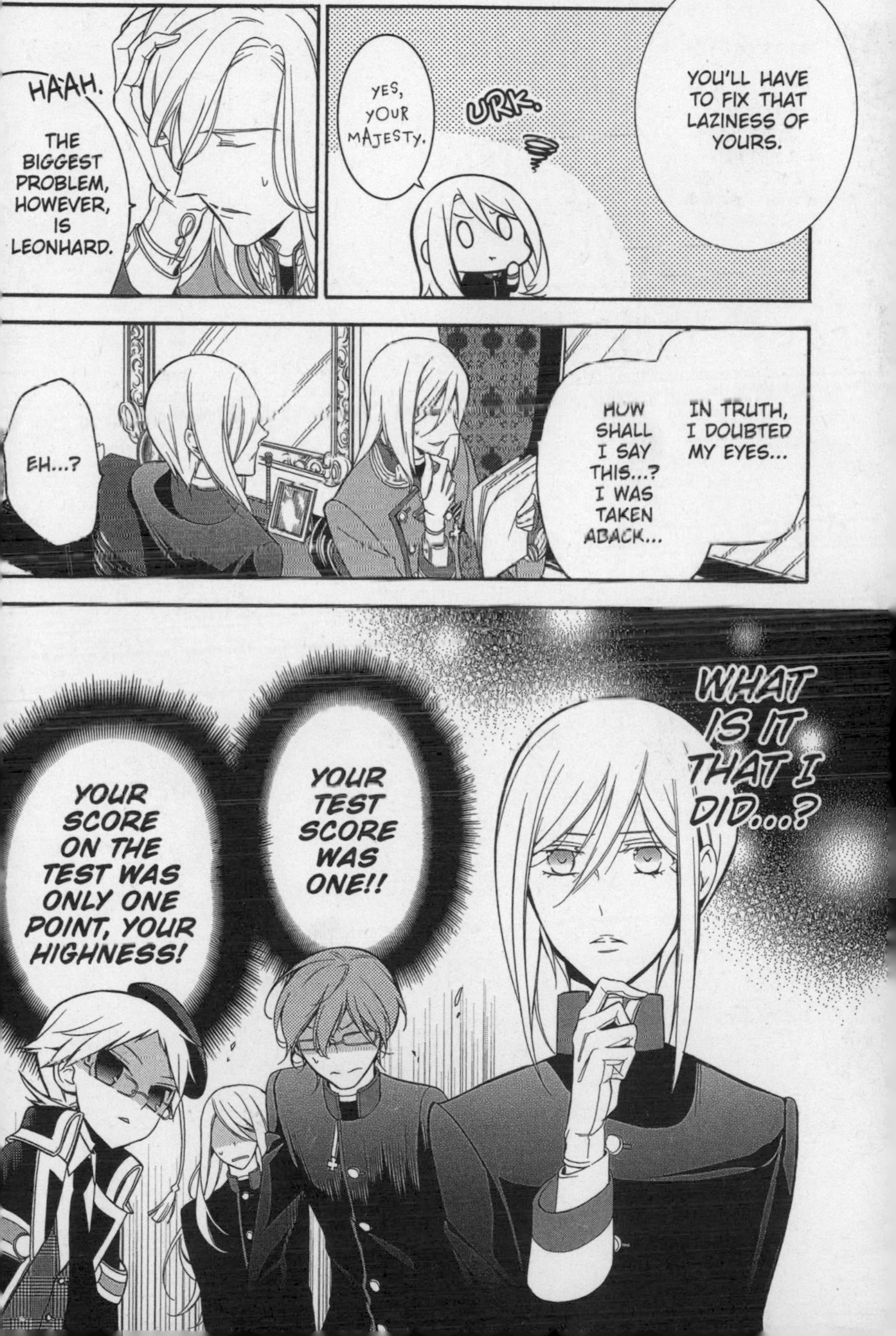
YOU'LL HAVE TO FIX THAT LAZINESS OF YOURS.
URK.
YES, YOUR MAJESTY.
HAAH.
THE BIGGEST PROBLEM, HOWEVER, IS LEONHARD.
IN TRUTH, I DOUBTED MY EYES...
HOW SHALL I SAY THIS...? I WAS TAKEN ABACK...
EH...?
WHAT IS IT THAT I DID...?
YOUR TEST SCORE WAS ONE!!
YOUR SCORE ON THE TEST WAS ONLY ONE POINT, YOUR HIGHNESS!

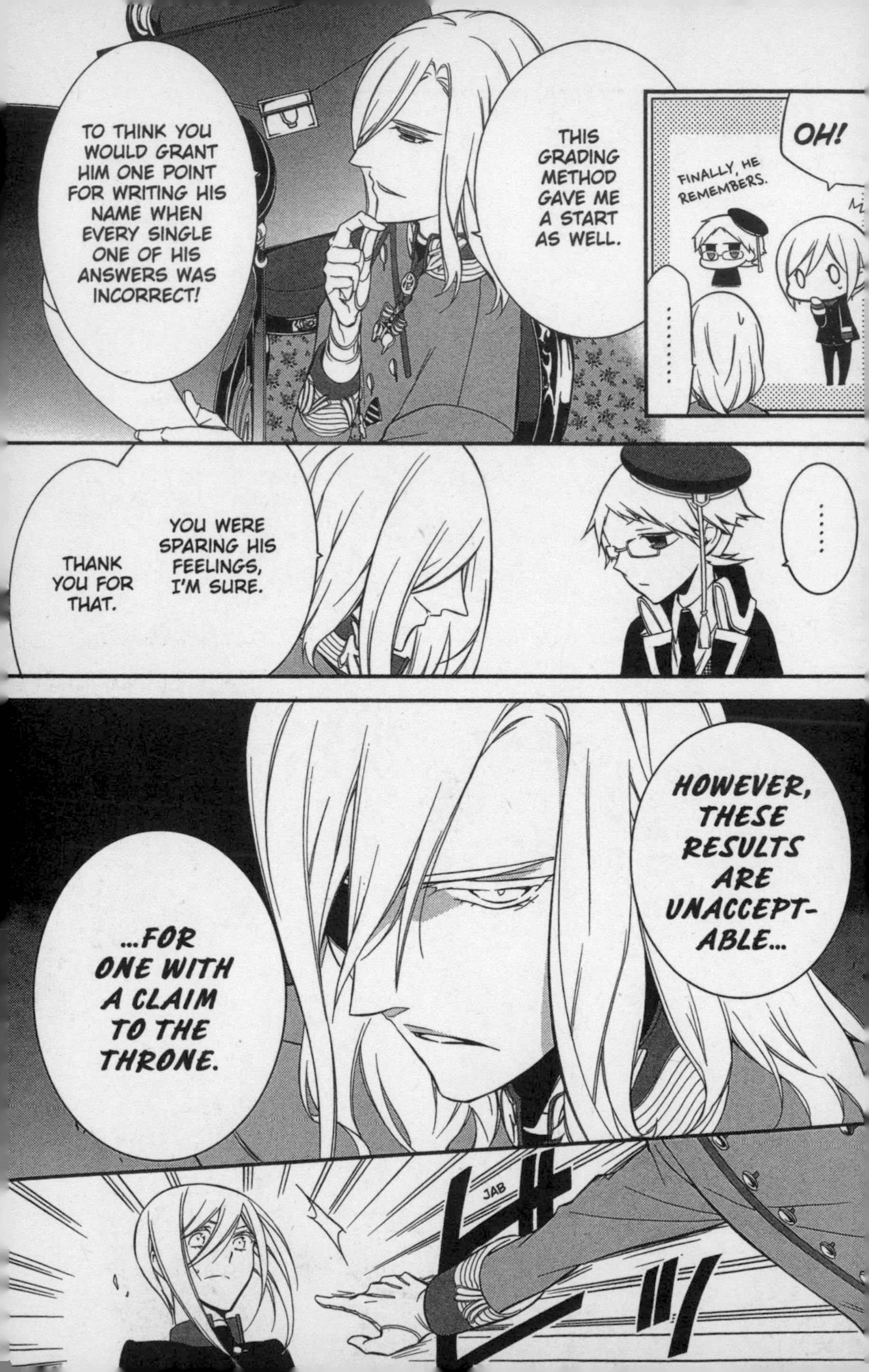

OH!
FINALLY, HE REMEMBERS.
......
THIS GRADING METHOD GAVE ME A START AS WELL.
TO THINK YOU WOULD GRANT HIM ONE POINT FOR WRITING HIS NAME WHEN EVERY SINGLE ONE OF HIS ANSWERS WAS INCORRECT!
......
YOU WERE SPARING HIS FEELINGS, I'M SURE.
THANK YOU FOR THAT.
HOWEVER, THESE RESULTS ARE UNACCEPTABLE...
...FOR ONE WITH A CLAIM TO THE THRONE.
JAB

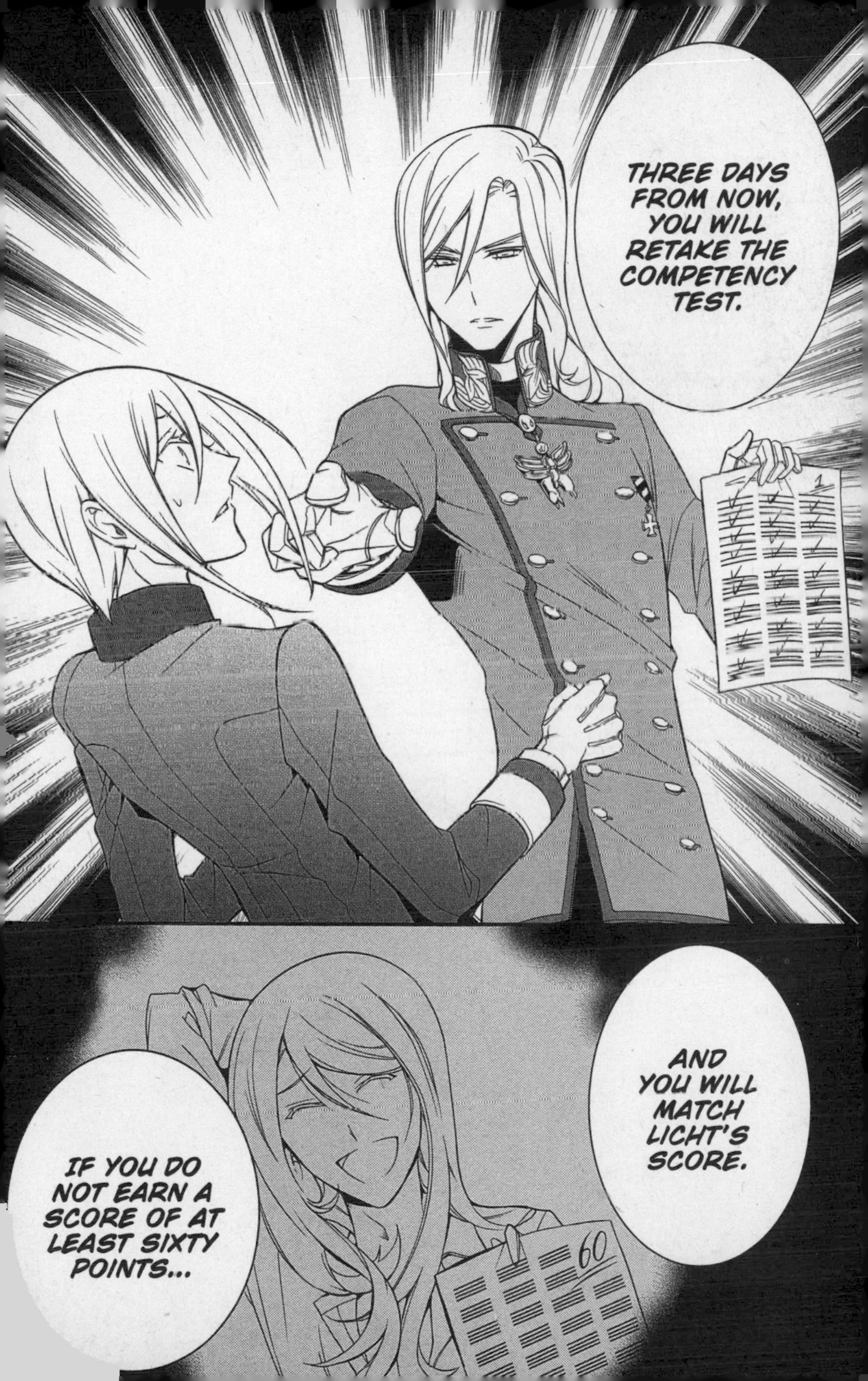
THREE DAYS FROM NOW, YOU WILL RETAKE THE COMPETENCY TEST.
AND YOU WILL MATCH LICHT'S SCORE.
IF YOU DO NOT EARN A SCORE OF AT LEAST SIXTY POINTS...

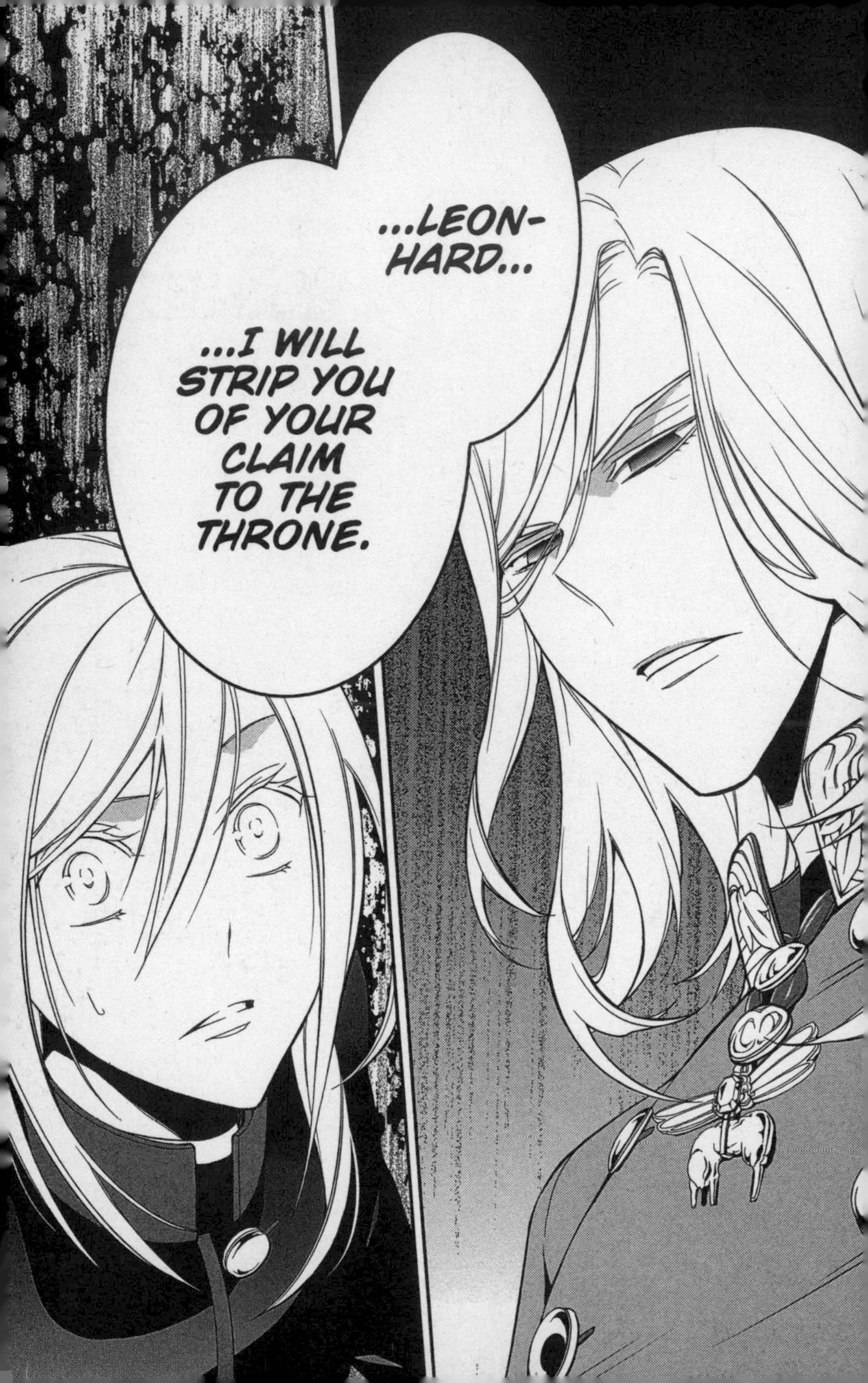
...LEON-HARD...
...I WILL STRIP YOU OF YOUR CLAIM TO THE THRONE.

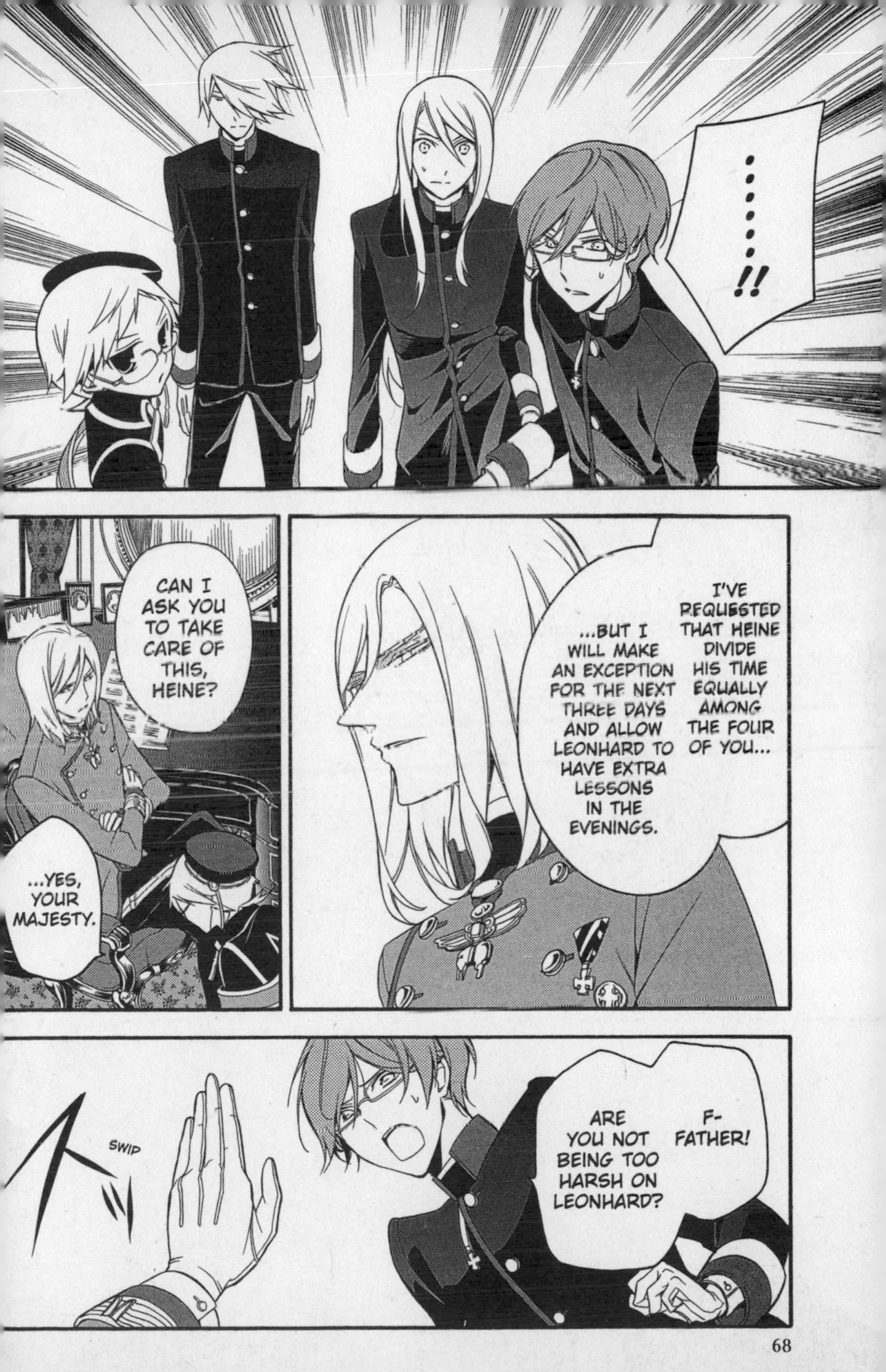
……!!
I'VE REQUESTED THAT HEINE DIVIDE HIS TIME EQUALLY AMONG THE FOUR OF YOU...
...BUT I WILL MAKE AN EXCEPTION FOR THE NEXT THREE DAYS AND ALLOW LEONHARD TO HAVE EXTRA LESSONS IN THE EVENINGS.
CAN I ASK YOU TO TAKE CARE OF THIS, HEINE?
...YES, YOUR MAJESTY.
F-FATHER!
ARE YOU NOT BEING TOO HARSH ON LEONHARD?
SWIP

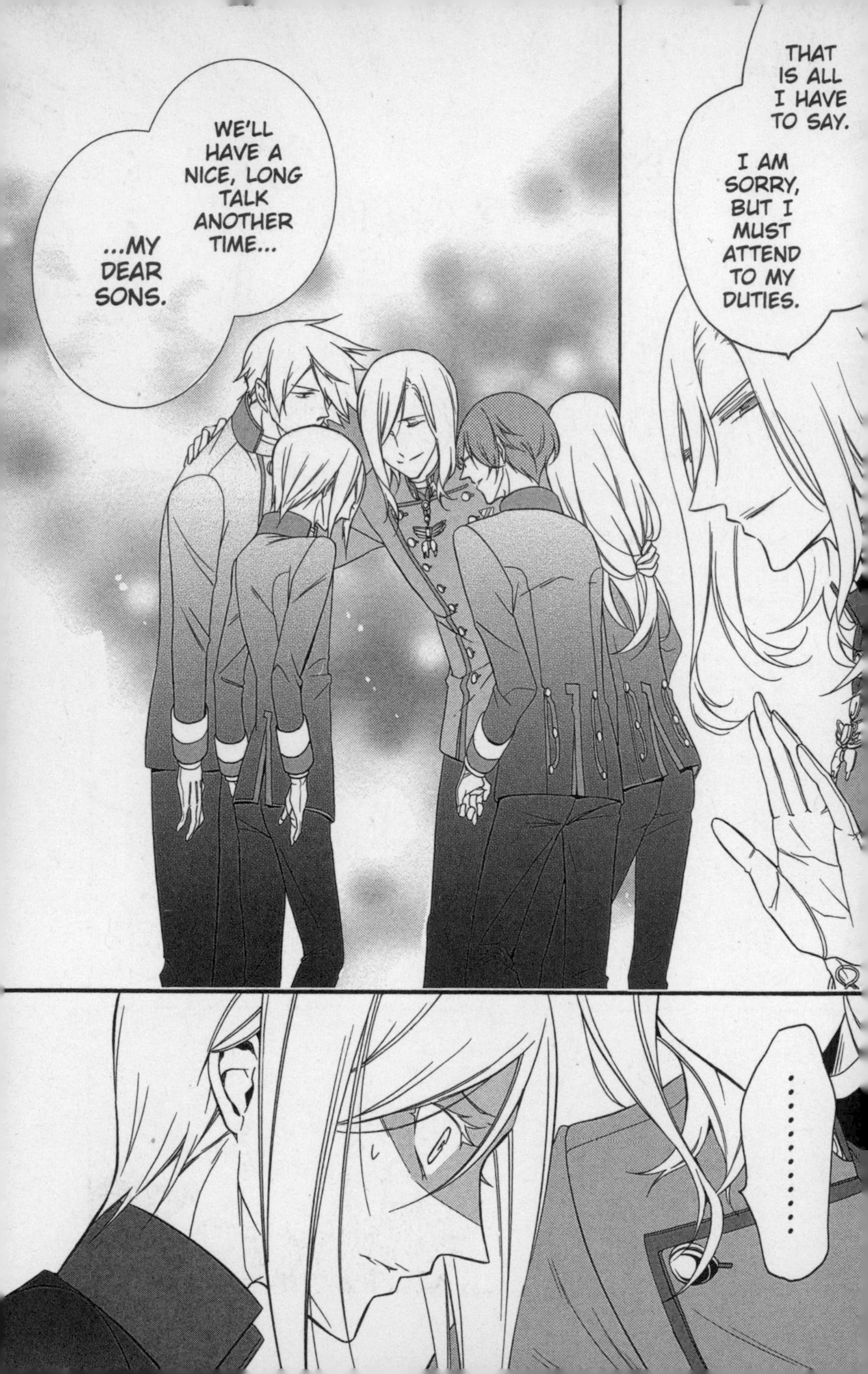
THAT IS ALL I HAVE TO SAY.
I AM SORRY, BUT I MUST ATTEND TO MY DUTIES.
WE'LL HAVE A NICE, LONG TALK ANOTHER TIME...
...MY DEAR SONS.
....

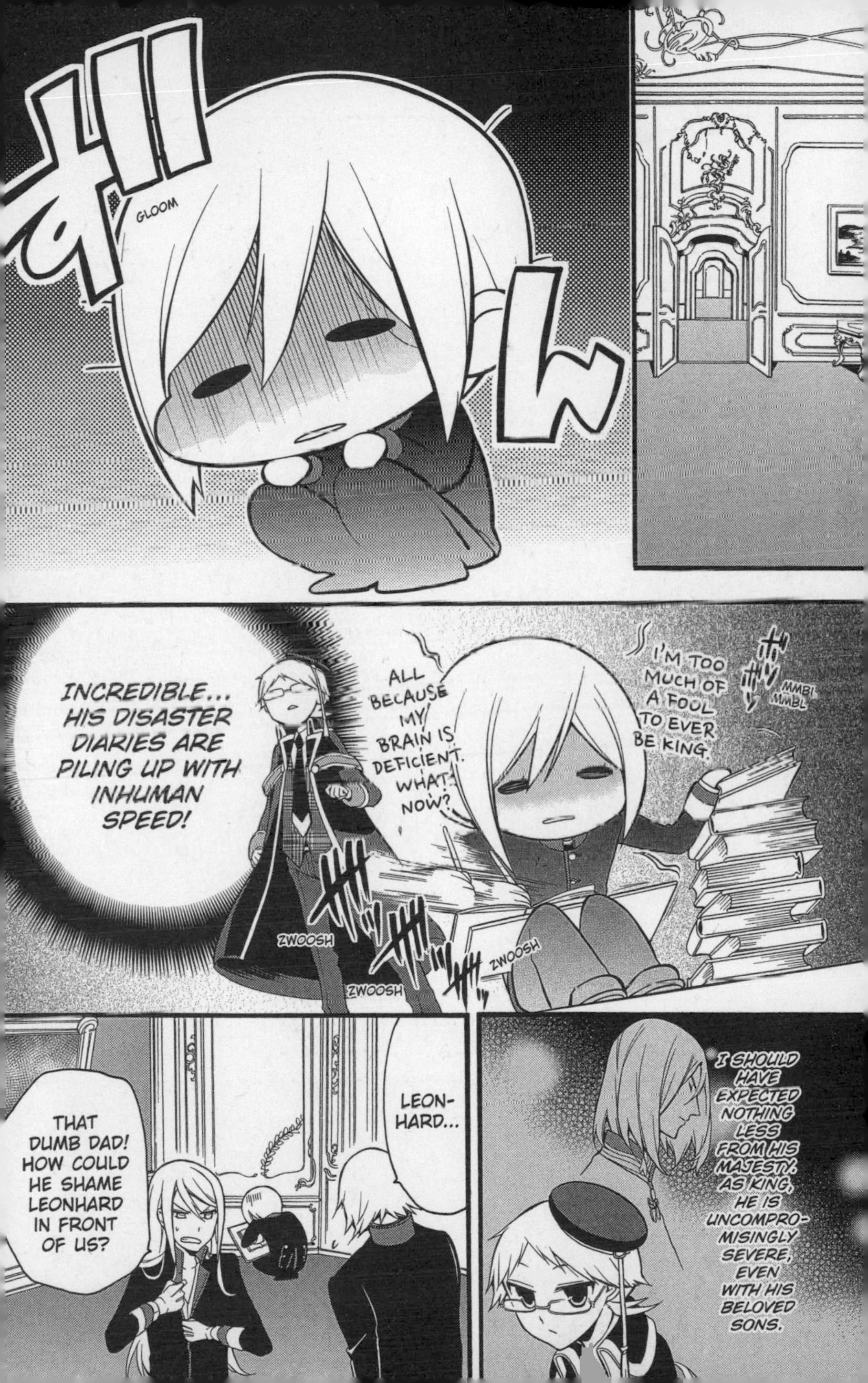
GLOOM
I'M TOO MUCH OF A FOOL TO EVER BE KING.
MMBL MMBL
ALL BECAUSE MY BRAIN IS DEFICIENT. WHAT NOW?
INCREDIBLE... HIS DISASTER DIARIES ARE PILING UP WITH INHUMAN SPEED!
ZWOOSH
ZWOOSH
ZWOOSH
I SHOULD HAVE EXPECTED NOTHING LESS FROM HIS MAJESTY. AS KING, HE IS UNCOMPROMISINGLY SEVERE, EVEN WITH HIS BELOVED SONS.
LEON-HARD...
THAT DUMB DAD! HOW COULD HE SHAME LEONHARD IN FRONT OF US?

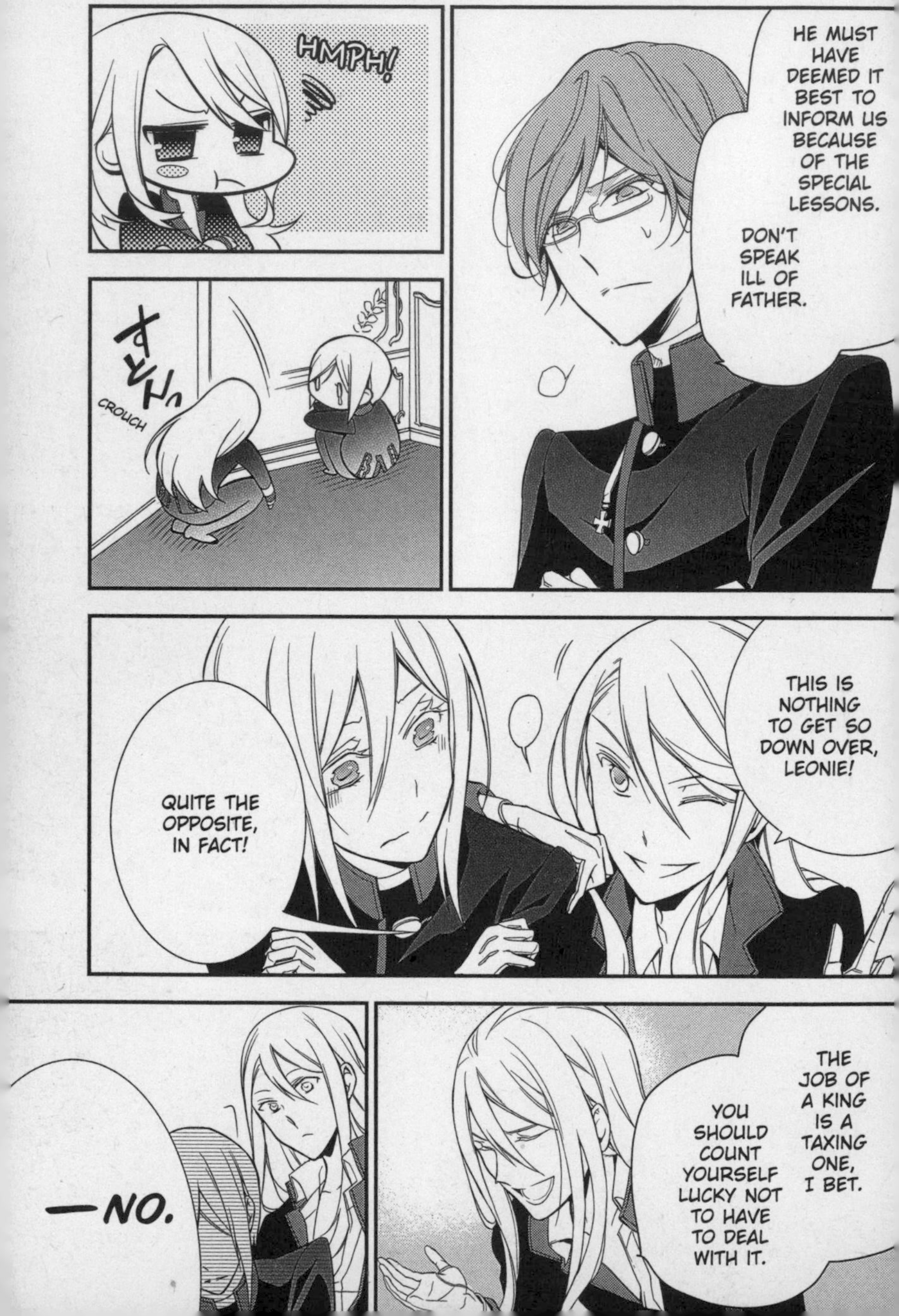
HE MUST HAVE DEEMED IT BEST TO INFORM US BECAUSE OF THE SPECIAL LESSONS.
DON'T SPEAK ILL OF FATHER.
HMPH!
すとん
CROUCH
THIS IS NOTHING TO GET SO DOWN OVER, LEONIE!
QUITE THE OPPOSITE, IN FACT!
THE JOB OF A KING IS A TAXING ONE, I BET.
YOU SHOULD COUNT YOURSELF LUCKY NOT TO HAVE TO DEAL WITH IT.
—NO.

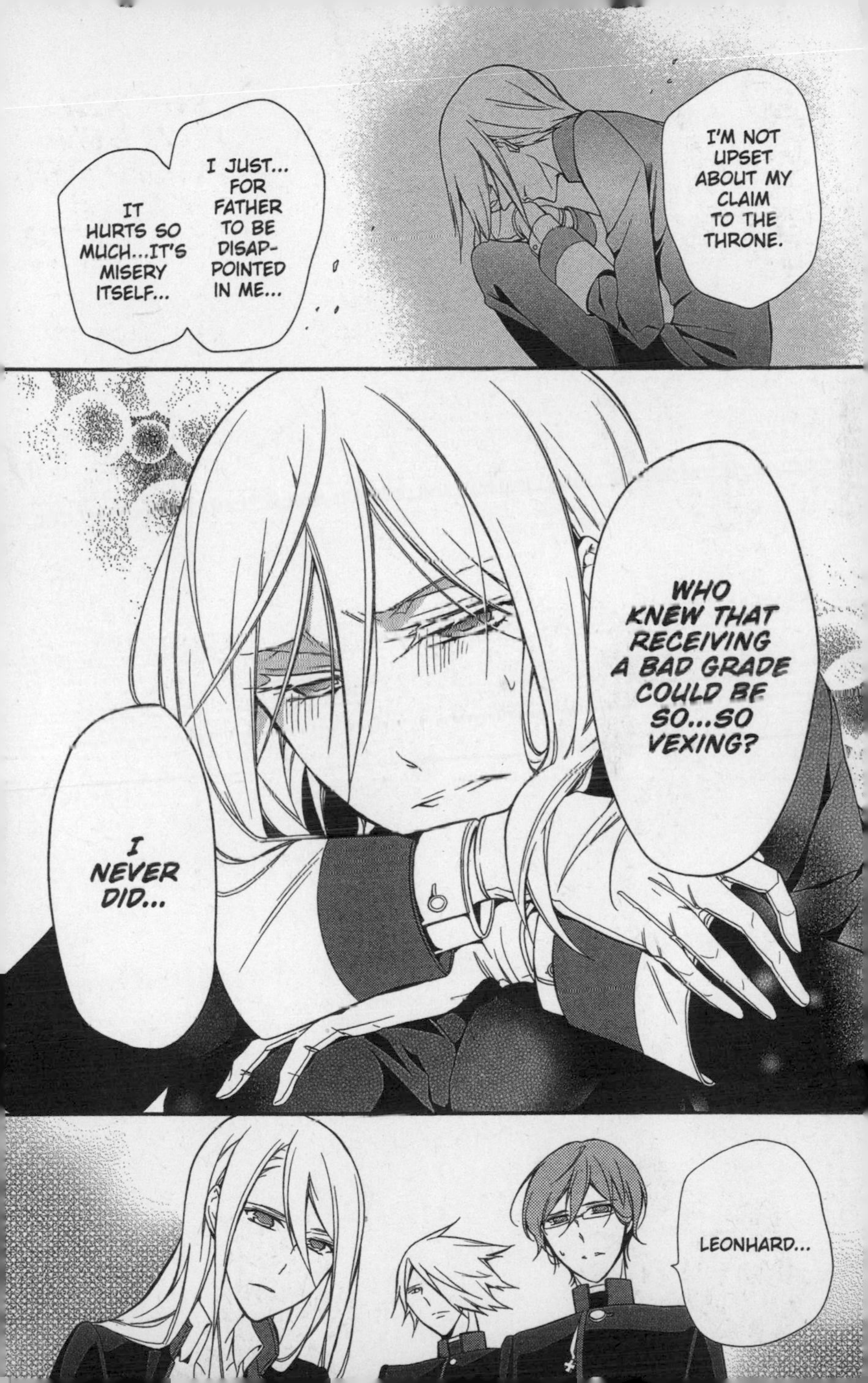

I'M NOT UPSET ABOUT MY CLAIM TO THE THRONE.
I JUST... FOR FATHER TO BE DISAP-POINTED IN ME...
IT HURTS SO MUCH...IT'S MISERY ITSELF...
WHO KNEW THAT RECEIVING A BAD GRADE COULD BE SO...SO VEXING?
I NEVER DID...
LEONHARD...

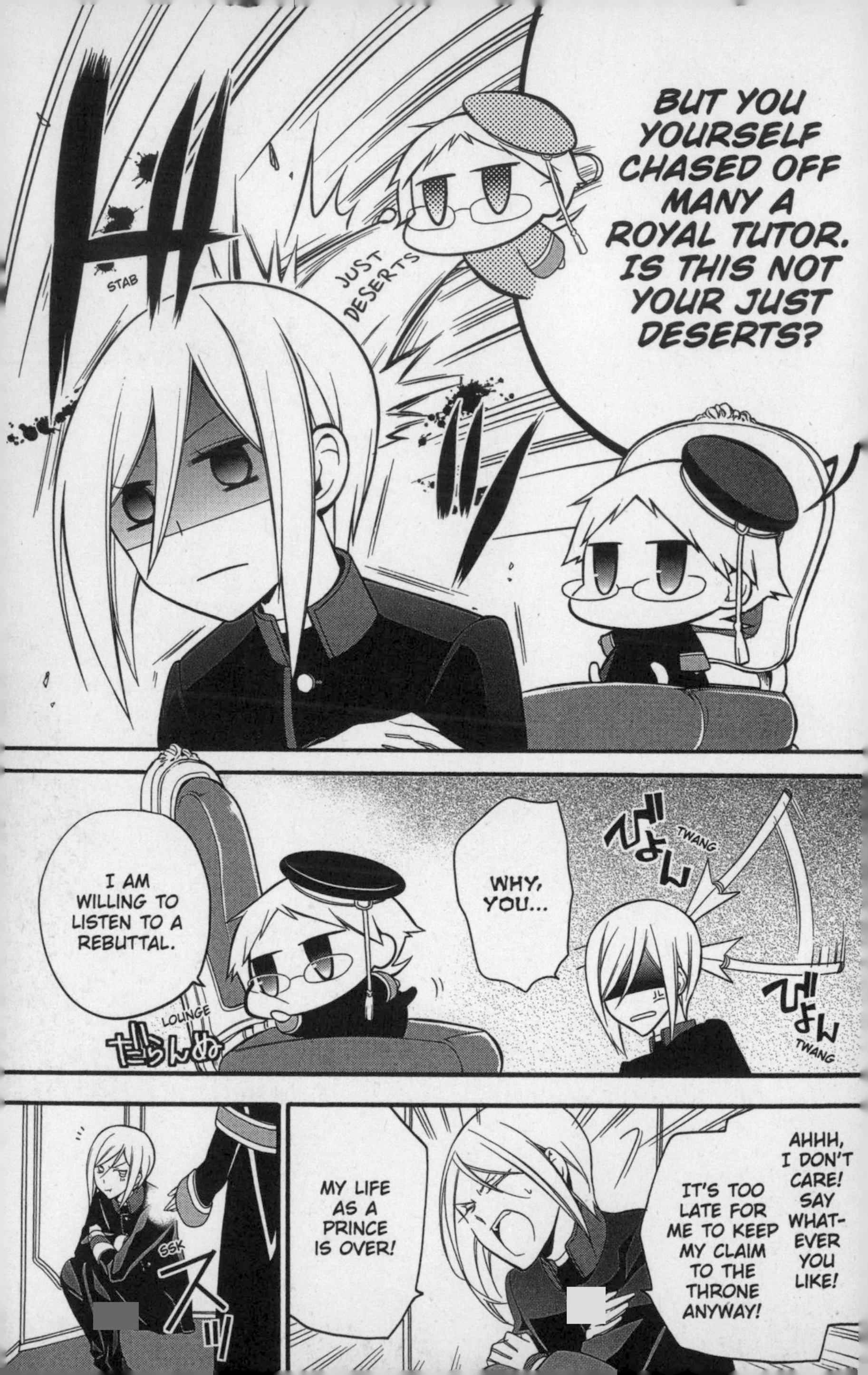
BUT YOU YOURSELF CHASED OFF MANY A ROYAL TUTOR. IS THIS NOT YOUR JUST DESERTS?
JUST DESERTS
STAB
TWANG
WHY, YOU...
TWANG
I AM WILLING TO LISTEN TO A REBUTTAL.
LOUNGE
AHHH, I DON'T CARE! SAY WHATEVER YOU LIKE!
IT'S TOO LATE FOR ME TO KEEP MY CLAIM TO THE THRONE ANYWAY!
MY LIFE AS A PRINCE IS OVER!
SSK

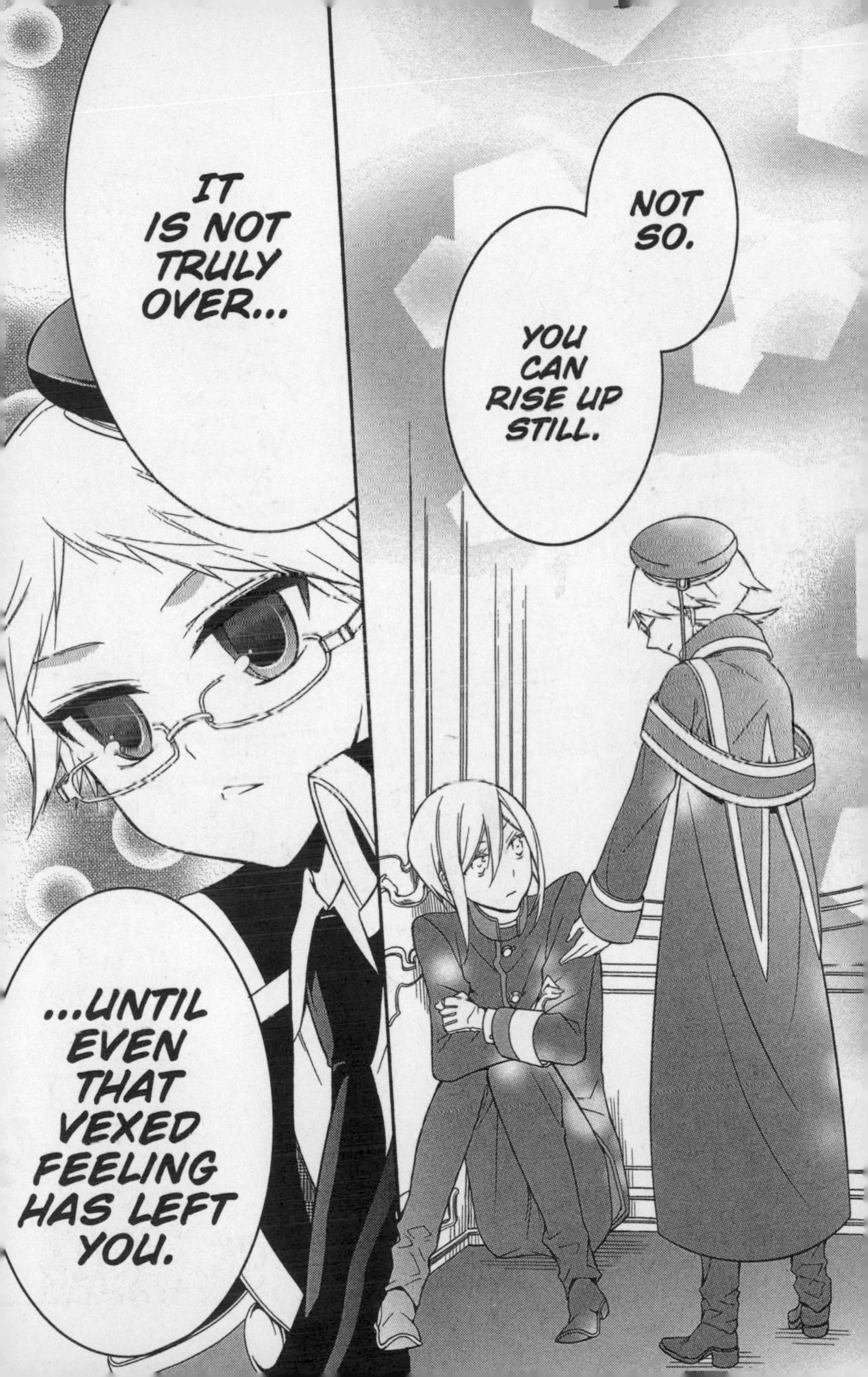
NOT SO.
YOU CAN RISE UP STILL.
IT IS NOT TRULY OVER...
...UNTIL EVEN THAT VEXED FEELING HAS LEFT YOU.

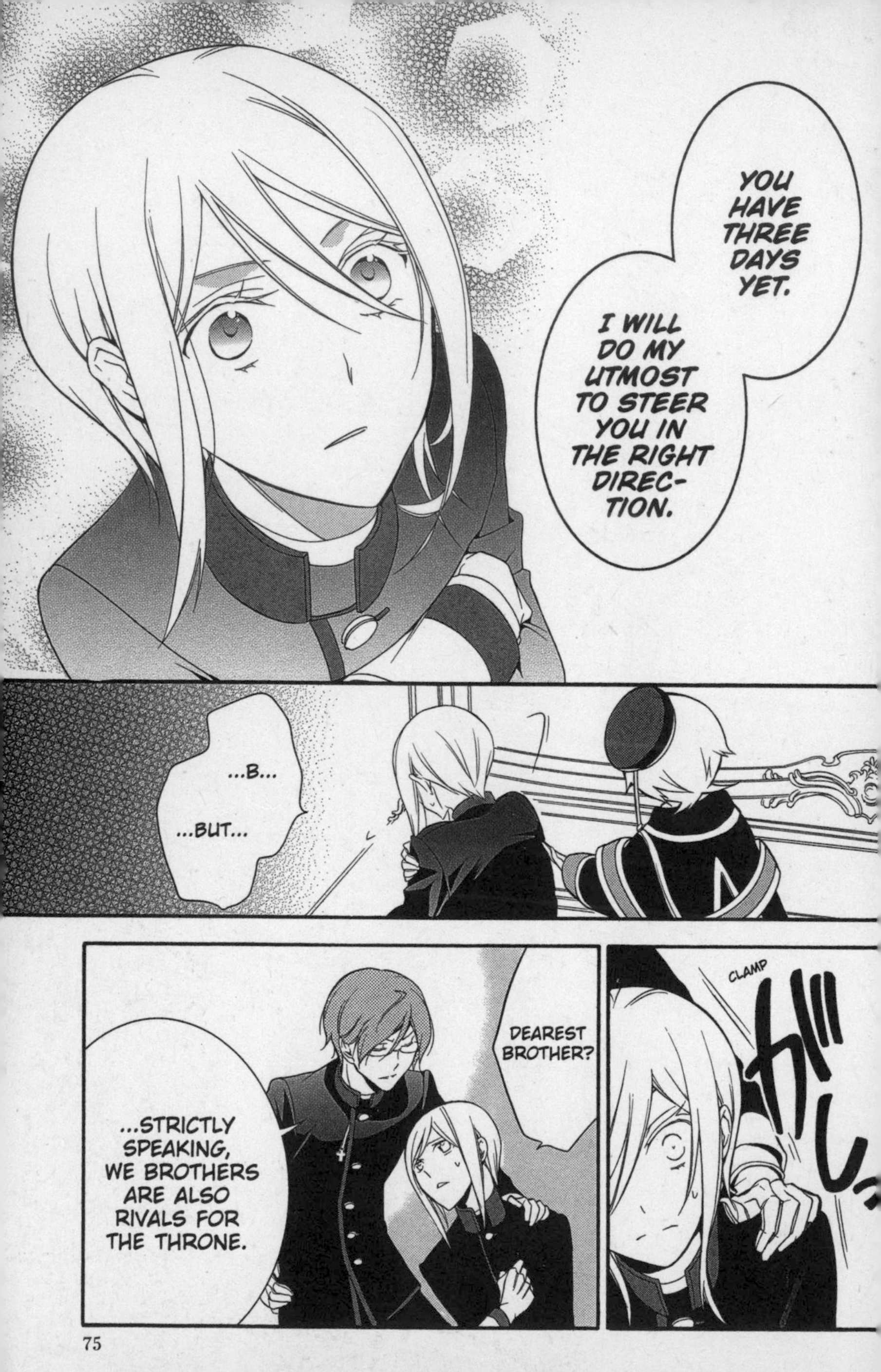
YOU HAVE THREE DAYS YET.
I WILL DO MY UTMOST TO STEER YOU IN THE RIGHT DIREC-TION.
...B...
...BUT...
CLAMP
DEAREST BROTHER?
...STRICTLY SPEAKING, WE BROTHERS ARE ALSO RIVALS FOR THE THRONE.

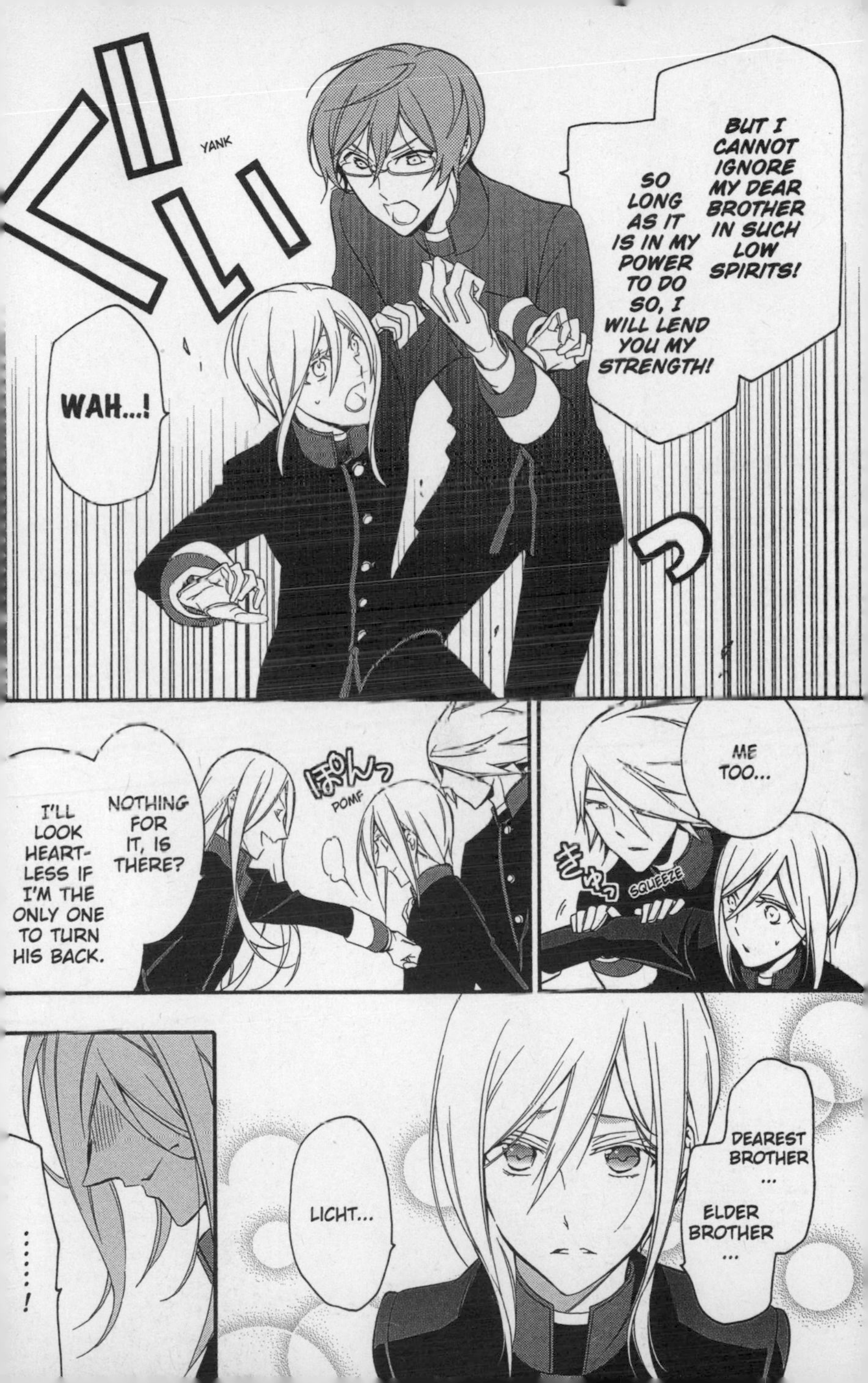
BUT I CANNOT IGNORE MY DEAR BROTHER IN SUCH LOW SPIRITS!
SO LONG AS IT IS IN MY POWER TO DO SO, I WILL LEND YOU MY STRENGTH!
ぐいっ
YANK
WAH...!
ME TOO...
きゅっ
SQUEEZE
ぽんっ
POMF
NOTHING FOR IT, IS THERE?
I'LL LOOK HEART-LESS IF I'M THE ONLY ONE TO TURN HIS BACK.
DEAREST BROTHER ... ELDER BROTHER ...
LICHT...
......!

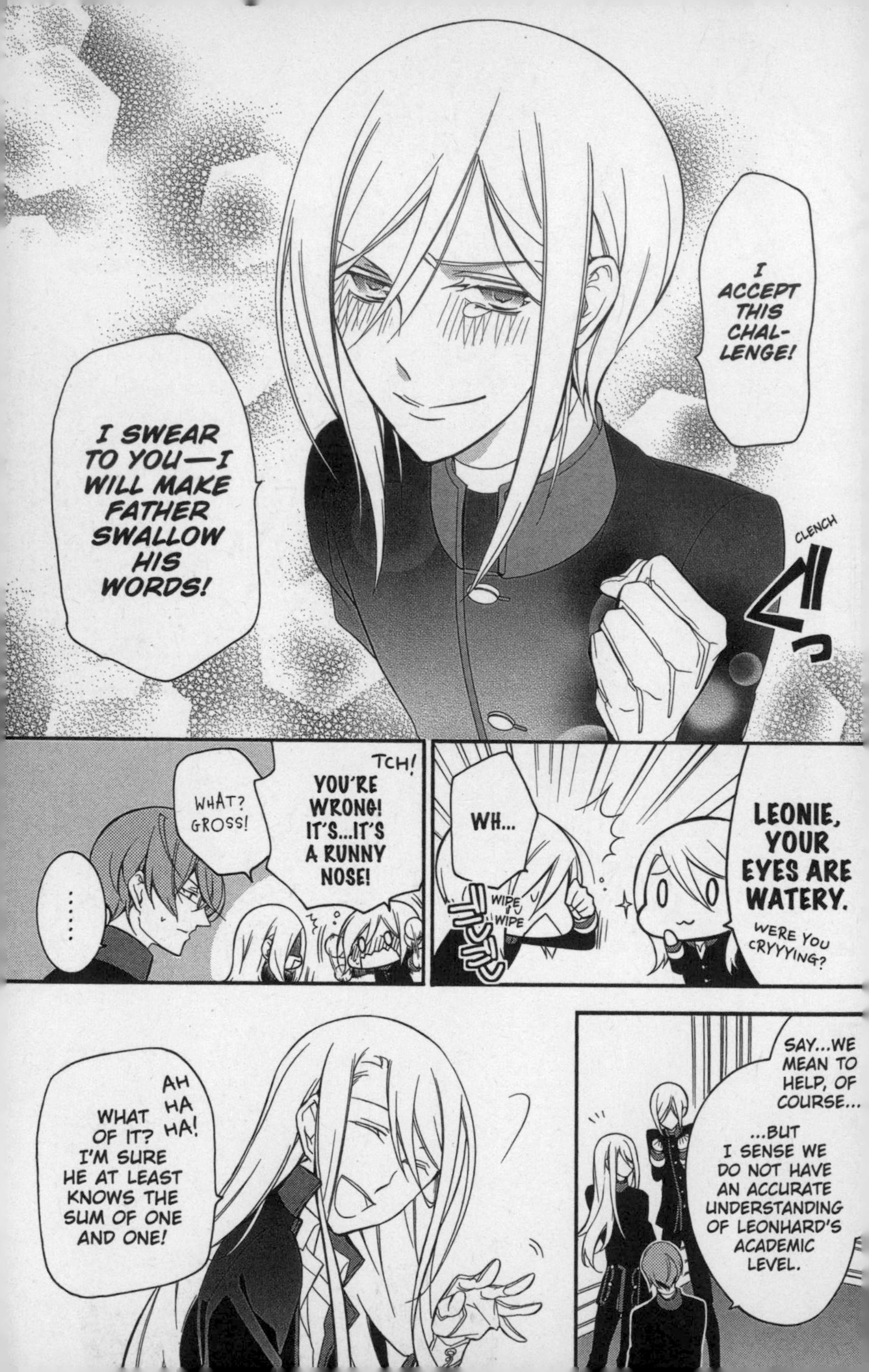
I ACCEPT THIS CHAL-LENGE!
CLENCH
I SWEAR TO YOU—I WILL MAKE FATHER SWALLOW HIS WORDS!
LEONIE, YOUR EYES ARE WATERY.
WERE YOU CRYYYING?
WH...
WIPE WIPE
TCH!
YOU'RE WRONG! IT'S...IT'S A RUNNY NOSE!
WHAT? GROSS!
......
SAY...WE MEAN TO HELP, OF COURSE...
...BUT I SENSE WE DO NOT HAVE AN ACCURATE UNDERSTANDING OF LEONHARD'S ACADEMIC LEVEL.
AH HA HA!
WHAT OF IT? I'M SURE HE AT LEAST KNOWS THE SUM OF ONE AND ONE!

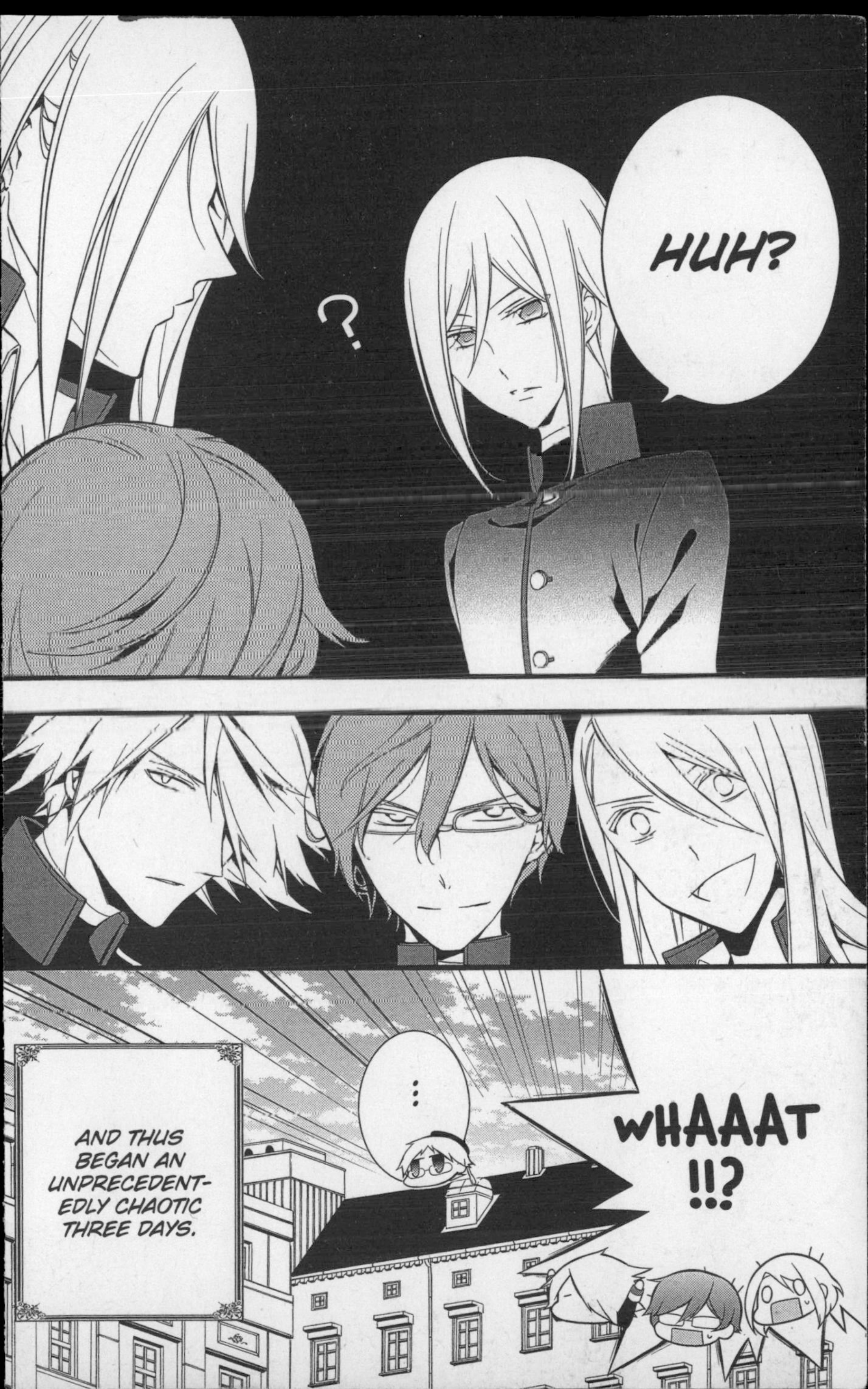
HUH?
?
WHAAAT !!?
...
AND THUS BEGAN AN UNPRECEDENTEDLY CHAOTIC THREE DAYS.

Chapter 10
Most Solemn Studying

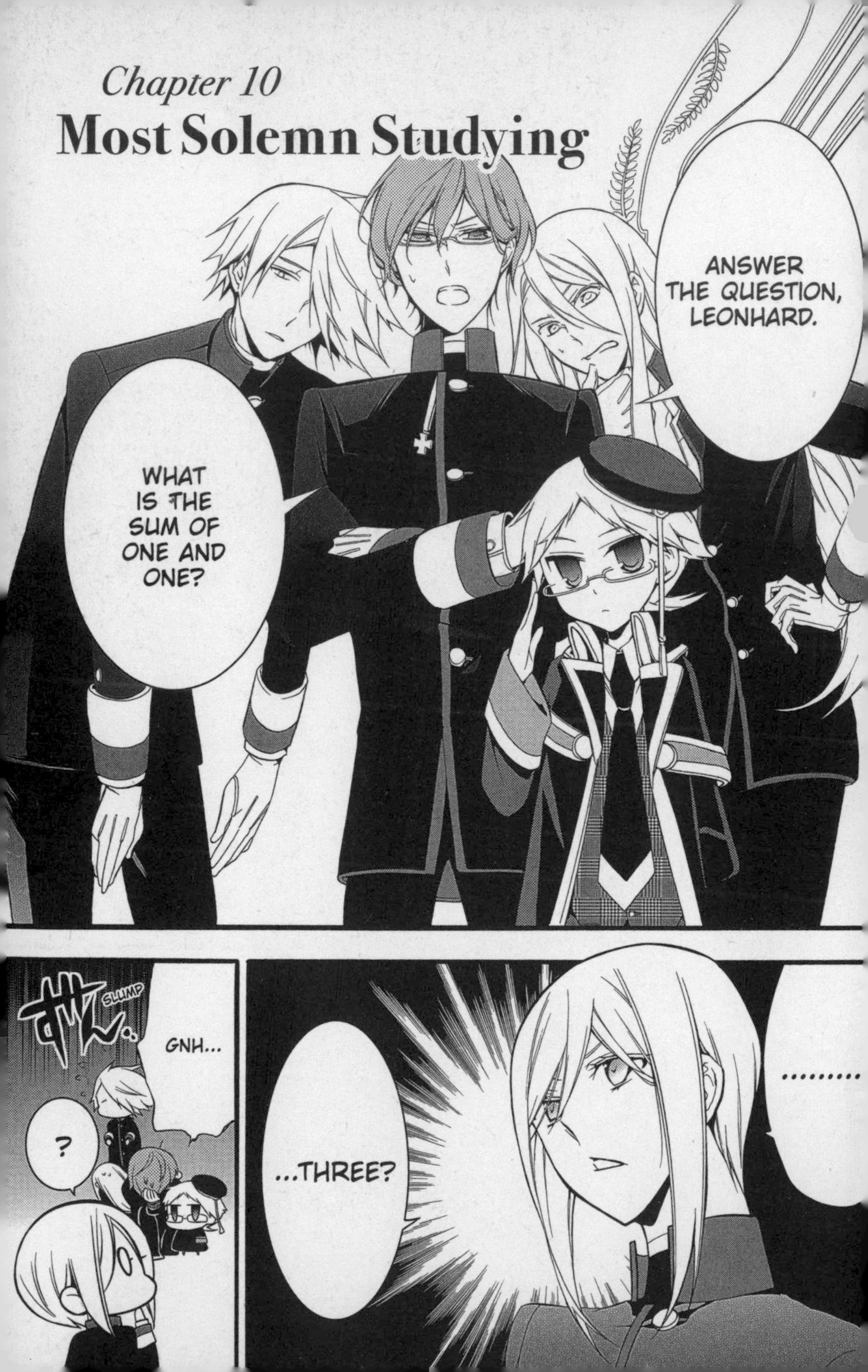
ANSWER THE QUESTION, LEONHARD.
WHAT IS THE SUM OF ONE AND ONE?
....
...THREE?
がん
SLUMP
GNH...
?

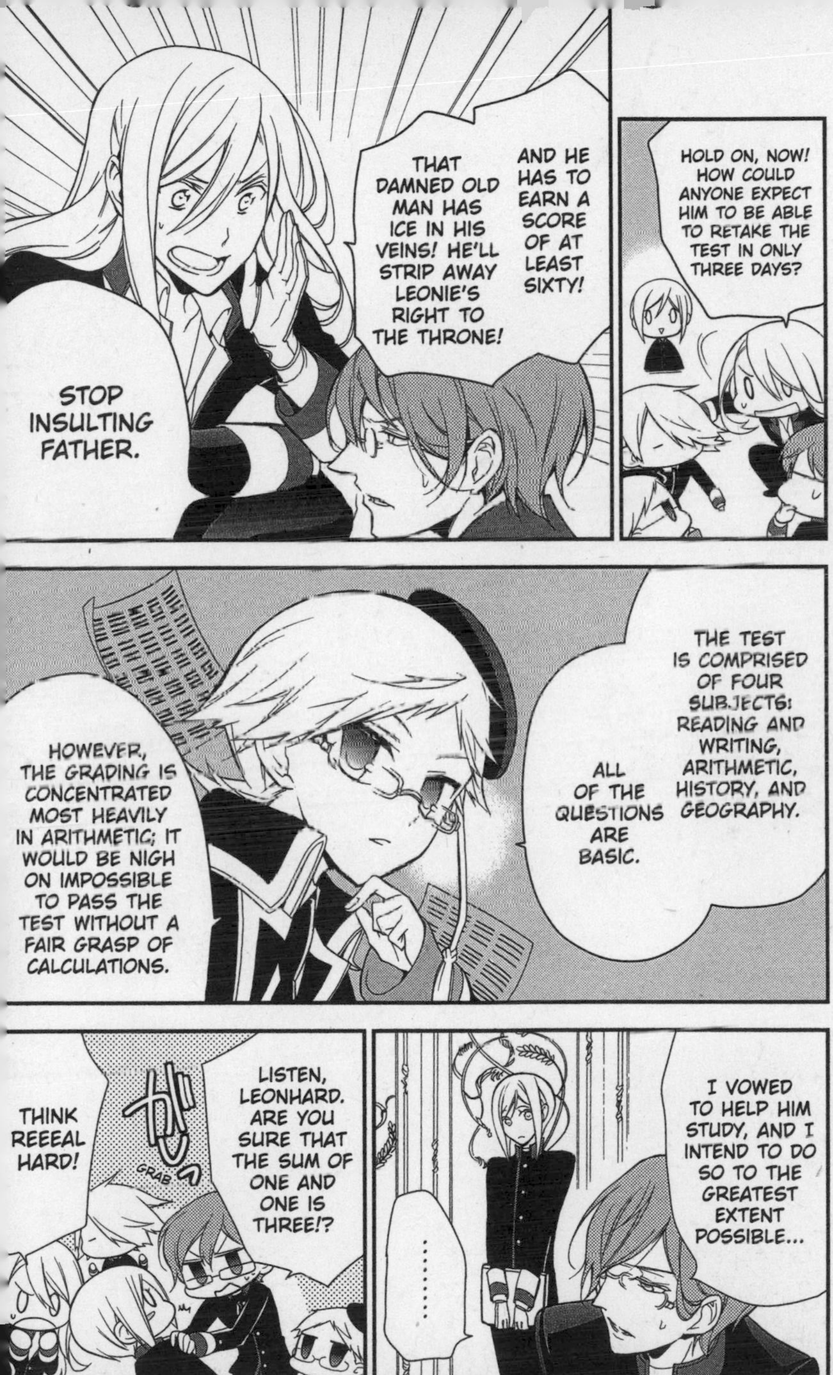
HOLD ON, NOW! HOW COULD ANYONE EXPECT HIM TO BE ABLE TO RETAKE THE TEST IN ONLY THREE DAYS?
AND HE HAS TO EARN A SCORE OF AT LEAST SIXTY!
THAT DAMNED OLD MAN HAS ICE IN HIS VEINS! HE'LL STRIP AWAY LEONIE'S RIGHT TO THE THRONE!
STOP INSULTING FATHER.
THE TEST IS COMPRISED OF FOUR SUBJECTS: READING AND WRITING, ARITHMETIC, HISTORY, AND GEOGRAPHY.
ALL OF THE QUESTIONS ARE BASIC.
HOWEVER, THE GRADING IS CONCENTRATED MOST HEAVILY IN ARITHMETIC; IT WOULD BE NIGH ON IMPOSSIBLE TO PASS THE TEST WITHOUT A FAIR GRASP OF CALCULATIONS.
I VOWED TO HELP HIM STUDY, AND I INTEND TO DO SO TO THE GREATEST EXTENT POSSIBLE...
......
LISTEN, LEONHARD. ARE YOU SURE THAT THE SUM OF ONE AND ONE IS THREE!?
THINK REEEAL HARD!
GRAB

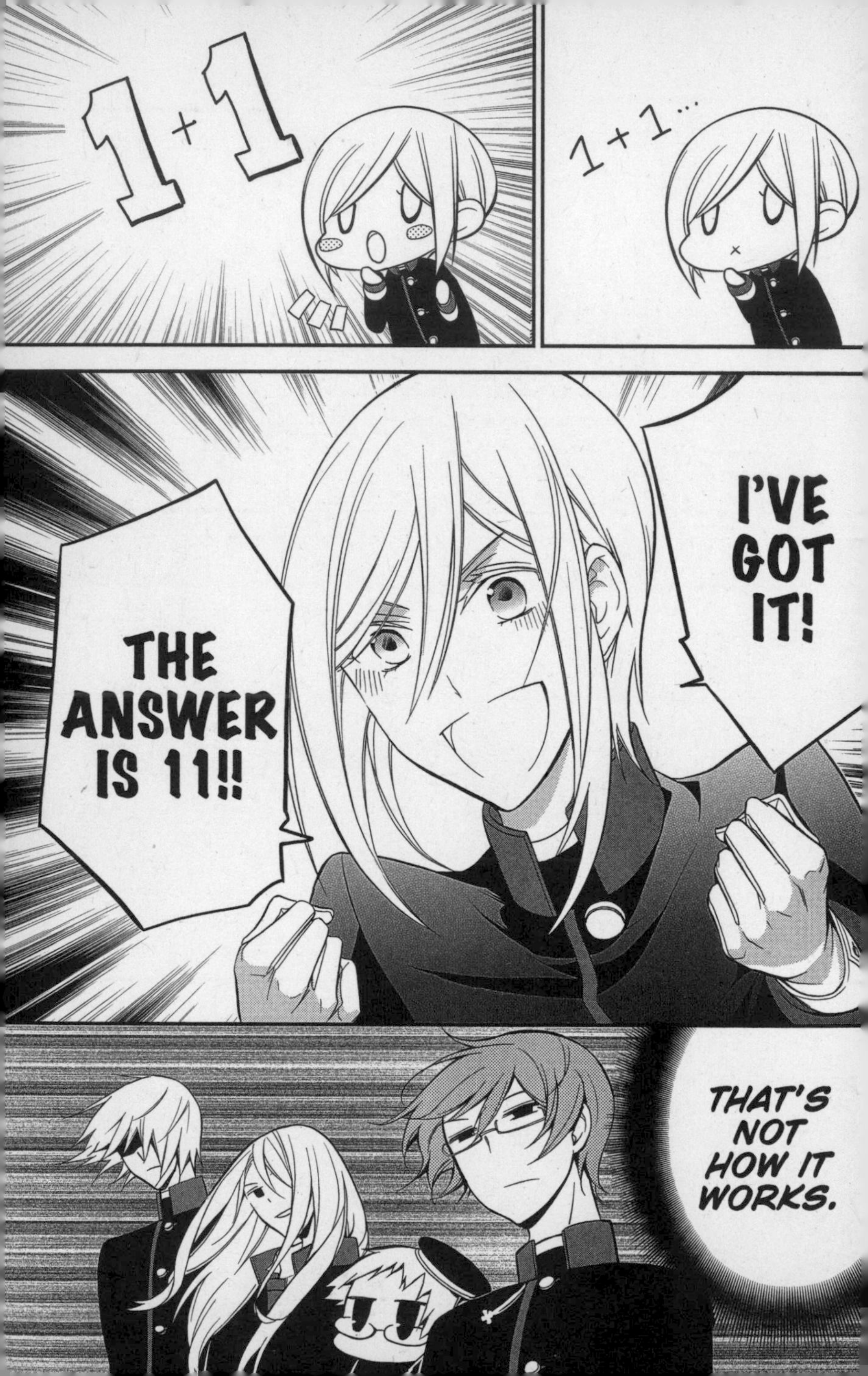
1+1...
1+1
I'VE GOT IT!
THE ANSWER IS 11!!
THAT'S NOT HOW IT WORKS.

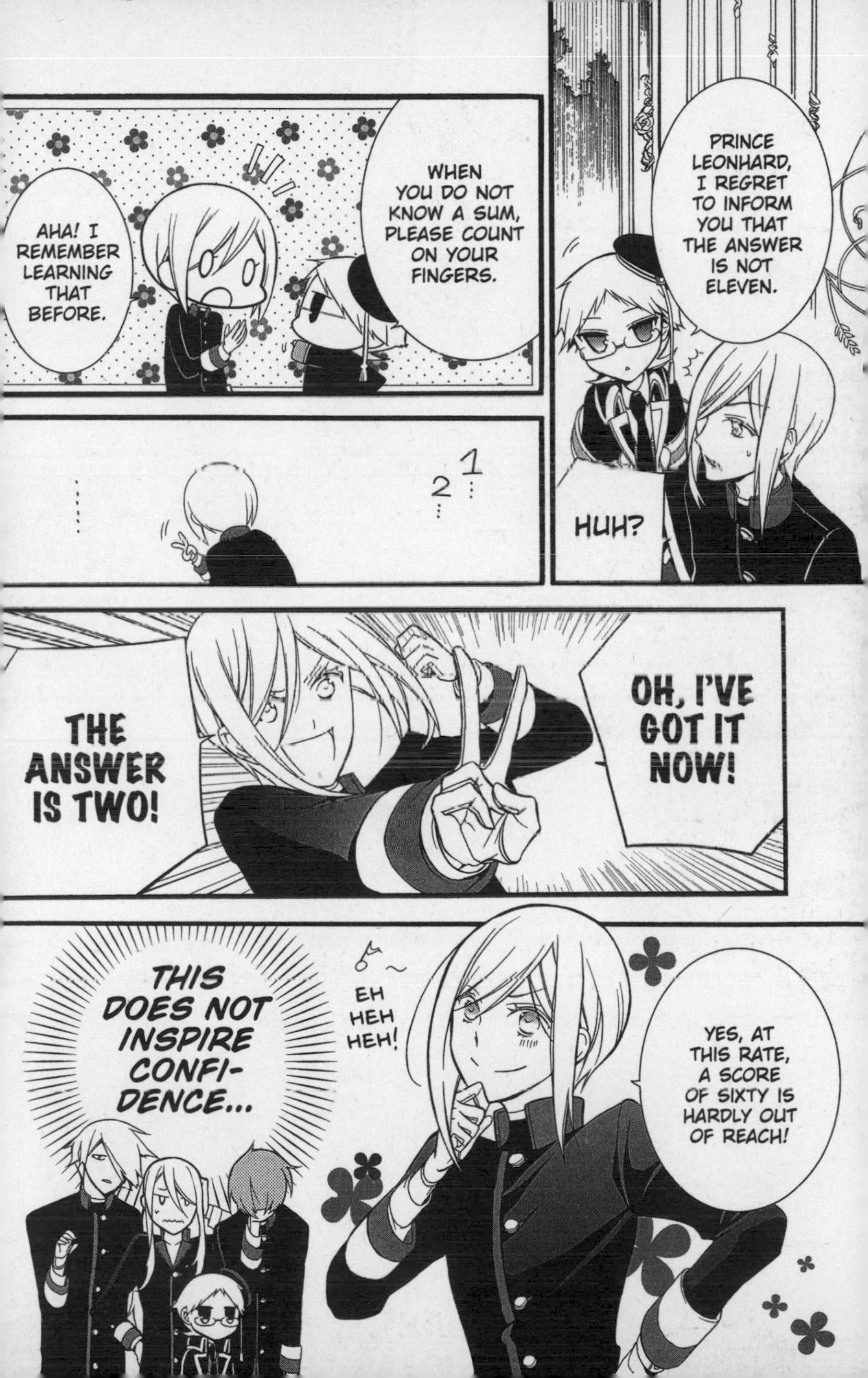
PRINCE LEONHARD, I REGRET TO INFORM YOU THAT THE ANSWER IS NOT ELEVEN.
HUH?
WHEN YOU DO NOT KNOW A SUM, PLEASE COUNT ON YOUR FINGERS.
AHA! I REMEMBER LEARNING THAT BEFORE.
1...
2...
......
OH, I'VE GOT IT NOW!
THE ANSWER IS TWO!
YES, AT THIS RATE, A SCORE OF SIXTY IS HARDLY OUT OF REACH!
EH HEH HEH!
THIS DOES NOT INSPIRE CONFI-DENCE...

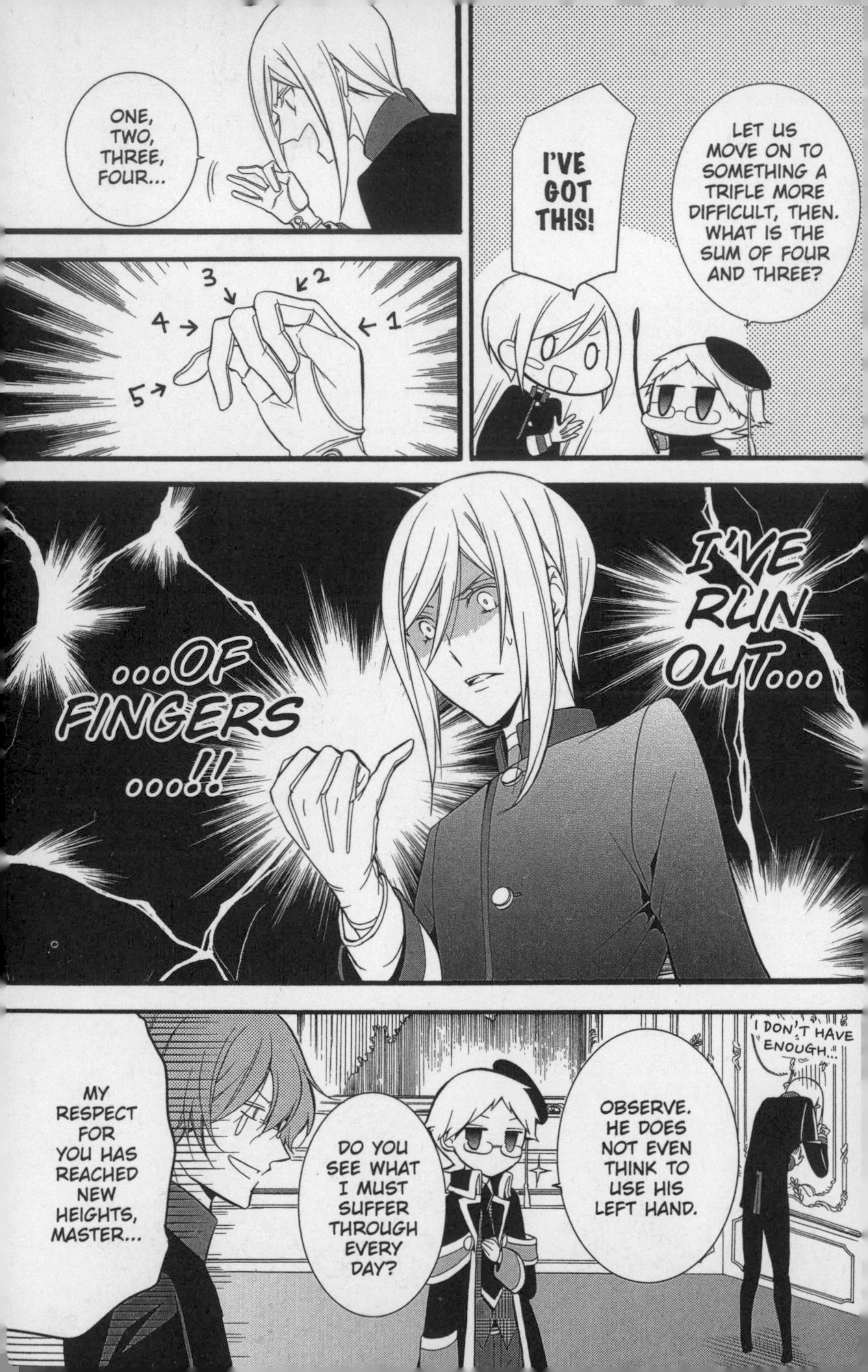
LET US MOVE ON TO SOMETHING A TRIFLE MORE DIFFICULT, THEN. WHAT IS THE SUM OF FOUR AND THREE?
I'VE GOT THIS!
ONE, TWO, THREE, FOUR...
1
2
3
4
5
I'VE RUN OUT...
...OF FINGERS...!!
I DON'T HAVE ENOUGH...
OBSERVE. HE DOES NOT EVEN THINK TO USE HIS LEFT HAND.
DO YOU SEE WHAT I MUST SUFFER THROUGH EVERY DAY?
MY RESPECT FOR YOU HAS REACHED NEW HEIGHTS, MASTER...

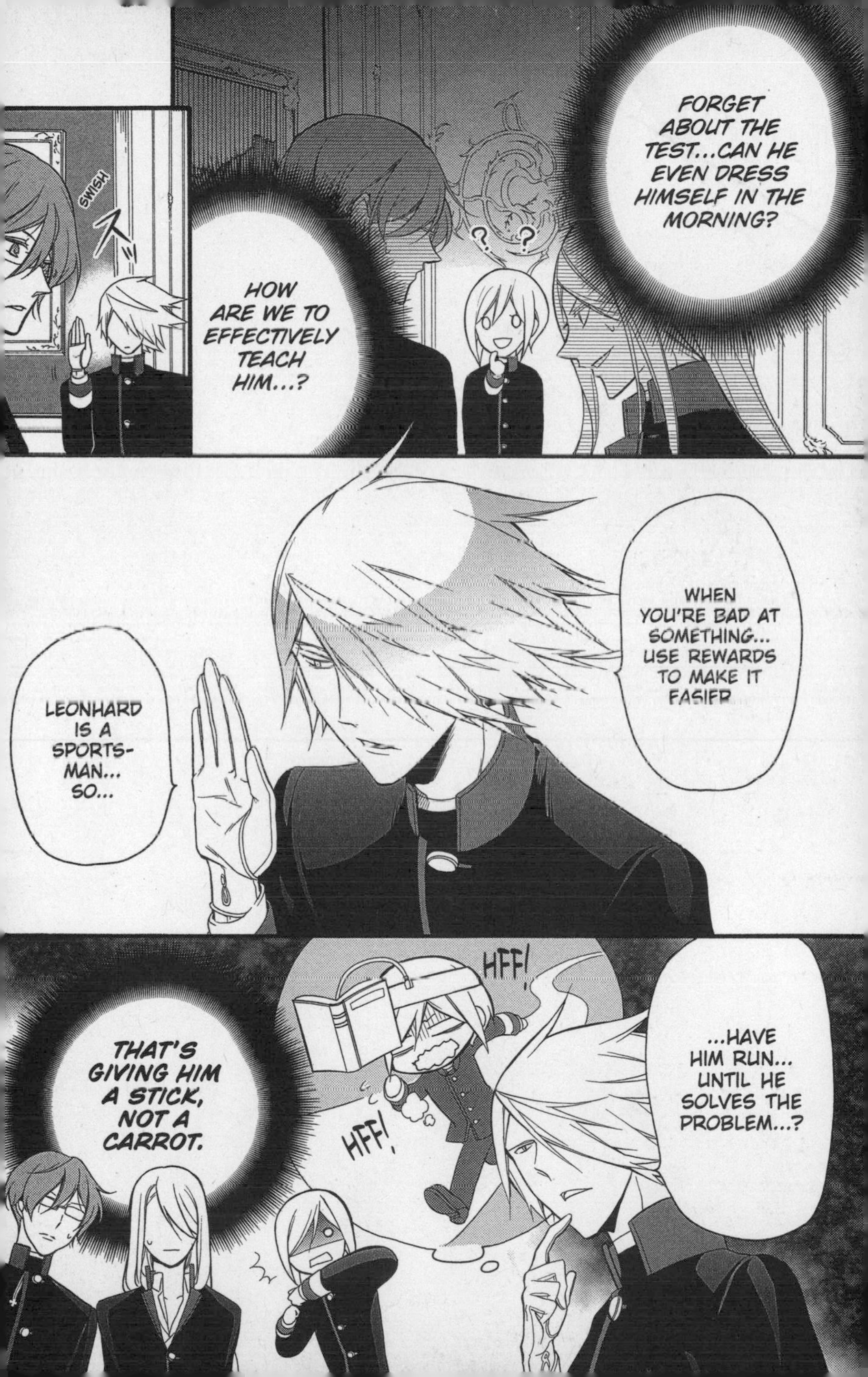
FORGET ABOUT THE TEST...CAN HE EVEN DRESS HIMSELF IN THE MORNING?
HOW ARE WE TO EFFECTIVELY TEACH HIM...?
SWISH
WHEN YOU'RE BAD AT SOMETHING... USE REWARDS TO MAKE IT EASIER
LEONHARD IS A SPORTS-MAN... SO...
...HAVE HIM RUN... UNTIL HE SOLVES THE PROBLEM...?
HFF!
HFF!
THAT'S GIVING HIM A STICK, NOT A CARROT.

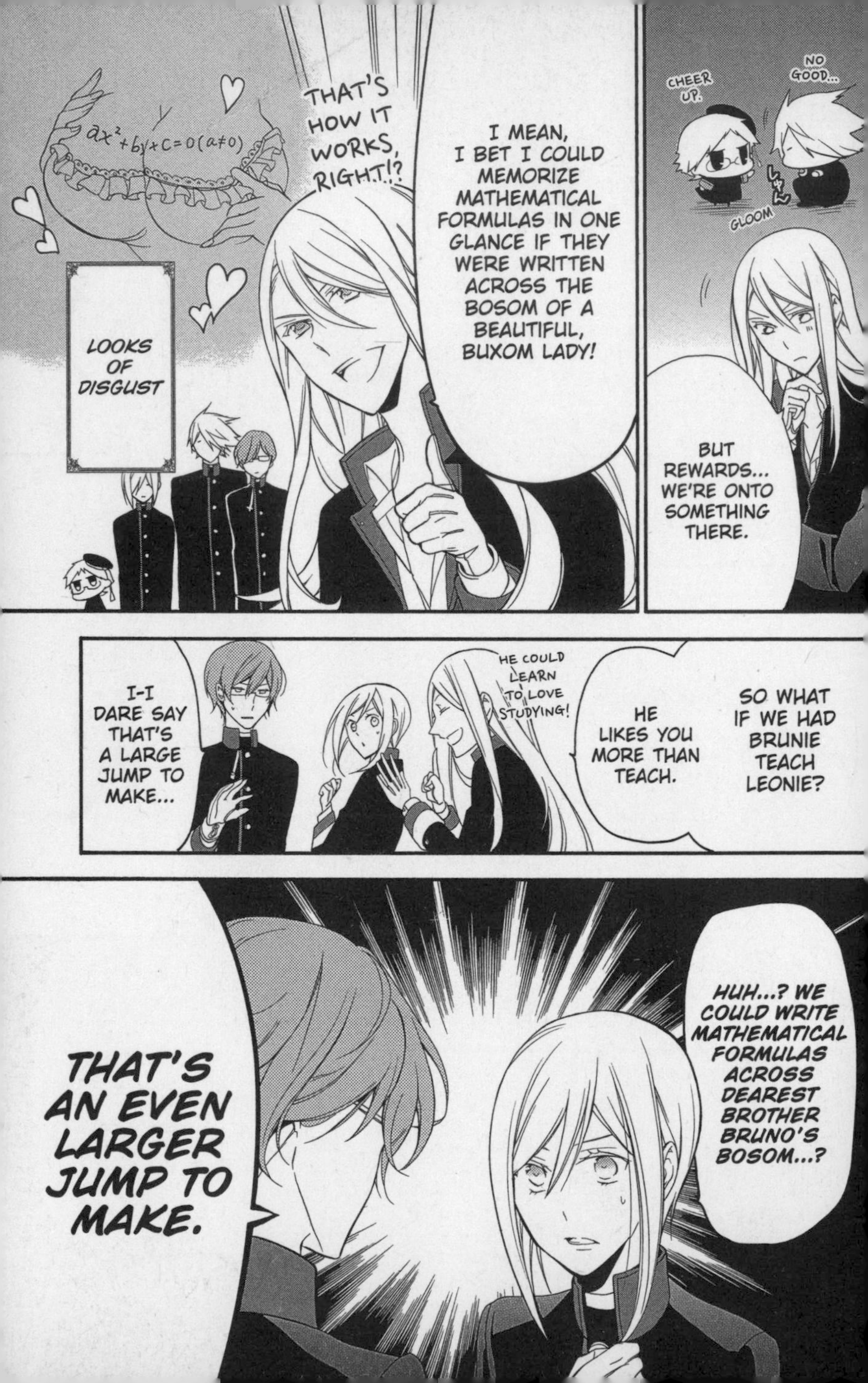
NO GOOD...
CHEER UP.
GLOOM
BUT REWARDS... WE'RE ONTO SOMETHING THERE.
I MEAN, I BET I COULD MEMORIZE MATHEMATICAL FORMULAS IN ONE GLANCE IF THEY WERE WRITTEN ACROSS THE BOSOM OF A BEAUTIFUL, BUXOM LADY!
THAT'S HOW IT WORKS, RIGHT!?
$ax^2+by+c=0(a\neq0)$
LOOKS OF DISGUST
SO WHAT IF WE HAD BRUNIE TEACH LEONIE?
HE LIKES YOU MORE THAN TEACH.
HE COULD LEARN TO LOVE STUDYING!
I-I DARE SAY THAT'S A LARGE JUMP TO MAKE...
HUH...? WE COULD WRITE MATHEMATICAL FORMULAS ACROSS DEAREST BROTHER BRUNO'S BOSOM...?
THAT'S AN EVEN LARGER JUMP TO MAKE.

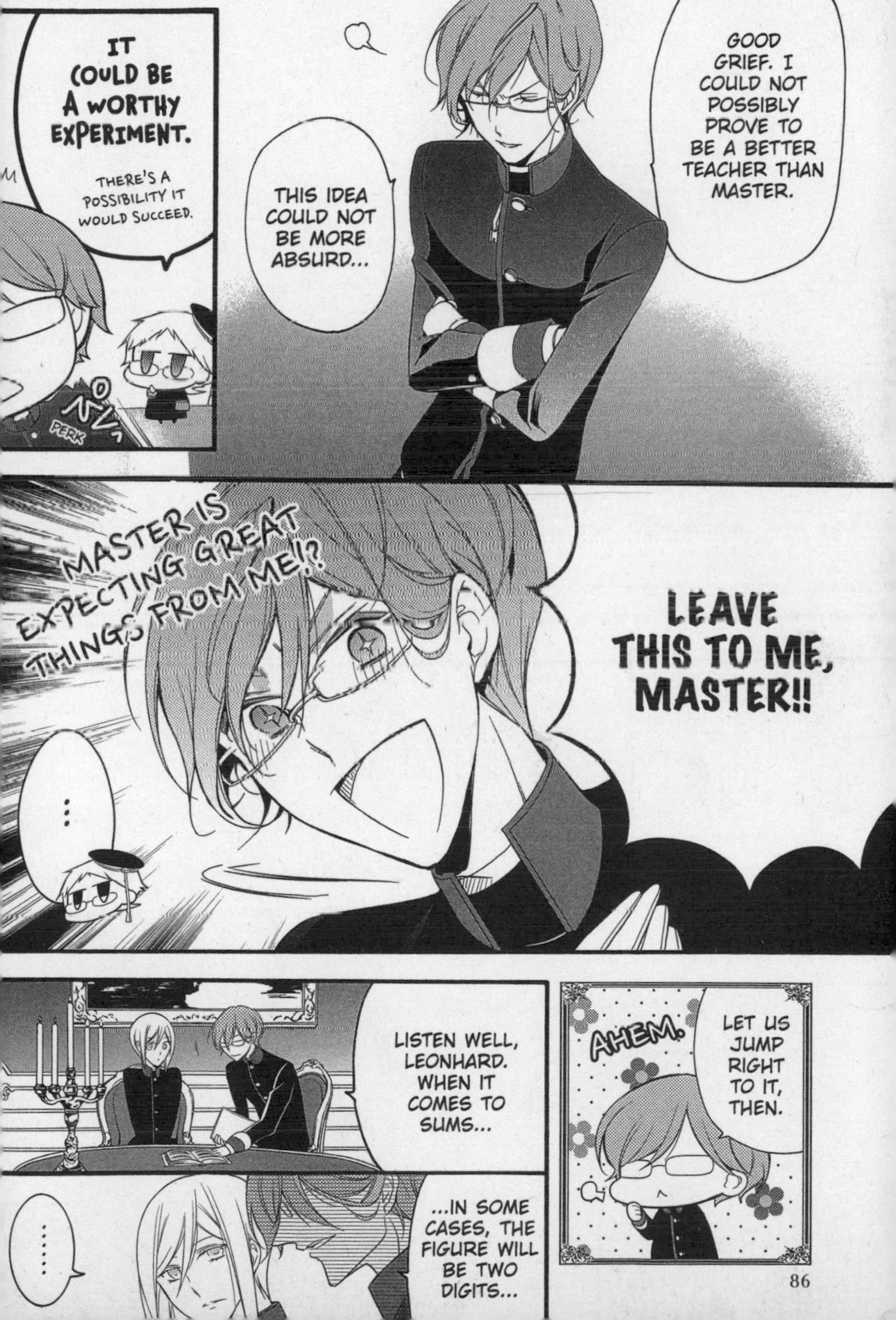
GOOD GRIEF. I COULD NOT POSSIBLY PROVE TO BE A BETTER TEACHER THAN MASTER.
THIS IDEA COULD NOT BE MORE ABSURD...
IT COULD BE A WORTHY EXPERIMENT.
THERE'S A POSSIBILITY IT WOULD SUCCEED.
PERK
LEAVE THIS TO ME, MASTER!!
MASTER IS EXPECTING GREAT THINGS FROM ME!?
...
AHEM.
LET US JUMP RIGHT TO IT, THEN.
LISTEN WELL, LEONHARD. WHEN IT COMES TO SUMS...
...IN SOME CASES, THE FIGURE WILL BE TWO DIGITS...
......

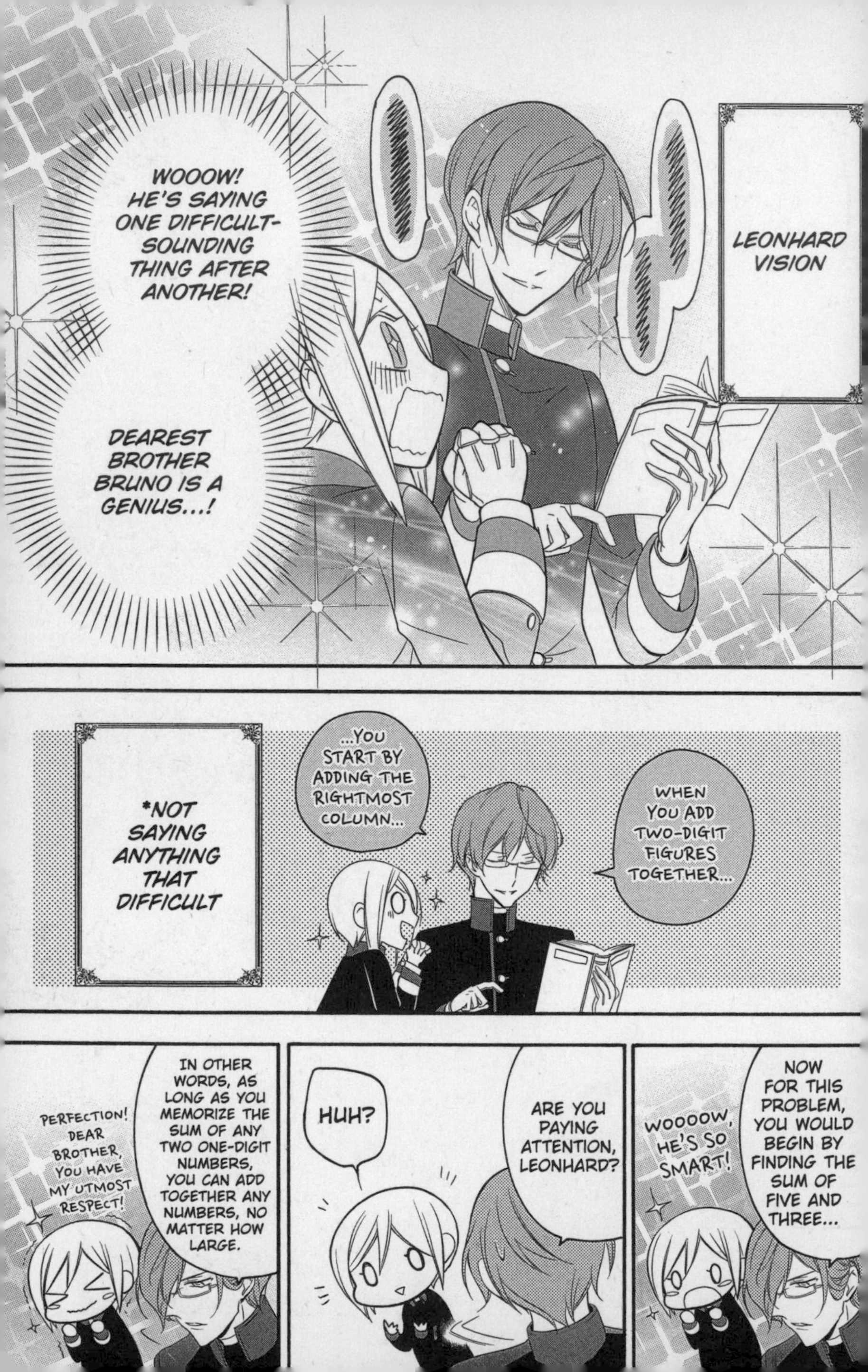
LEONHARD VISION
WOOOW! HE'S SAYING ONE DIFFICULT-SOUNDING THING AFTER ANOTHER!
DEAREST BROTHER BRUNO IS A GENIUS...!
WHEN YOU ADD TWO-DIGIT FIGURES TOGETHER...
...YOU START BY ADDING THE RIGHTMOST COLUMN...
*NOT SAYING ANYTHING THAT DIFFICULT
NOW FOR THIS PROBLEM, YOU WOULD BEGIN BY FINDING THE SUM OF FIVE AND THREE...
WOOOOW, HE'S SO SMART!
ARE YOU PAYING ATTENTION, LEONHARD?
HUH?
IN OTHER WORDS, AS LONG AS YOU MEMORIZE THE SUM OF ANY TWO ONE-DIGIT NUMBERS, YOU CAN ADD TOGETHER ANY NUMBERS, NO MATTER HOW LARGE.
PERFECTION! DEAR BROTHER, YOU HAVE MY UTMOST RESPECT!

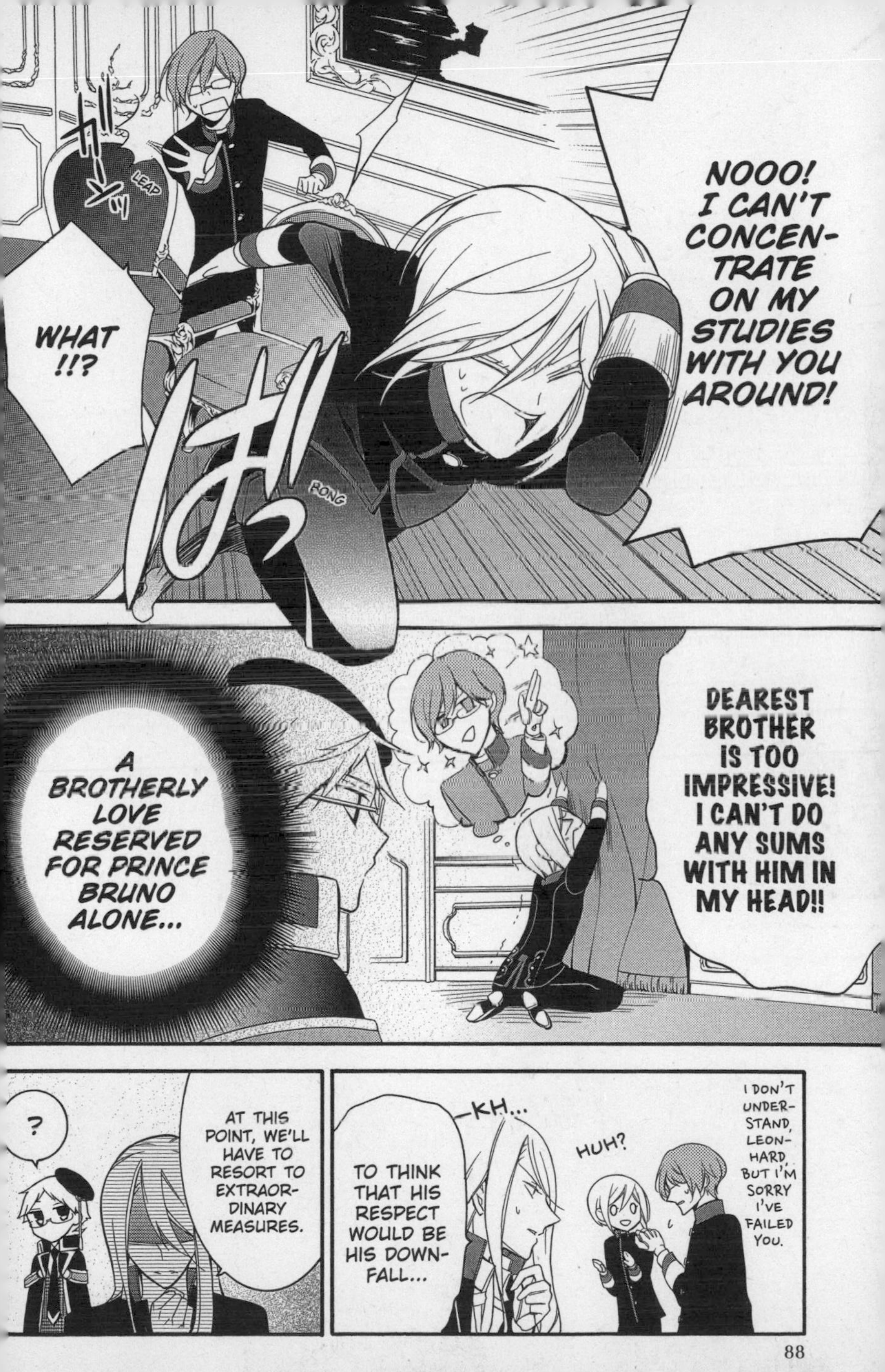
NOOO! I CAN'T CONCEN-TRATE ON MY STUDIES WITH YOU AROUND!
LEAP
WHAT!!?
DEAREST BROTHER IS TOO IMPRESSIVE! I CAN'T DO ANY SUMS WITH HIM IN MY HEAD!!
A BROTHERLY LOVE RESERVED FOR PRINCE BRUNO ALONE...
I DON'T UNDER-STAND, LEON-HARD, BUT I'M SORRY I'VE FAILED YOU.
HUH?
-KH...
TO THINK THAT HIS RESPECT WOULD BE HIS DOWN-FALL...
AT THIS POINT, WE'LL HAVE TO RESORT TO EXTRAOR-DINARY MEASURES.
?

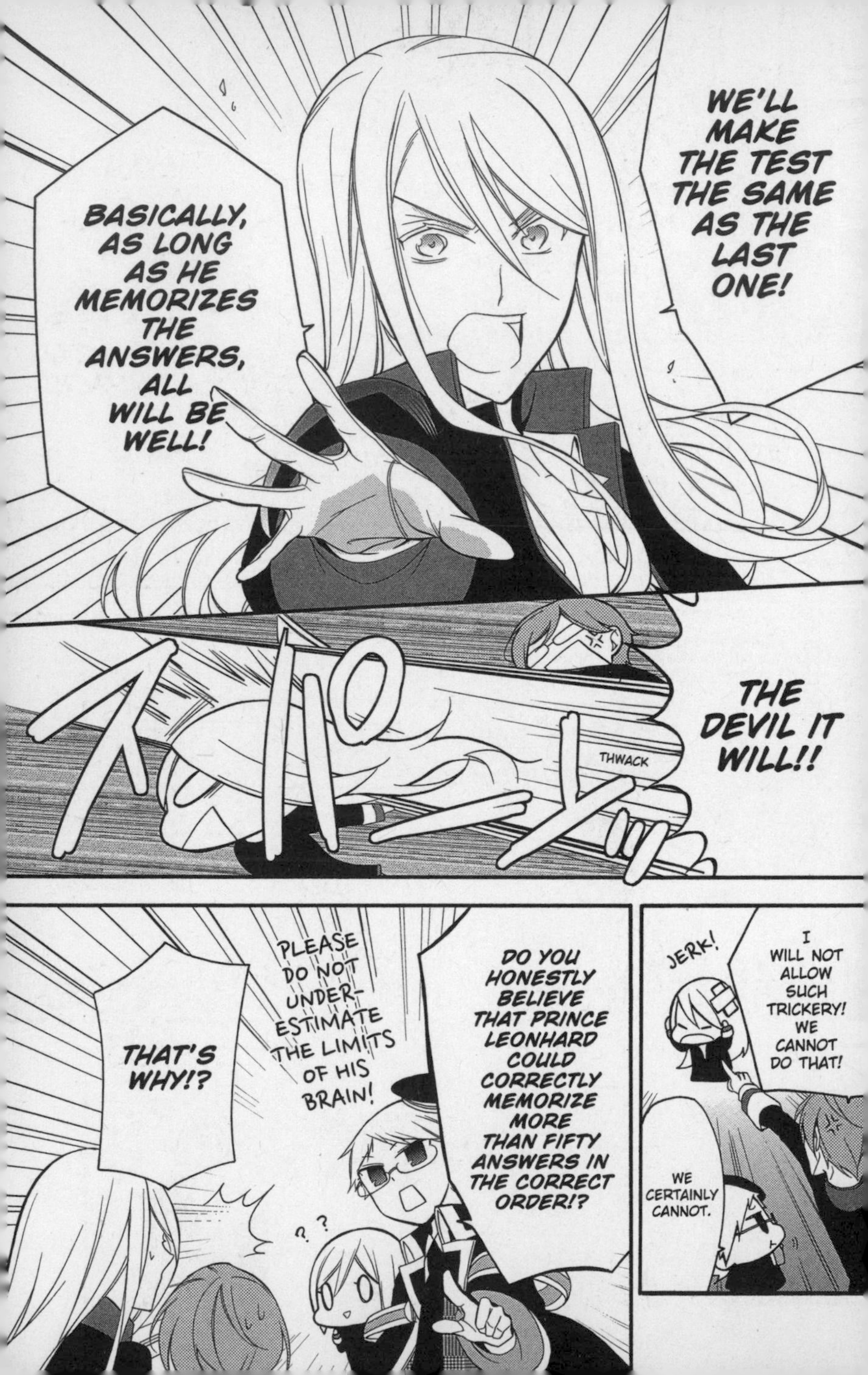
WE'LL MAKE THE TEST THE SAME AS THE LAST ONE!
BASICALLY, AS LONG AS HE MEMORIZES THE ANSWERS, ALL WILL BE WELL!
THE DEVIL IT WILL!!
THWACK
I WILL NOT ALLOW SUCH TRICKERY! WE CANNOT DO THAT!
JERK!
WE CERTAINLY CANNOT.
DO YOU HONESTLY BELIEVE THAT PRINCE LEONHARD COULD CORRECTLY MEMORIZE MORE THAN FIFTY ANSWERS IN THE CORRECT ORDER!?
PLEASE DO NOT UNDER-ESTIMATE THE LIMITS OF HIS BRAIN!
THAT'S WHY!?

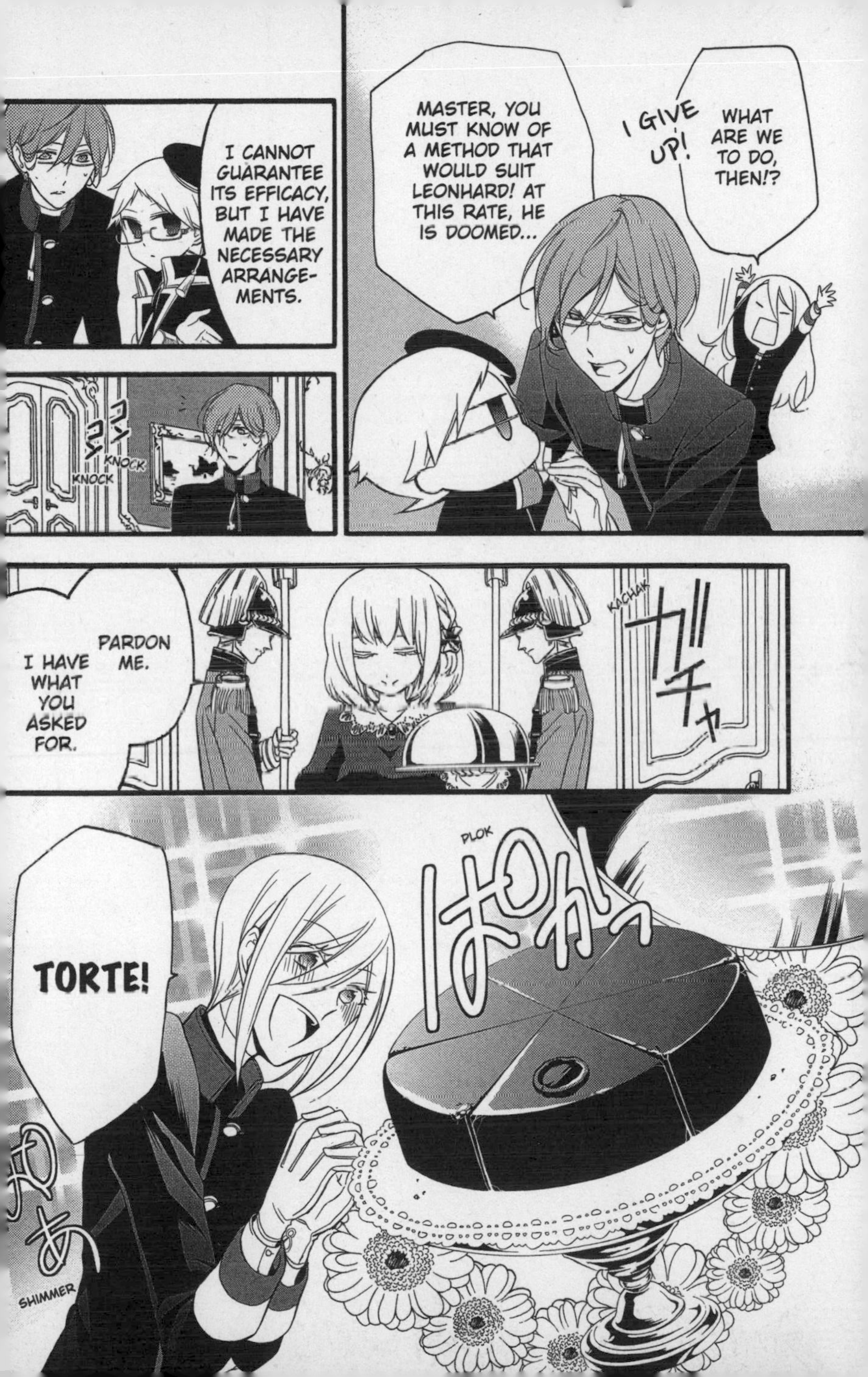
WHAT ARE WE TO DO, THEN!?
I GIVE UP!
MASTER, YOU MUST KNOW OF A METHOD THAT WOULD SUIT LEONHARD! AT THIS RATE, HE IS DOOMED...
I CANNOT GUARANTEE ITS EFFICACY, BUT I HAVE MADE THE NECESSARY ARRANGE-MENTS.
コン
KNOCK
コン
KNOCK
ガチャ
KACHAK
PARDON ME.
I HAVE WHAT YOU ASKED FOR.
はわっ
PLOK
TORTE!
ゆあ
SHIMMER

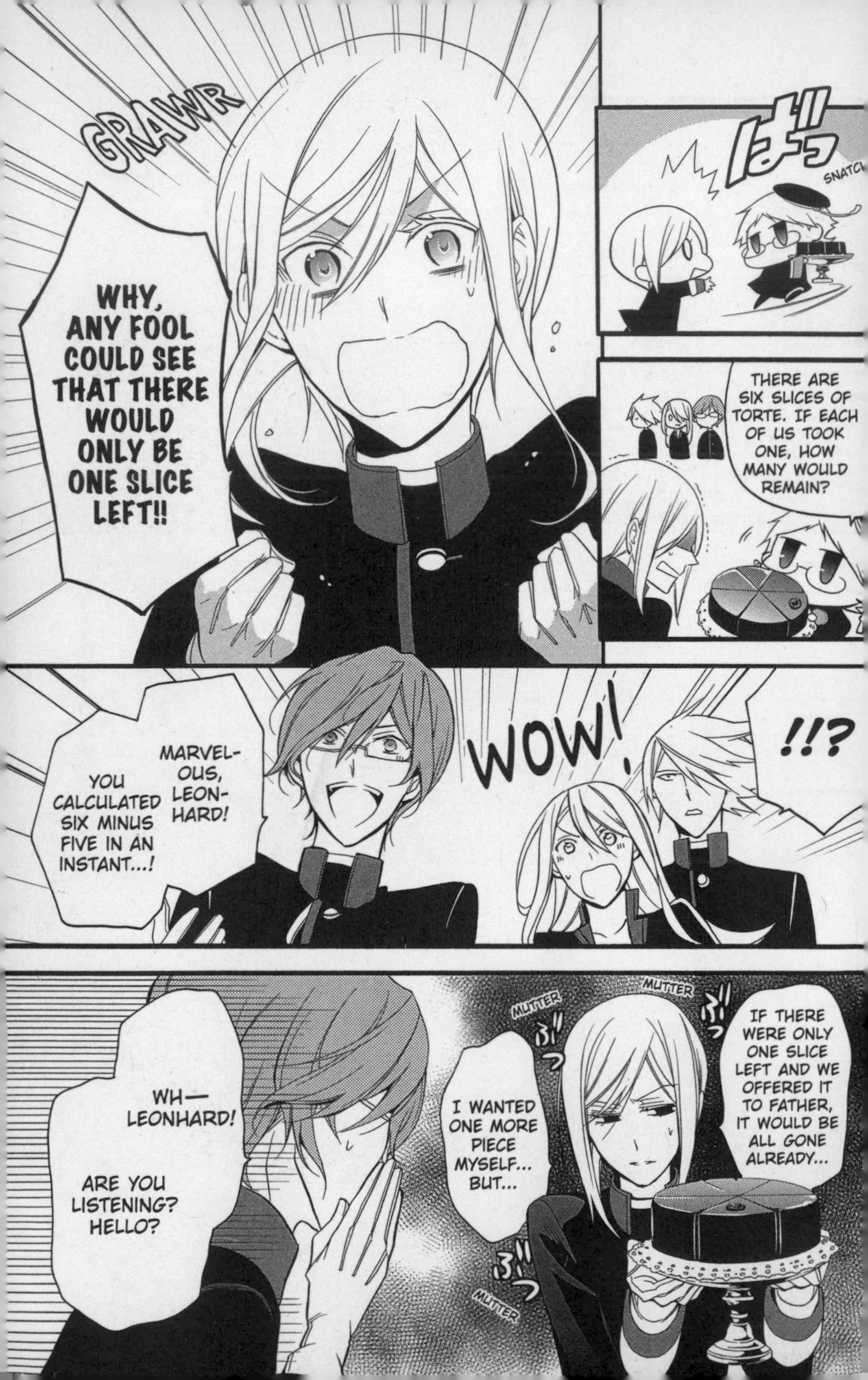

ぱっ
SNATC
THERE ARE SIX SLICES OF TORTE. IF EACH OF US TOOK ONE, HOW MANY WOULD REMAIN?
GRAWR
WHY, ANY FOOL COULD SEE THAT THERE WOULD ONLY BE ONE SLICE LEFT!!
!!?
WOW!
MARVEL-OUS, LEON-HARD!
YOU CALCULATED SIX MINUS FIVE IN AN INSTANT...!
IF THERE WERE ONLY ONE SLICE LEFT AND WE OFFERED IT TO FATHER, IT WOULD BE ALL GONE ALREADY...
MUTTER
ぶつ
MUTTER
ぶつ
I WANTED ONE MORE PIECE MYSELF... BUT...
ぶつ
MUTTER
WH— LEONHARD!
ARE YOU LISTENING? HELLO?

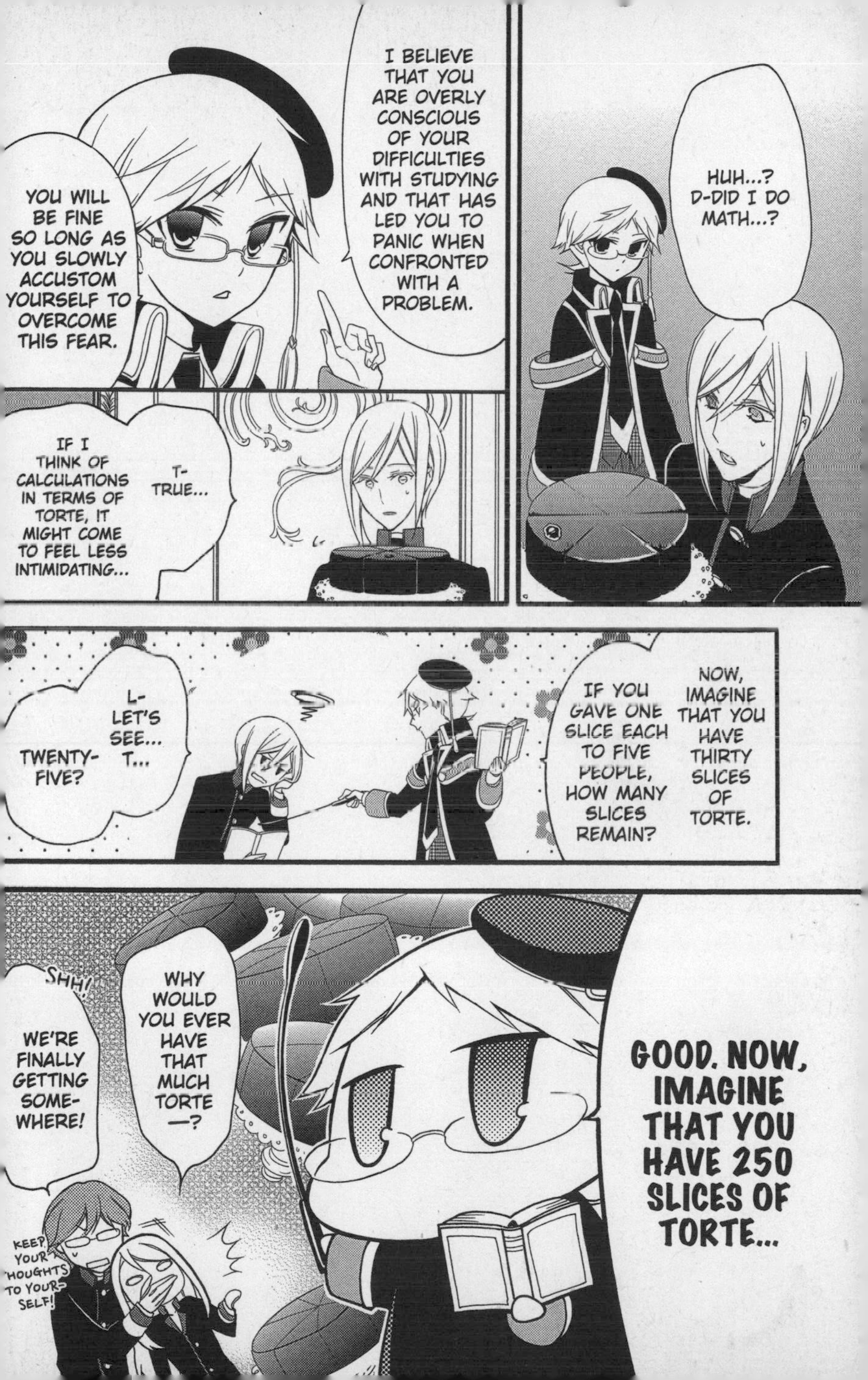
HUH...? D-DID I DO MATH...?
I BELIEVE THAT YOU ARE OVERLY CONSCIOUS OF YOUR DIFFICULTIES WITH STUDYING AND THAT HAS LED YOU TO PANIC WHEN CONFRONTED WITH A PROBLEM.
YOU WILL BE FINE SO LONG AS YOU SLOWLY ACCUSTOM YOURSELF TO OVERCOME THIS FEAR.
T-TRUE...
IF I THINK OF CALCULATIONS IN TERMS OF TORTE, IT MIGHT COME TO FEEL LESS INTIMIDATING...
NOW, IMAGINE THAT YOU HAVE THIRTY SLICES OF TORTE.
IF YOU GAVE ONE SLICE EACH TO FIVE PEOPLE, HOW MANY SLICES REMAIN?
L-LET'S SEE... T...
TWENTY-FIVE?
GOOD. NOW, IMAGINE THAT YOU HAVE 250 SLICES OF TORTE...
WHY WOULD YOU EVER HAVE THAT MUCH TORTE—?
SHH!
WE'RE FINALLY GETTING SOME-WHERE!
KEEP YOUR THOUGHTS TO YOUR-SELF!

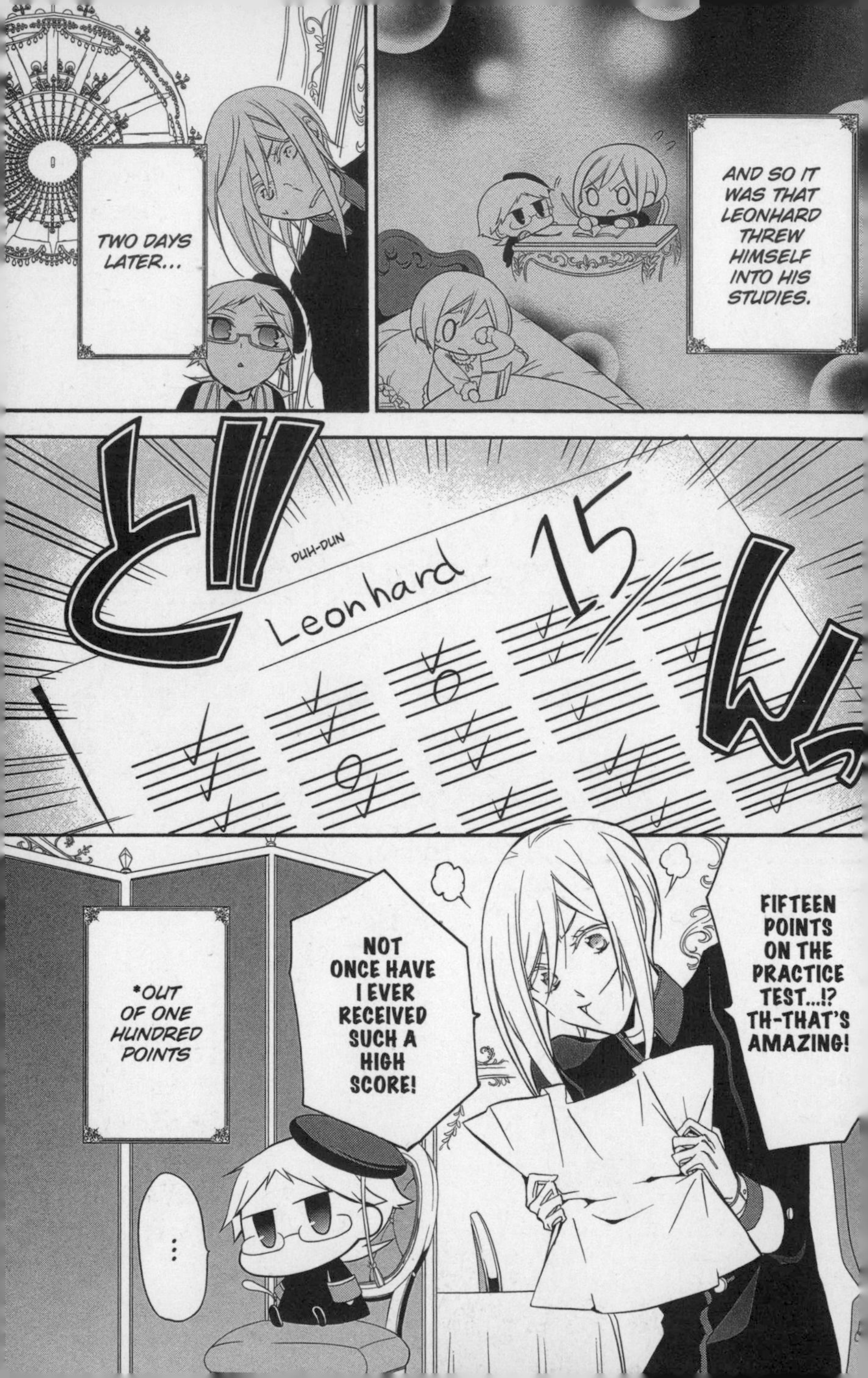
AND SO IT WAS THAT LEONHARD THREW HIMSELF INTO HIS STUDIES.
TWO DAYS LATER...
DUH-DUN
Leonhard
15
FIFTEEN POINTS ON THE PRACTICE TEST...!? TH-THAT'S AMAZING!
NOT ONCE HAVE I EVER RECEIVED SUCH A HIGH SCORE!
*OUT OF ONE HUNDRED POINTS
...

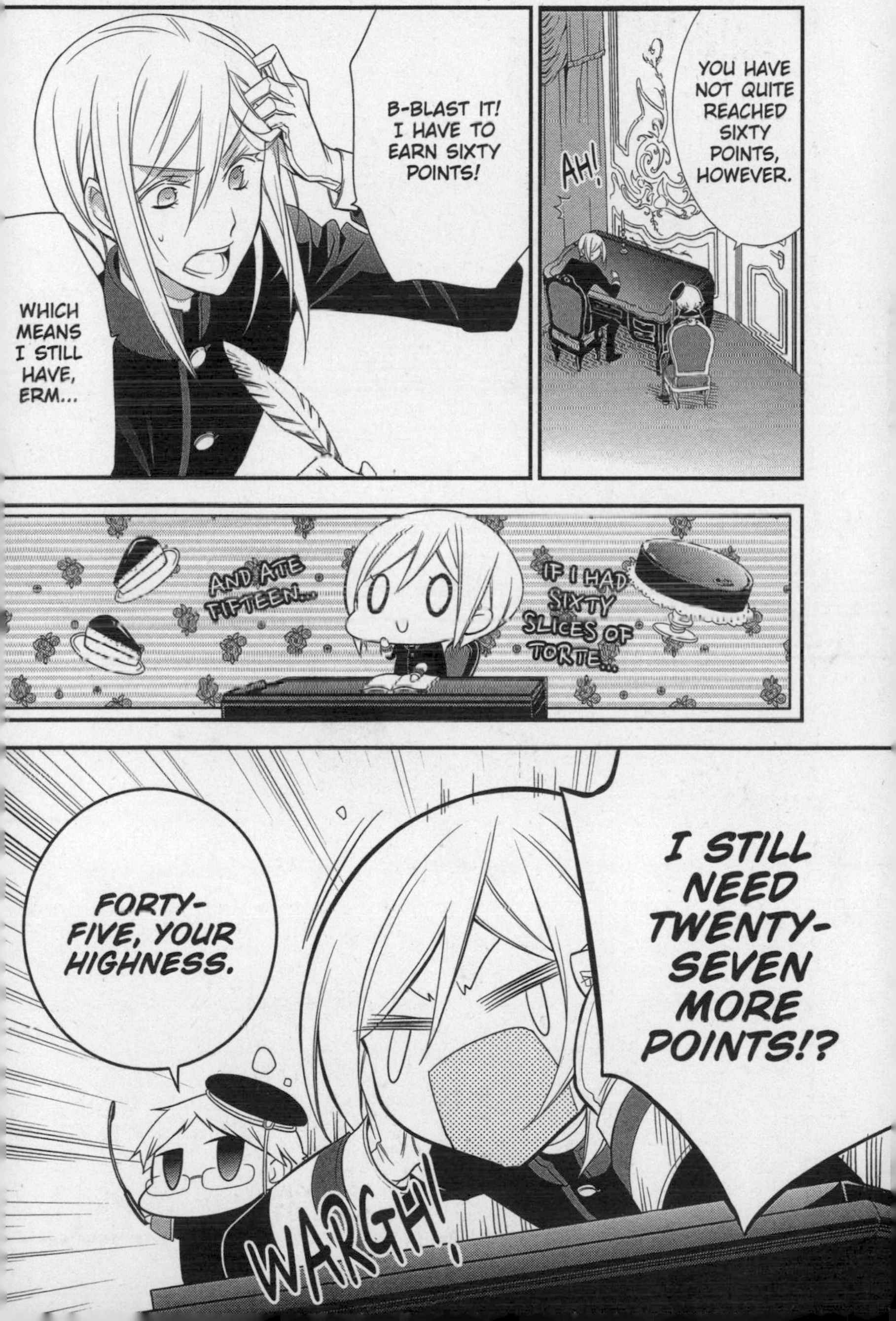
YOU HAVE NOT QUITE REACHED SIXTY POINTS, HOWEVER.
AH!
B-BLAST IT! I HAVE TO EARN SIXTY POINTS!
WHICH MEANS I STILL HAVE, ERM...
IF I HAD SIXTY SLICES OF TORTE...
AND ATE FIFTEEN...
I STILL NEED TWENTY-SEVEN MORE POINTS!?
FORTY-FIVE, YOUR HIGHNESS.
WARGH!

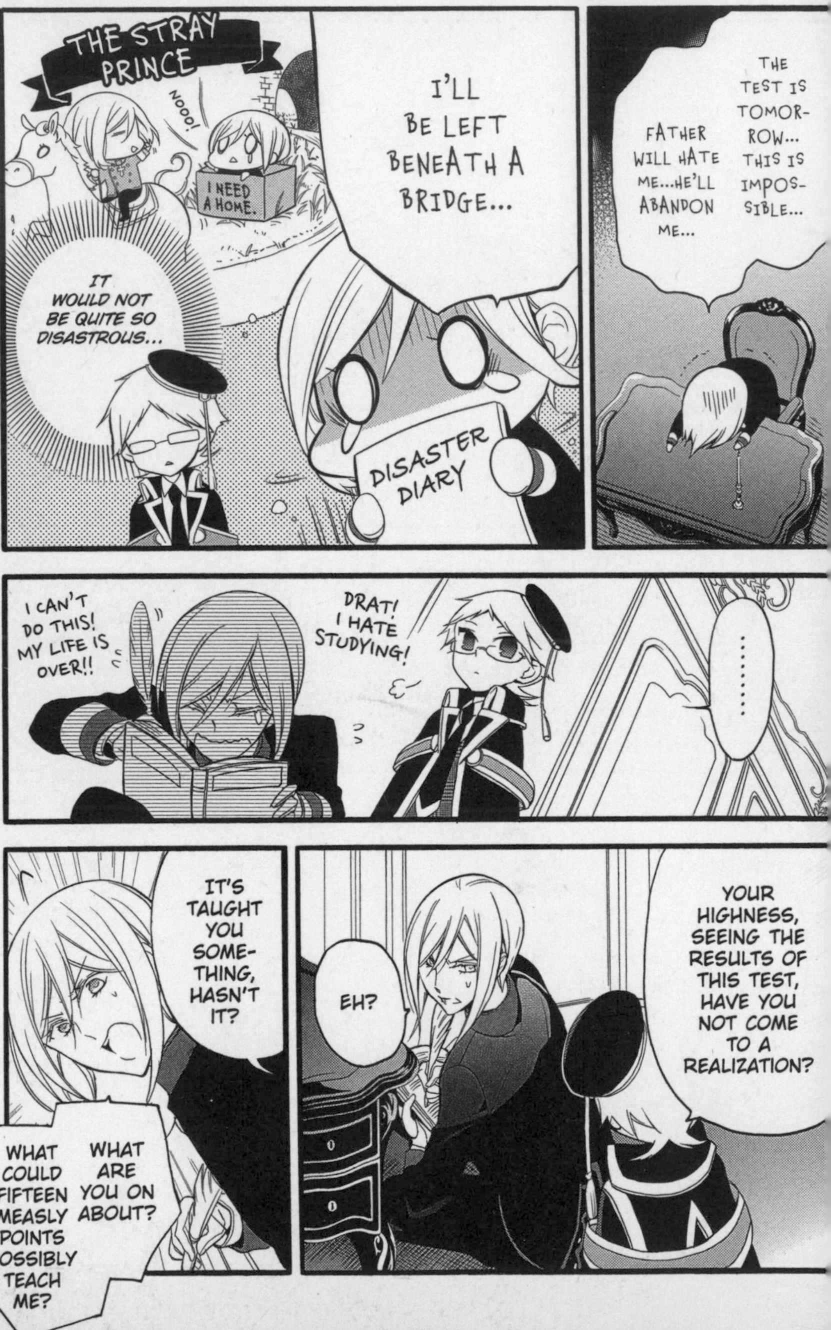
THE TEST IS TOMORROW... THIS IS IMPOSSIBLE...
FATHER WILL HATE ME...HE'LL ABANDON ME...
I'LL BE LEFT BENEATH A BRIDGE...
DISASTER DIARY
THE STRAY PRINCE
NOOOO!
I NEED A HOME.
IT WOULD NOT BE QUITE SO DISASTROUS...
......
DRAT! I HATE STUDYING!
I CAN'T DO THIS! MY LIFE IS OVER!!
YOUR HIGHNESS, SEEING THE RESULTS OF THIS TEST, HAVE YOU NOT COME TO A REALIZATION?
EH?
IT'S TAUGHT YOU SOMETHING, HASN'T IT?
WHAT ARE YOU ON ABOUT?
WHAT COULD FIFTEEN MEASLY POINTS POSSIBLY TEACH ME?

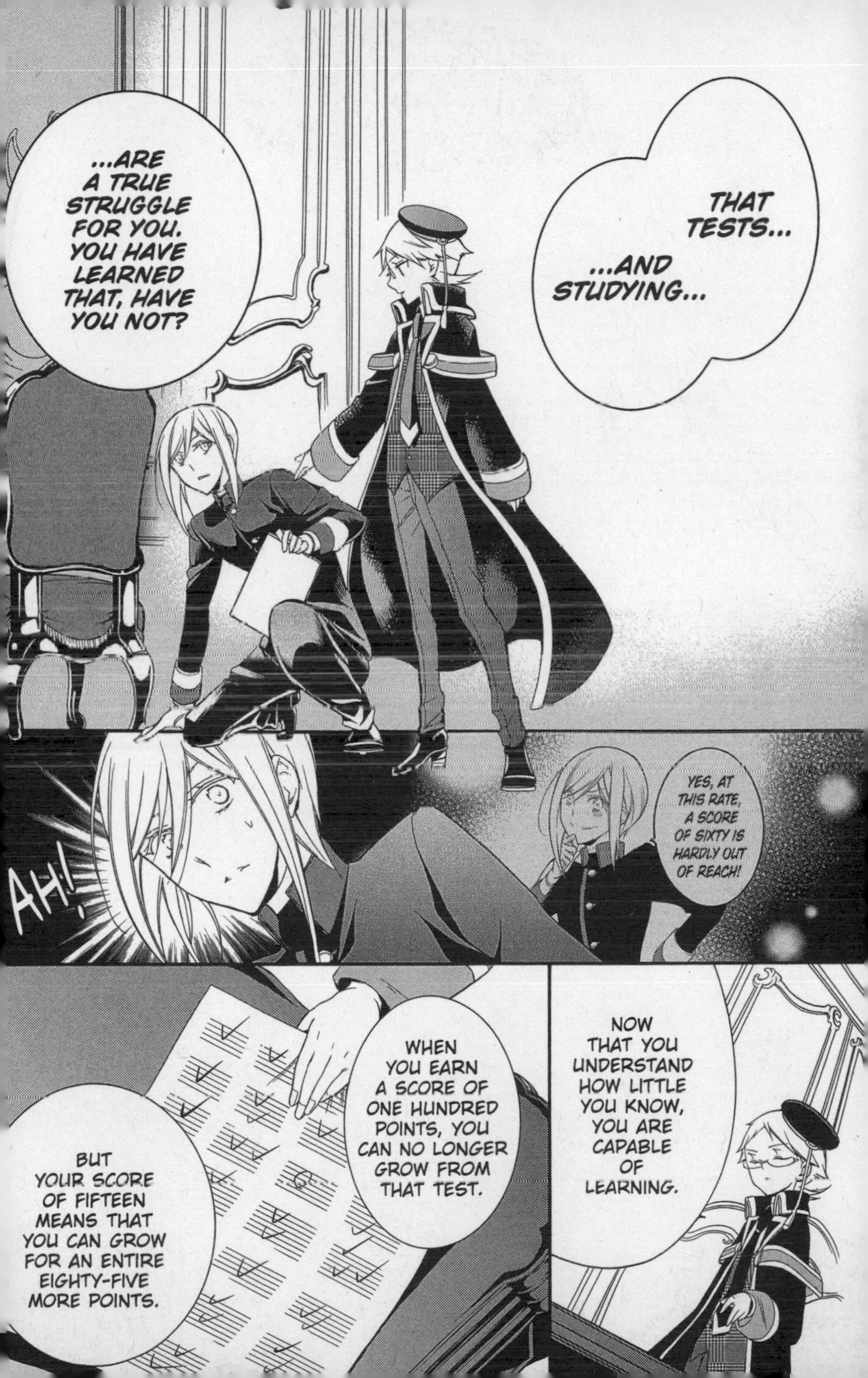
THAT TESTS...
...AND STUDYING...
...ARE A TRUE STRUGGLE FOR YOU. YOU HAVE LEARNED THAT, HAVE YOU NOT?
YES, AT THIS RATE, A SCORE OF SIXTY IS HARDLY OUT OF REACH!
AH!
NOW THAT YOU UNDERSTAND HOW LITTLE YOU KNOW, YOU ARE CAPABLE OF LEARNING.
WHEN YOU EARN A SCORE OF ONE HUNDRED POINTS, YOU CAN NO LONGER GROW FROM THAT TEST.
BUT YOUR SCORE OF FIFTEEN MEANS THAT YOU CAN GROW FOR AN ENTIRE EIGHTY-FIVE MORE POINTS.

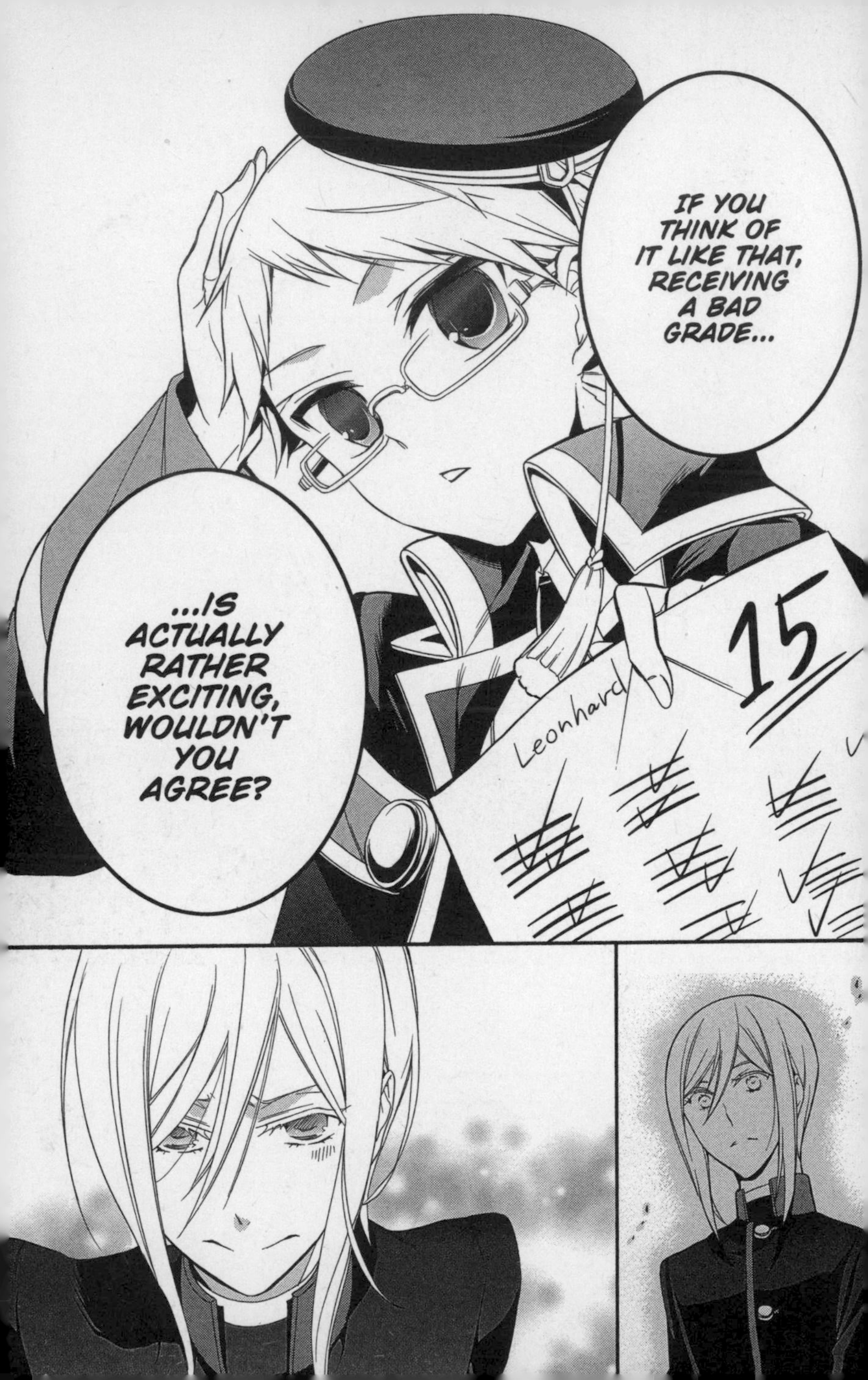
IF YOU THINK OF IT LIKE THAT, RECEIVING A BAD GRADE...
15
Leonhard
...IS ACTUALLY RATHER EXCITING, WOULDN'T YOU AGREE?

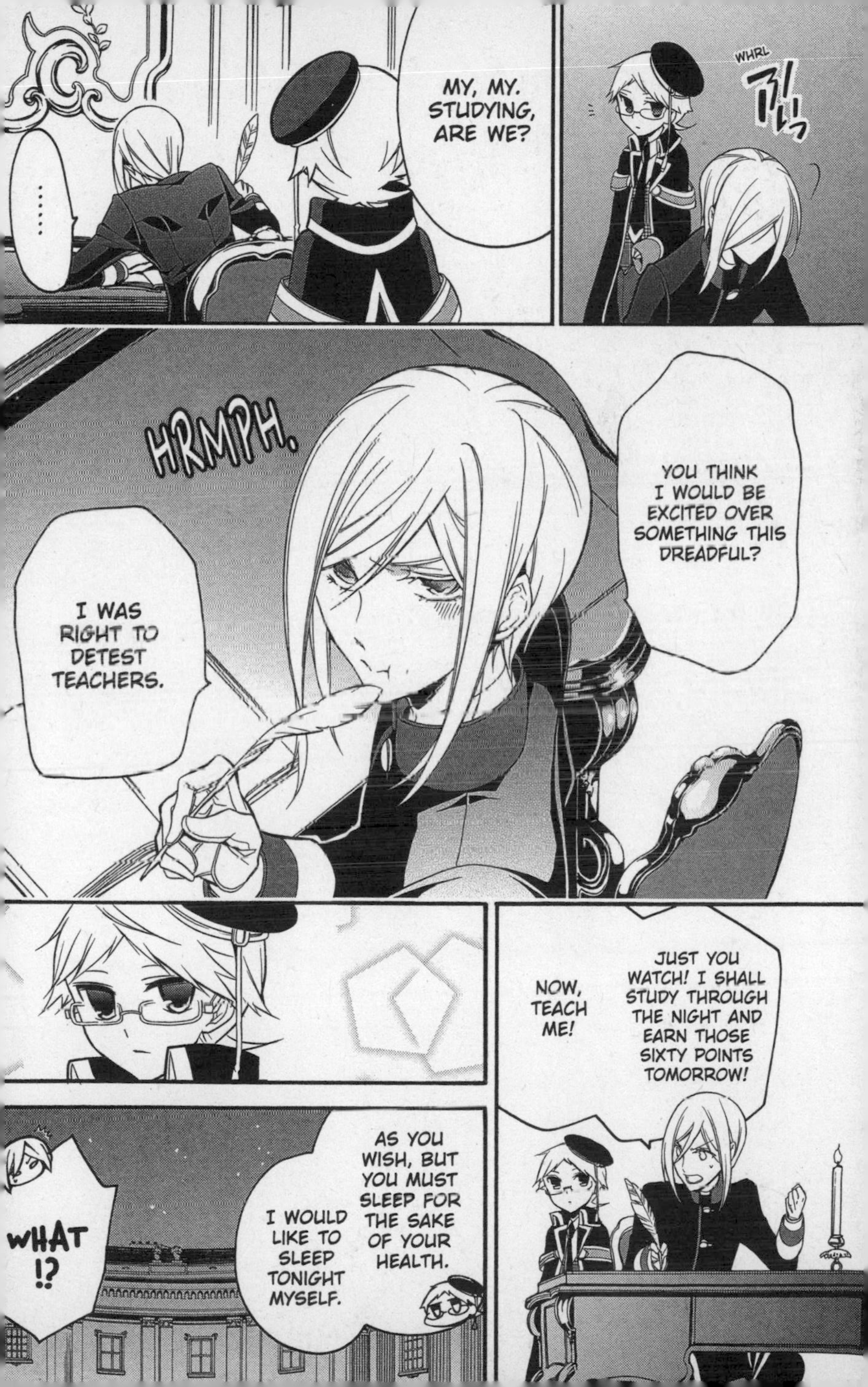
WHRL
MY, MY. STUDYING, ARE WE?
......
YOU THINK I WOULD BE EXCITED OVER SOMETHING THIS DREADFUL?
HRMPH.
I WAS RIGHT TO DETEST TEACHERS.
JUST YOU WATCH! I SHALL STUDY THROUGH THE NIGHT AND EARN THOSE SIXTY POINTS TOMORROW!
NOW, TEACH ME!
AS YOU WISH, BUT YOU MUST SLEEP FOR THE SAKE OF YOUR HEALTH.
I WOULD LIKE TO SLEEP TONIGHT MYSELF.
WHAT !?

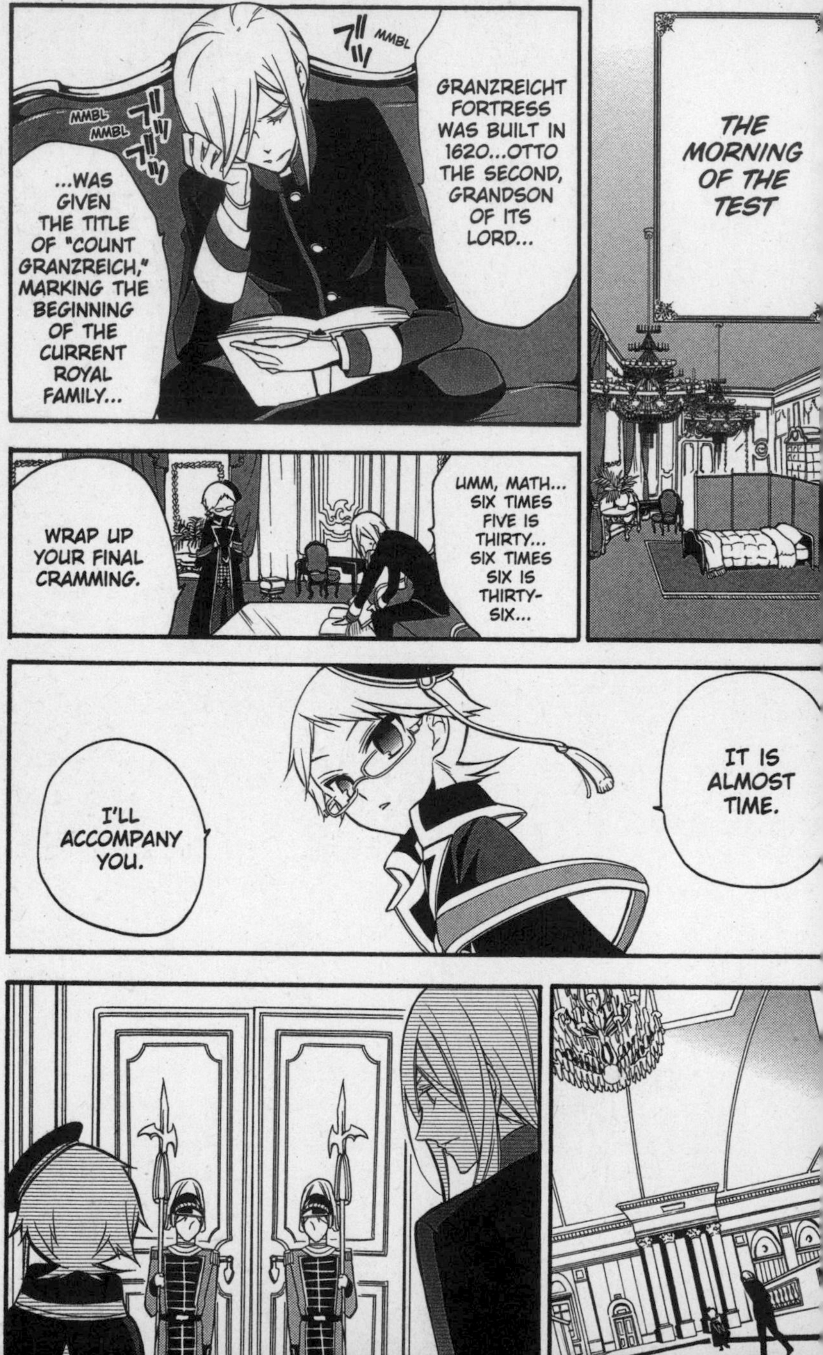
THE MORNING OF THE TEST
MMBL
GRANZREICHT FORTRESS WAS BUILT IN 1620...OTTO THE SECOND, GRANDSON OF ITS LORD...
MMBL MMBL
...WAS GIVEN THE TITLE OF "COUNT GRANZREICH," MARKING THE BEGINNING OF THE CURRENT ROYAL FAMILY...
UMM, MATH... SIX TIMES FIVE IS THIRTY... SIX TIMES SIX IS THIRTY-SIX...
WRAP UP YOUR FINAL CRAMMING.
IT IS ALMOST TIME.
I'LL ACCOMPANY YOU.

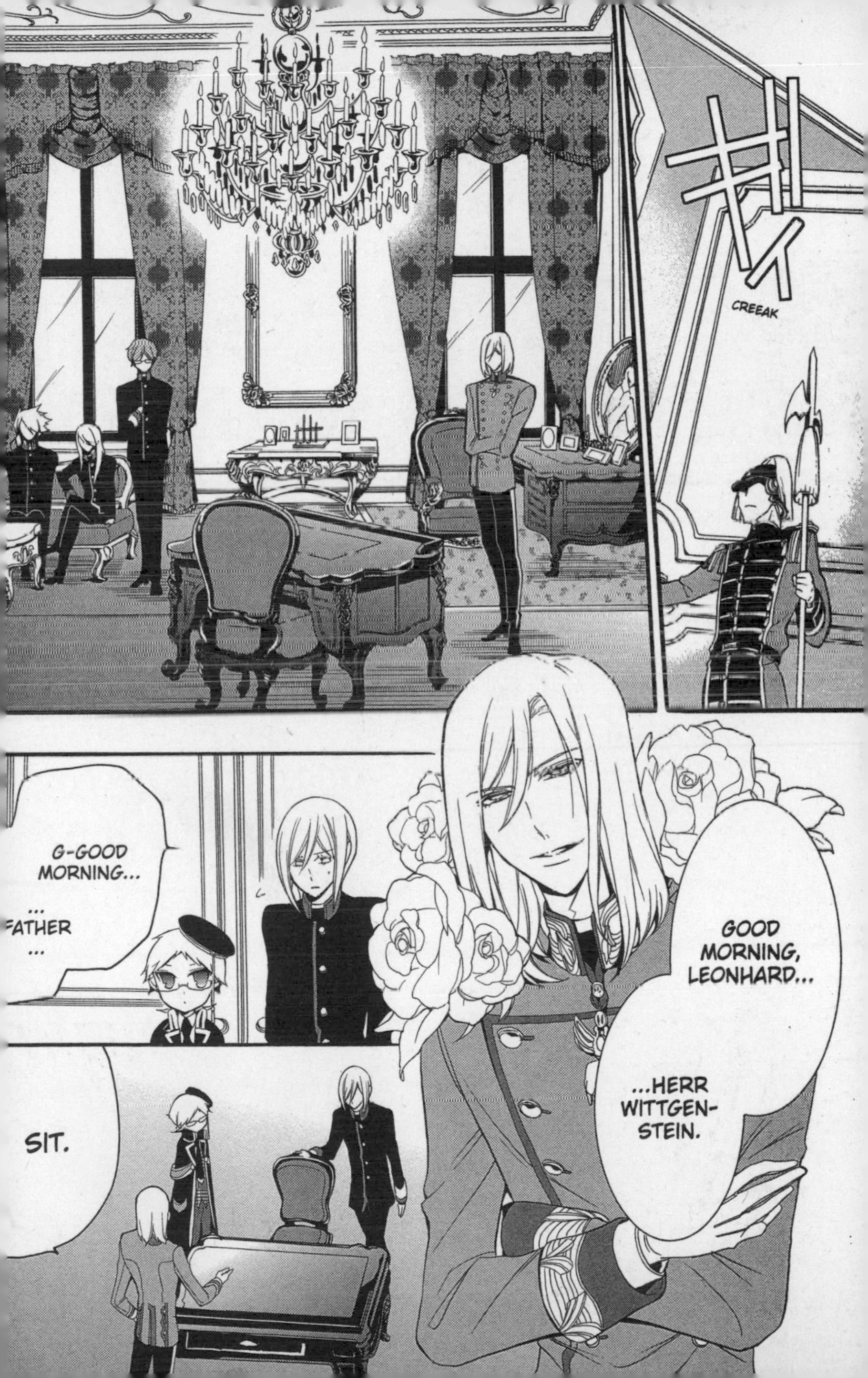

ギィ
CREEAK
GOOD MORNING, LEONHARD...
...HERR WITTGEN-STEIN.
G-GOOD MORNING...
...FATHER...
SIT.

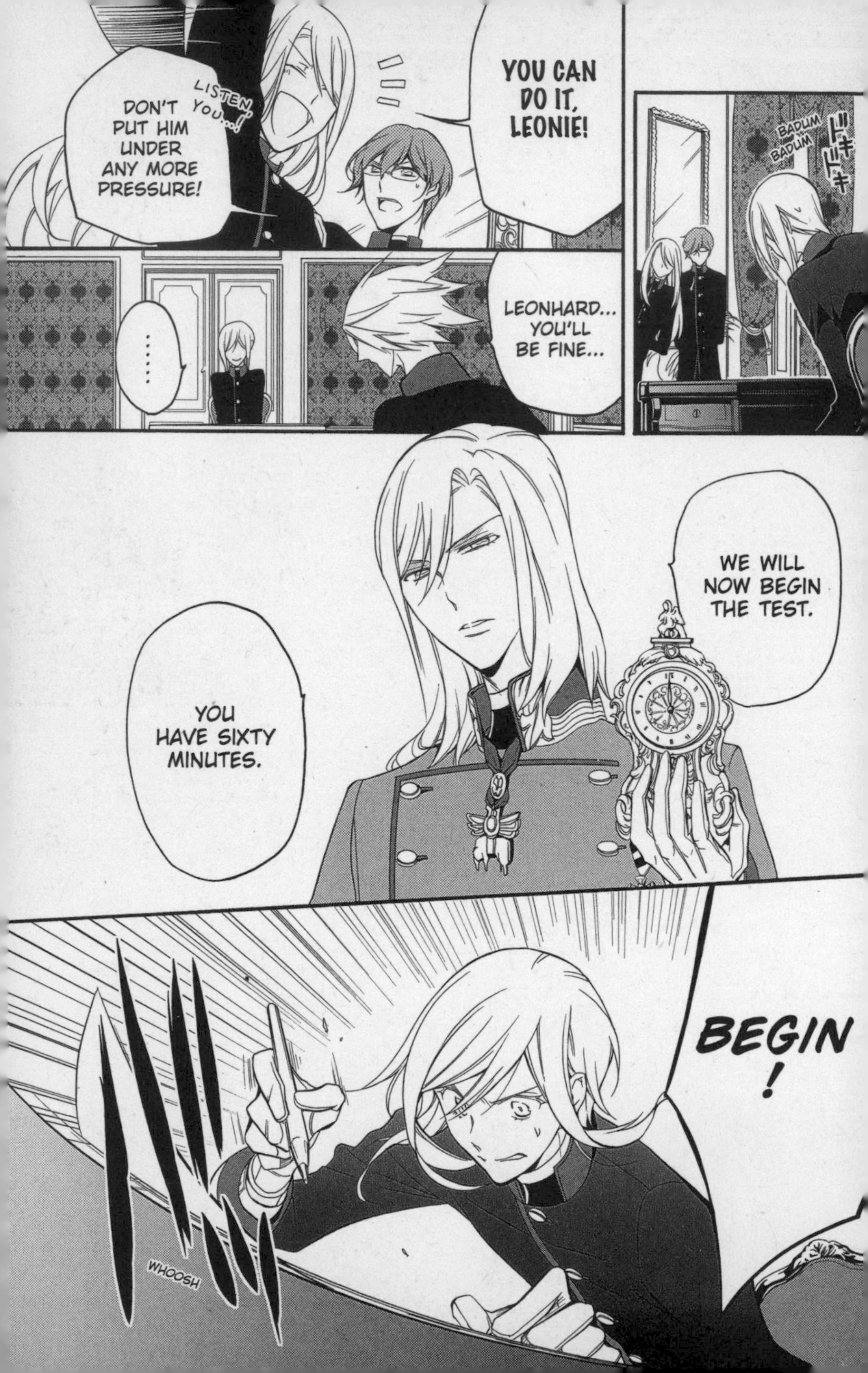
YOU CAN DO IT, LEONIE!
LISTEN, YOU...!
DON'T PUT HIM UNDER ANY MORE PRESSURE!
LEONHARD... YOU'LL BE FINE...
......
BADUM BADUM
ドキドキ
WE WILL NOW BEGIN THE TEST.
YOU HAVE SIXTY MINUTES.
BEGIN!
WHOOSH

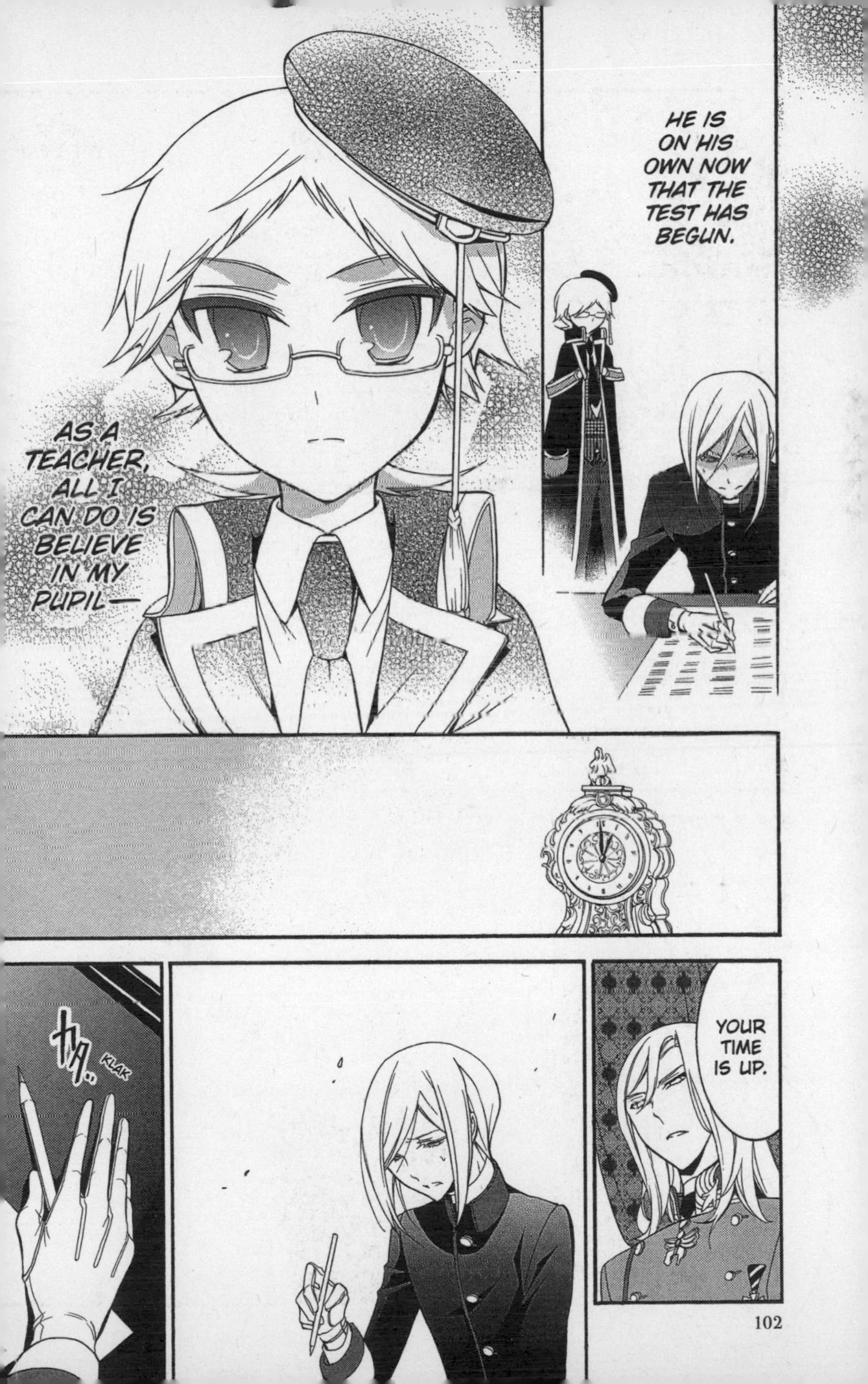
HE IS ON HIS OWN NOW THAT THE TEST HAS BEGUN.
AS A TEACHER, ALL I CAN DO IS BELIEVE IN MY PUPIL—
YOUR TIME IS UP.
カタ..
KLAK

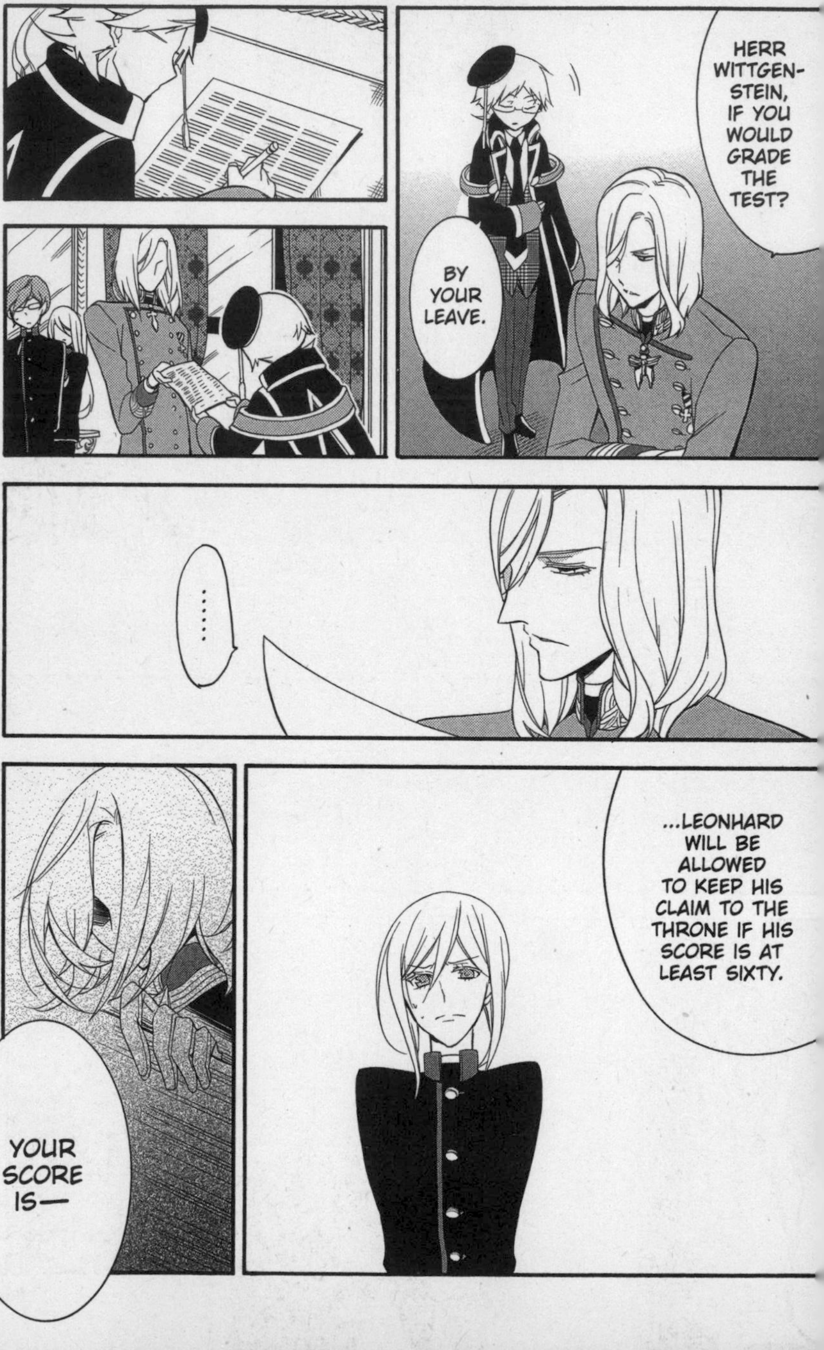
HERR WITTGENSTEIN, IF YOU WOULD GRADE THE TEST?
BY YOUR LEAVE.
......
...LEONHARD WILL BE ALLOWED TO KEEP HIS CLAIM TO THE THRONE IF HIS SCORE IS AT LEAST SIXTY.
YOUR SCORE IS—

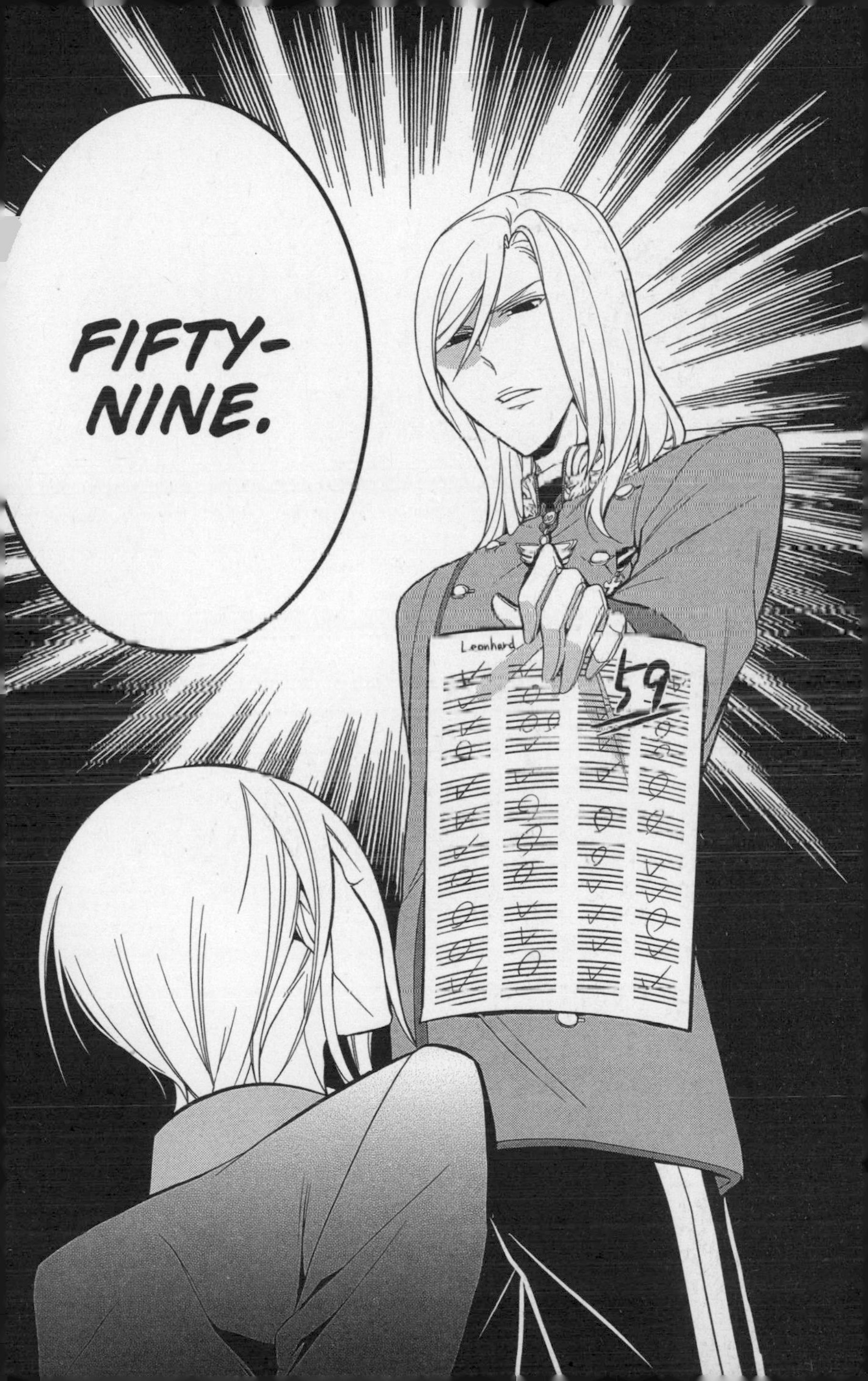
FIFTY-NINE.
Leonhard
59

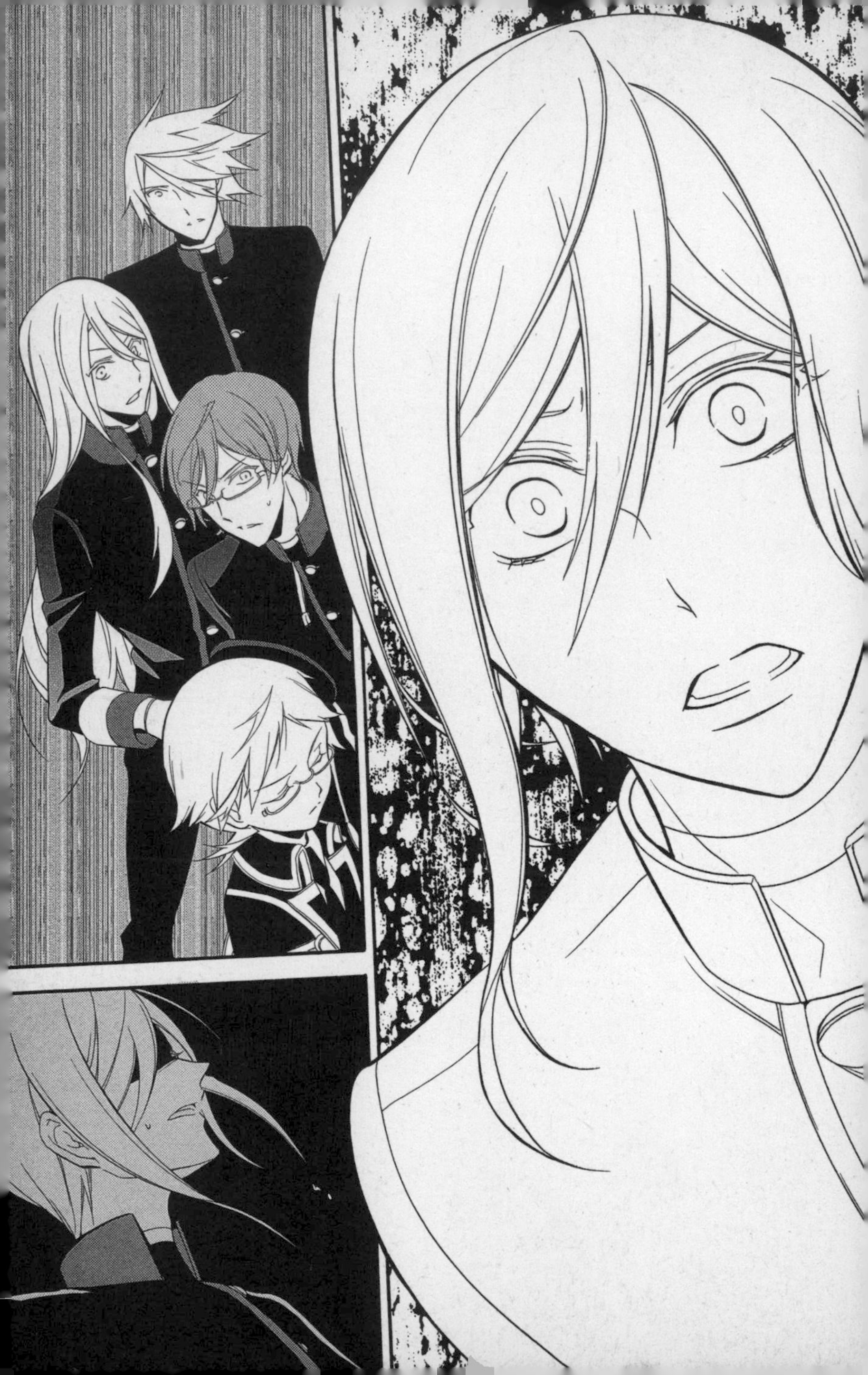

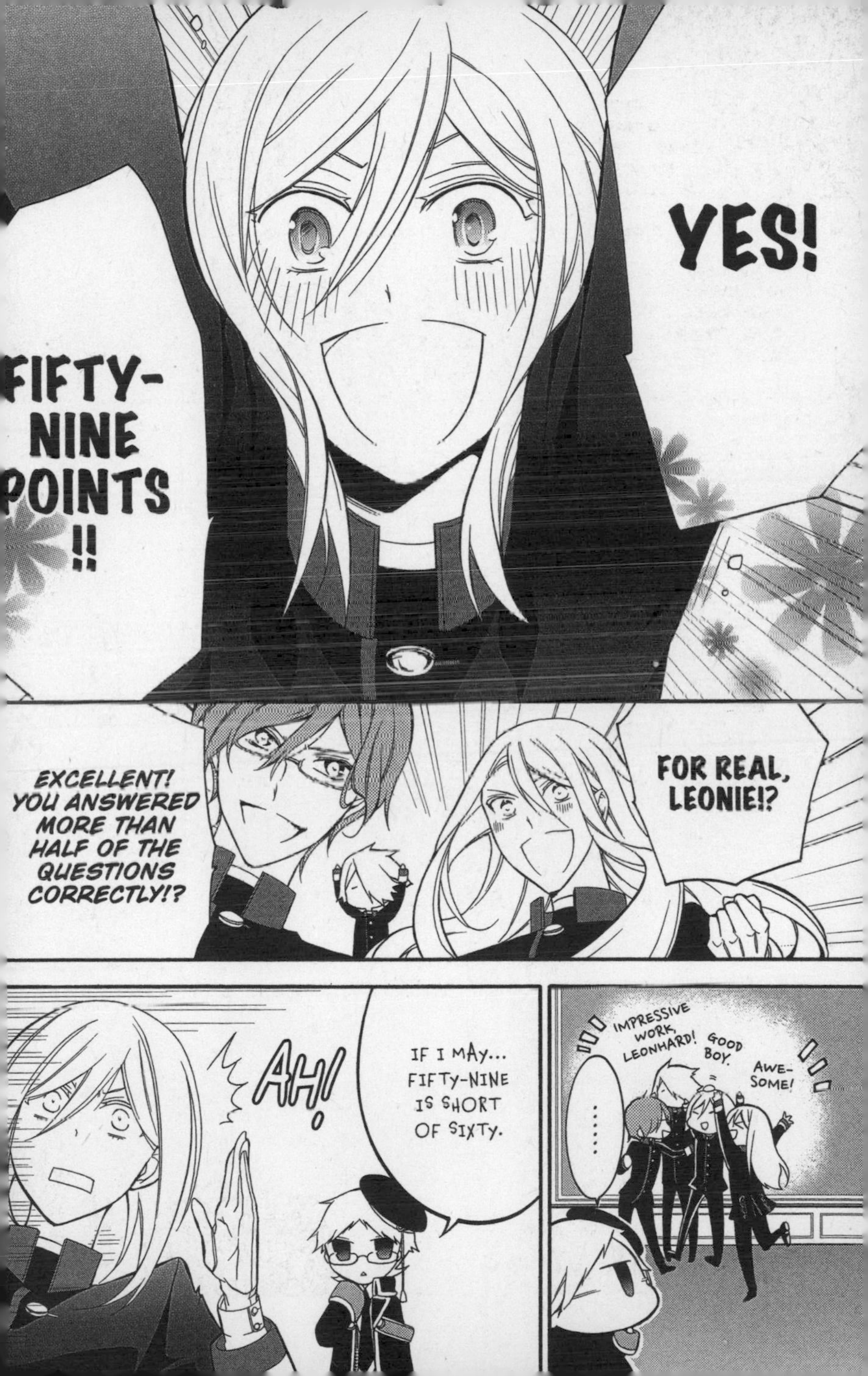
YES!
FIFTY-NINE POINTS!!
FOR REAL, LEONIE!?
EXCELLENT! YOU ANSWERED MORE THAN HALF OF THE QUESTIONS CORRECTLY!?
AWE-SOME!
GOOD BOY.
IMPRESSIVE WORK, LEONHARD!
......
IF I MAY... FIFTY-NINE IS SHORT OF SIXTY.
AH!

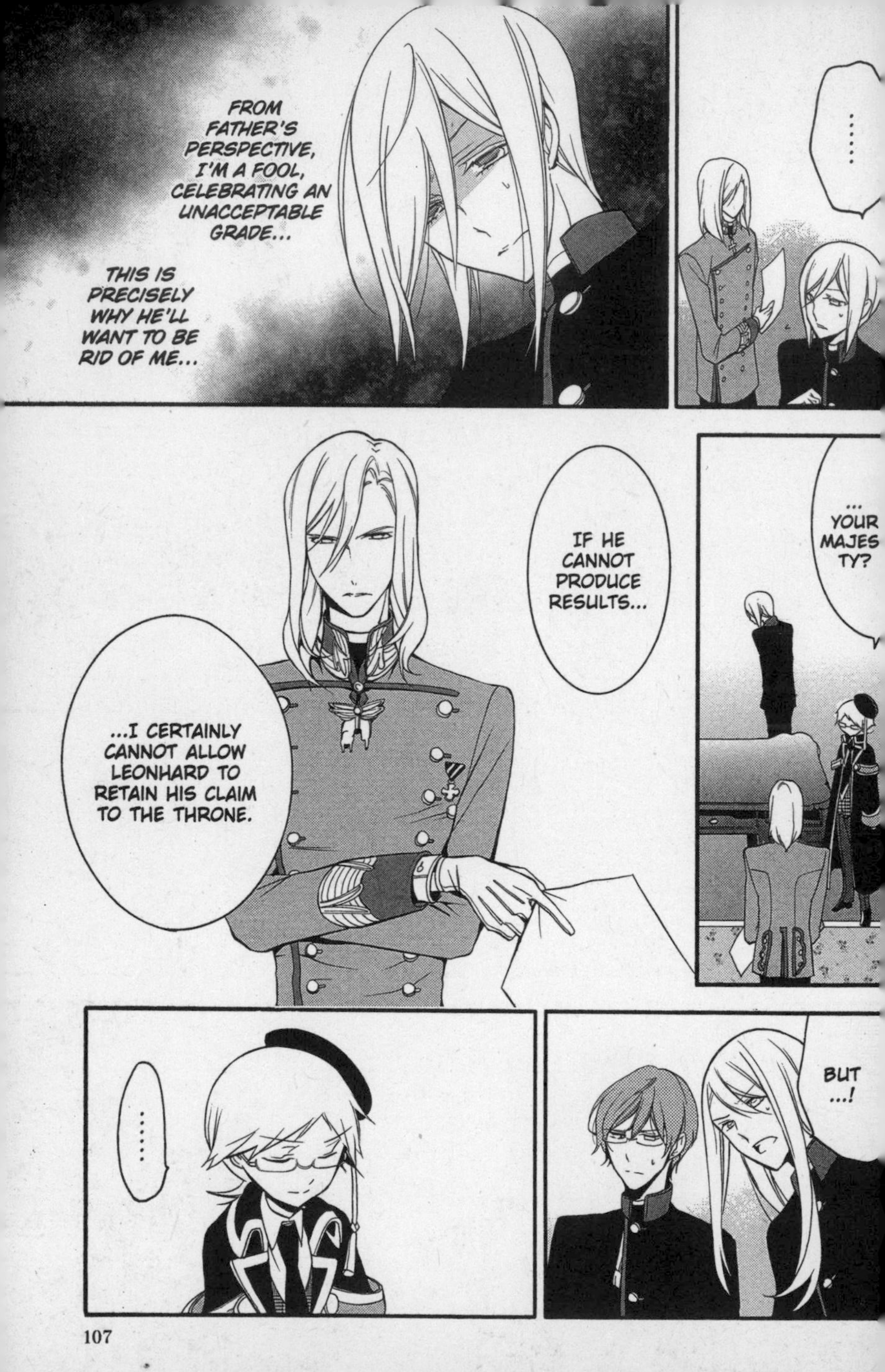
......
FROM FATHER'S PERSPECTIVE, I'M A FOOL, CELEBRATING AN UNACCEPTABLE GRADE...
THIS IS PRECISELY WHY HE'LL WANT TO BE RID OF ME...
...YOUR MAJESTY?
IF HE CANNOT PRODUCE RESULTS...
...I CERTAINLY CANNOT ALLOW LEONHARD TO RETAIN HIS CLAIM TO THE THRONE.
BUT ...!
......

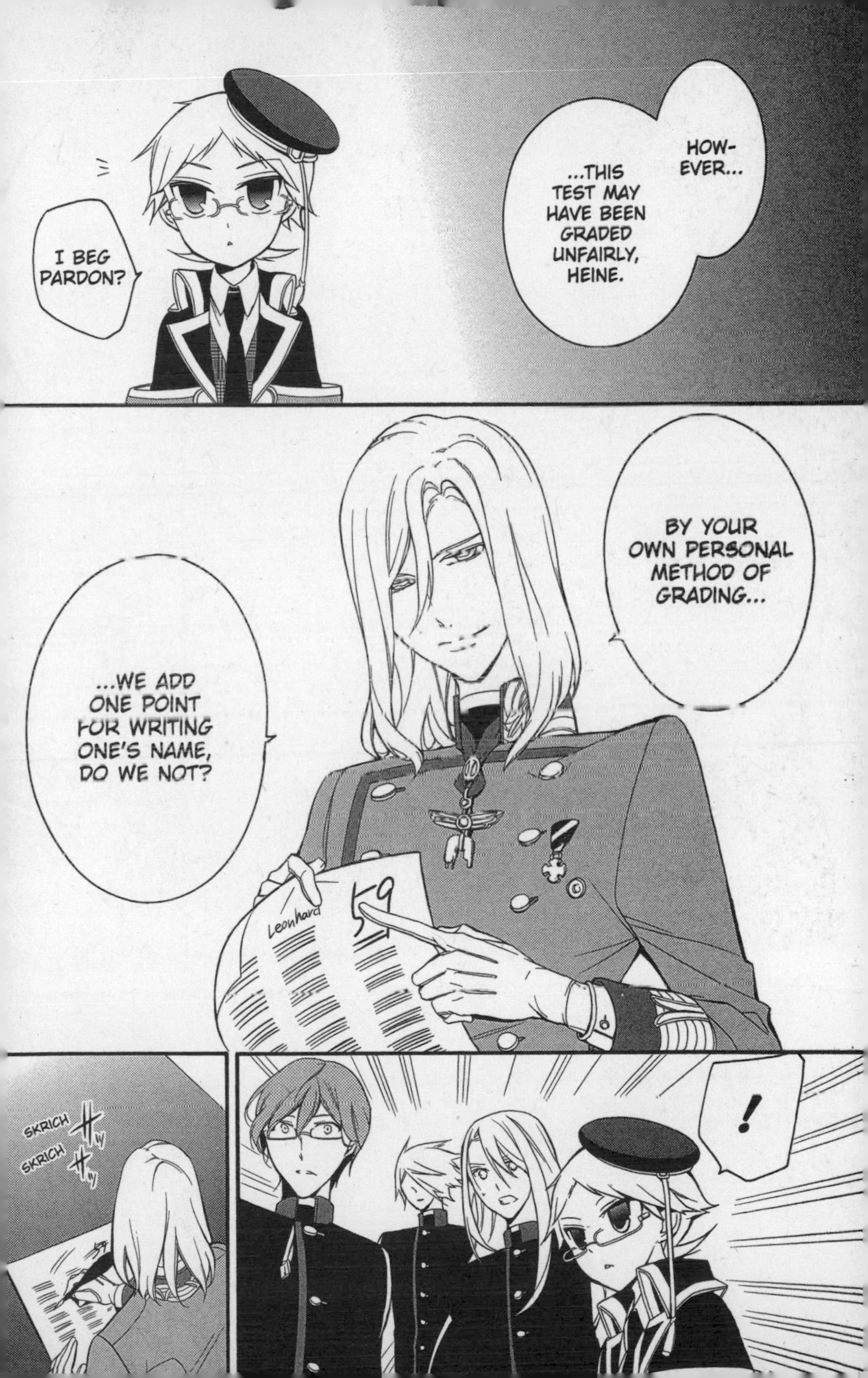
HOW-EVER...
...THIS TEST MAY HAVE BEEN GRADED UNFAIRLY, HEINE.
I BEG PARDON?
BY YOUR OWN PERSONAL METHOD OF GRADING...
...WE ADD ONE POINT FOR WRITING ONE'S NAME, DO WE NOT?
Leonhard
59
!
SKRICH
SKRICH

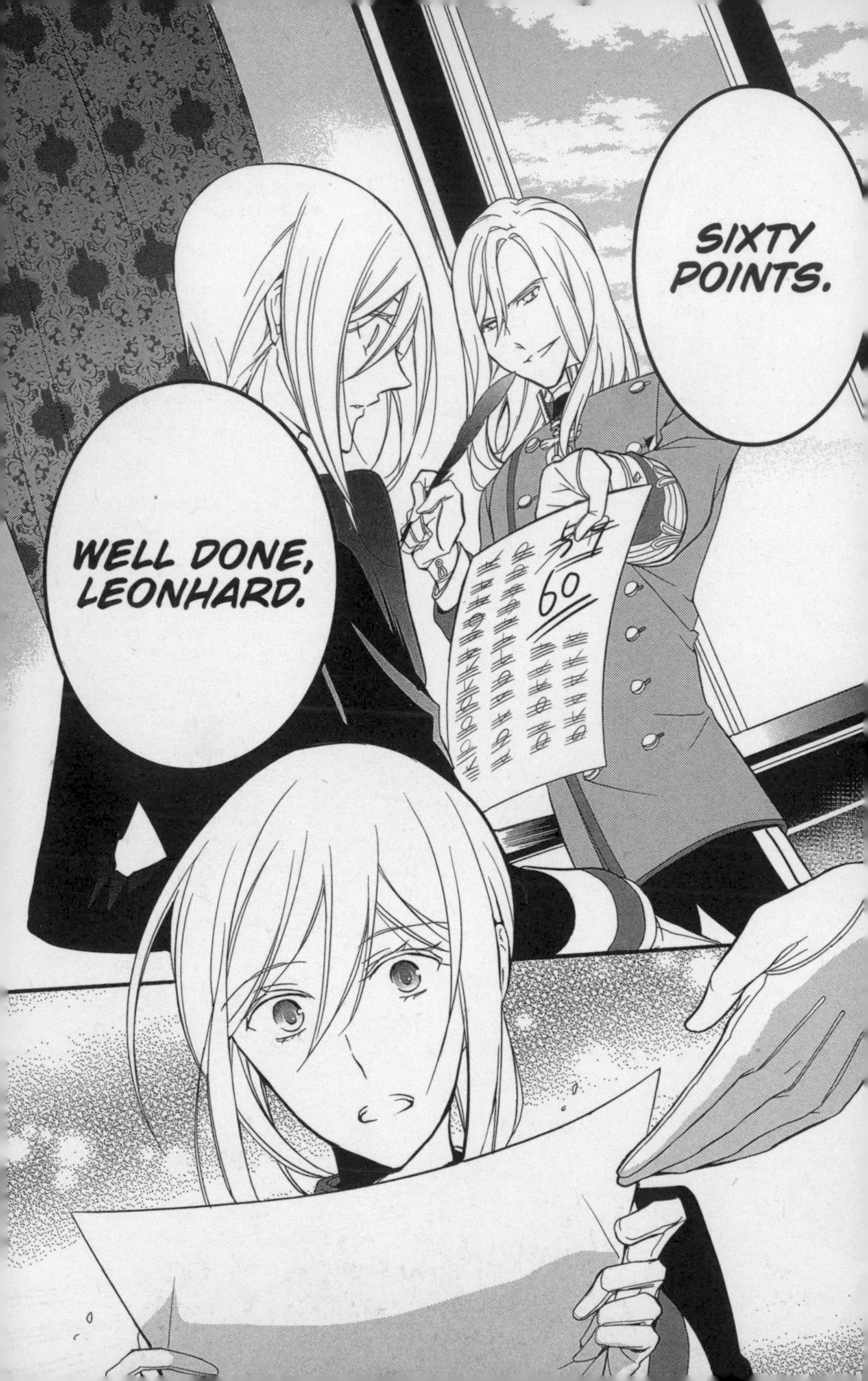
SIXTY POINTS.
60
WELL DONE, LEONHARD.

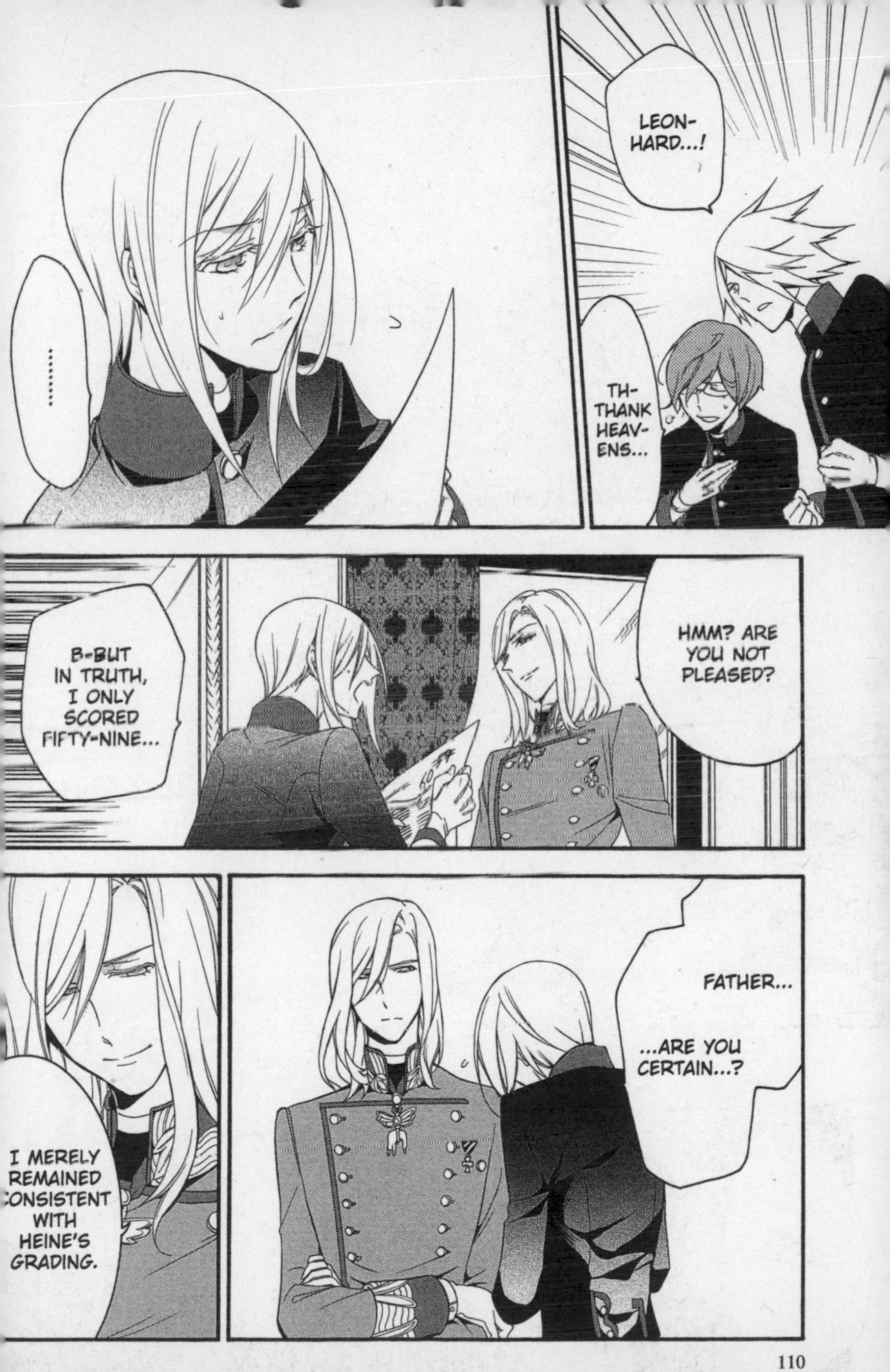
LEON-HARD...!
TH-THANK HEAV-ENS...
......
HMM? ARE YOU NOT PLEASED?
B-BUT IN TRUTH, I ONLY SCORED FIFTY-NINE...
FATHER...
...ARE YOU CERTAIN...?
I MERELY REMAINED CONSISTENT WITH HEINE'S GRADING.

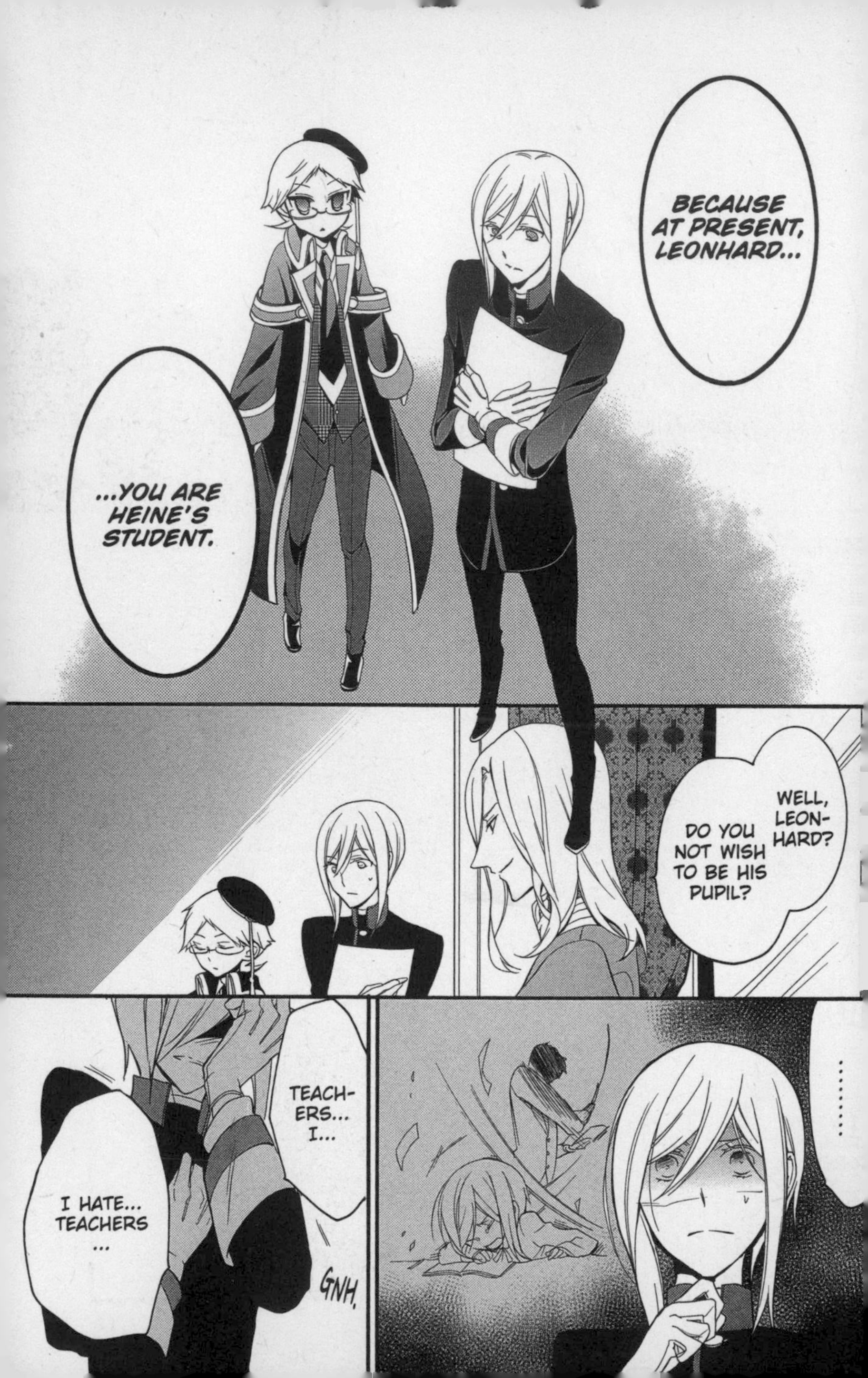
BECAUSE AT PRESENT, LEONHARD...
...YOU ARE HEINE'S STUDENT.
WELL, LEONHARD?
DO YOU NOT WISH TO BE HIS PUPIL?
......
TEACHERS... I...
I HATE... TEACHERS ...
GNH

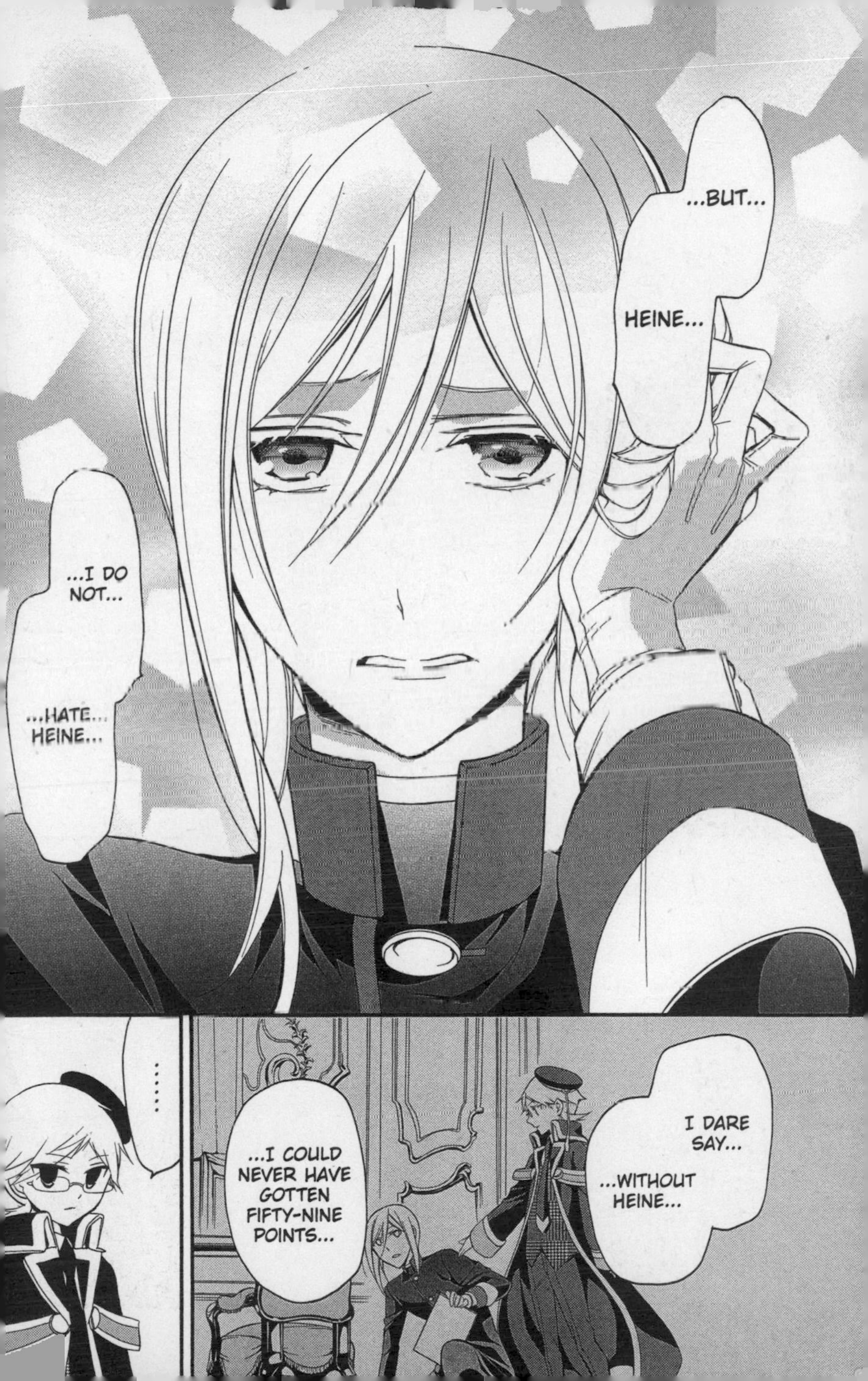
...BUT... HEINE...
...I DO NOT... ...HATE... HEINE...
I DARE SAY... ...WITHOUT HEINE...
...I COULD NEVER HAVE GOTTEN FIFTY-NINE POINTS...
......

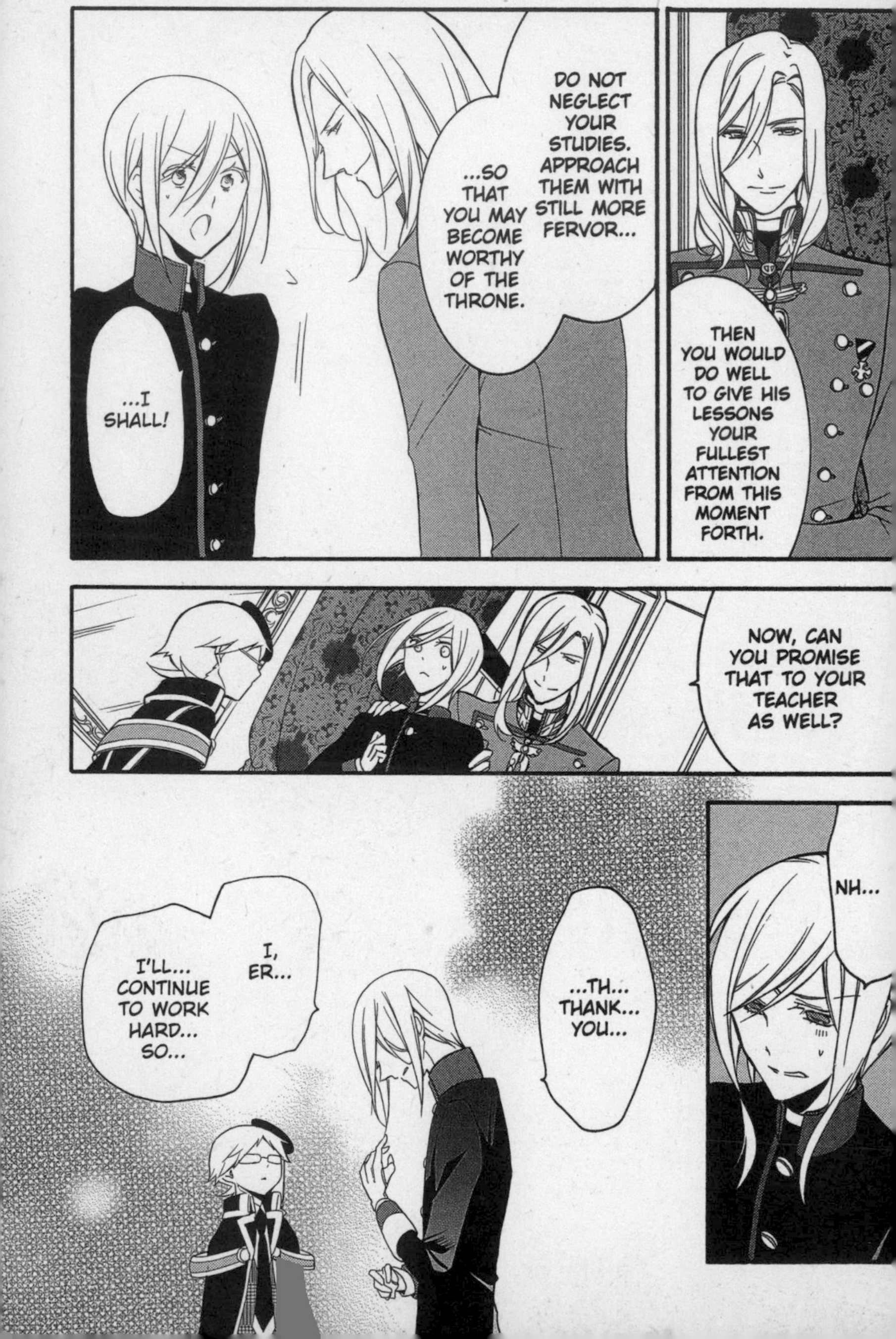
THEN YOU WOULD DO WELL TO GIVE HIS LESSONS YOUR FULLEST ATTENTION FROM THIS MOMENT FORTH.
DO NOT NEGLECT YOUR STUDIES. APPROACH THEM WITH STILL MORE FERVOR...
...SO THAT YOU MAY BECOME WORTHY OF THE THRONE.
...I SHALL!
NOW, CAN YOU PROMISE THAT TO YOUR TEACHER AS WELL?
NH...
...TH... THANK... YOU...
I, ER...
I'LL... CONTINUE TO WORK HARD... SO...

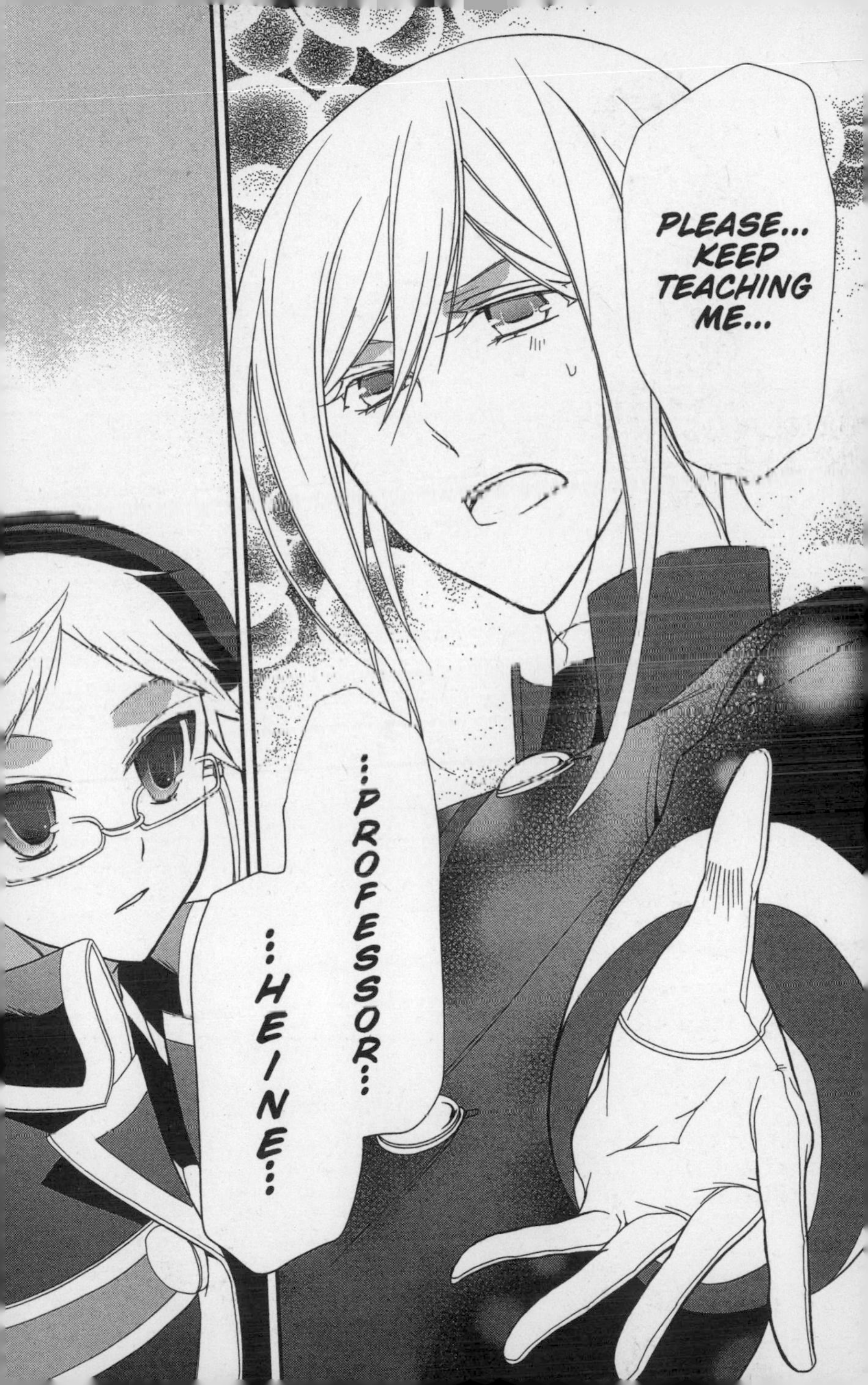
PLEASE... KEEP TEACHING ME...
...PROFESSOR...
...HEINE...

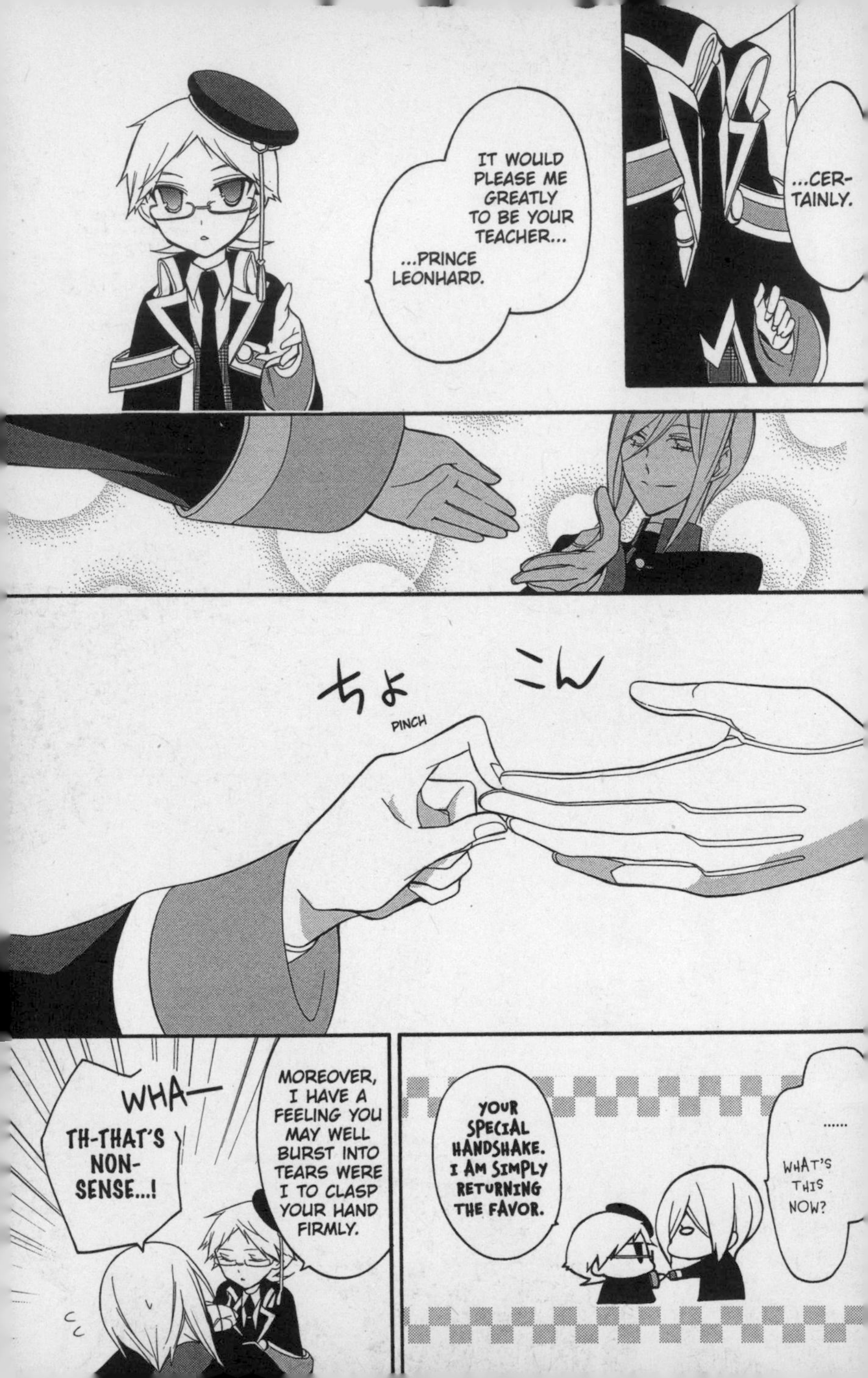
...CERTAINLY.
IT WOULD PLEASE ME GREATLY TO BE YOUR TEACHER...
...PRINCE LEONHARD.
ちょこん
PINCH
......
WHAT'S THIS NOW?
YOUR SPECIAL HANDSHAKE. I AM SIMPLY RETURNING THE FAVOR.
MOREOVER, I HAVE A FEELING YOU MAY WELL BURST INTO TEARS WERE I TO CLASP YOUR HAND FIRMLY.
WHA—
TH-THAT'S NON-SENSE...!

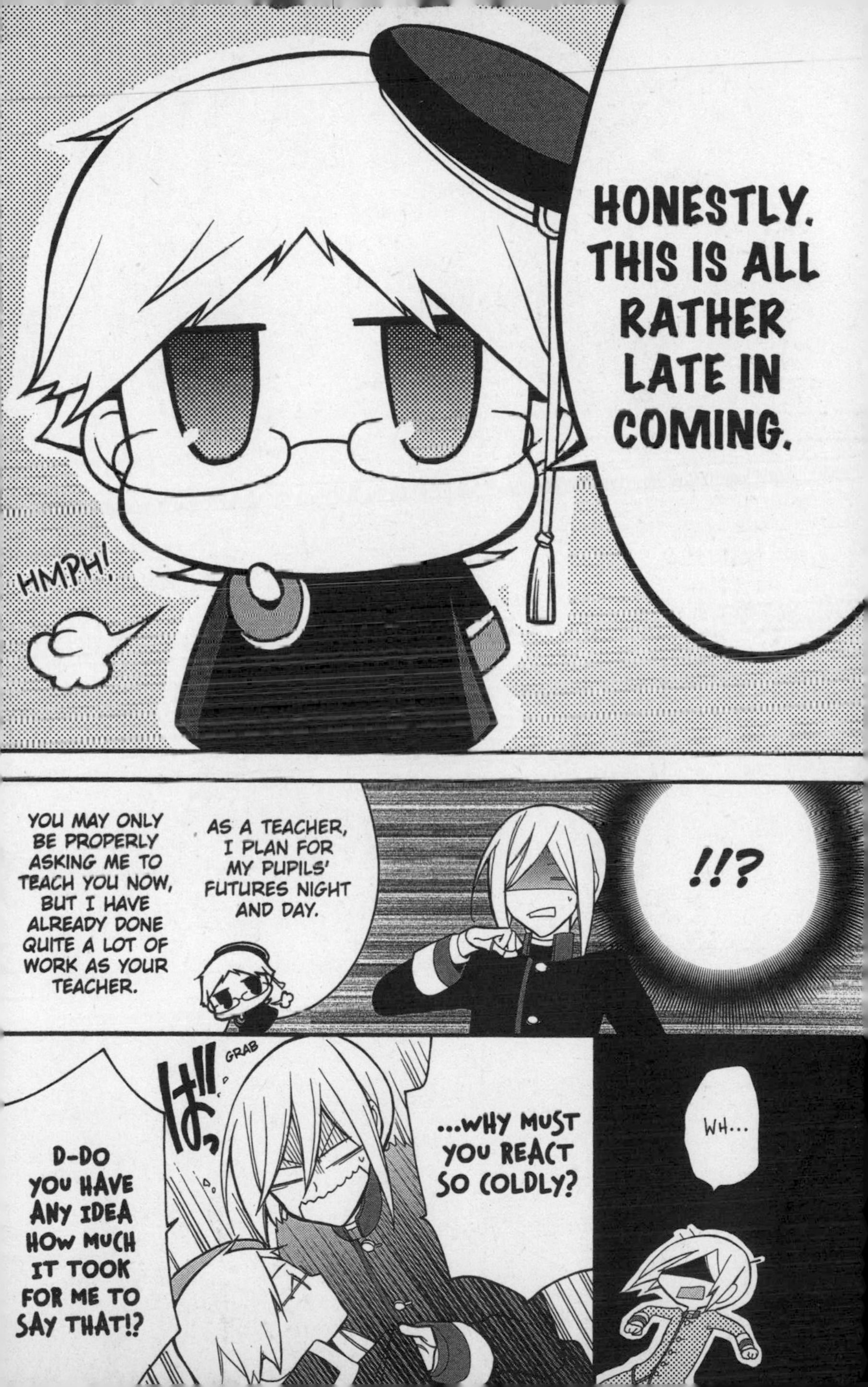
HONESTLY. THIS IS ALL RATHER LATE IN COMING.
HMPH!
!!?
AS A TEACHER, I PLAN FOR MY PUPILS' FUTURES NIGHT AND DAY.
YOU MAY ONLY BE PROPERLY ASKING ME TO TEACH YOU NOW, BUT I HAVE ALREADY DONE QUITE A LOT OF WORK AS YOUR TEACHER.
WH...
...WHY MUST YOU REACT SO COLDLY?
GRAB
は
D-DO YOU HAVE ANY IDEA HOW MUCH IT TOOK FOR ME TO SAY THAT!?

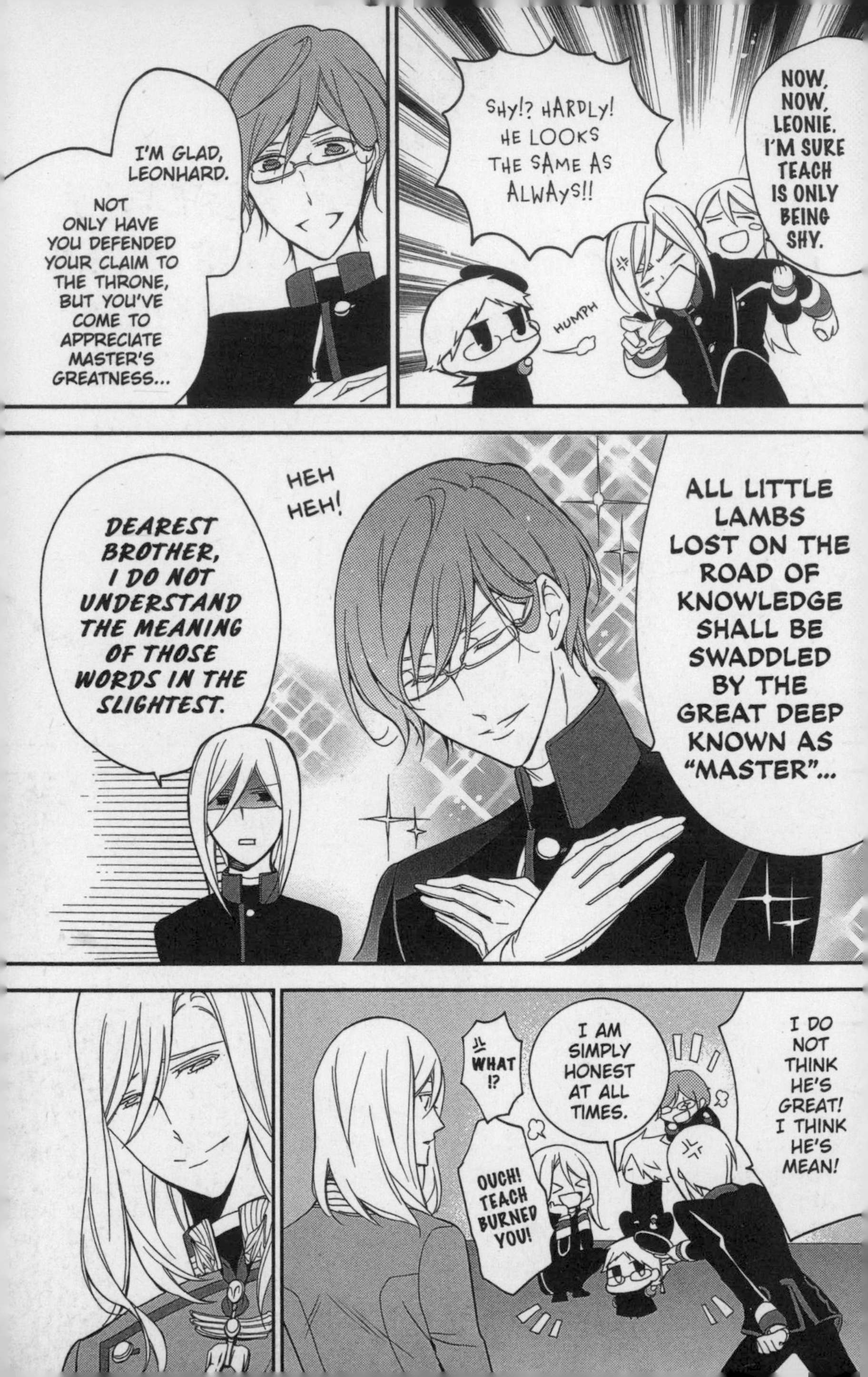
NOW, NOW, LEONIE. I'M SURE TEACH IS ONLY BEING SHY.
SHY!? HARDLY! HE LOOKS THE SAME AS ALWAYS!!
HUMPH
I'M GLAD, LEONHARD.
NOT ONLY HAVE YOU DEFENDED YOUR CLAIM TO THE THRONE, BUT YOU'VE COME TO APPRECIATE MASTER'S GREATNESS...
ALL LITTLE LAMBS LOST ON THE ROAD OF KNOWLEDGE SHALL BE SWADDLED BY THE GREAT DEEP KNOWN AS "MASTER"...
HEH HEH!
DEAREST BROTHER, I DO NOT UNDERSTAND THE MEANING OF THOSE WORDS IN THE SLIGHTEST.
I DO NOT THINK HE'S GREAT! I THINK HE'S MEAN!
I AM SIMPLY HONEST AT ALL TIMES.
WHAT!?
OUCH! TEACH BURNED YOU!

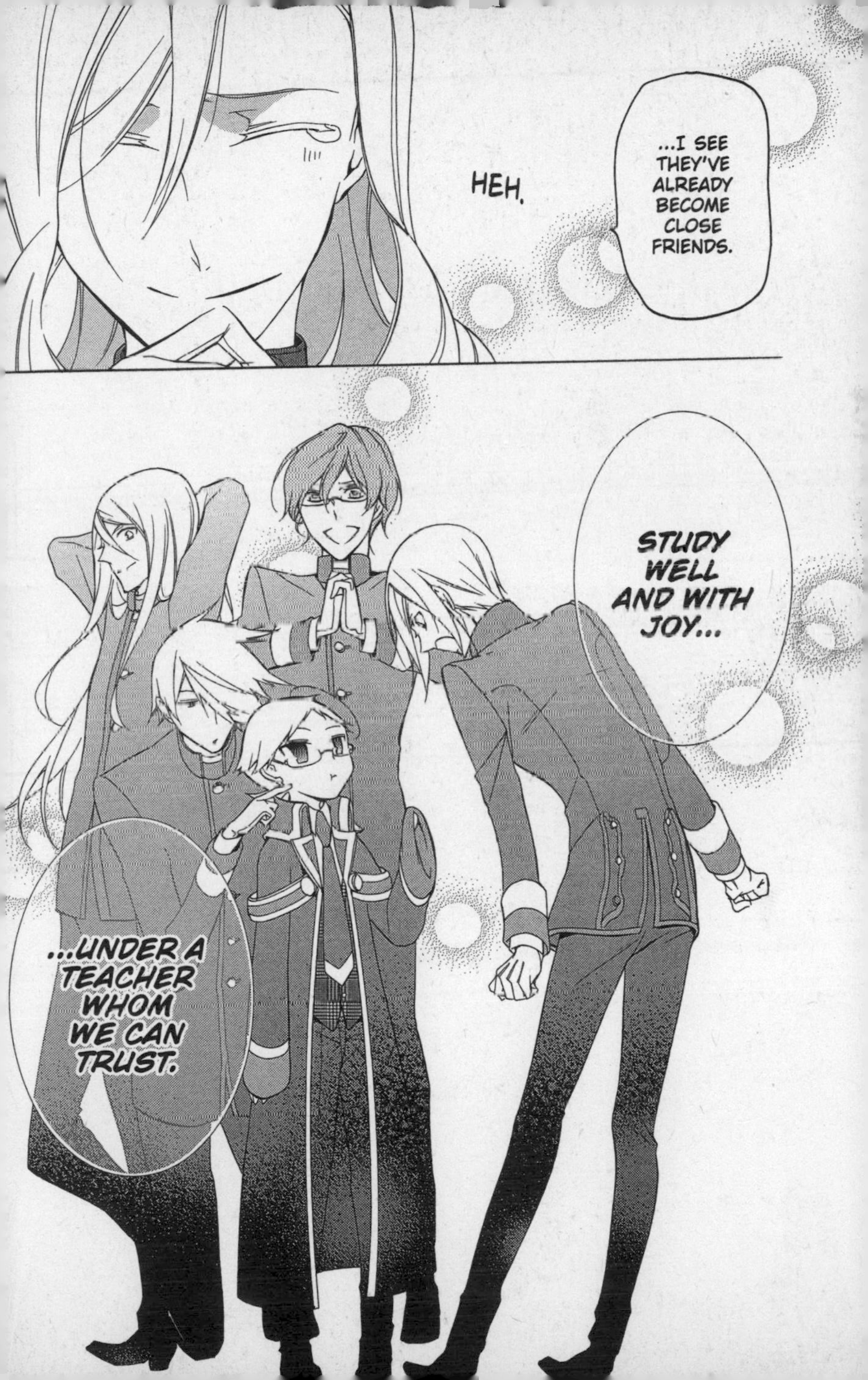
...I SEE THEY'VE ALREADY BECOME CLOSE FRIENDS.
HEH.
STUDY WELL AND WITH JOY...
...UNDER A TEACHER WHOM WE CAN TRUST.

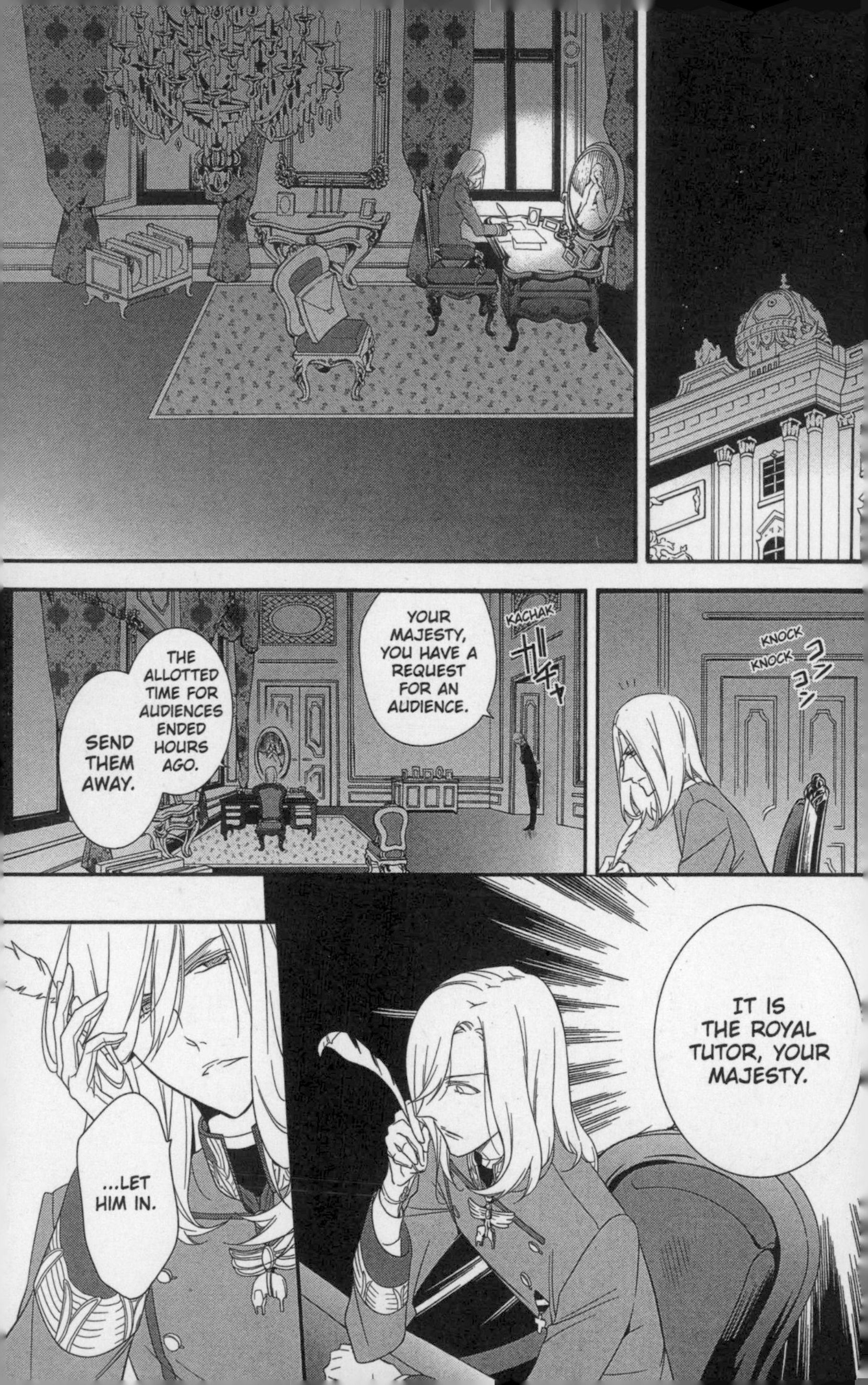
KNOCK
KNOCK
KACHAK
YOUR MAJESTY, YOU HAVE A REQUEST FOR AN AUDIENCE.
THE ALLOTTED TIME FOR AUDIENCES ENDED HOURS AGO.
SEND THEM AWAY.
IT IS THE ROYAL TUTOR, YOUR MAJESTY.
...LET HIM IN.

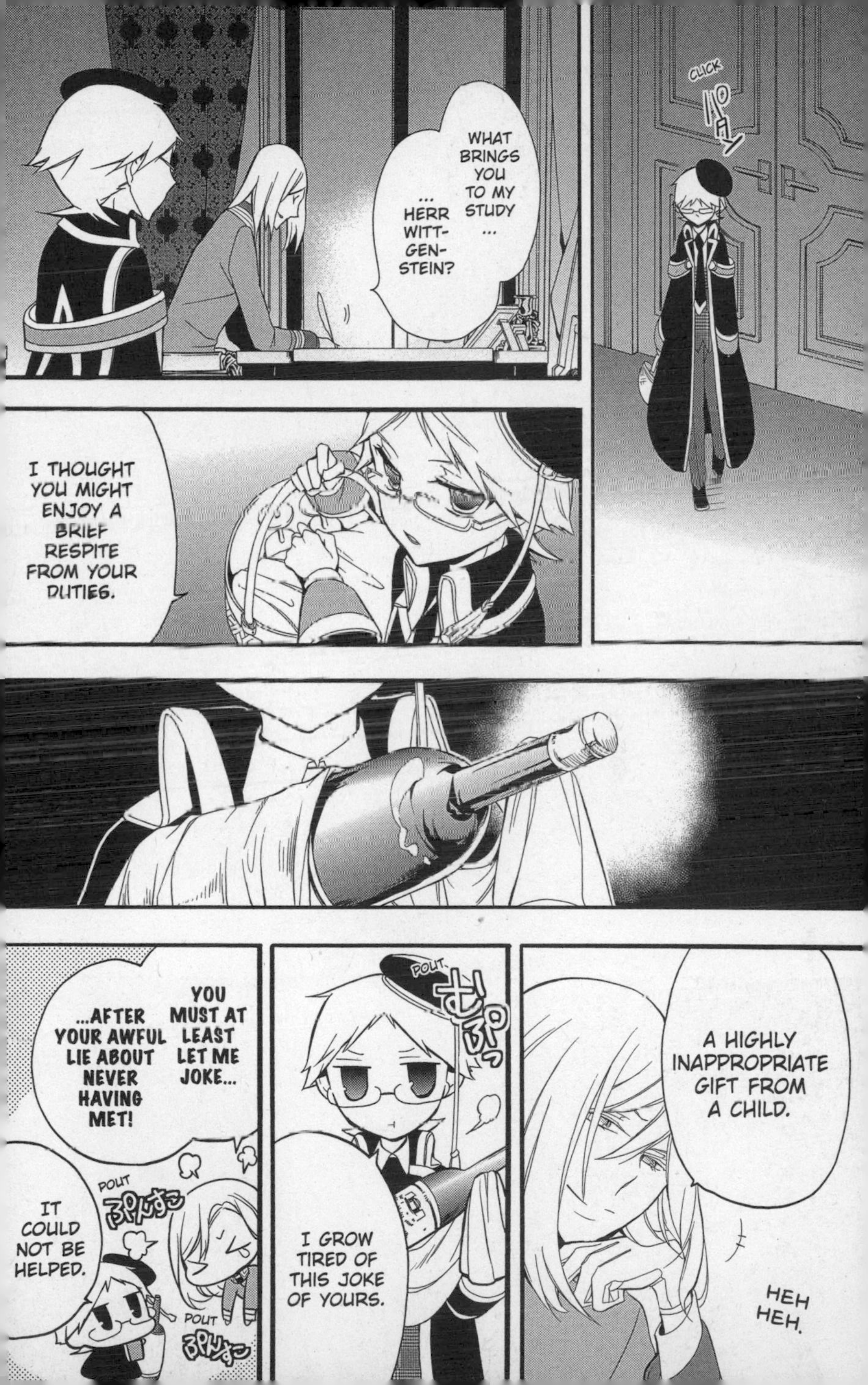
CLICK
WHAT BRINGS YOU TO MY STUDY ...
... HERR WITTGENSTEIN?
I THOUGHT YOU MIGHT ENJOY A BRIEF RESPITE FROM YOUR DUTIES.
A HIGHLY INAPPROPRIATE GIFT FROM A CHILD.
HEH HEH.
POUT.
I GROW TIRED OF THIS JOKE OF YOURS.
YOU MUST AT LEAST LET ME JOKE...
...AFTER YOUR AWFUL LIE ABOUT NEVER HAVING MET!
POUT
IT COULD NOT BE HELPED.
POUT

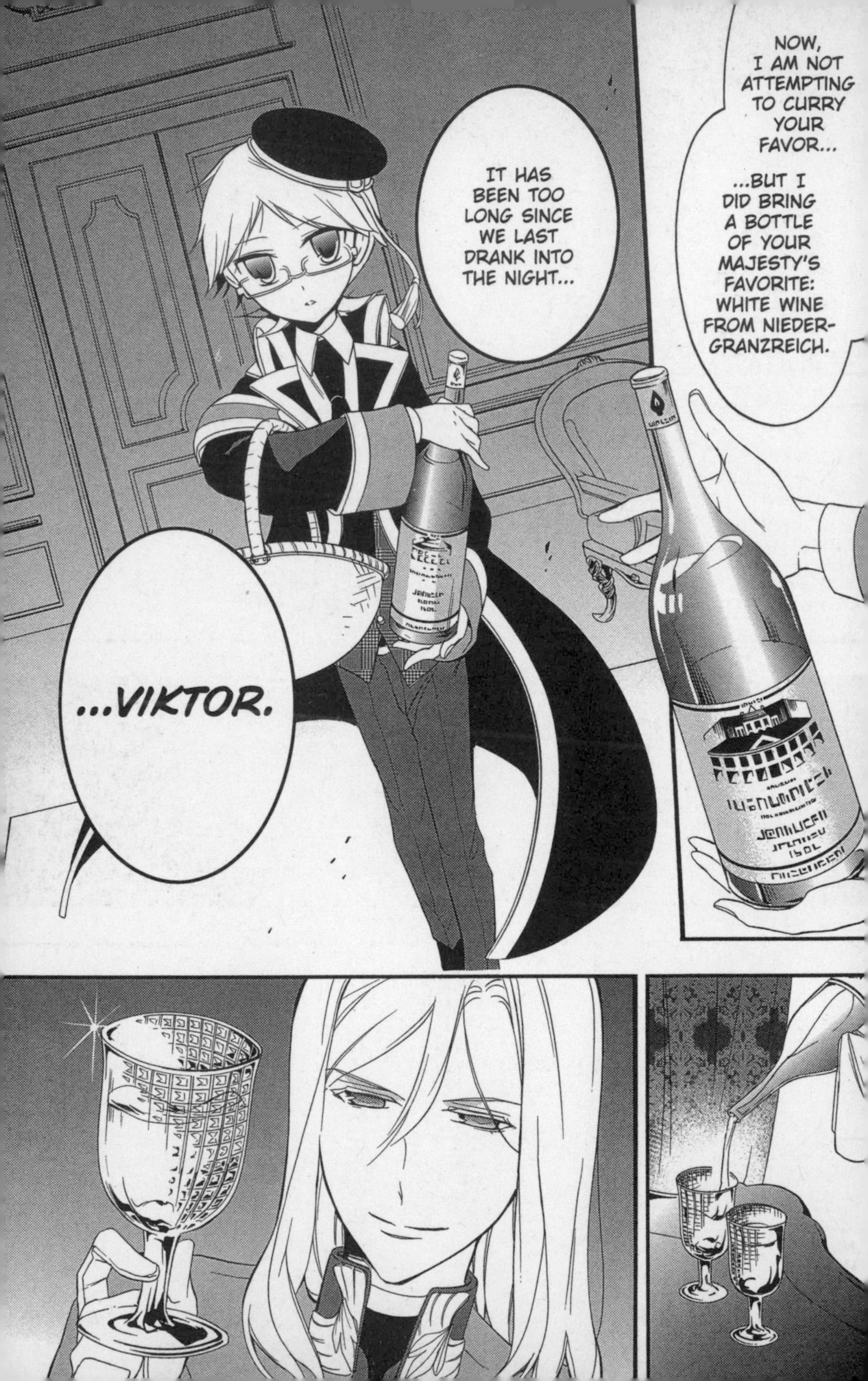
NOW, I AM NOT ATTEMPTING TO CURRY YOUR FAVOR...
...BUT I DID BRING A BOTTLE OF YOUR MAJESTY'S FAVORITE: WHITE WINE FROM NIEDER-GRANZREICH.
IT HAS BEEN TOO LONG SINCE WE LAST DRANK INTO THE NIGHT...
...VIKTOR.

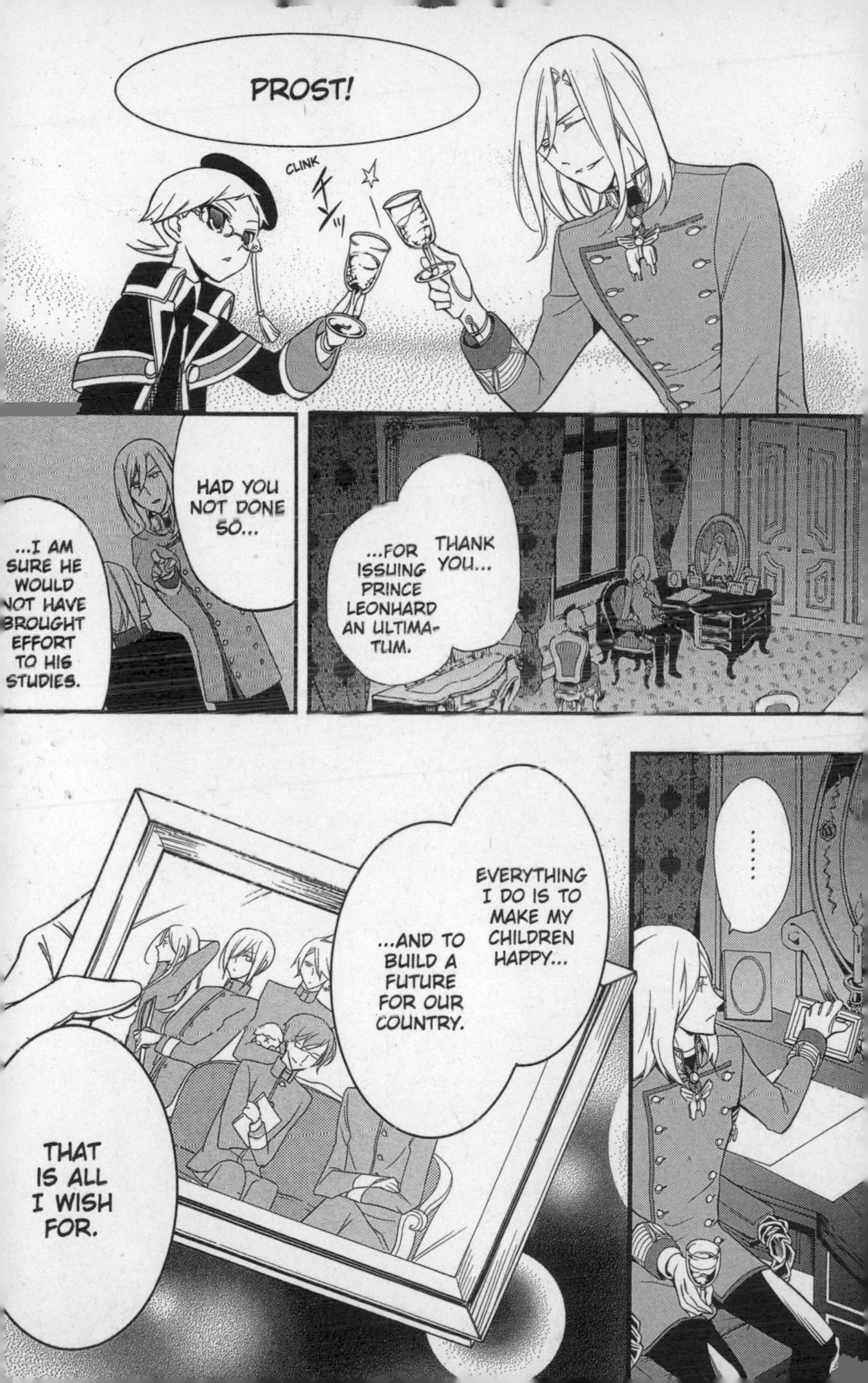
PROST!
CLINK
THANK YOU...
...FOR ISSUING PRINCE LEONHARD AN ULTIMA-TUM.
HAD YOU NOT DONE SO...
...I AM SURE HE WOULD NOT HAVE BROUGHT EFFORT TO HIS STUDIES.
......
EVERYTHING I DO IS TO MAKE MY CHILDREN HAPPY...
...AND TO BUILD A FUTURE FOR OUR COUNTRY.
THAT IS ALL I WISH FOR.

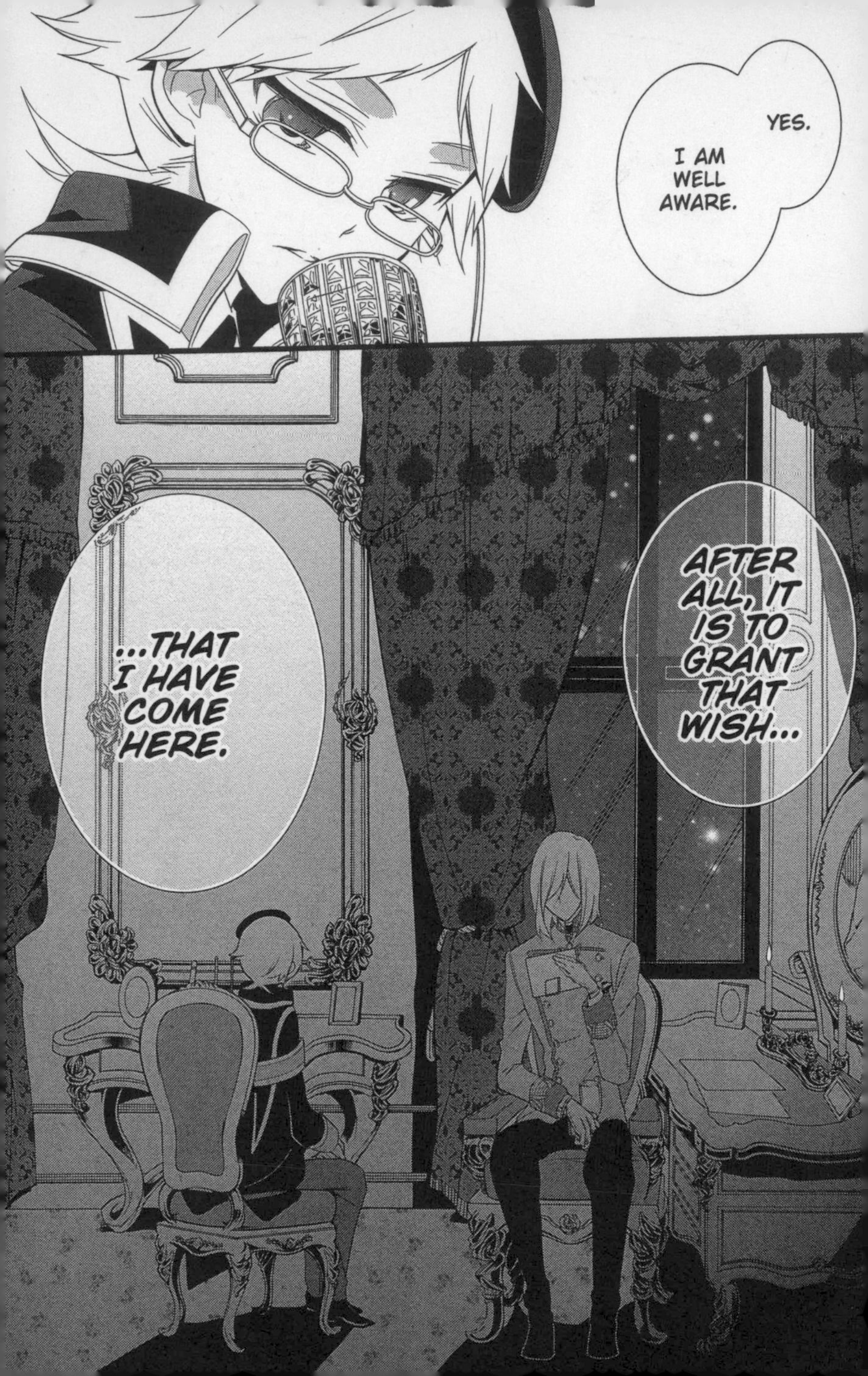
YES.
I AM WELL AWARE.
AFTER ALL, IT IS TO GRANT THAT WISH...
...THAT I HAVE COME HERE.

THE
ROYAL
TUTOR

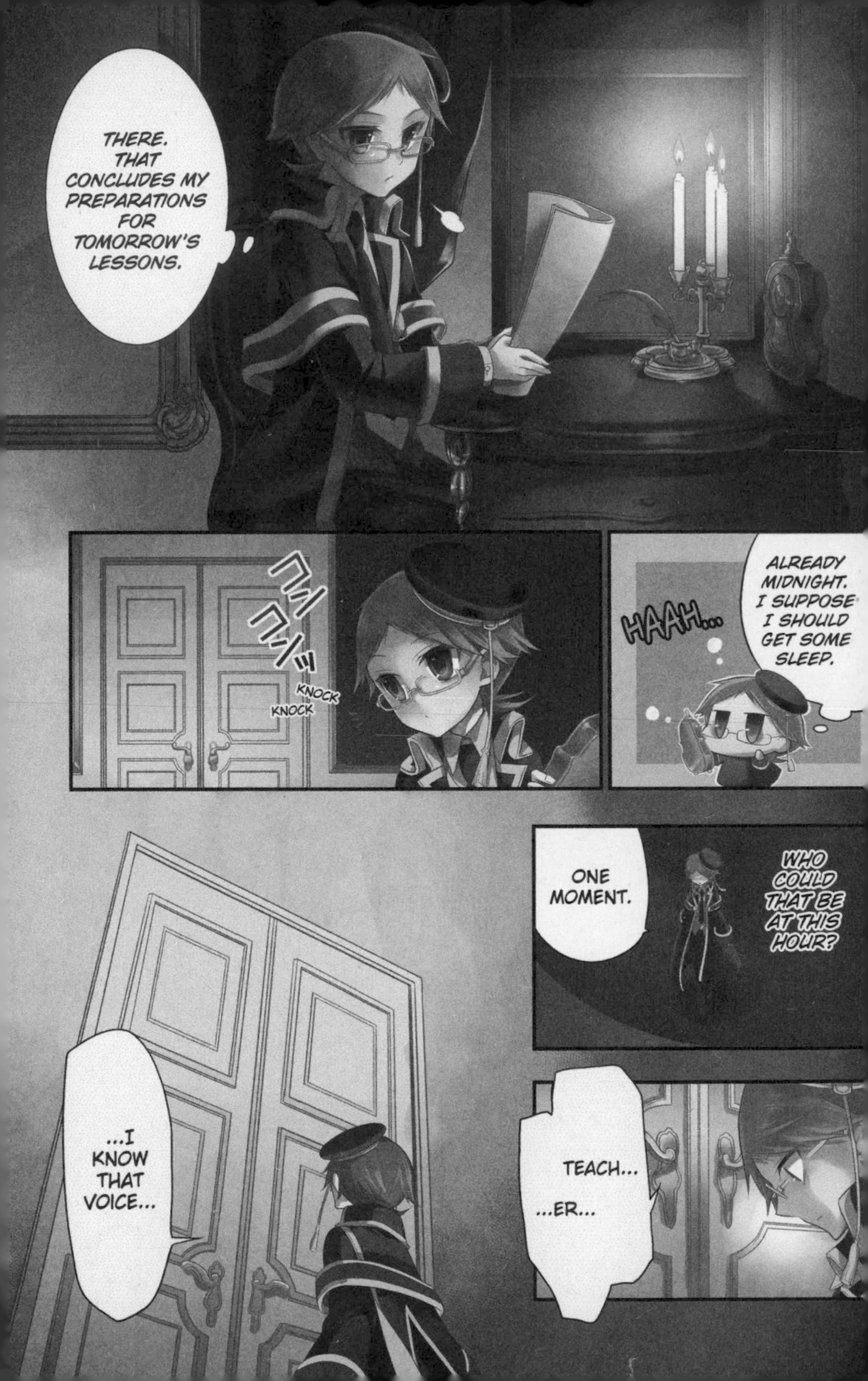
THERE. THAT CONCLUDES MY PREPARATIONS FOR TOMORROW'S LESSONS.
ALREADY MIDNIGHT. I SUPPOSE I SHOULD GET SOME SLEEP.
HAAH...
コンコンッ
KNOCK KNOCK
WHO COULD THAT BE AT THIS HOUR?
ONE MOMENT.
TEACH...
...ER...
...I KNOW THAT VOICE...

Chapter 11
A Cowardly Heart

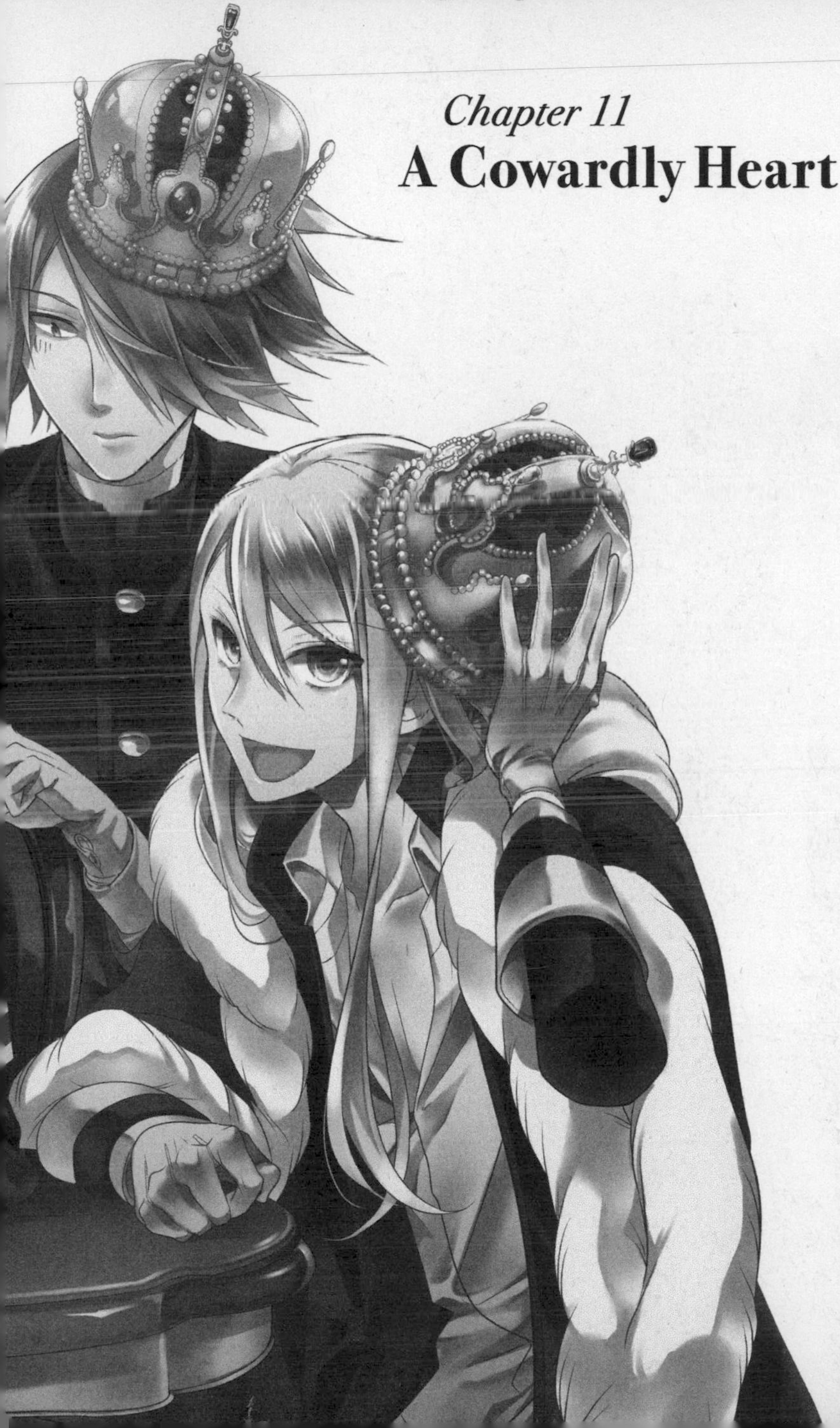

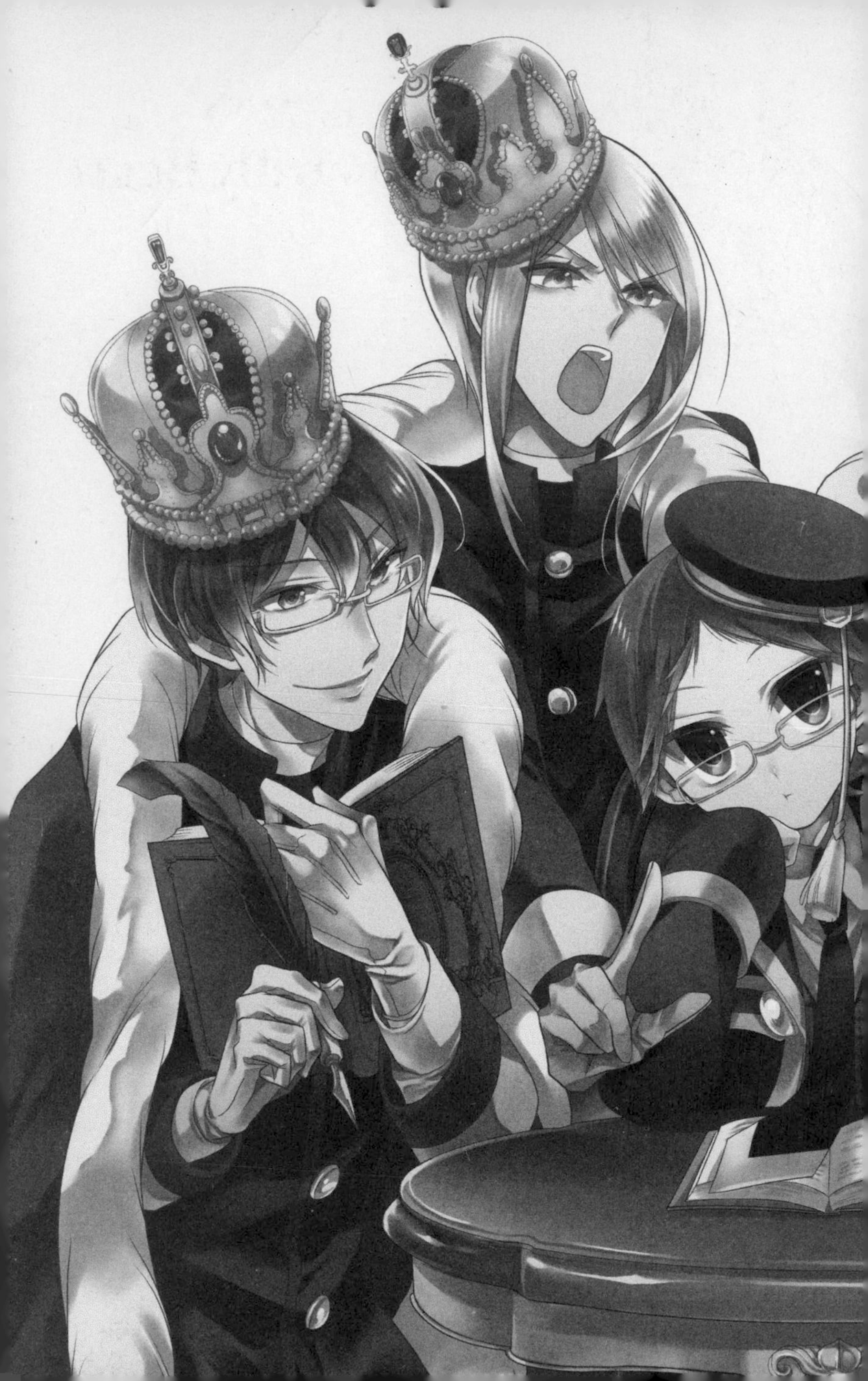

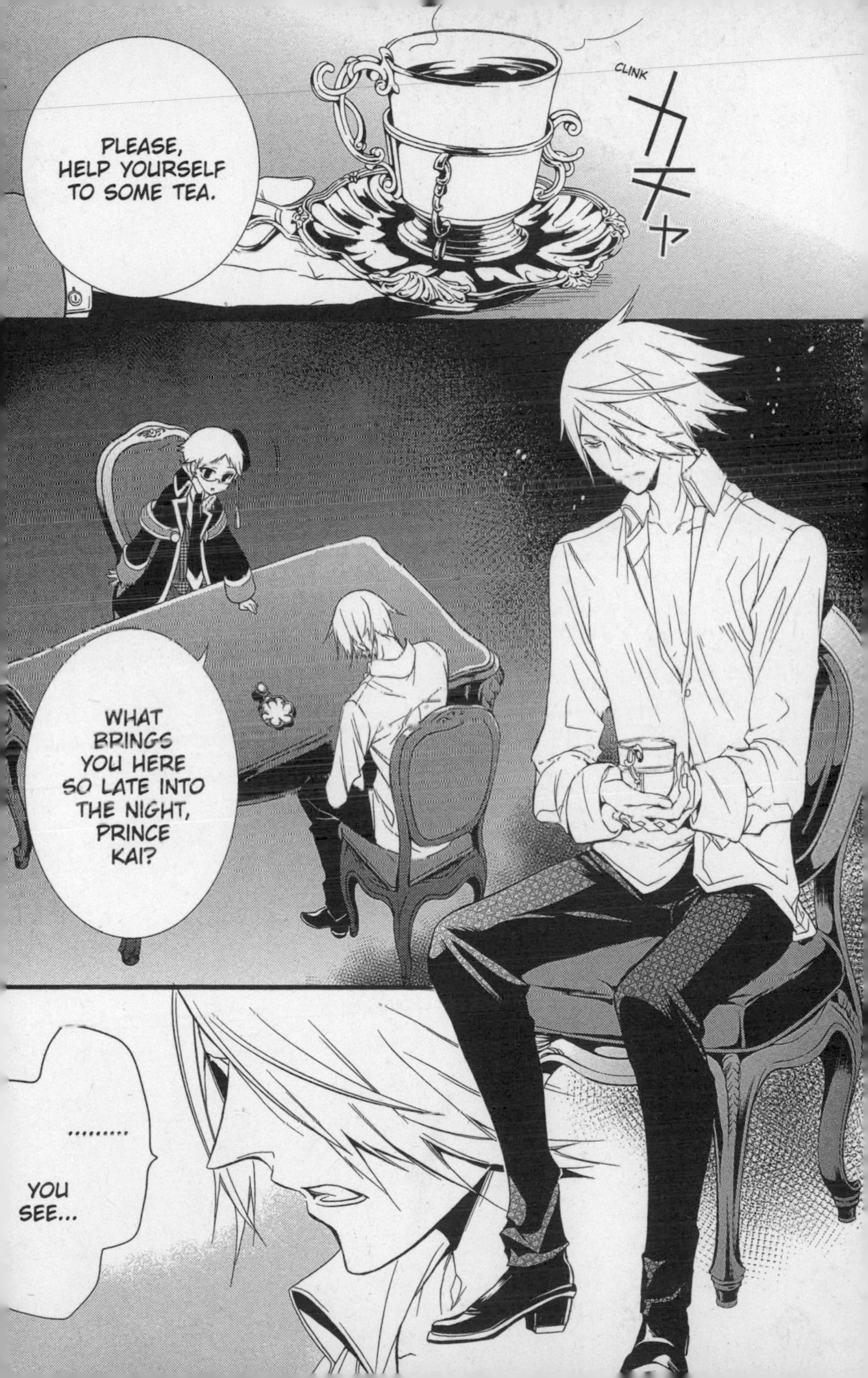
CLINK
カチャ
PLEASE, HELP YOURSELF TO SOME TEA.
WHAT BRINGS YOU HERE SO LATE INTO THE NIGHT, PRINCE KAI?
....
YOU SEE...

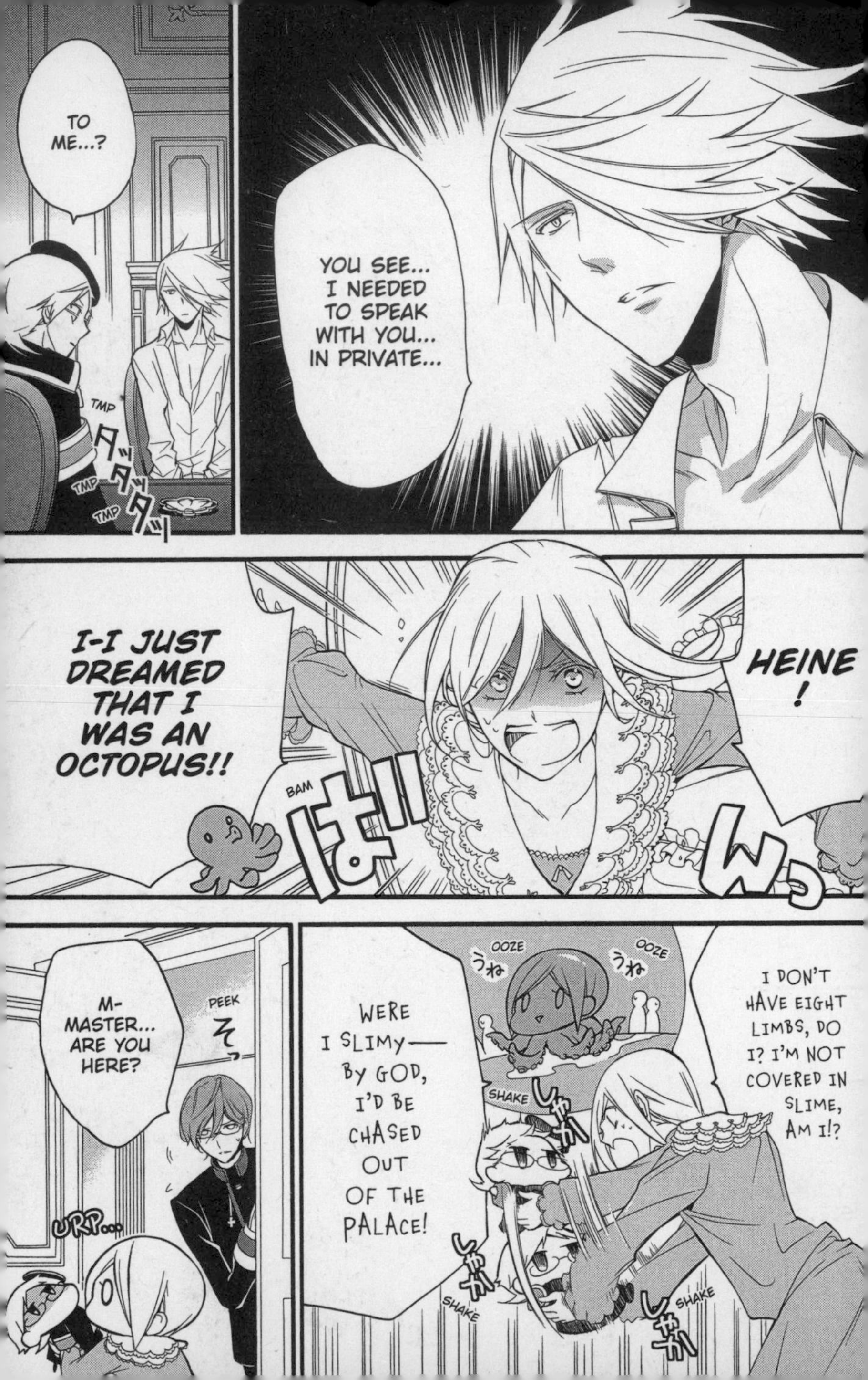
YOU SEE... I NEEDED TO SPEAK WITH YOU... IN PRIVATE...
TO ME...?
TMP
TMP
TMP
HEINE!
I-I JUST DREAMED THAT I WAS AN OCTOPUS!!
BAM
I DON'T HAVE EIGHT LIMBS, DO I? I'M NOT COVERED IN SLIME, AM I!?
OOZE
OOZE
WERE I SLIMY— BY GOD, I'D BE CHASED OUT OF THE PALACE!
SHAKE
SHAKE
SHAKE
PEEK
M-MASTER... ARE YOU HERE?
URP...

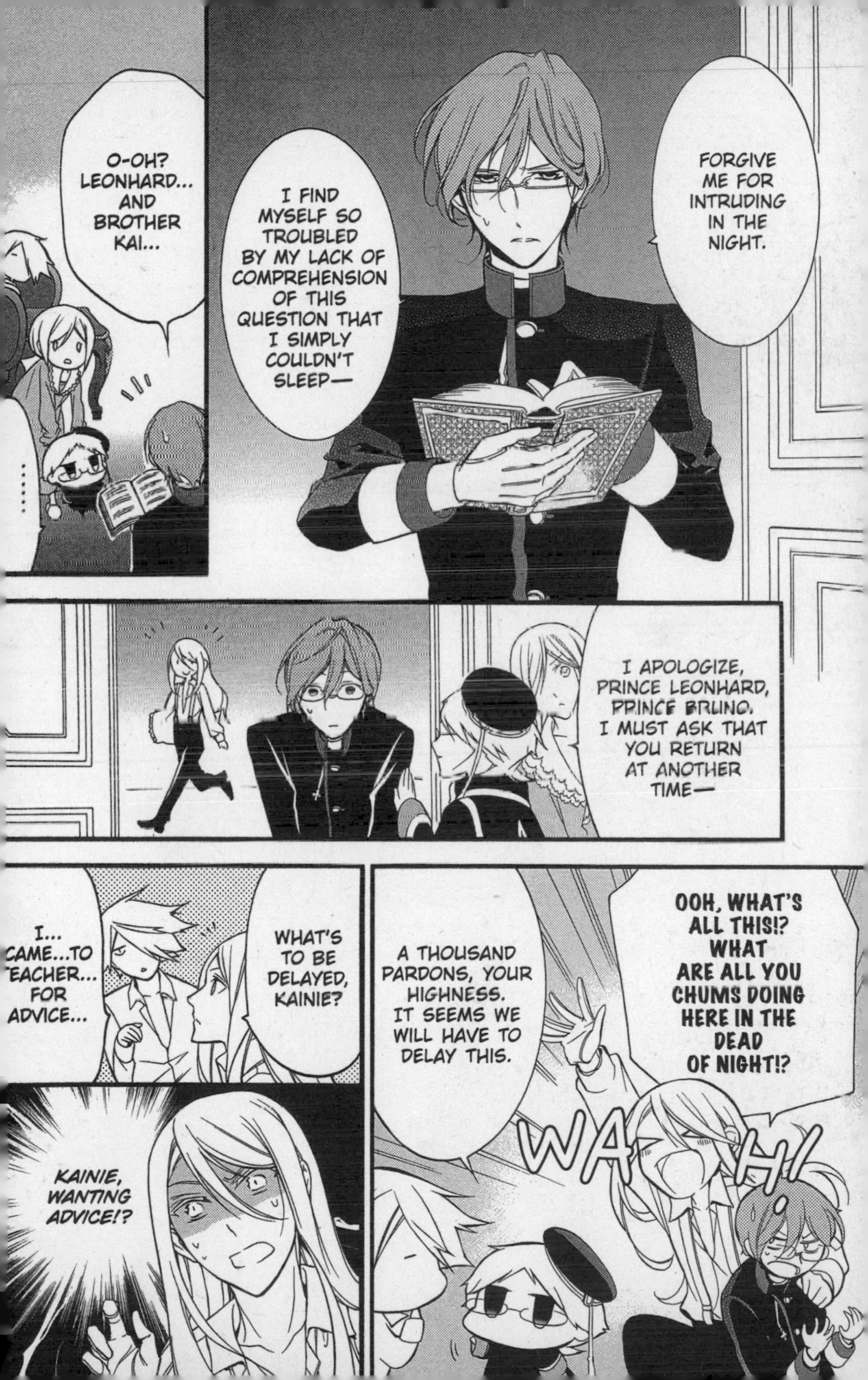
FORGIVE ME FOR INTRUDING IN THE NIGHT.
I FIND MYSELF SO TROUBLED BY MY LACK OF COMPREHENSION OF THIS QUESTION THAT I SIMPLY COULDN'T SLEEP—
O-OH? LEONHARD... AND BROTHER KAI...
......
I APOLOGIZE, PRINCE LEONHARD, PRINCE BRUNO. I MUST ASK THAT YOU RETURN AT ANOTHER TIME—
OOH, WHAT'S ALL THIS!? WHAT ARE ALL YOU CHUMS DOING HERE IN THE DEAD OF NIGHT!?
A THOUSAND PARDONS, YOUR HIGHNESS. IT SEEMS WE WILL HAVE TO DELAY THIS.
WHAT'S TO BE DELAYED, KAINIE?
I... CAME...TO TEACHER... FOR ADVICE...
KAINIE, WANTING ADVICE!?

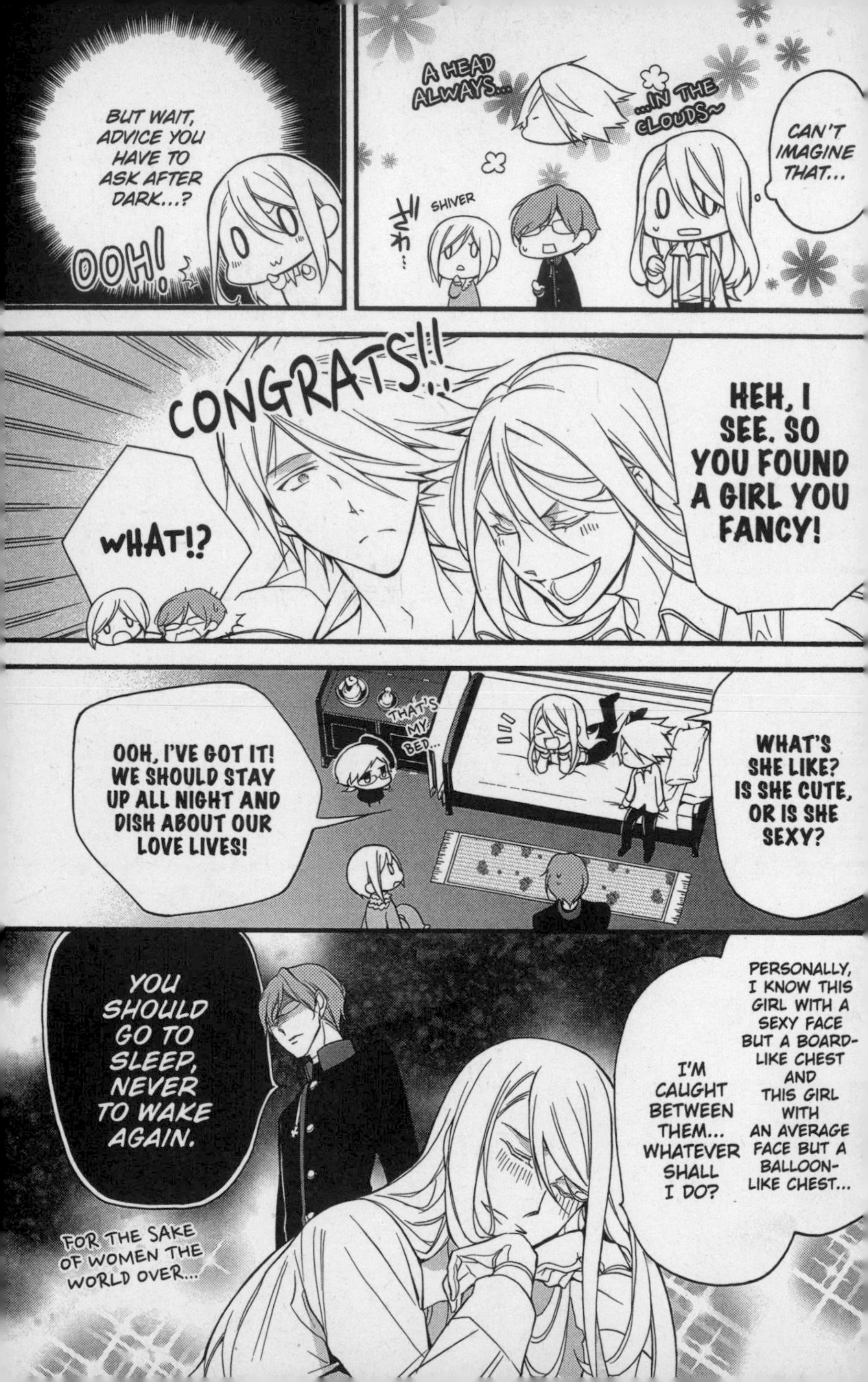
A HEAD ALWAYS...
...IN THE CLOUDS~
CAN'T IMAGINE THAT...
SHIVER
BUT WAIT, ADVICE YOU HAVE TO ASK AFTER DARK...?
OOH!
HEH, I SEE. SO YOU FOUND A GIRL YOU FANCY!
CONGRATS!!
WHAT!?
WHAT'S SHE LIKE? IS SHE CUTE, OR IS SHE SEXY?
THAT'S MY BED...
OOH, I'VE GOT IT! WE SHOULD STAY UP ALL NIGHT AND DISH ABOUT OUR LOVE LIVES!
PERSONALLY, I KNOW THIS GIRL WITH A SEXY FACE BUT A BOARD-LIKE CHEST AND THIS GIRL WITH AN AVERAGE FACE BUT A BALLOON-LIKE CHEST...
I'M CAUGHT BETWEEN THEM... WHATEVER SHALL I DO?
YOU SHOULD GO TO SLEEP, NEVER TO WAKE AGAIN.
FOR THE SAKE OF WOMEN THE WORLD OVER...

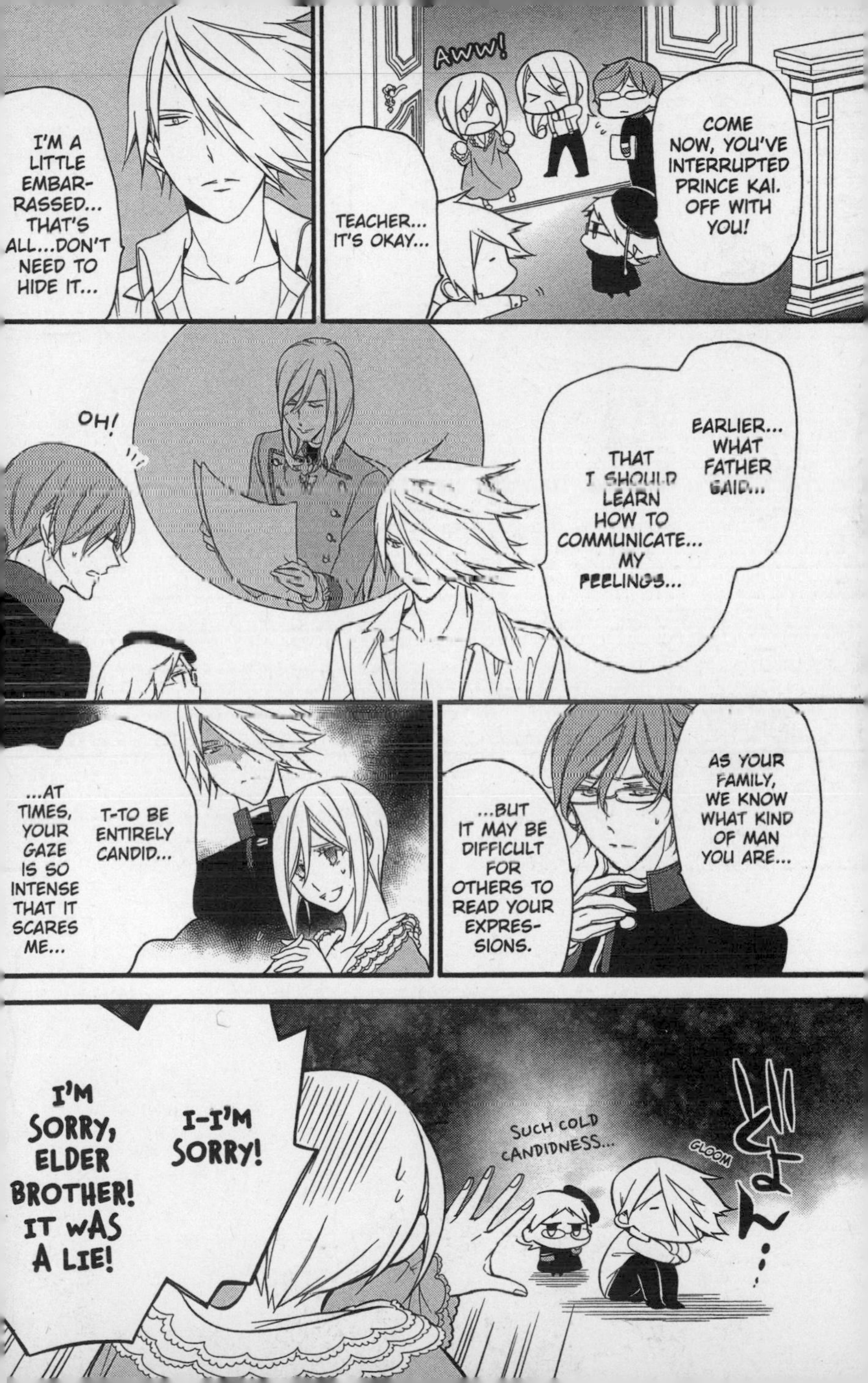
AWW!
COME NOW, YOU'VE INTERRUPTED PRINCE KAI. OFF WITH YOU!
TEACHER... IT'S OKAY...
I'M A LITTLE EMBARRASSED... THAT'S ALL...DON'T NEED TO HIDE IT...
EARLIER... WHAT FATHER SAID...
THAT I SHOULD LEARN HOW TO COMMUNICATE... MY FEELINGS...
OH!
AS YOUR FAMILY, WE KNOW WHAT KIND OF MAN YOU ARE...
...BUT IT MAY BE DIFFICULT FOR OTHERS TO READ YOUR EXPRESSIONS.
T-TO BE ENTIRELY CANDID...
...AT TIMES, YOUR GAZE IS SO INTENSE THAT IT SCARES ME...
どよ〜ん…
GLOOM
SUCH COLD CANDIDNESS...
I-I'M SORRY!
I'M SORRY, ELDER BROTHER! IT WAS A LIE!

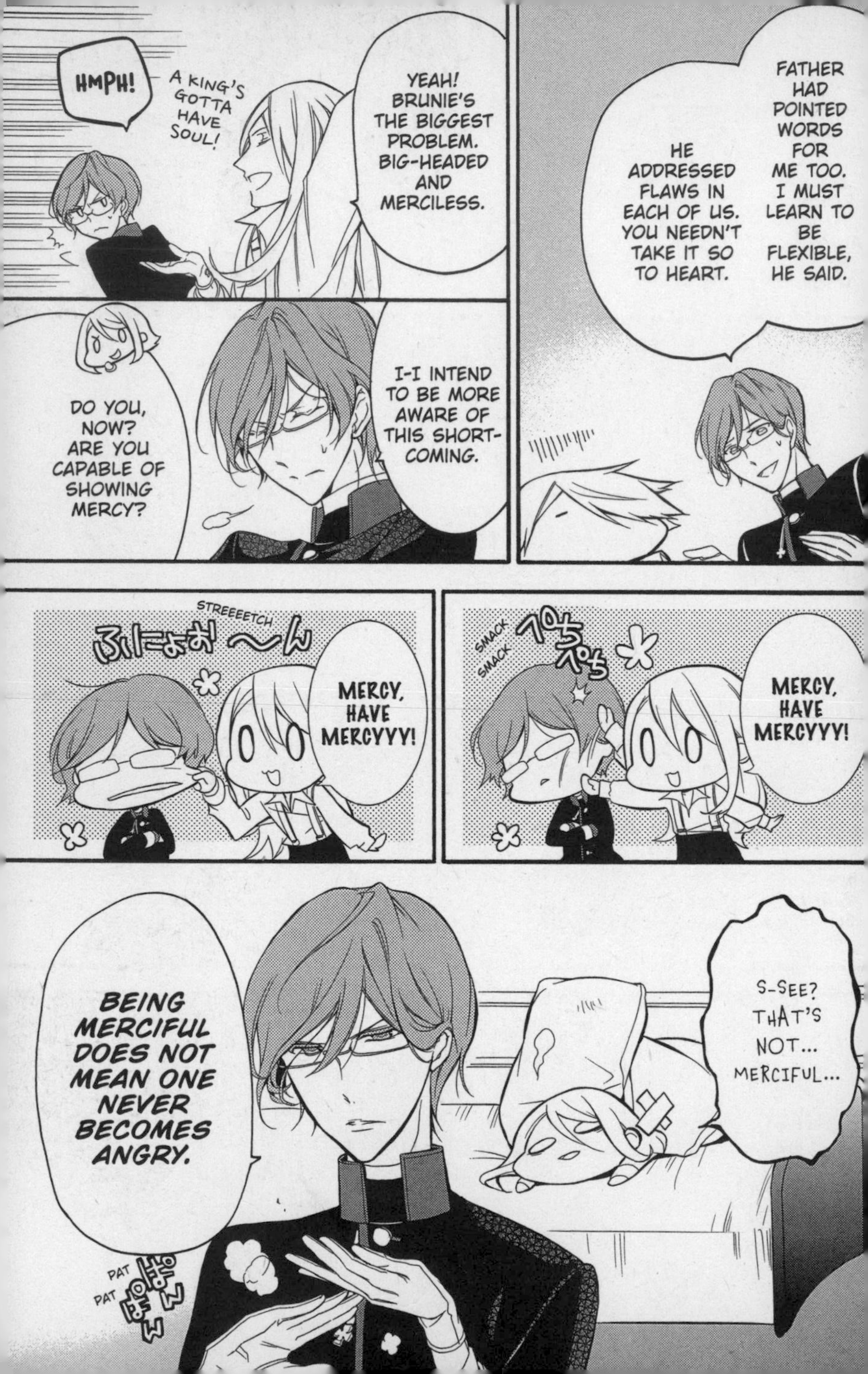

FATHER HAD POINTED WORDS FOR ME TOO. I MUST LEARN TO BE FLEXIBLE, HE SAID.
HE ADDRESSED FLAWS IN EACH OF US. YOU NEEDN'T TAKE IT SO TO HEART.
YEAH! BRUNIE'S THE BIGGEST PROBLEM. BIG-HEADED AND MERCILESS.
A KING'S GOTTA HAVE SOUL!
HMPH!
I-I INTEND TO BE MORE AWARE OF THIS SHORT-COMING.
DO YOU, NOW? ARE YOU CAPABLE OF SHOWING MERCY?
SMACK SMACK
ぺちぺち
MERCY, HAVE MERCYYY!
STREEEETCH
ふにょお～ん
MERCY, HAVE MERCYYY!
S-SEE? THAT'S NOT... MERCIFUL...
BEING MERCIFUL DOES NOT MEAN ONE NEVER BECOMES ANGRY.
PAT PAT
ぽんぽん

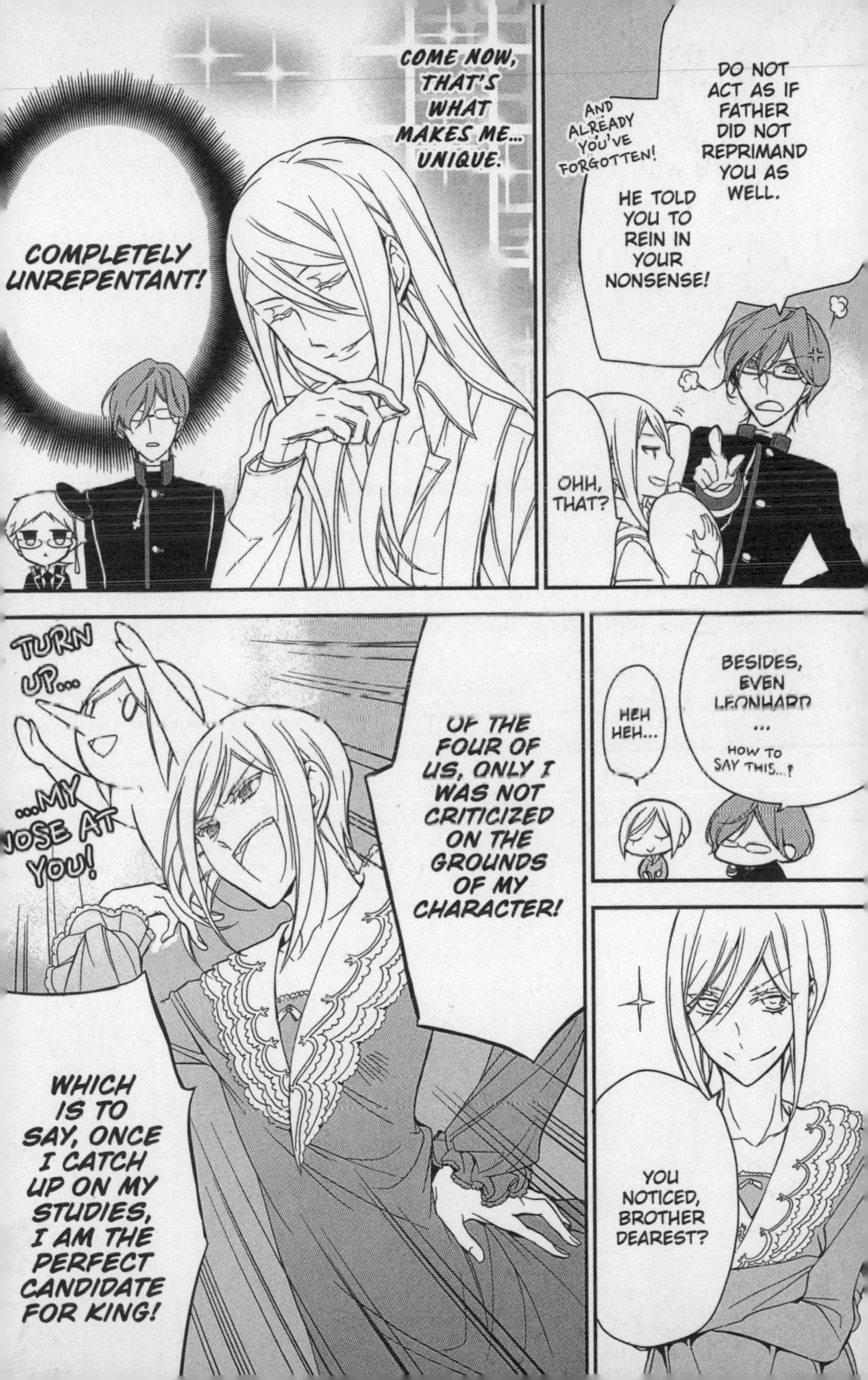
DO NOT ACT AS IF FATHER DID NOT REPRIMAND YOU AS WELL.
AND ALREADY YOU'VE FORGOTTEN!
HE TOLD YOU TO REIN IN YOUR NONSENSE!
OHH, THAT?
COME NOW, THAT'S WHAT MAKES ME... UNIQUE.
COMPLETELY UNREPENTANT!
BESIDES, EVEN LEONHARD...
HOW TO SAY THIS...?
HEH HEH...
YOU NOTICED, BROTHER DEAREST?
OF THE FOUR OF US, ONLY I WAS NOT CRITICIZED ON THE GROUNDS OF MY CHARACTER!
TURN UP...
...MY NOSE AT YOU!
WHICH IS TO SAY, ONCE I CATCH UP ON MY STUDIES, I AM THE PERFECT CANDIDATE FOR KING!

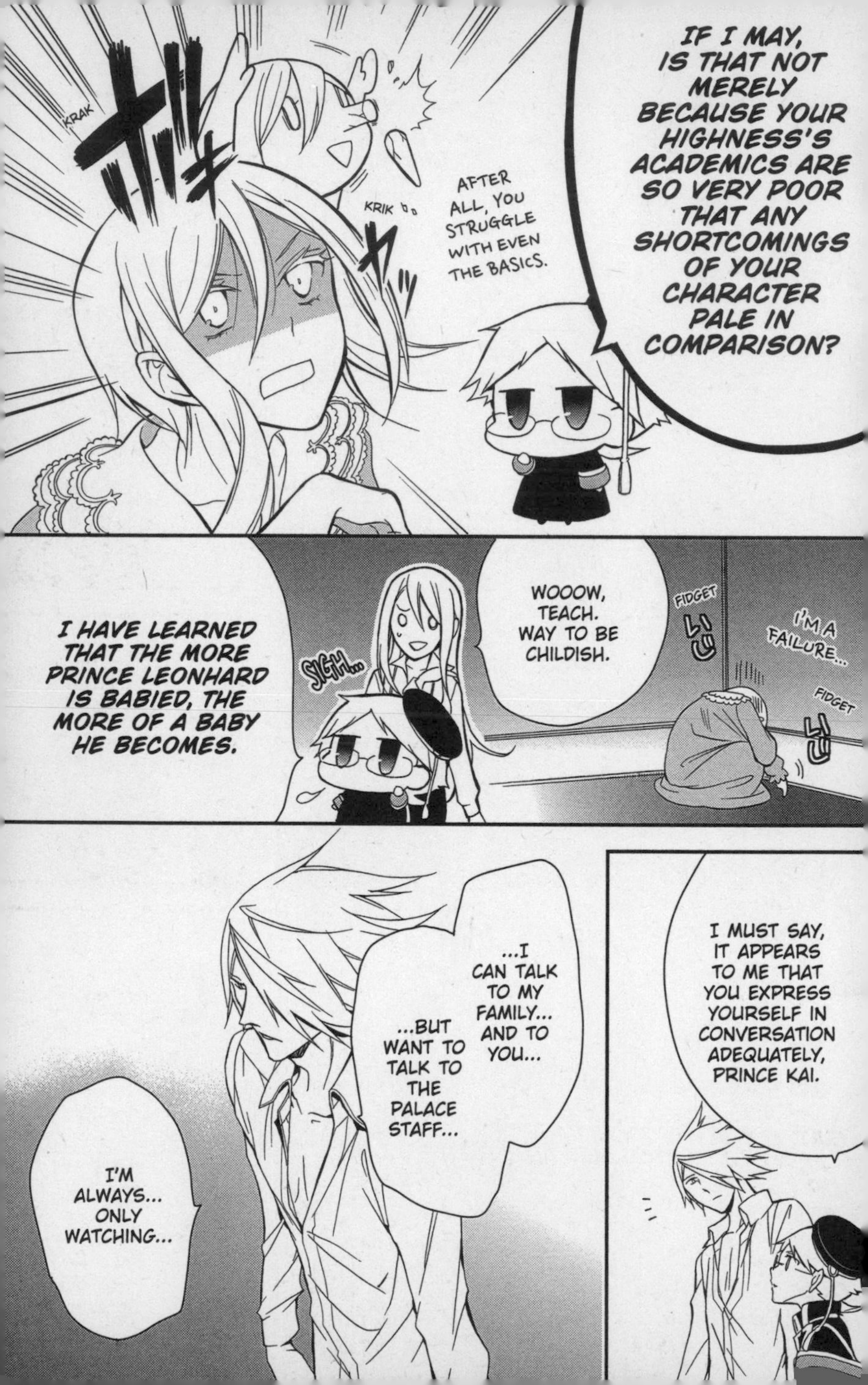
IF I MAY, IS THAT NOT MERELY BECAUSE YOUR HIGHNESS'S ACADEMICS ARE SO VERY POOR THAT ANY SHORTCOMINGS OF YOUR CHARACTER PALE IN COMPARISON?
AFTER ALL, YOU STRUGGLE WITH EVEN THE BASICS.
KRIK
KRAK
FIDGET
I'M A FAILURE...
FIDGET
WOOOW, TEACH. WAY TO BE CHILDISH.
SIGH...
I HAVE LEARNED THAT THE MORE PRINCE LEONHARD IS BABIED, THE MORE OF A BABY HE BECOMES.
I MUST SAY, IT APPEARS TO ME THAT YOU EXPRESS YOURSELF IN CONVERSATION ADEQUATELY, PRINCE KAI.
...I CAN TALK TO MY FAMILY... AND TO YOU...
...BUT WANT TO TALK TO THE PALACE STAFF...
I'M ALWAYS... ONLY WATCHING...

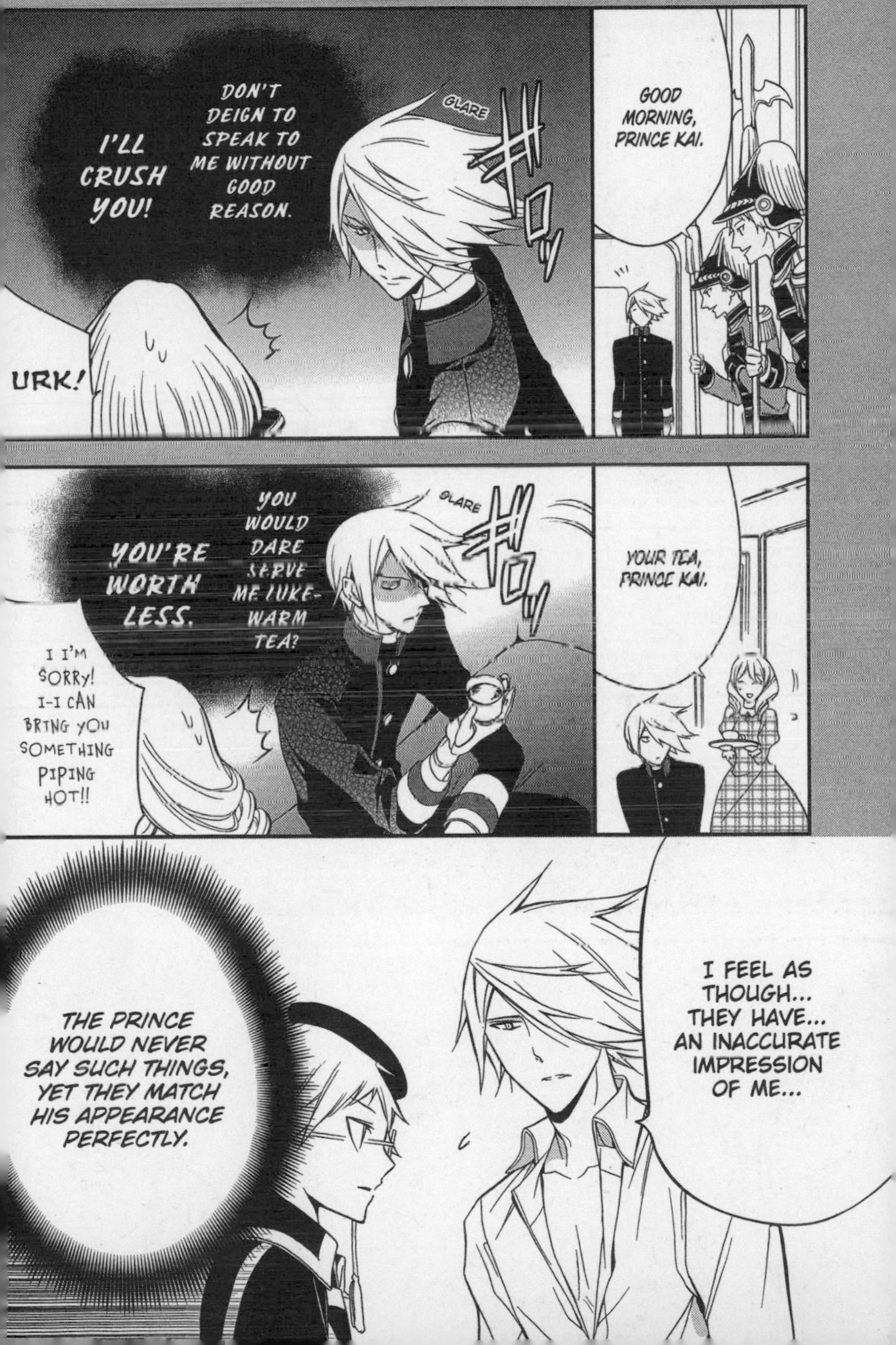
GOOD MORNING, PRINCE KAI.
GLARE
DON'T DEIGN TO SPEAK TO ME WITHOUT GOOD REASON.
I'LL CRUSH YOU!
URK!
YOUR TEA, PRINCE KAI.
GLARE
YOU WOULD DARE SERVE ME LUKE-WARM TEA?
YOU'RE WORTH LESS.
I I'M SORRY! I-I CAN BRING YOU SOMETHING PIPING HOT!!
I FEEL AS THOUGH... THEY HAVE... AN INACCURATE IMPRESSION OF ME...
THE PRINCE WOULD NEVER SAY SUCH THINGS, YET THEY MATCH HIS APPEARANCE PERFECTLY.

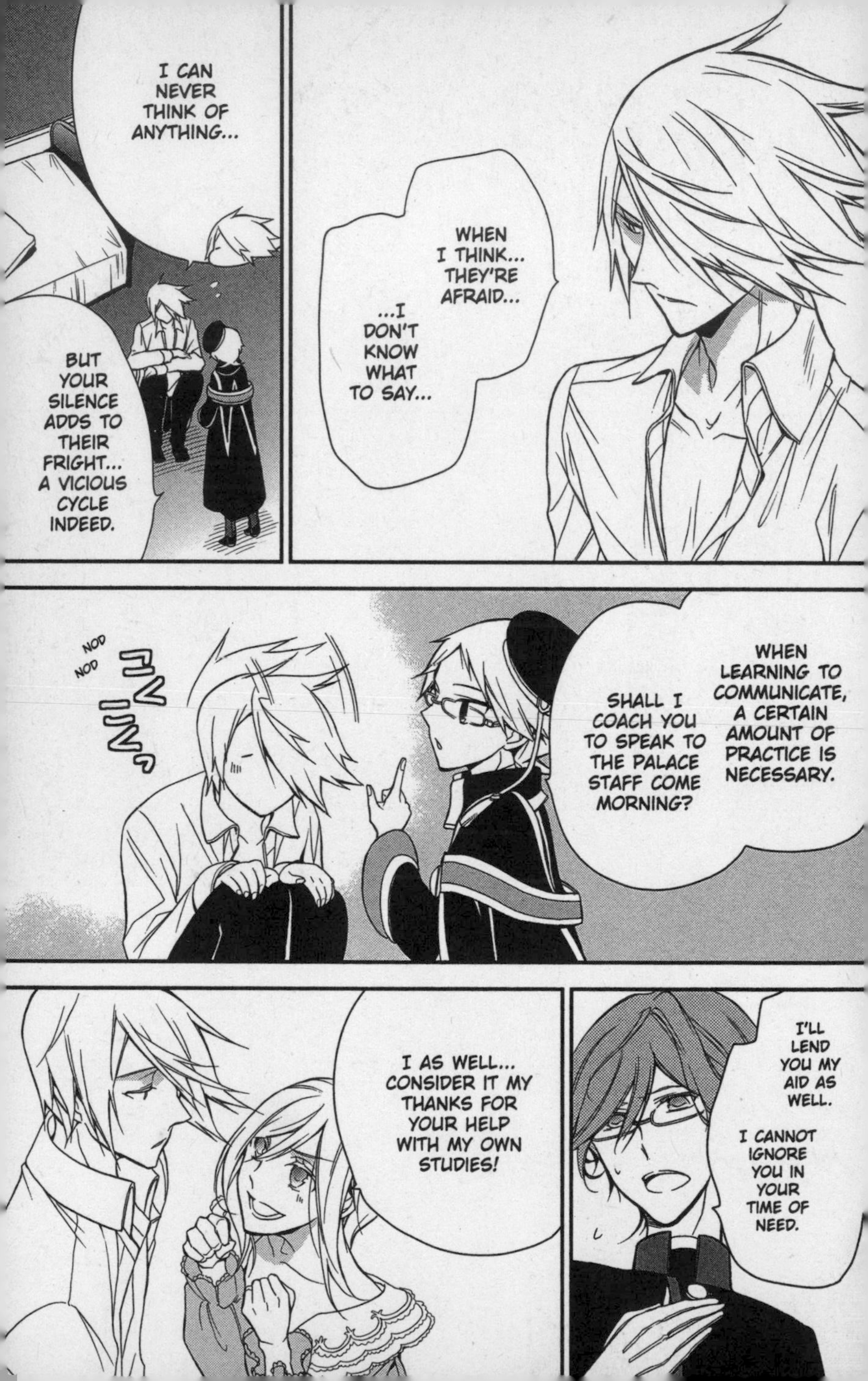
WHEN I THINK... THEY'RE AFRAID...
...I DON'T KNOW WHAT TO SAY...
I CAN NEVER THINK OF ANYTHING...
BUT YOUR SILENCE ADDS TO THEIR FRIGHT... A VICIOUS CYCLE INDEED.
WHEN LEARNING TO COMMUNICATE, A CERTAIN AMOUNT OF PRACTICE IS NECESSARY.
SHALL I COACH YOU TO SPEAK TO THE PALACE STAFF COME MORNING?
NOD NOD
I'LL LEND YOU MY AID AS WELL.
I CANNOT IGNORE YOU IN YOUR TIME OF NEED.
I AS WELL... CONSIDER IT MY THANKS FOR YOUR HELP WITH MY OWN STUDIES!

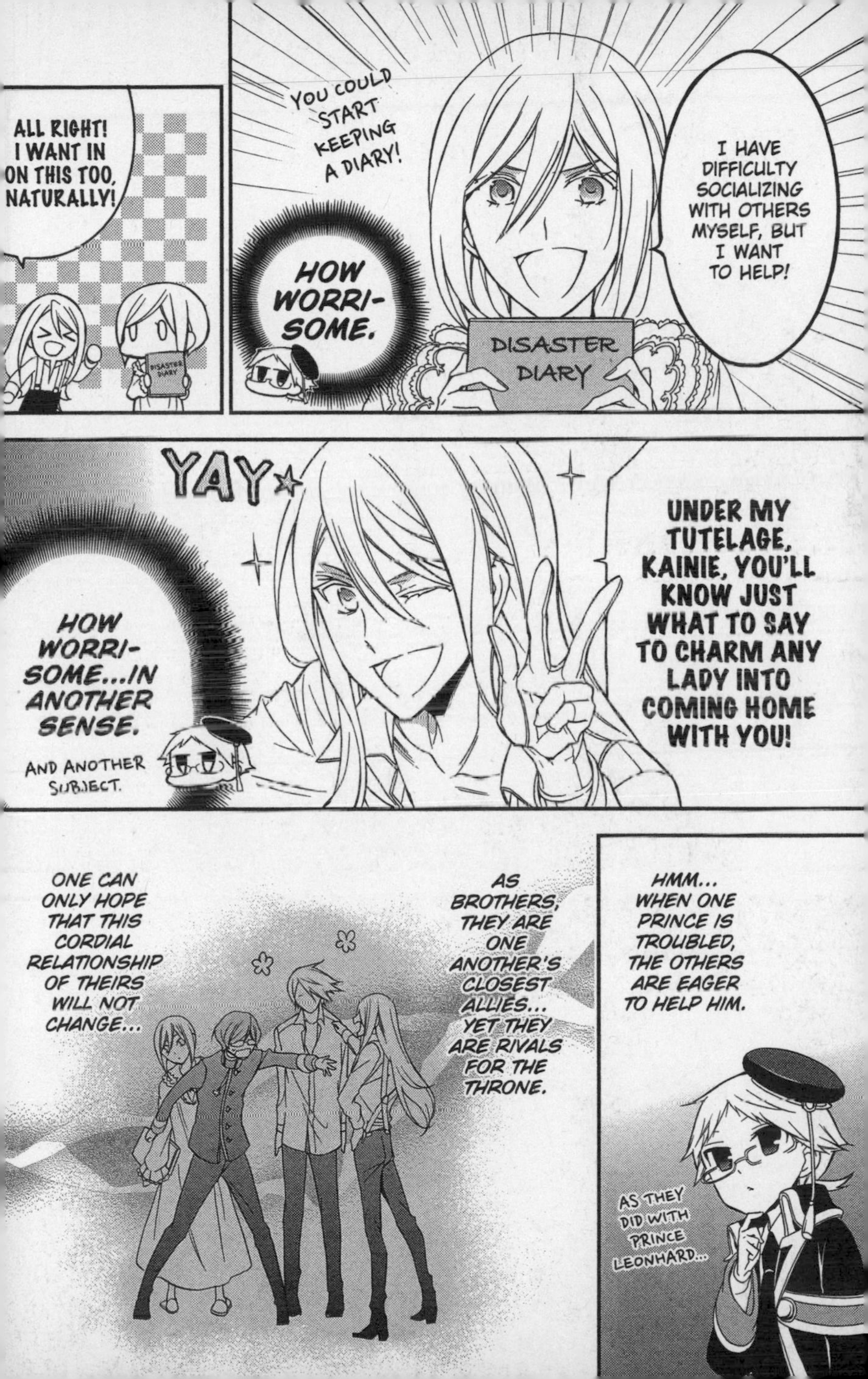
I HAVE DIFFICULTY SOCIALIZING WITH OTHERS MYSELF, BUT I WANT TO HELP!
YOU COULD START KEEPING A DIARY!
DISASTER DIARY
HOW WORRI-SOME.
ALL RIGHT! I WANT IN ON THIS TOO, NATURALLY!
DISASTER DIARY
UNDER MY TUTELAGE, KAINIE, YOU'LL KNOW JUST WHAT TO SAY TO CHARM ANY LADY INTO COMING HOME WITH YOU!
YAY
HOW WORRI-SOME...IN ANOTHER SENSE.
AND ANOTHER SUBJECT.
HMM... WHEN ONE PRINCE IS TROUBLED, THE OTHERS ARE EAGER TO HELP HIM.
AS THEY DID WITH PRINCE LEONHARD...
AS BROTHERS, THEY ARE ONE ANOTHER'S CLOSEST ALLIES... YET THEY ARE RIVALS FOR THE THRONE.
ONE CAN ONLY HOPE THAT THIS CORDIAL RELATIONSHIP OF THEIRS WILL NOT CHANGE...

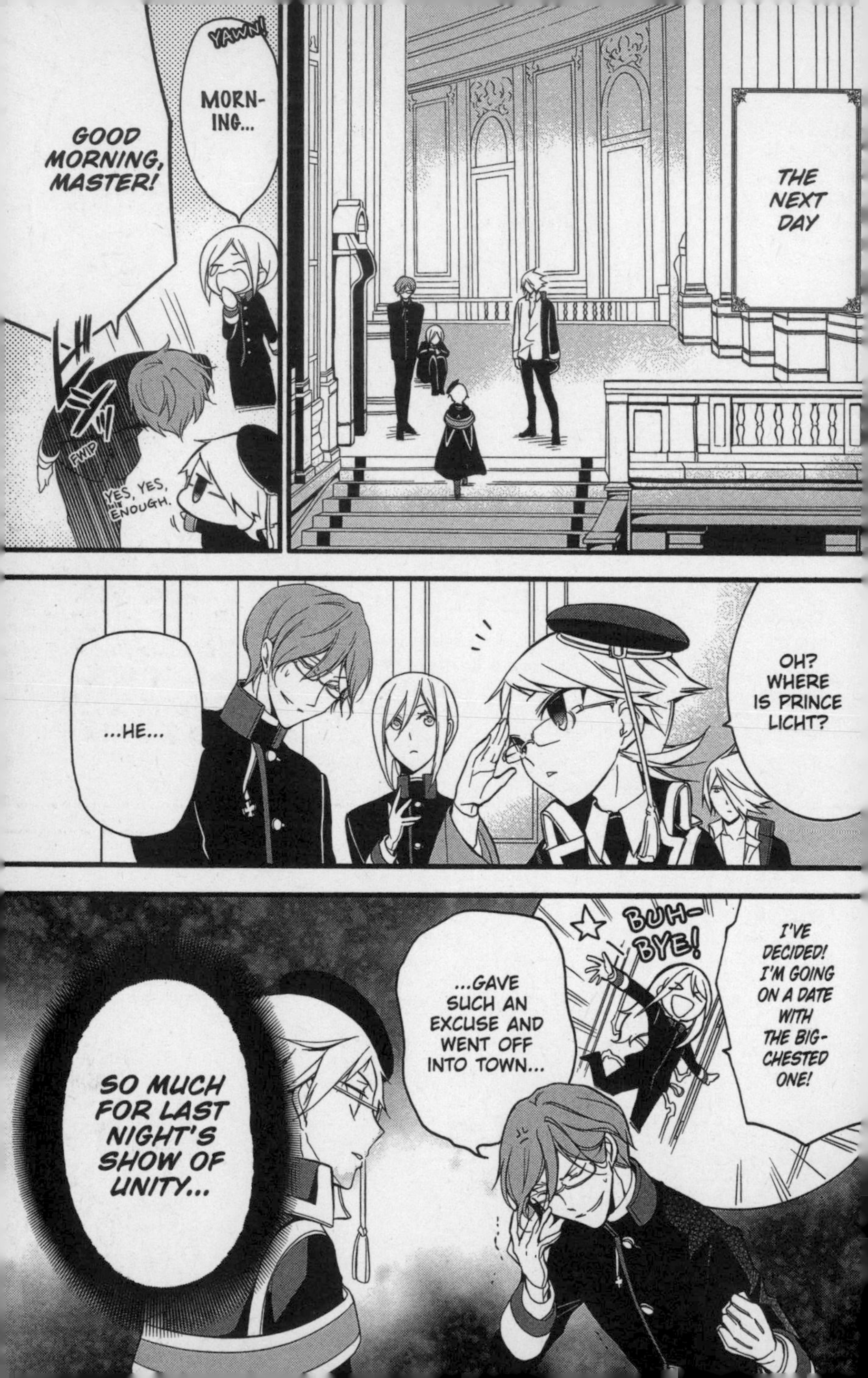
THE NEXT DAY
YAWN!
MORN-ING...
GOOD MORNING, MASTER!
FWIP
YES, YES, ENOUGH.
OH? WHERE IS PRINCE LICHT?
...HE...
I'VE DECIDED! I'M GOING ON A DATE WITH THE BIG-CHESTED ONE!
BUH-BYE!
...GAVE SUCH AN EXCUSE AND WENT OFF INTO TOWN...
SO MUCH FOR LAST NIGHT'S SHOW OF UNITY...

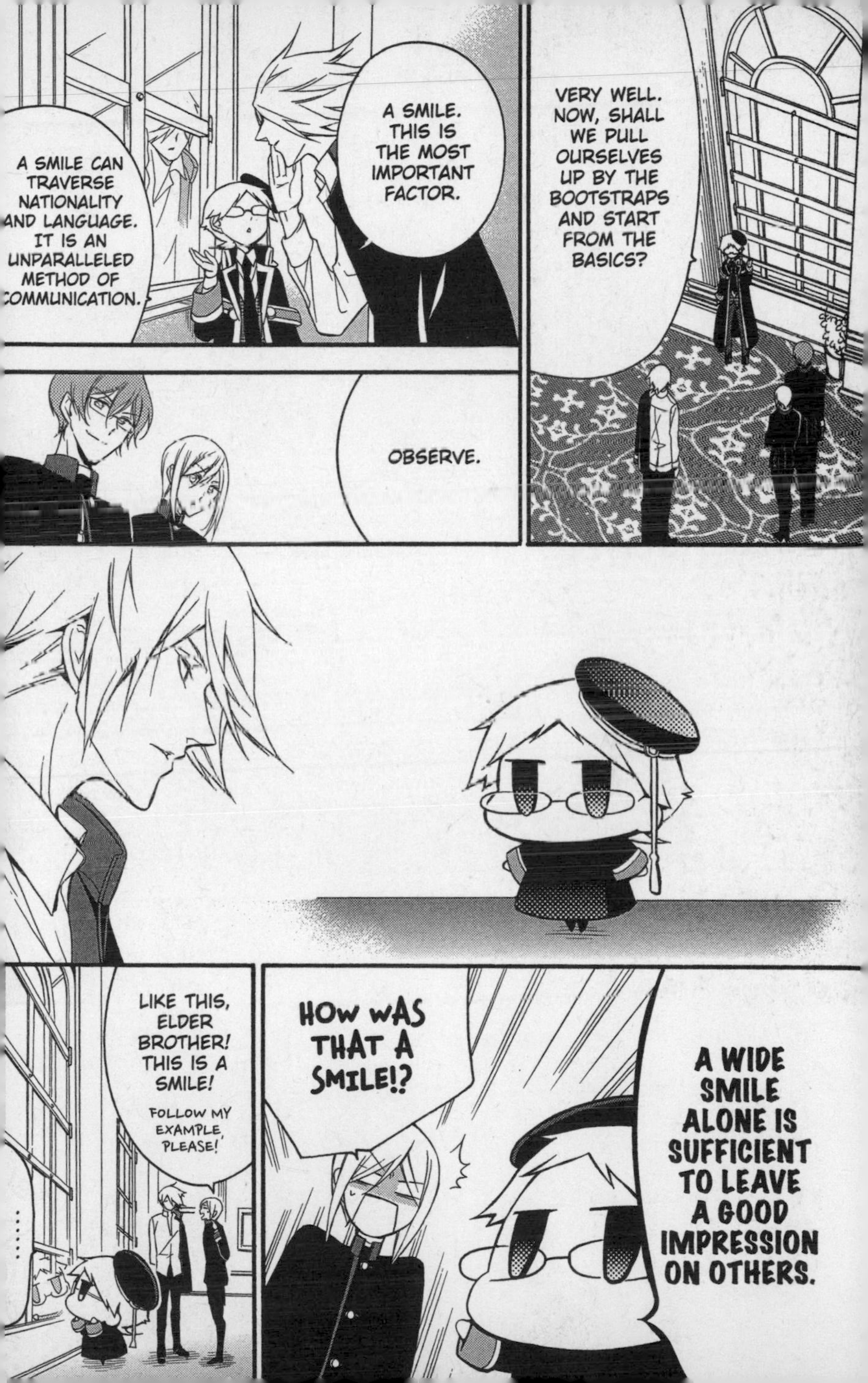

VERY WELL. NOW, SHALL WE PULL OURSELVES UP BY THE BOOTSTRAPS AND START FROM THE BASICS?
A SMILE. THIS IS THE MOST IMPORTANT FACTOR.
A SMILE CAN TRAVERSE NATIONALITY AND LANGUAGE. IT IS AN UNPARALLELED METHOD OF COMMUNICATION.
OBSERVE.
A WIDE SMILE ALONE IS SUFFICIENT TO LEAVE A GOOD IMPRESSION ON OTHERS.
HOW WAS THAT A SMILE!?
LIKE THIS, ELDER BROTHER! THIS IS A SMILE!
FOLLOW MY EXAMPLE, PLEASE!
......

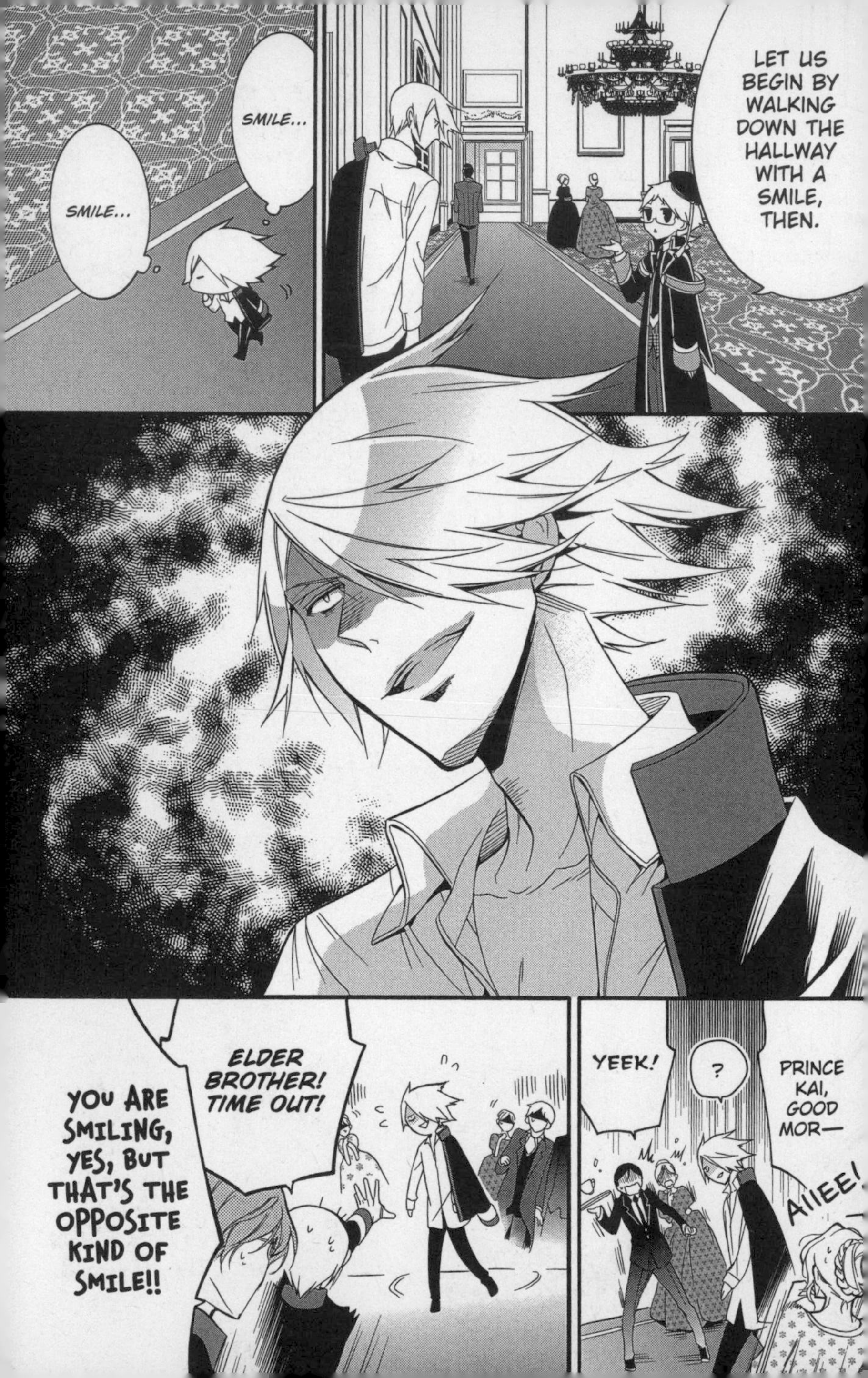
LET US BEGIN BY WALKING DOWN THE HALLWAY WITH A SMILE, THEN.
SMILE...
SMILE...
PRINCE KAI, GOOD MOR—
?
YEEK!
AIIEE!
ELDER BROTHER! TIME OUT!
YOU ARE SMILING, YES, BUT THAT'S THE OPPOSITE KIND OF SMILE!!

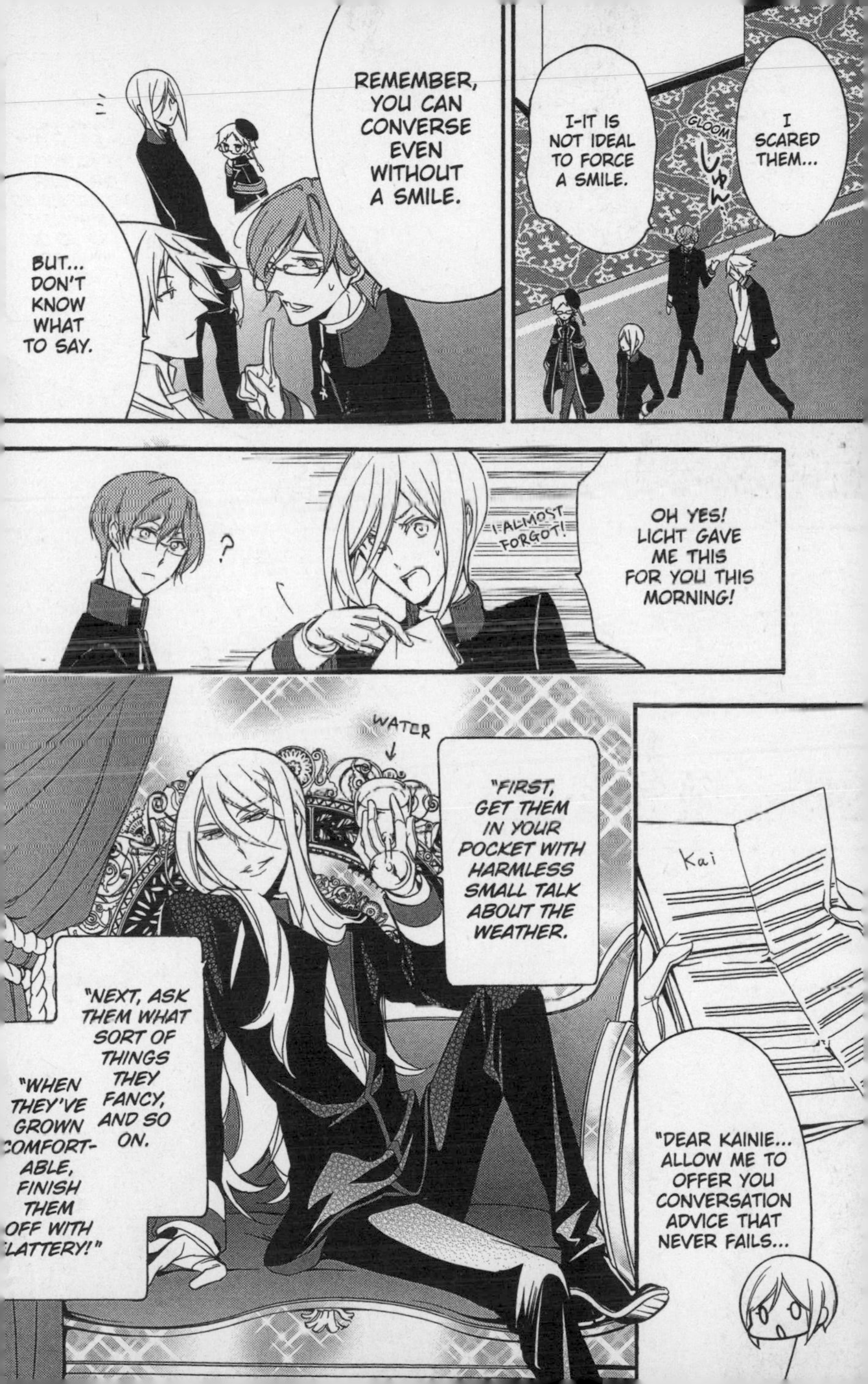
I SCARED THEM...
GLOOM
じゅん
I-IT IS NOT IDEAL TO FORCE A SMILE.
REMEMBER, YOU CAN CONVERSE EVEN WITHOUT A SMILE.
BUT... DON'T KNOW WHAT TO SAY.
OH YES! LICHT GAVE ME THIS FOR YOU THIS MORNING!
I ALMOST FORGOT!
Kai
"DEAR KAINIE... ALLOW ME TO OFFER YOU CONVERSATION ADVICE THAT NEVER FAILS...
WATER
"FIRST, GET THEM IN YOUR POCKET WITH HARMLESS SMALL TALK ABOUT THE WEATHER.
"NEXT, ASK THEM WHAT SORT OF THINGS THEY FANCY, AND SO ON.
"WHEN THEY'VE GROWN OMFORT-ABLE, FINISH THEM OFF WITH LATTERY!"

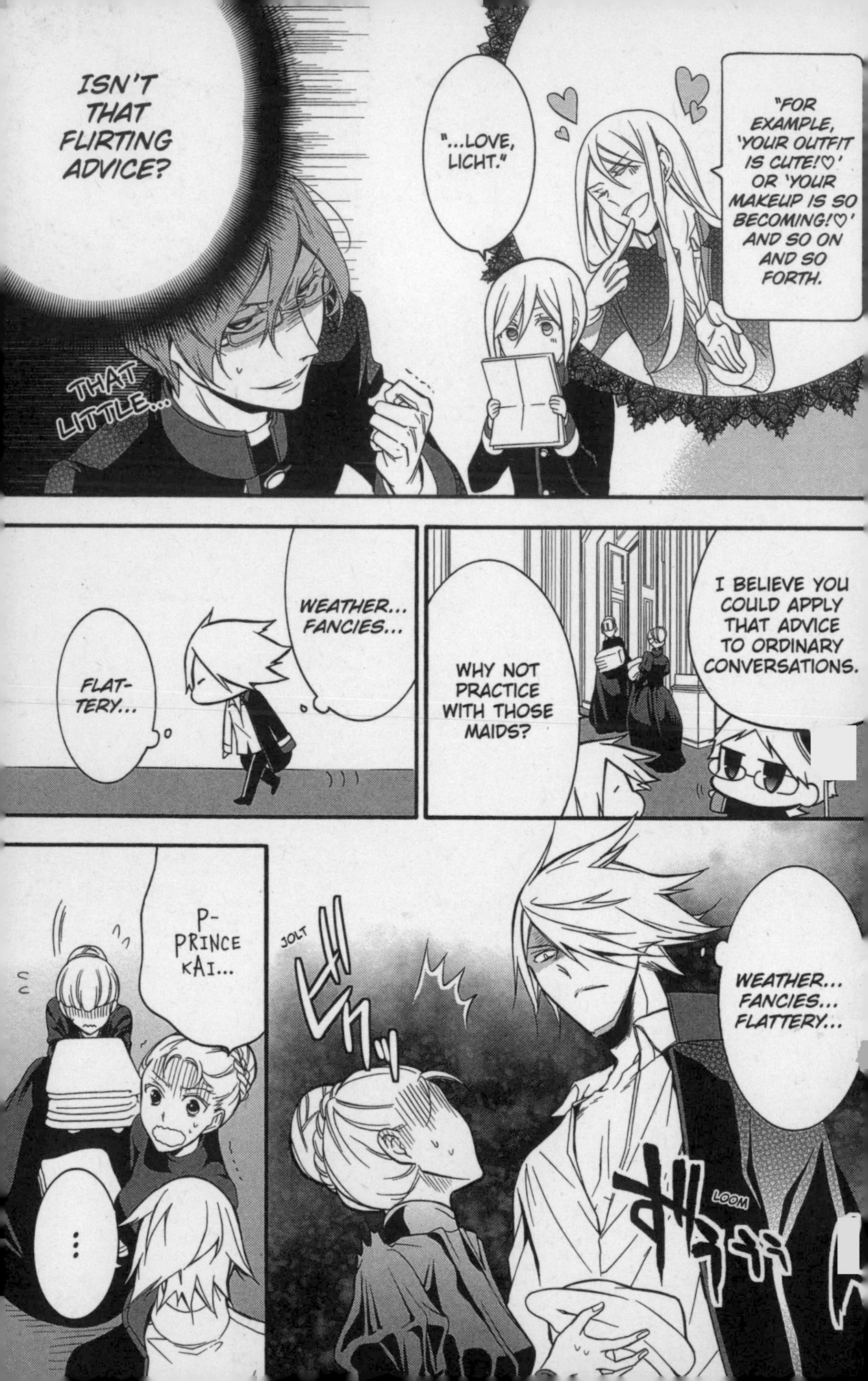
"FOR EXAMPLE, 'YOUR OUTFIT IS CUTE!♡' OR 'YOUR MAKEUP IS SO BECOMING!♡' AND SO ON AND SO FORTH.
"...LOVE, LICHT."
ISN'T THAT FLIRTING ADVICE?
THAT LITTLE...
I BELIEVE YOU COULD APPLY THAT ADVICE TO ORDINARY CONVERSATIONS.
WHY NOT PRACTICE WITH THOSE MAIDS?
WEATHER... FANCIES...
FLAT-TERY...
WEATHER... FANCIES... FLATTERY...
LOOM
JOLT
P-PRINCE KAI...
...

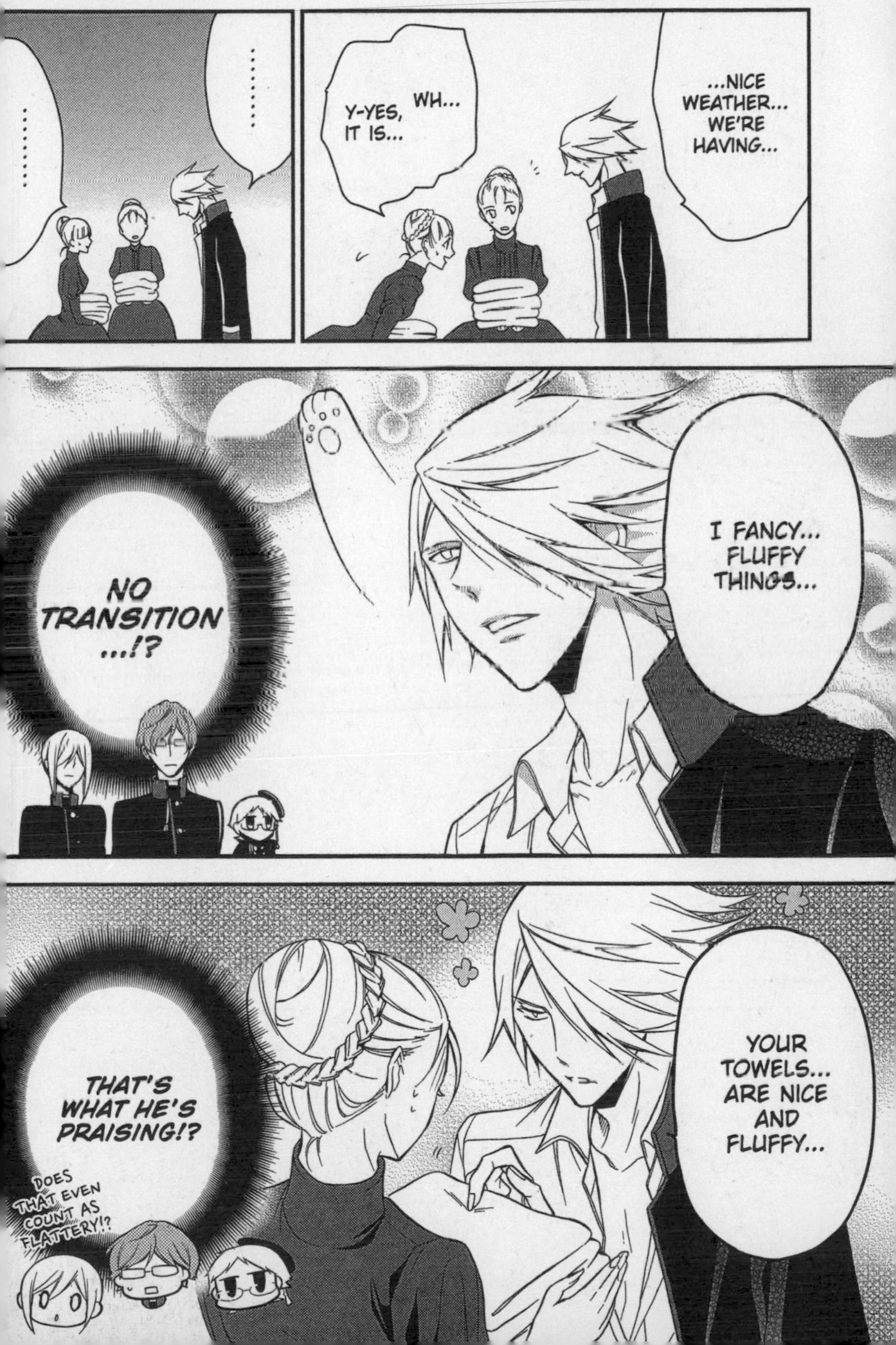
...NICE WEATHER... WE'RE HAVING...
WH...
Y-YES, IT IS...
....
....
I FANCY... FLUFFY THINGS...
NO TRANSITION ...!?
YOUR TOWELS... ARE NICE AND FLUFFY...
THAT'S WHAT HE'S PRAISING!?
DOES THAT EVEN COUNT AS FLATTERY!?

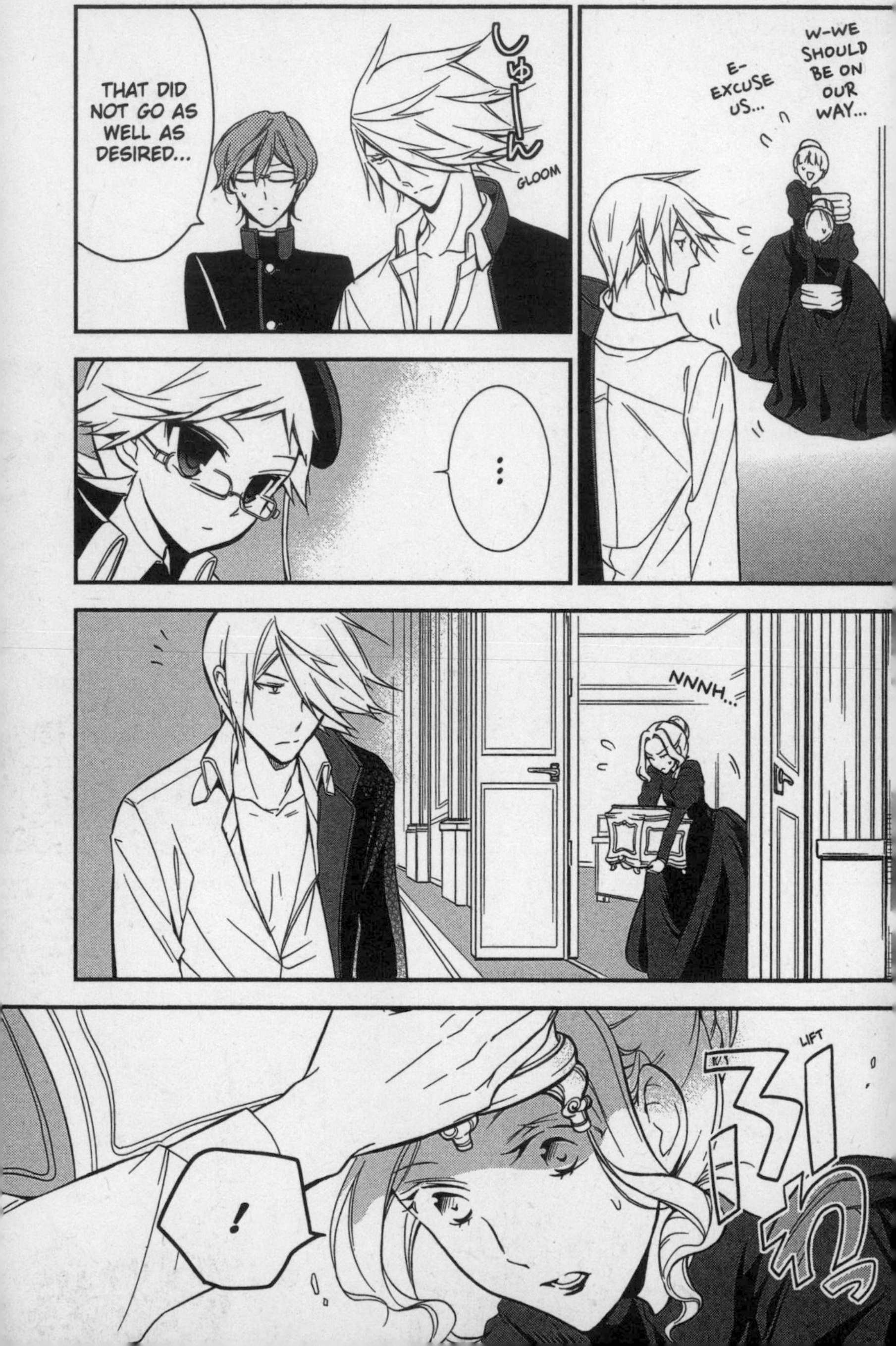
W-WE SHOULD BE ON OUR WAY...
E-EXCUSE US...
THAT DID NOT GO AS WELL AS DESIRED...
しゅーん
GLOOM
...
NNNH...
LIFT
ふわ
!

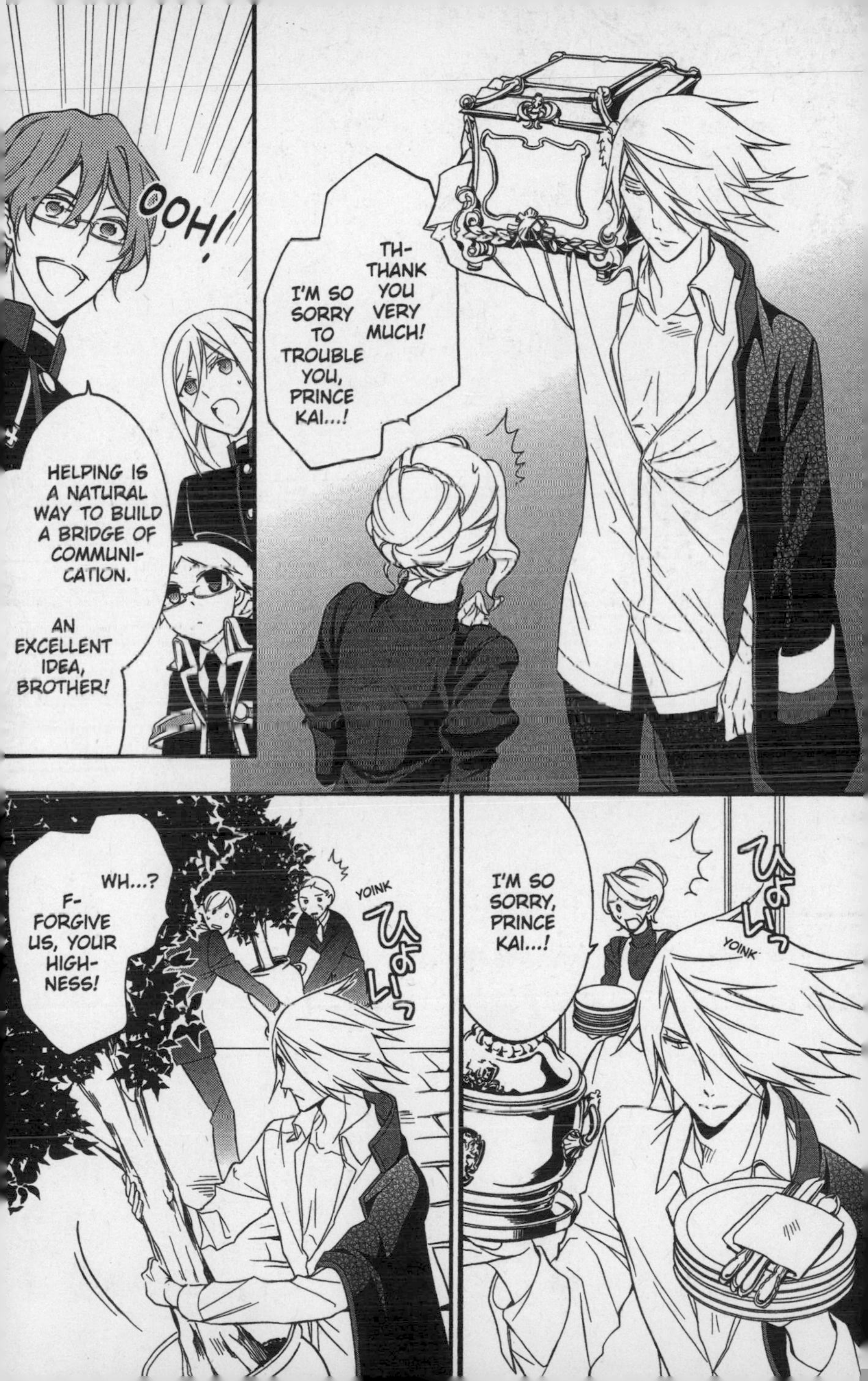
TH-THANK YOU VERY MUCH!
I'M SO SORRY TO TROUBLE YOU, PRINCE KAI...!
OOH!
HELPING IS A NATURAL WAY TO BUILD A BRIDGE OF COMMUNI-CATION.
AN EXCELLENT IDEA, BROTHER!
ひょいっ
YOINK
I'M SO SORRY, PRINCE KAI...!
WH...?
F-FORGIVE US, YOUR HIGHNESS!
YOINK
ひょいっ

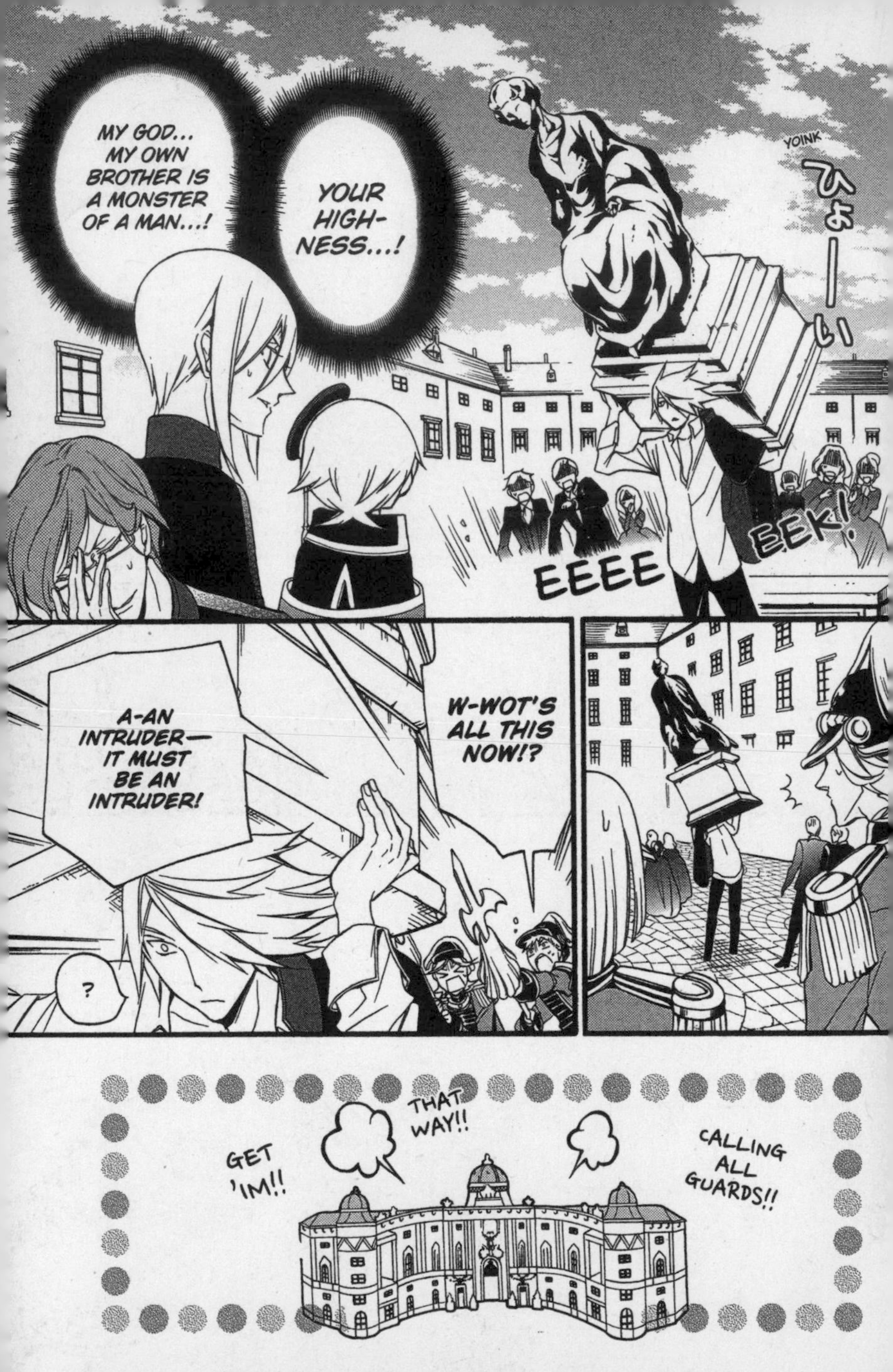
YOINK
ひょーーい
EEK!
EEEE
YOUR HIGHNESS...!
MY GOD... MY OWN BROTHER IS A MONSTER OF A MAN...!
W-WOT'S ALL THIS NOW!?
A-AN INTRUDER— IT MUST BE AN INTRUDER!
?
CALLING ALL GUARDS!!
THAT WAY!!
GET 'IM!!

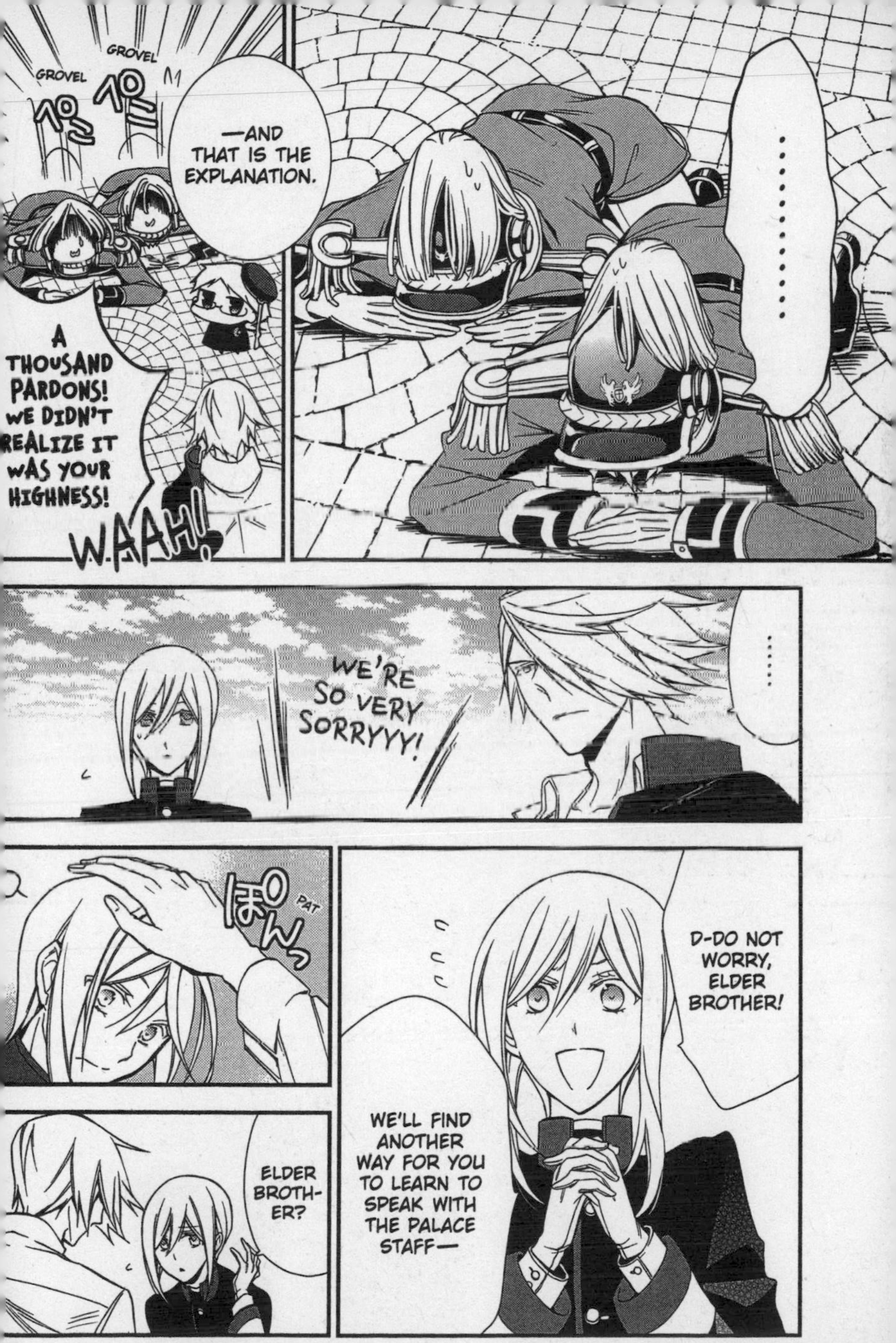
......
—AND THAT IS THE EXPLANATION.
GROVEL
GROVEL
A THOUSAND PARDONS! WE DIDN'T REALIZE IT WAS YOUR HIGHNESS!
WAAH!
......
WE'RE SO VERY SORRYYY!
D-DO NOT WORRY, ELDER BROTHER!
WE'LL FIND ANOTHER WAY FOR YOU TO LEARN TO SPEAK WITH THE PALACE STAFF—
PAT
ELDER BROTHER?

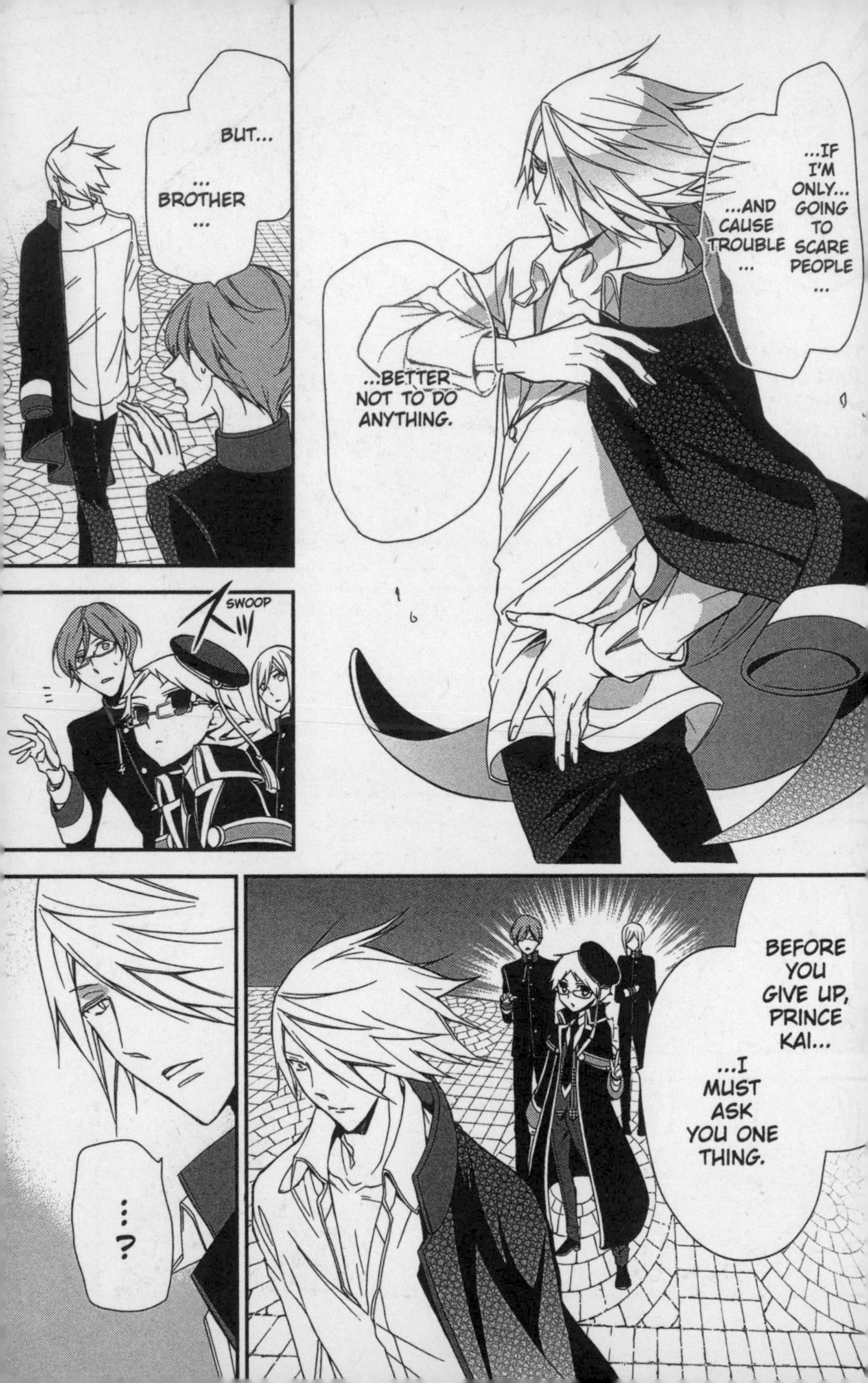
...IF I'M ONLY... GOING TO SCARE PEOPLE...
...AND CAUSE TROUBLE...
...BETTER NOT TO DO ANYTHING.
BUT...
... BROTHER ...
SWOOP
BEFORE YOU GIVE UP, PRINCE KAI...
...I MUST ASK YOU ONE THING.
...?

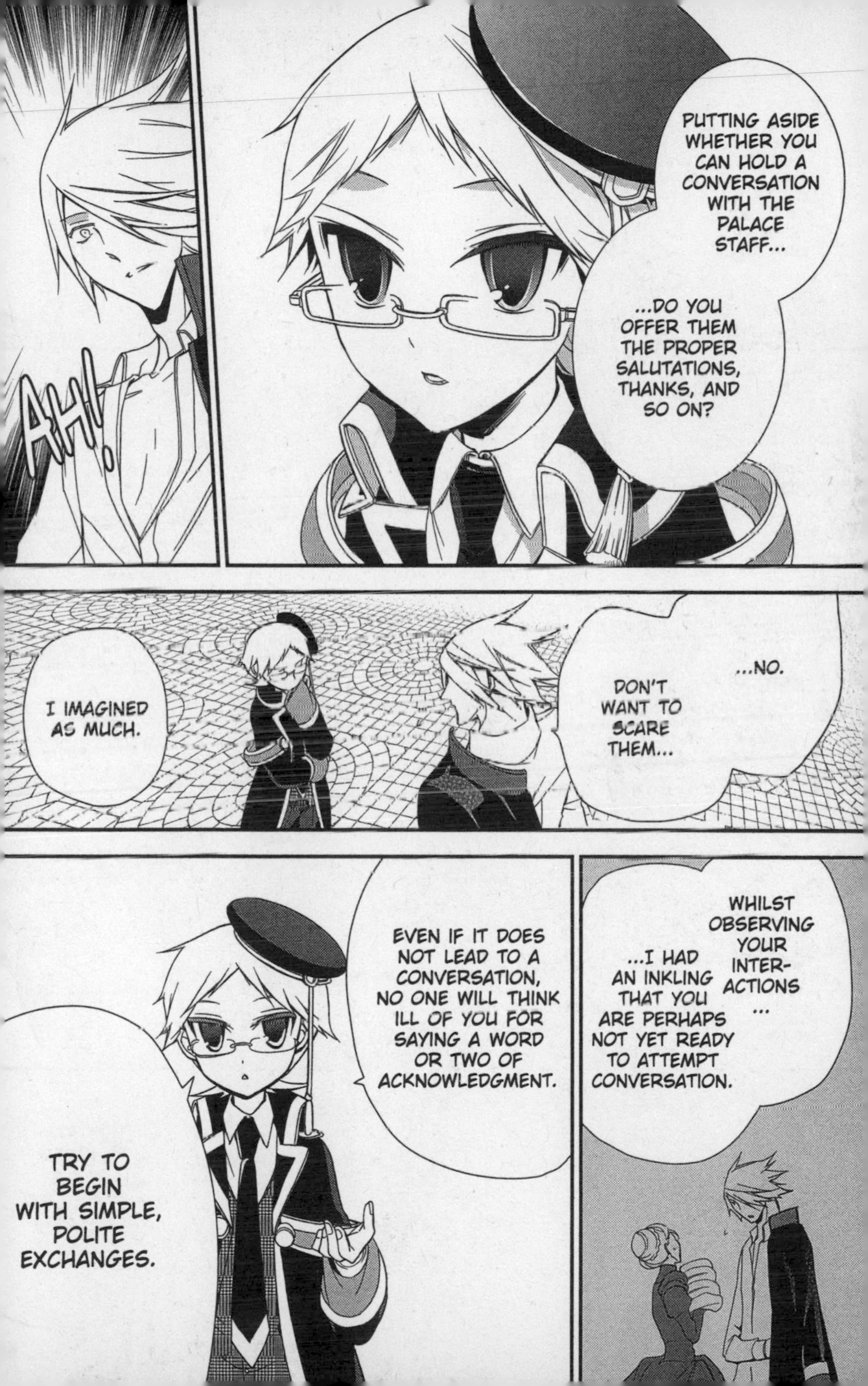
PUTTING ASIDE WHETHER YOU CAN HOLD A CONVERSATION WITH THE PALACE STAFF...
...DO YOU OFFER THEM THE PROPER SALUTATIONS, THANKS, AND SO ON?
AH!
...NO.
DON'T WANT TO SCARE THEM...
I IMAGINED AS MUCH.
WHILST OBSERVING YOUR INTER-ACTIONS...
...I HAD AN INKLING THAT YOU ARE PERHAPS NOT YET READY TO ATTEMPT CONVERSATION.
EVEN IF IT DOES NOT LEAD TO A CONVERSATION, NO ONE WILL THINK ILL OF YOU FOR SAYING A WORD OR TWO OF ACKNOWLEDGMENT.
TRY TO BEGIN WITH SIMPLE, POLITE EXCHANGES.

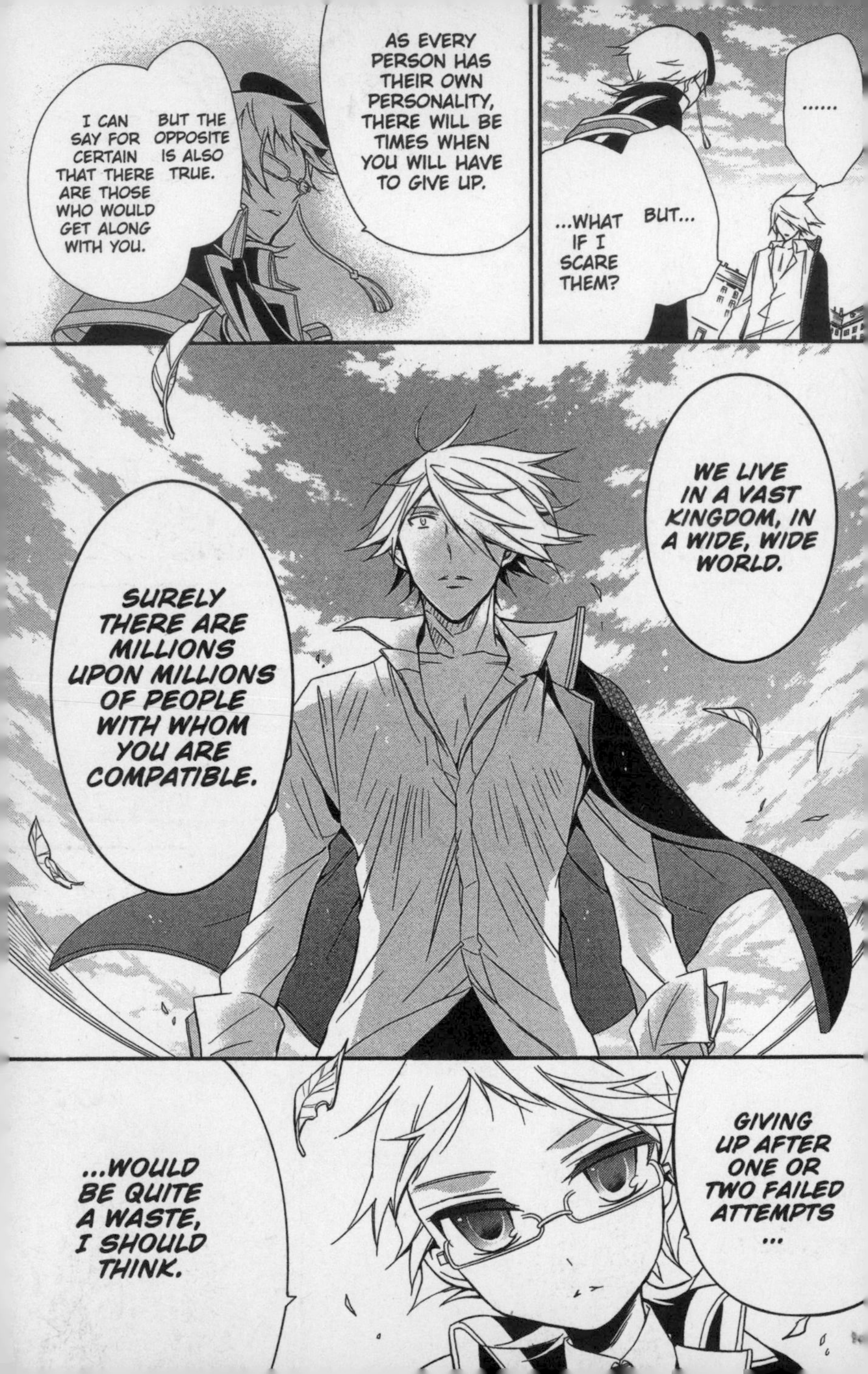
......
BUT...
...WHAT IF I SCARE THEM?
AS EVERY PERSON HAS THEIR OWN PERSONALITY, THERE WILL BE TIMES WHEN YOU WILL HAVE TO GIVE UP.
I CAN SAY FOR CERTAIN THAT THERE ARE THOSE WHO WOULD GET ALONG WITH YOU.
BUT THE OPPOSITE IS ALSO TRUE.
WE LIVE IN A VAST KINGDOM, IN A WIDE, WIDE WORLD.
SURELY THERE ARE MILLIONS UPON MILLIONS OF PEOPLE WITH WHOM YOU ARE COMPATIBLE.
GIVING UP AFTER ONE OR TWO FAILED ATTEMPTS...
...WOULD BE QUITE A WASTE, I SHOULD THINK.

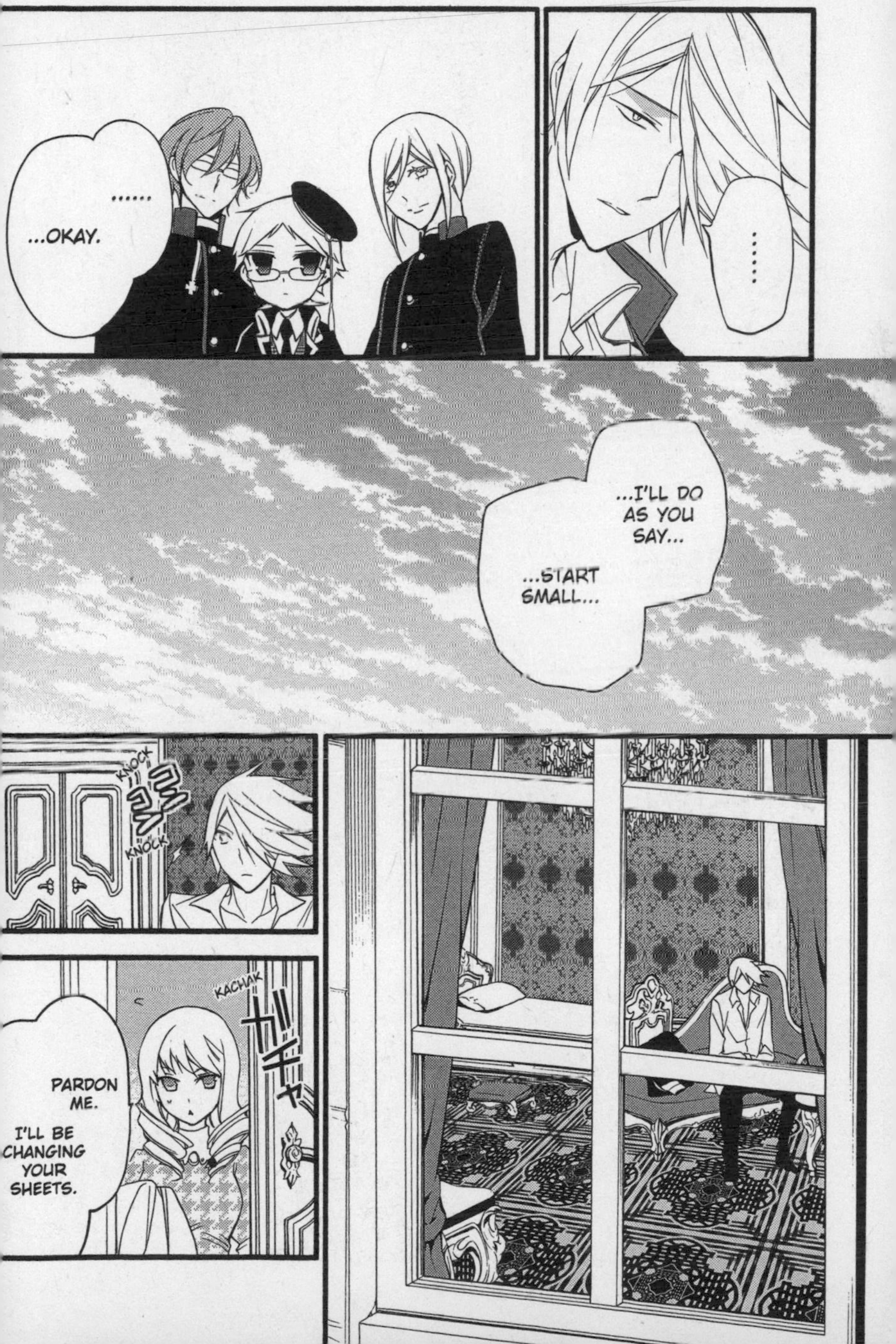
......
......
...OKAY.
...I'LL DO AS YOU SAY...
...START SMALL...
KNOCK KNOCK
KACHAK
PARDON ME.
I'LL BE CHANGING YOUR SHEETS.

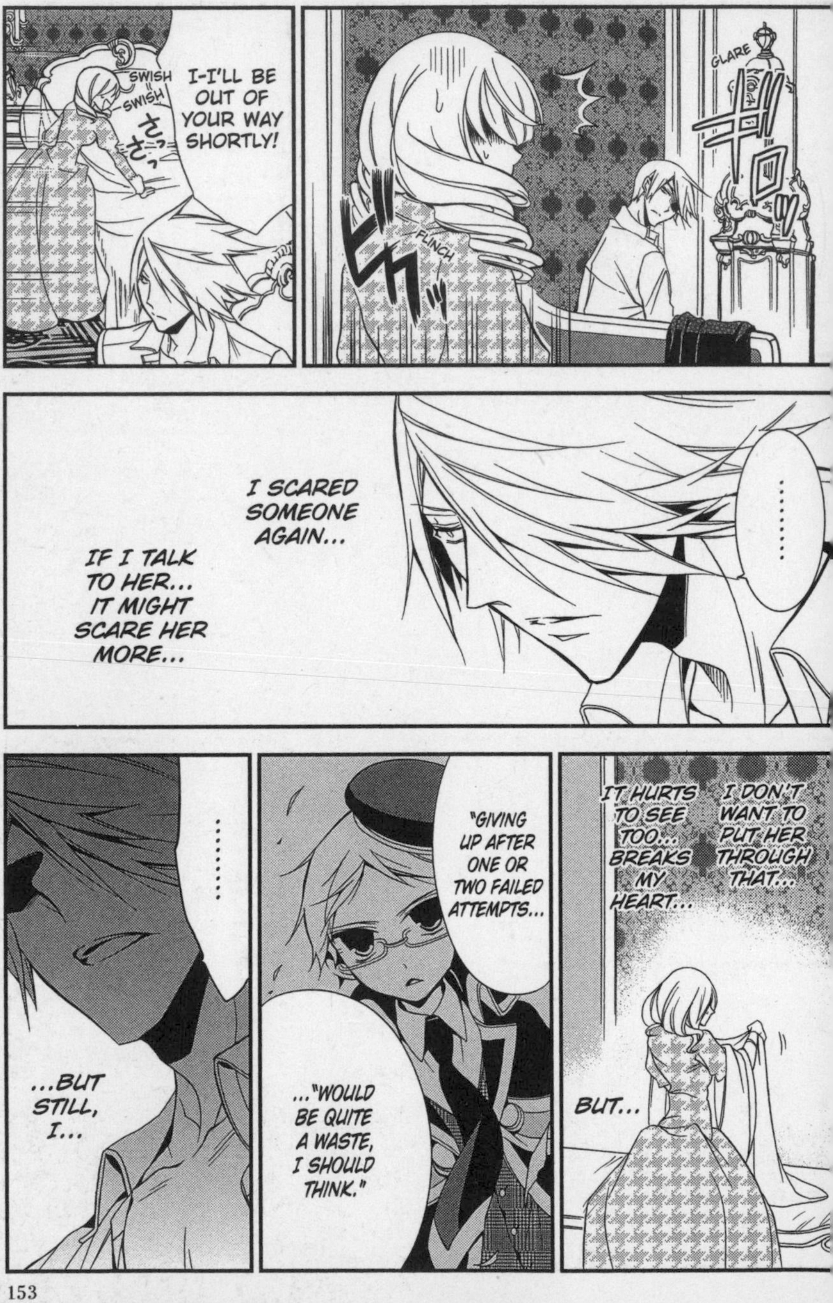
GLARE
FLINCH
SWISH
SWISH
I-I'LL BE OUT OF YOUR WAY SHORTLY!
......
I SCARED SOMEONE AGAIN...
IF I TALK TO HER... IT MIGHT SCARE HER MORE...
I DON'T WANT TO PUT HER THROUGH THAT...
IT HURTS TO SEE TOO... BREAKS MY HEART...
BUT...
"GIVING UP AFTER ONE OR TWO FAILED ATTEMPTS...
..."WOULD BE QUITE A WASTE, I SHOULD THINK."
......
...BUT STILL, I...

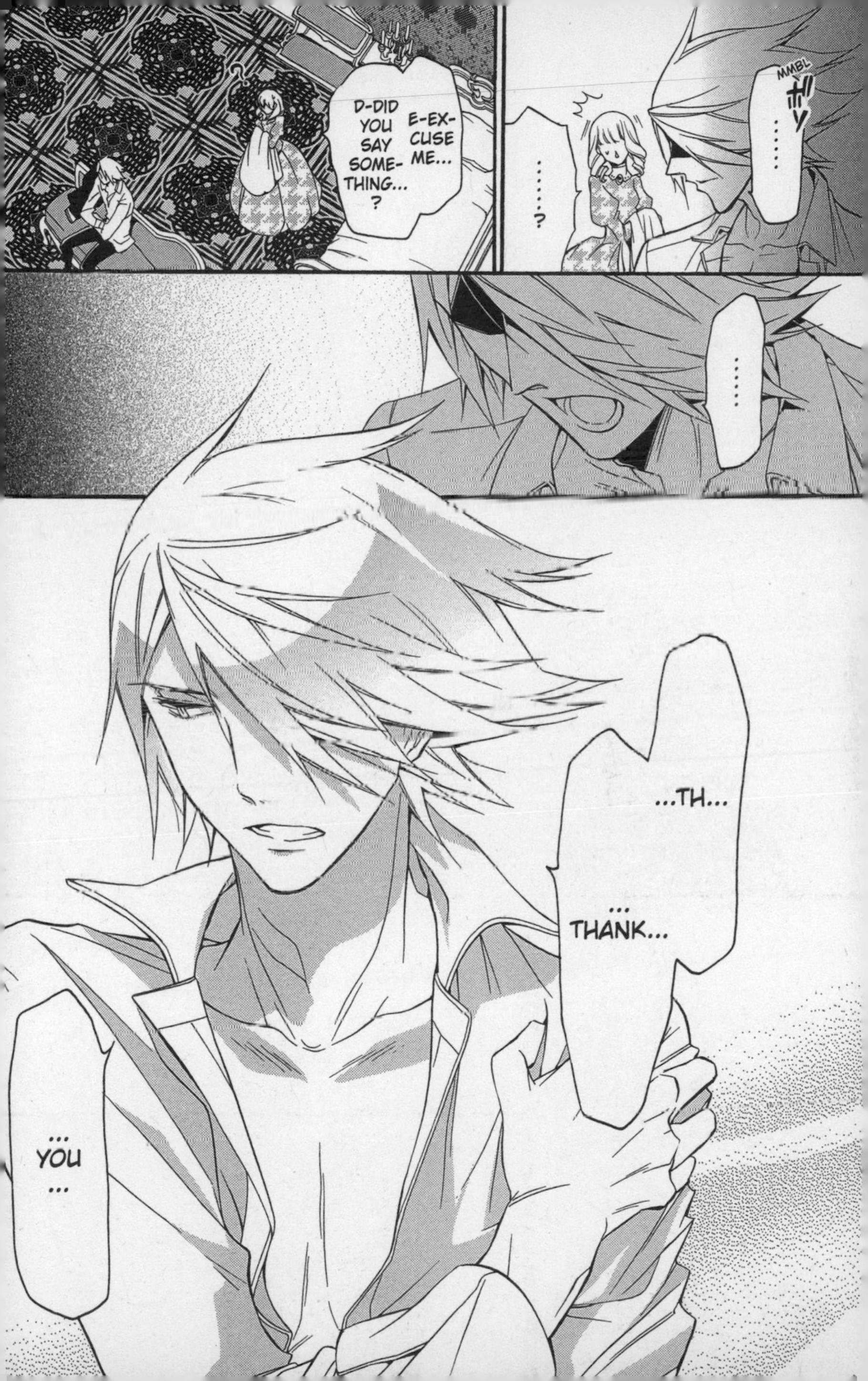
MMBL
ボソ
......
......?
E-EX-CUSE ME...
D-DID YOU SAY SOME-THING...?
......
...TH...
...THANK...
...YOU...

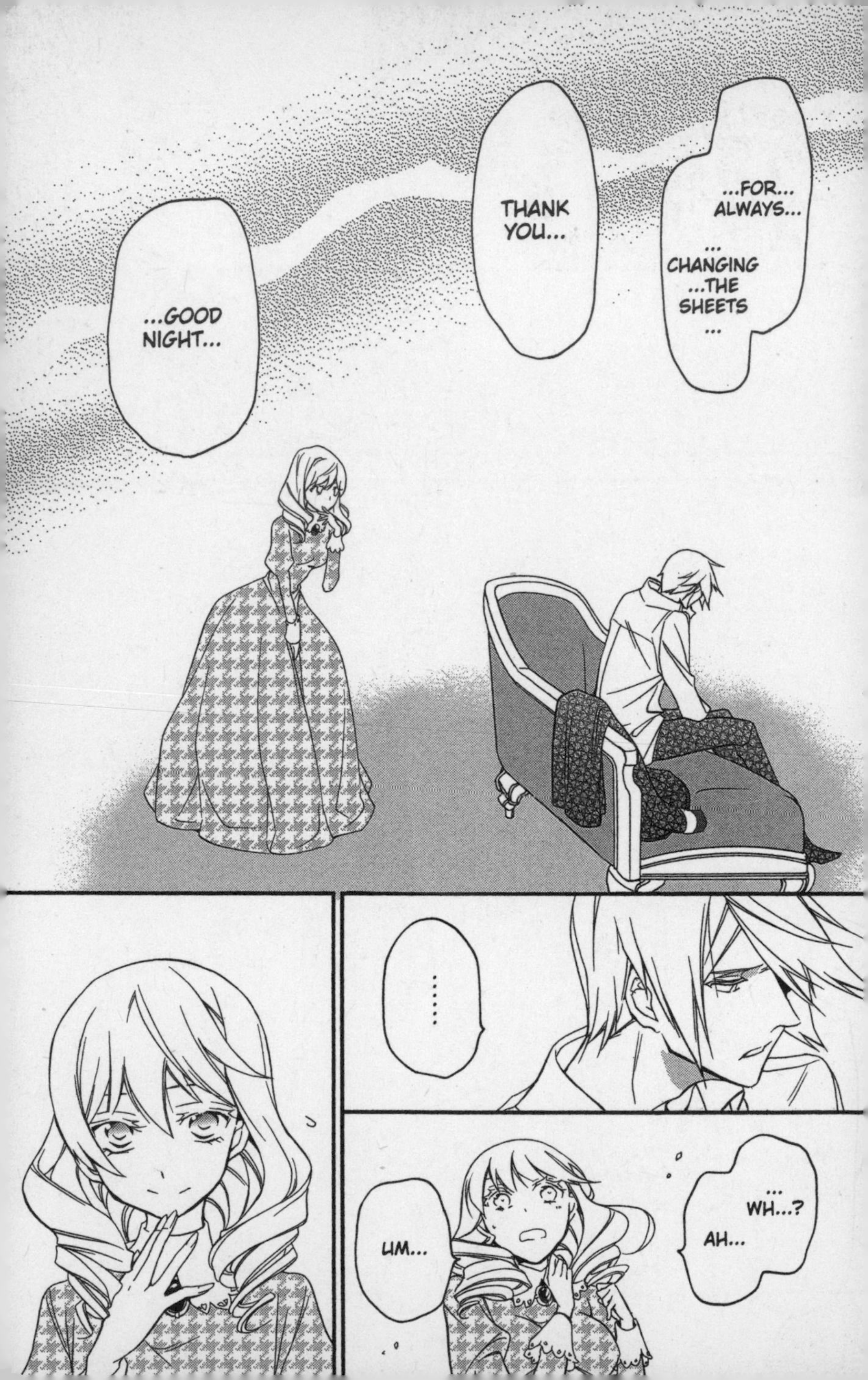
...FOR... ALWAYS... ...CHANGING ...THE SHEETS ...
THANK YOU...
...GOOD NIGHT...
......
... WH...? AH...
UM...

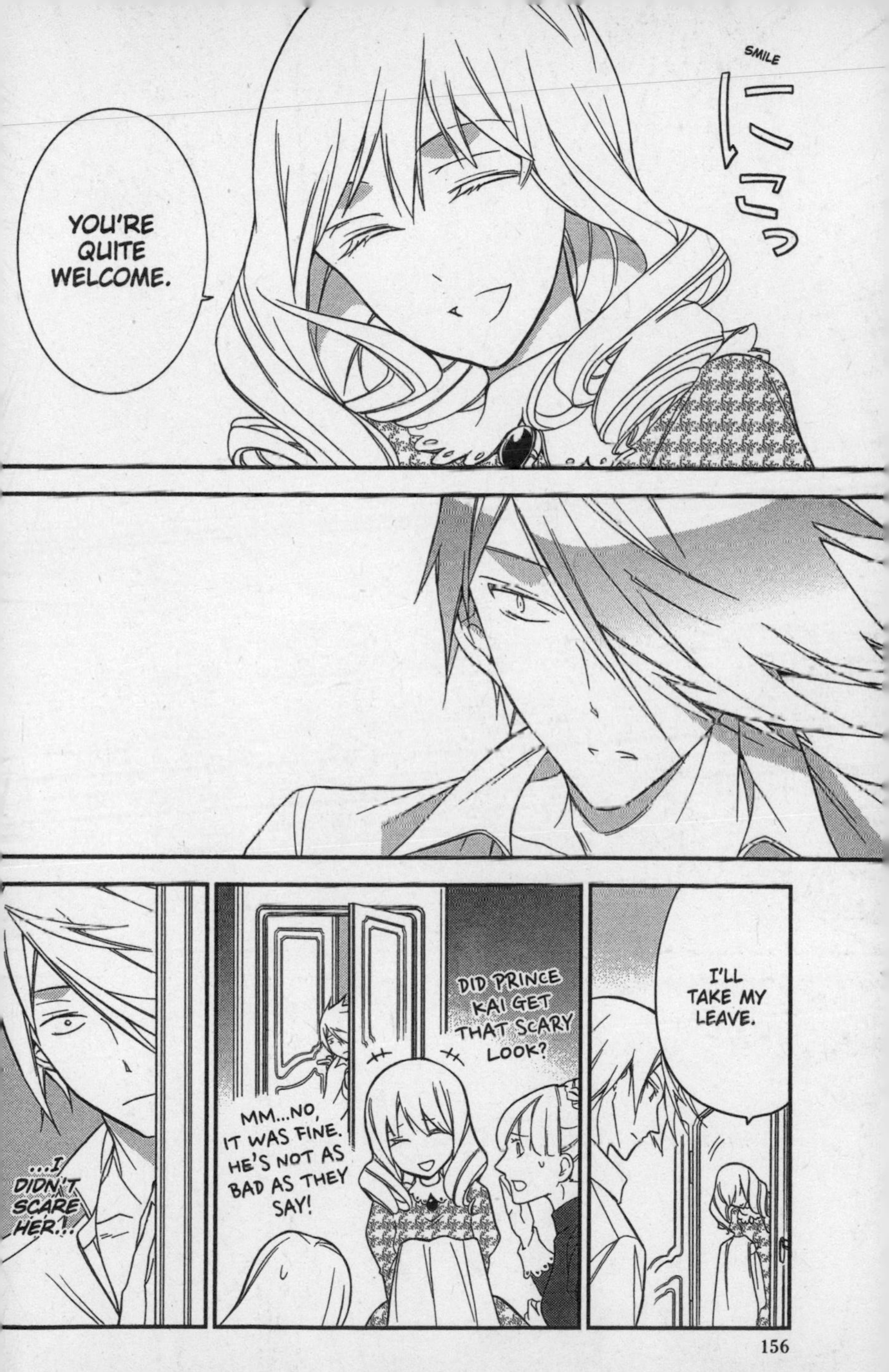
SMILE
YOU'RE QUITE WELCOME.
I'LL TAKE MY LEAVE.
DID PRINCE KAI GET THAT SCARY LOOK?
MM...NO, IT WAS FINE. HE'S NOT AS BAD AS THEY SAY!
...I DIDN'T SCARE HER...!

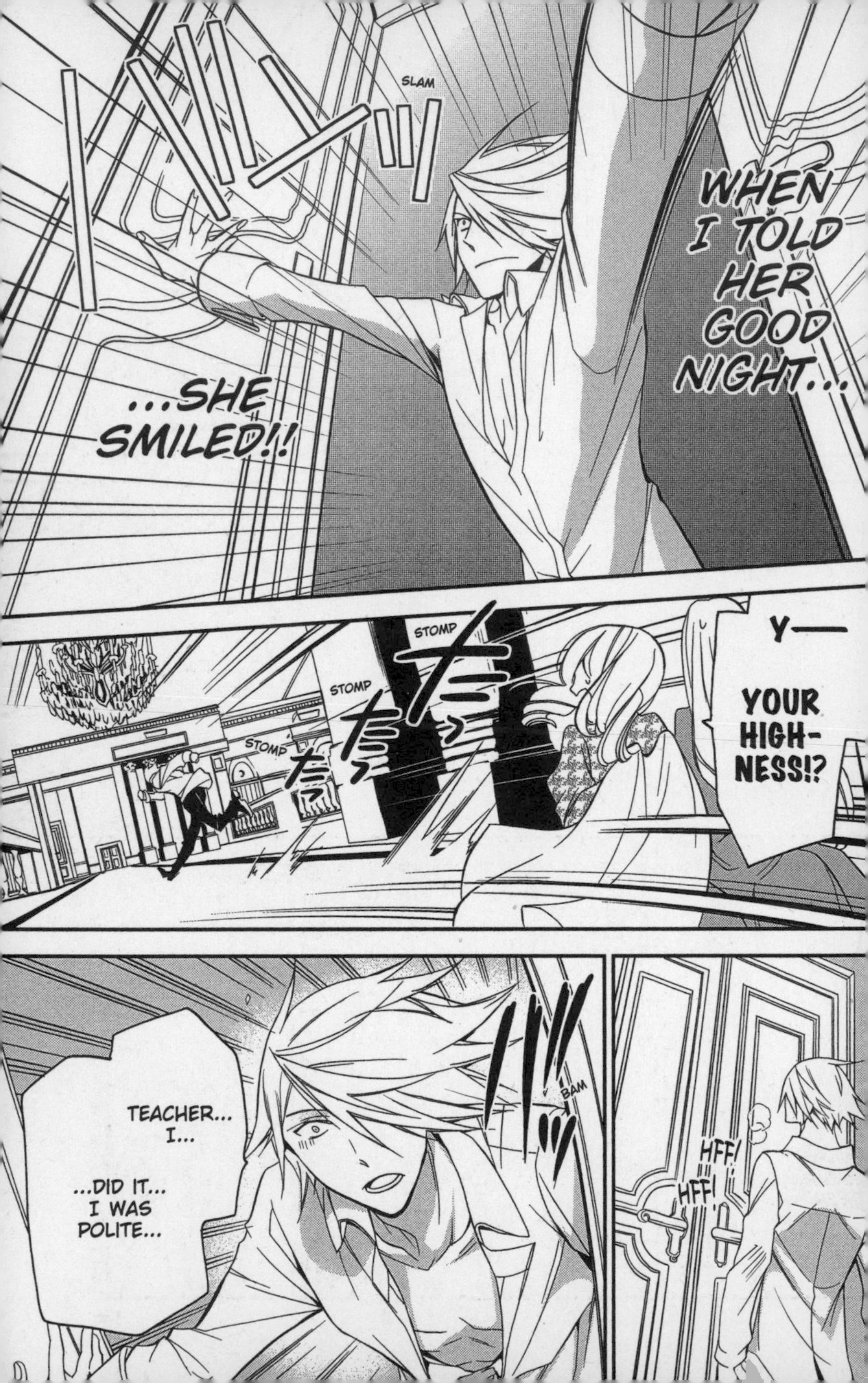
WHEN I TOLD HER GOOD NIGHT...
SLAM
...SHE SMILED!!
Y——
YOUR HIGH-NESS!?
STOMP
STOMP
STOMP
HFF!
HFF!
BAM
TEACHER... I...
...DID IT... I WAS POLITE...

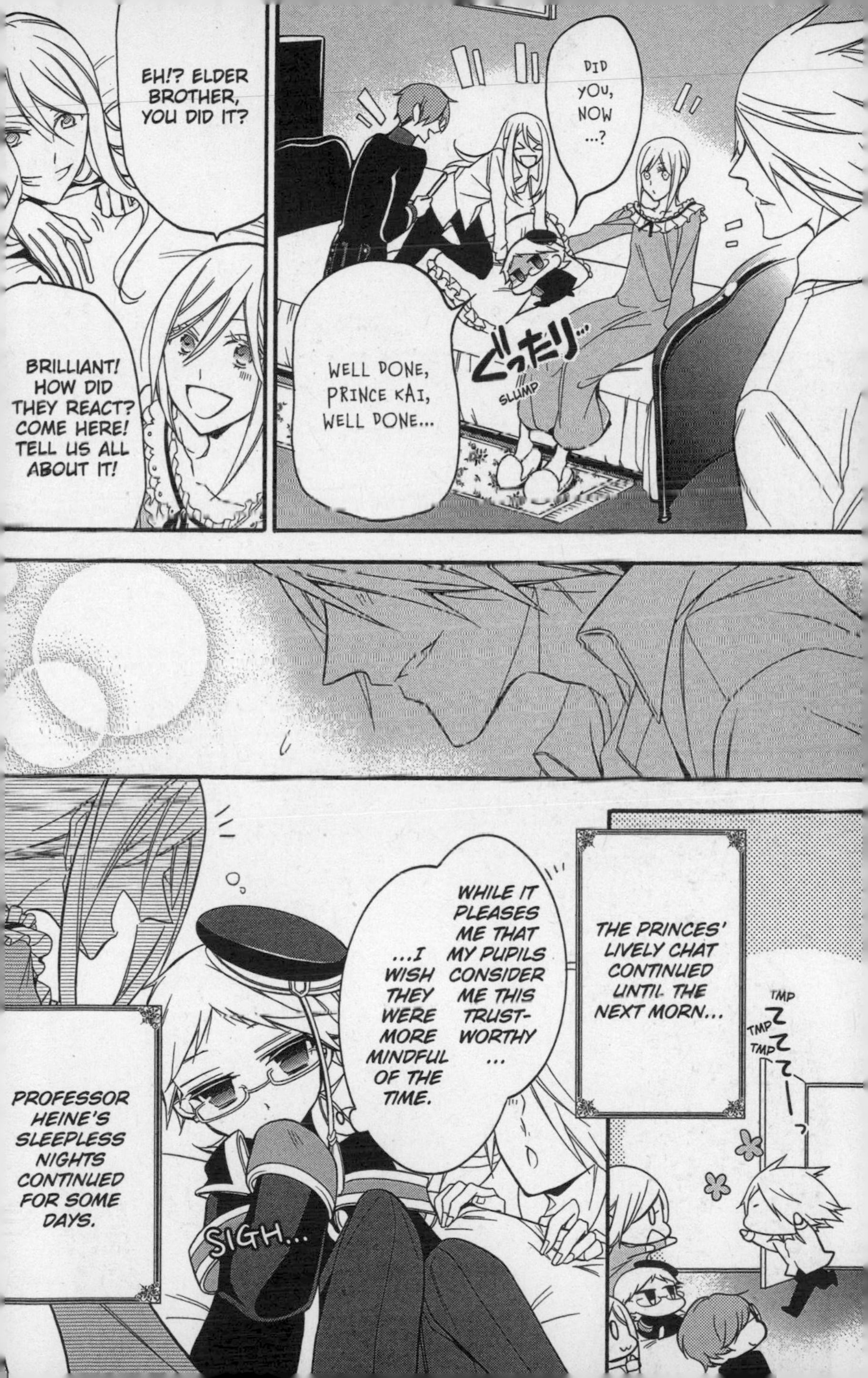
DID YOU, NOW ...?
WELL DONE, PRINCE KAI, WELL DONE...
ぐったり
SLUMP
EH!? ELDER BROTHER, YOU DID IT?
BRILLIANT! HOW DID THEY REACT? COME HERE! TELL US ALL ABOUT IT!
THE PRINCES' LIVELY CHAT CONTINUED UNTIL THE NEXT MORN...
TMP
TMP
TMP
WHILE IT PLEASES ME THAT MY PUPILS CONSIDER ME THIS TRUST-WORTHY ...
...I WISH THEY WERE MORE MINDFUL OF THE TIME.
PROFESSOR HEINE'S SLEEPLESS NIGHTS CONTINUED FOR SOME DAYS.
SIGH...

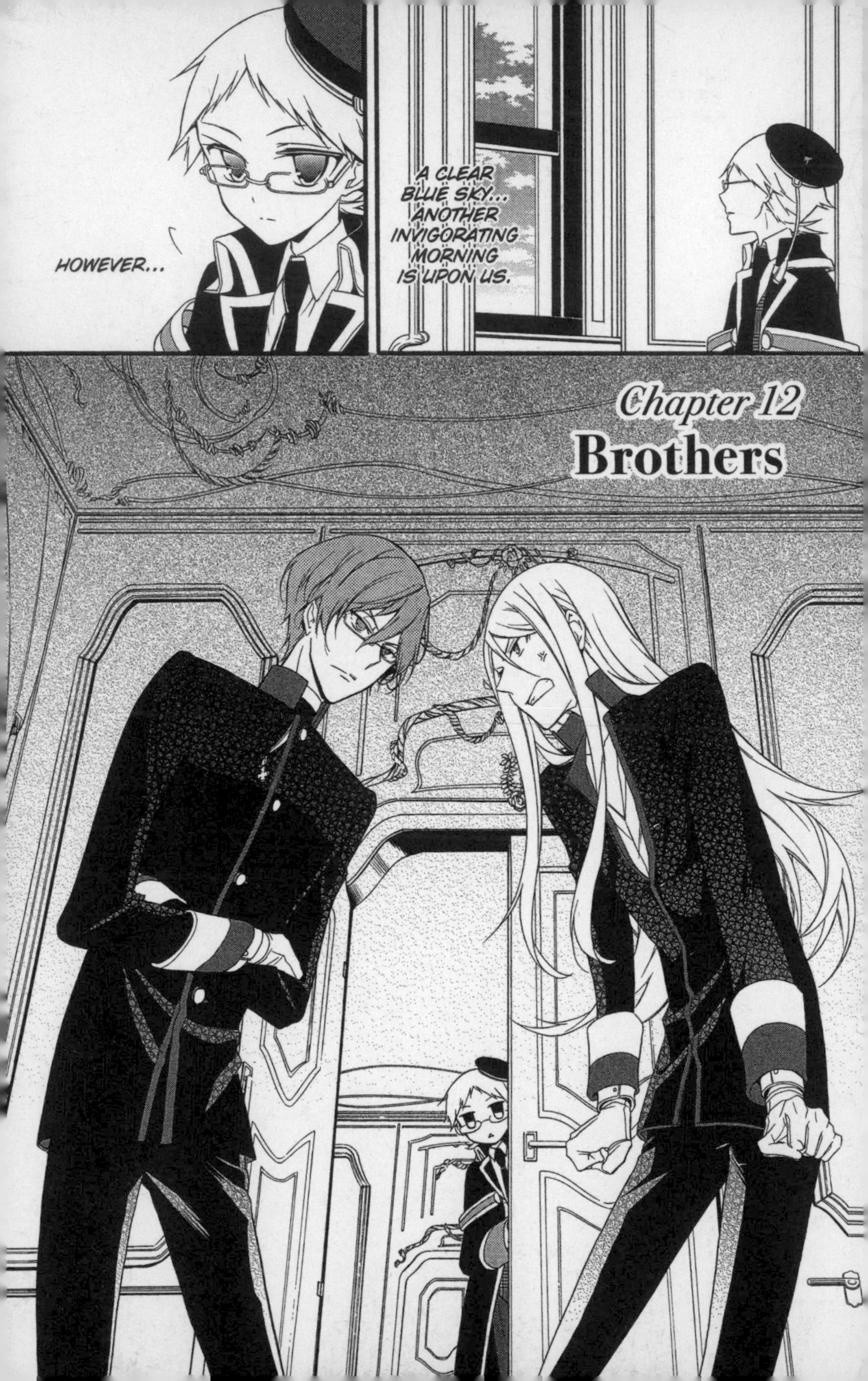
A CLEAR BLUE SKY... ANOTHER INVIGORATING MORNING IS UPON US.
HOWEVER...
Chapter 12
Brothers

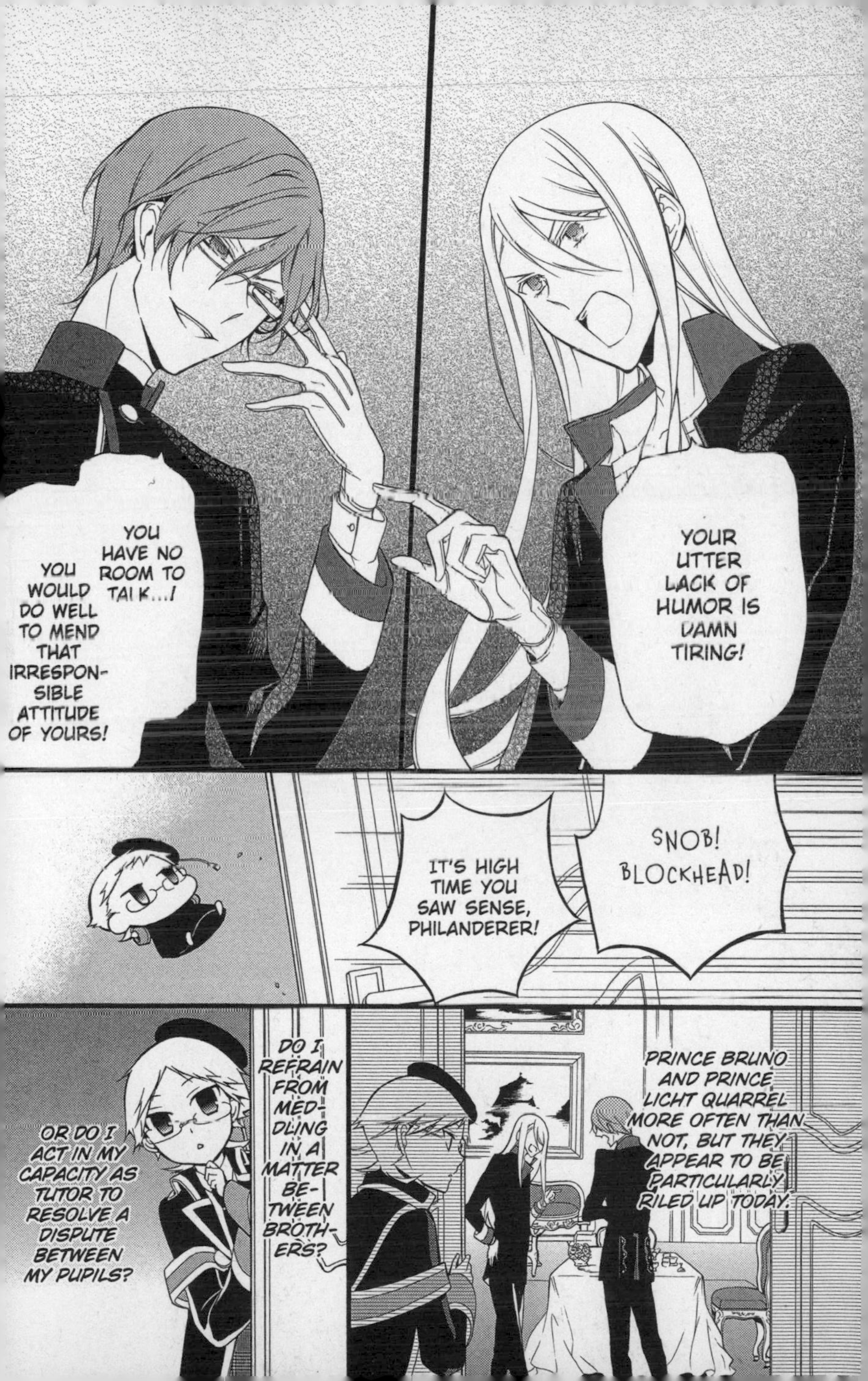
YOUR UTTER LACK OF HUMOR IS DAMN TIRING!
YOU HAVE NO ROOM TO TALK...!
YOU WOULD DO WELL TO MEND THAT IRRESPONSIBLE ATTITUDE OF YOURS!
SNOB! BLOCKHEAD!
IT'S HIGH TIME YOU SAW SENSE, PHILANDERER!
PRINCE BRUNO AND PRINCE LICHT QUARREL MORE OFTEN THAN NOT, BUT THEY APPEAR TO BE PARTICULARLY RILED UP TODAY.
DO I REFRAIN FROM MEDDLING IN A MATTER BETWEEN BROTHERS?
OR DO I ACT IN MY CAPACITY AS TUTOR TO RESOLVE A DISPUTE BETWEEN MY PUPILS?

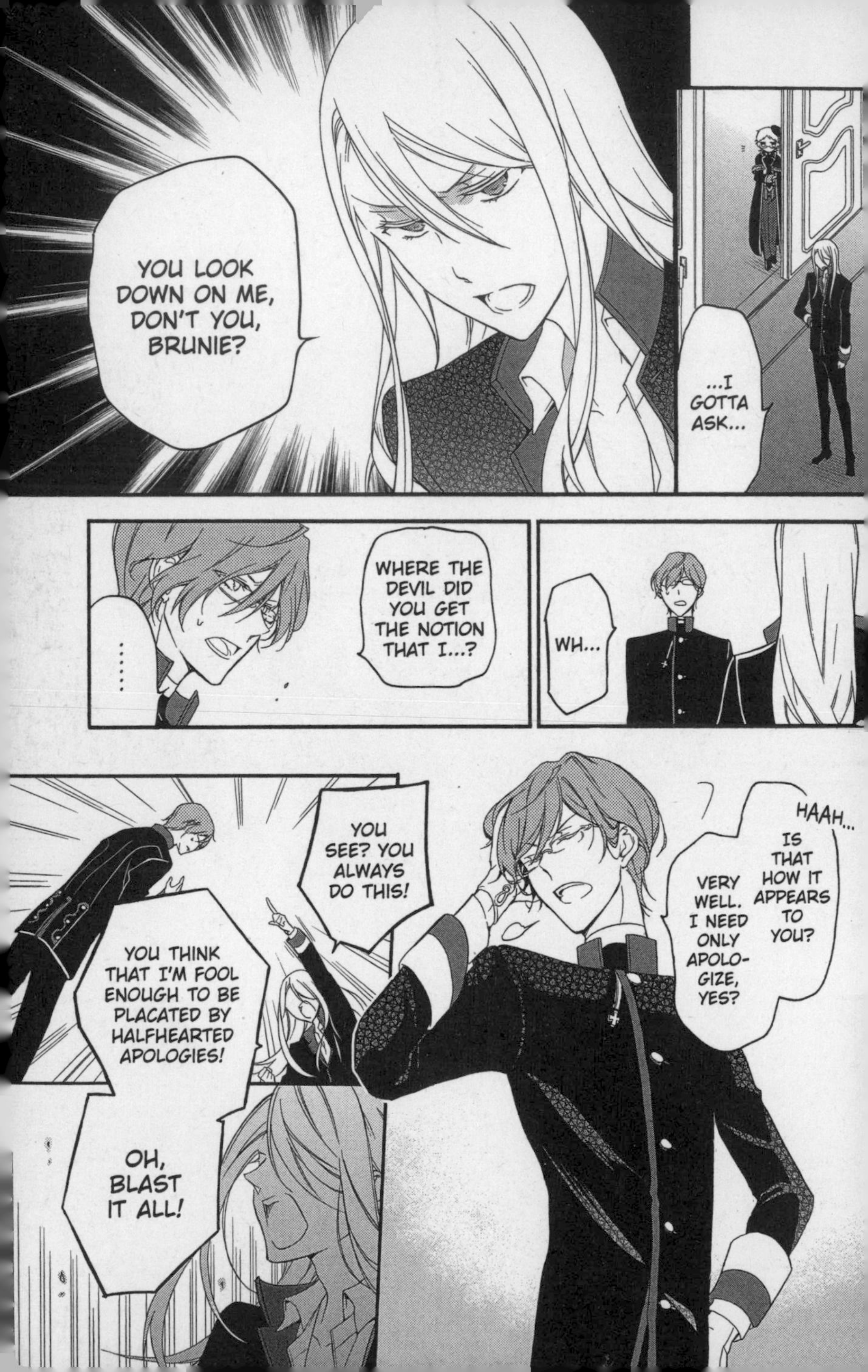
...I GOTTA ASK...
YOU LOOK DOWN ON ME, DON'T YOU, BRUNIE?
WH...
WHERE THE DEVIL DID YOU GET THE NOTION THAT I...?
......
HAAH... IS THAT HOW IT APPEARS TO YOU?
VERY WELL. I NEED ONLY APOLOGIZE, YES?
YOU SEE? YOU ALWAYS DO THIS!
YOU THINK THAT I'M FOOL ENOUGH TO BE PLACATED BY HALFHEARTED APOLOGIES!
OH, BLAST IT ALL!

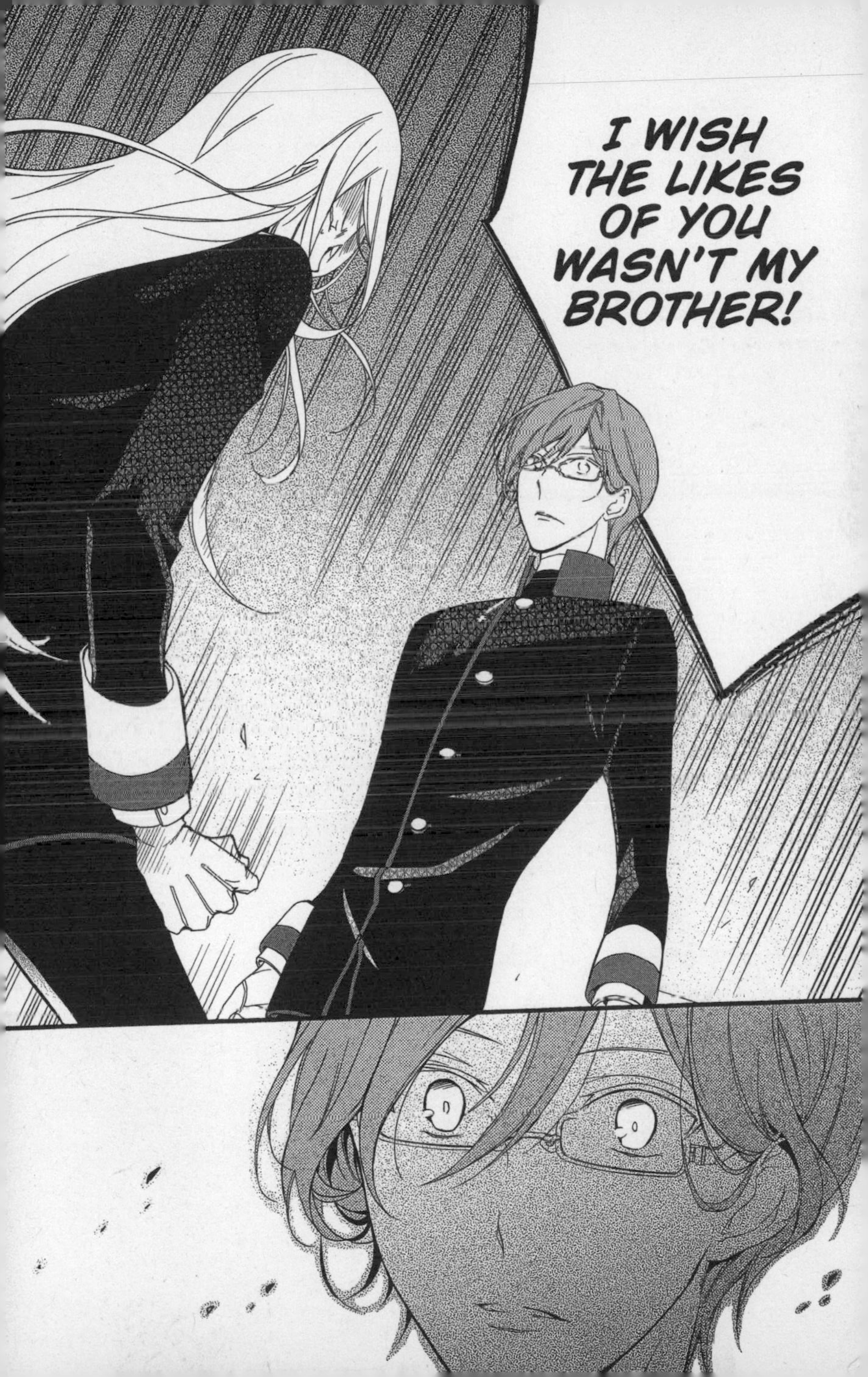
I WISH THE LIKES OF YOU WASN'T MY BROTHER!

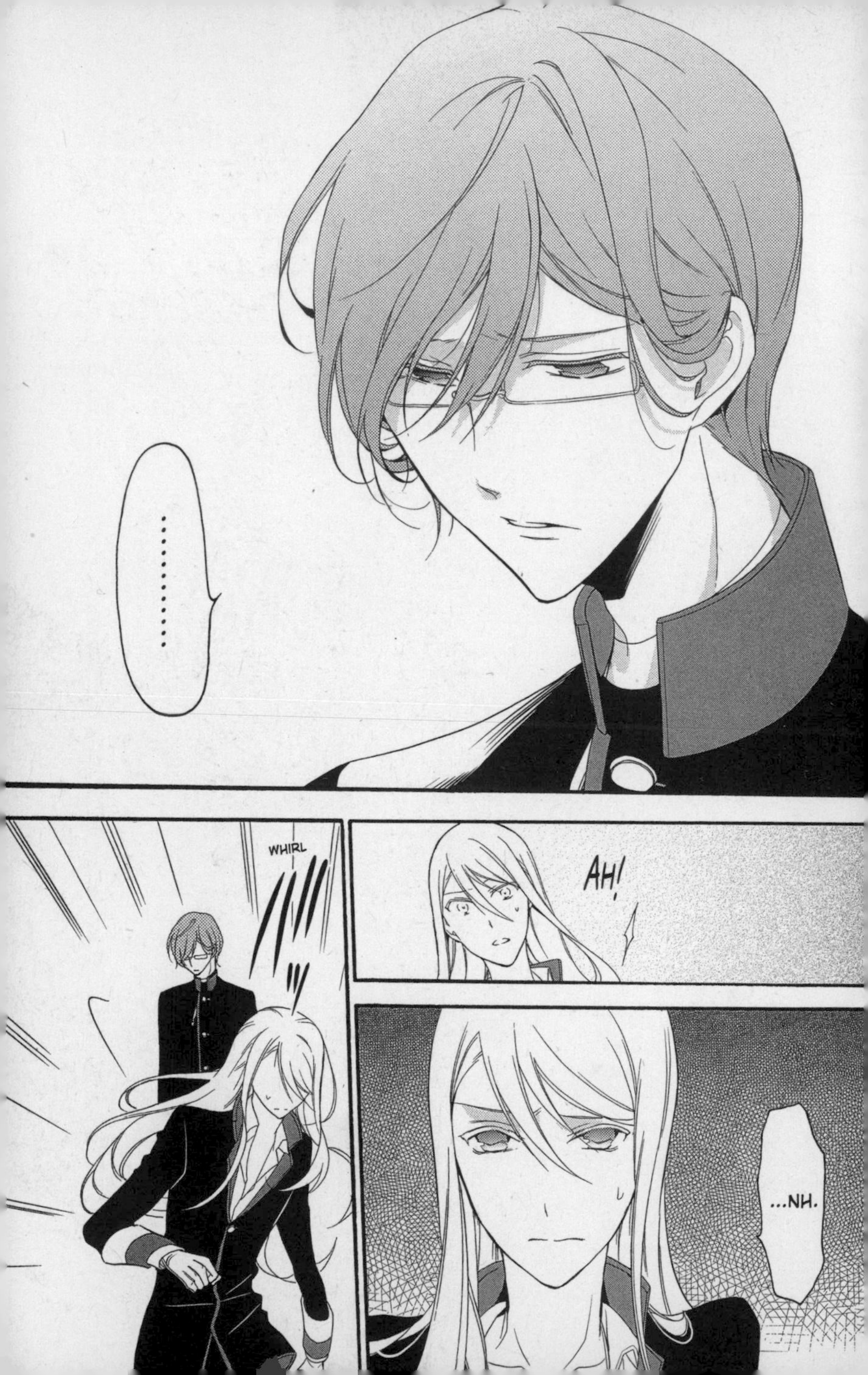
......
AH!
...NH.
WHIRL

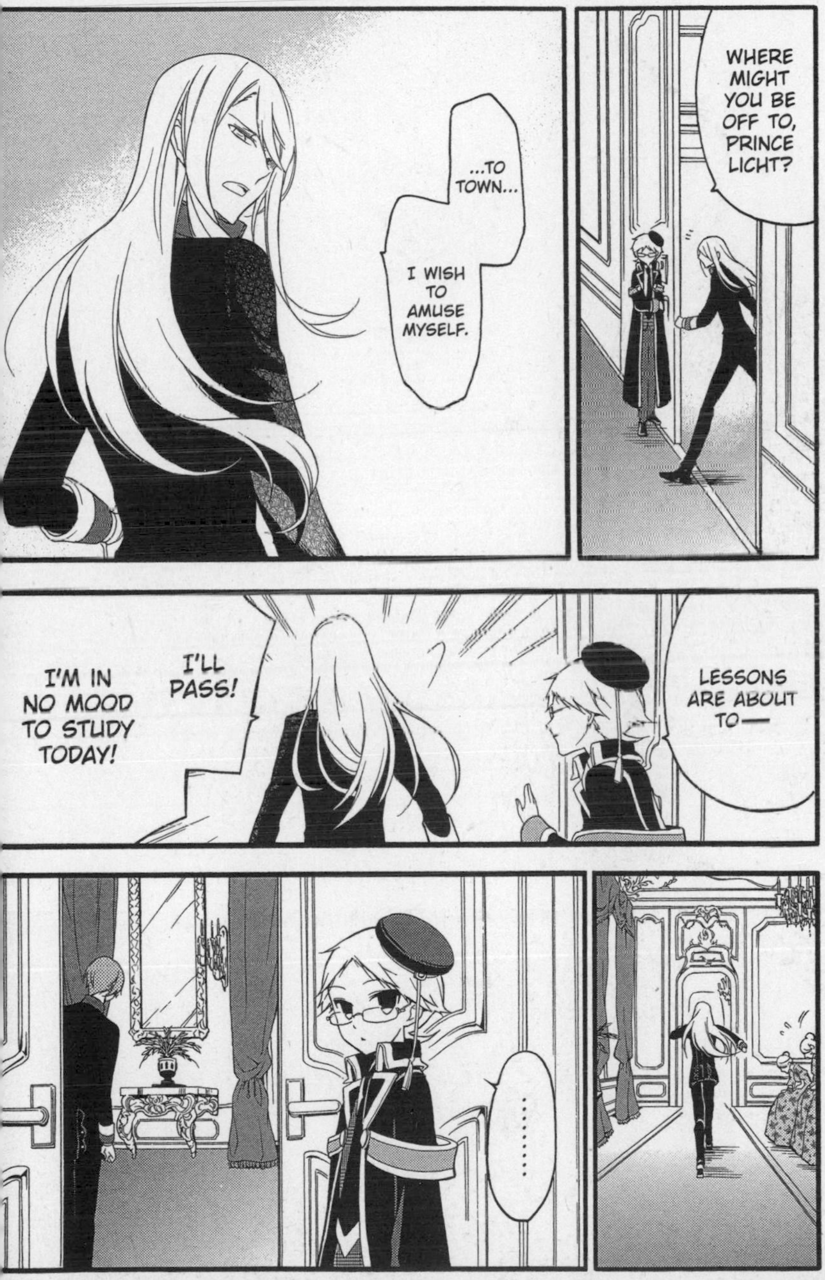

WHERE MIGHT YOU BE OFF TO, PRINCE LICHT?
...TO TOWN...
I WISH TO AMUSE MYSELF.
LESSONS ARE ABOUT TO—
I'LL PASS!
I'M IN NO MOOD TO STUDY TODAY!
......

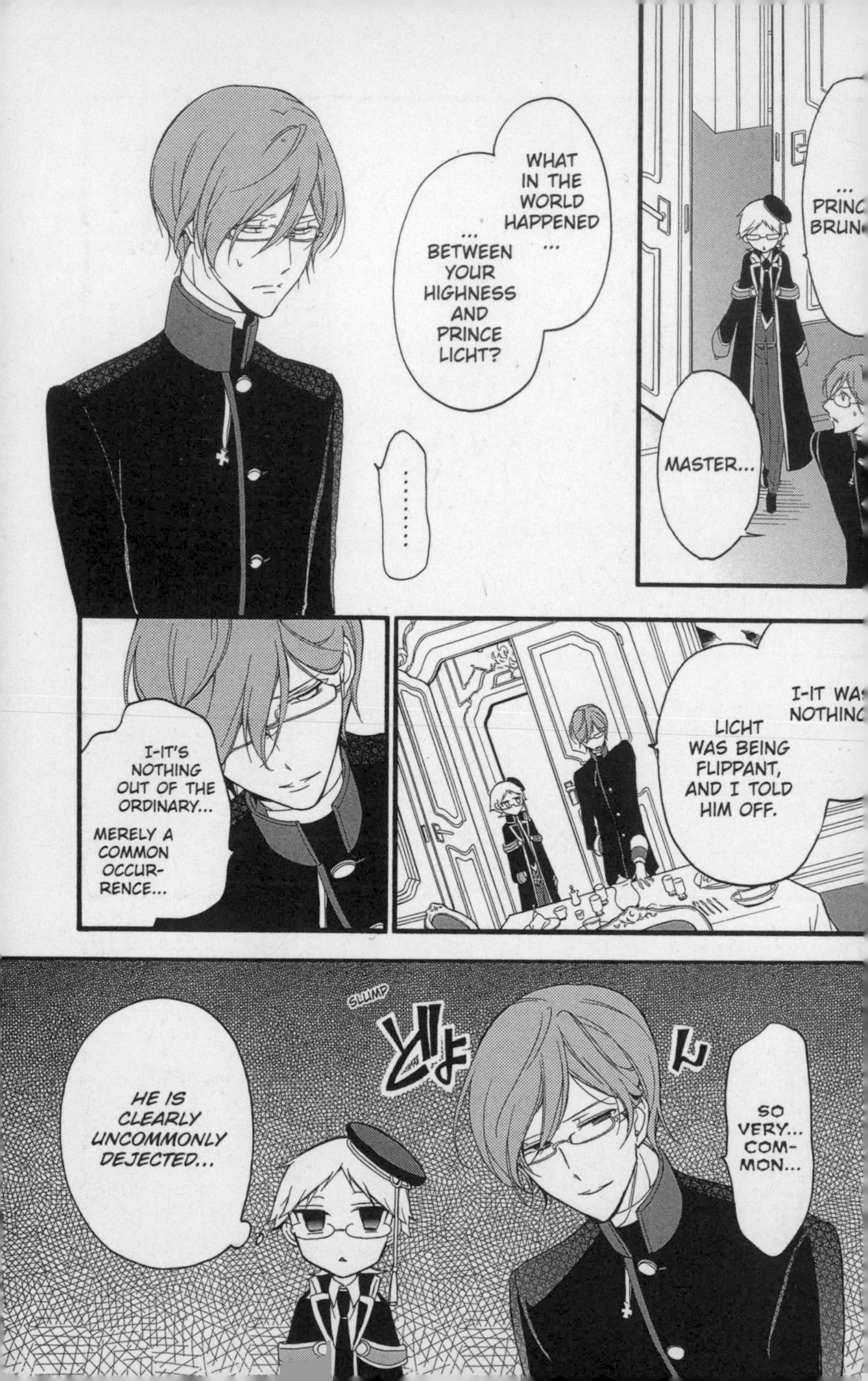
... PRINC BRUN
MASTER...
WHAT IN THE WORLD HAPPENED ... ... BETWEEN YOUR HIGHNESS AND PRINCE LICHT?
......
I-IT WA NOTHIN
LICHT WAS BEING FLIPPANT, AND I TOLD HIM OFF.
I-IT'S NOTHING OUT OF THE ORDINARY...
MERELY A COMMON OCCURRENCE...
SO VERY... COMMON...
SLUMP
どよん
HE IS CLEARLY UNCOMMONLY DEJECTED...

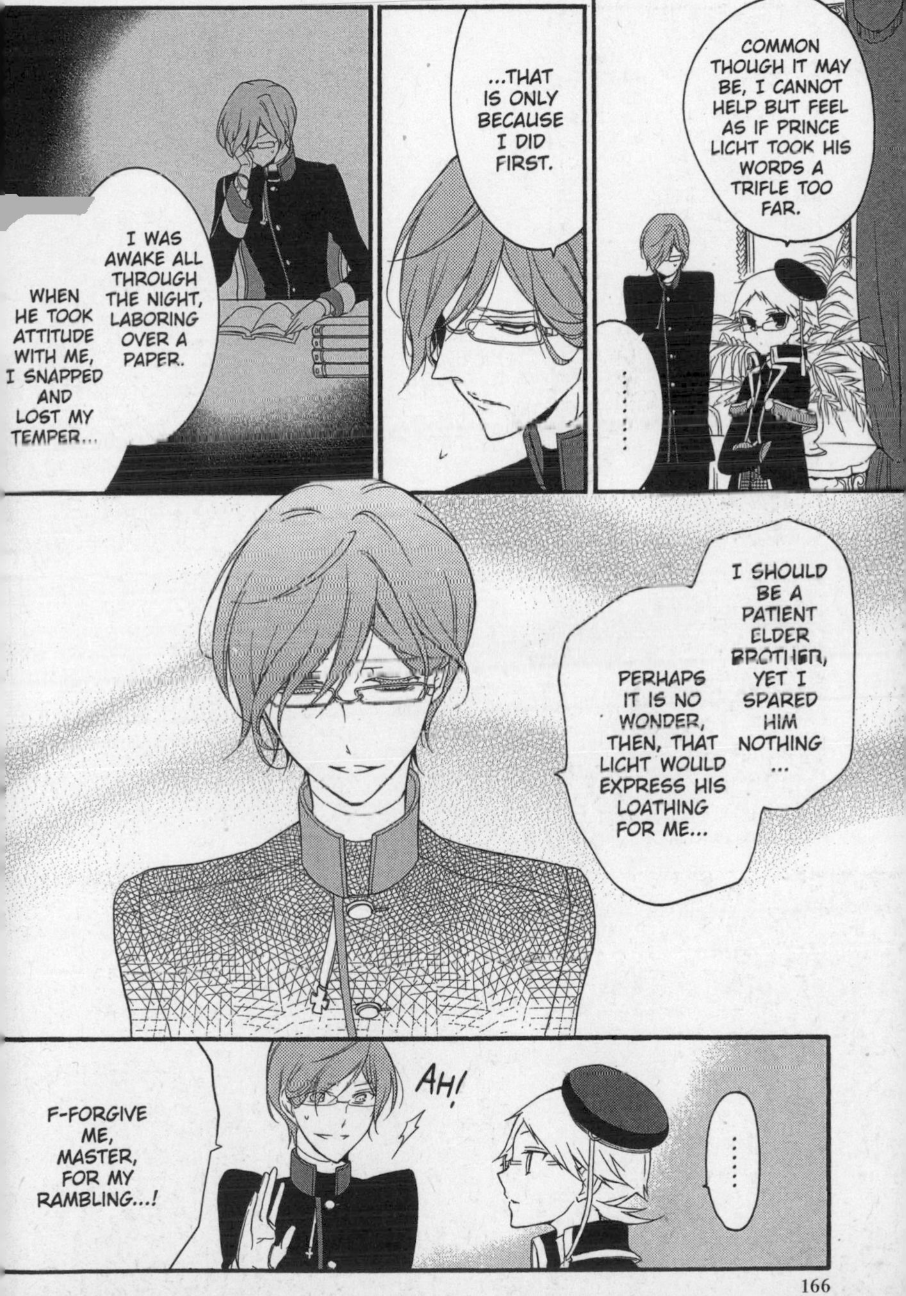
COMMON THOUGH IT MAY BE, I CANNOT HELP BUT FEEL AS IF PRINCE LICHT TOOK HIS WORDS A TRIFLE TOO FAR.
......
...THAT IS ONLY BECAUSE I DID FIRST.
I WAS AWAKE ALL THROUGH THE NIGHT, LABORING OVER A PAPER.
WHEN HE TOOK ATTITUDE WITH ME, I SNAPPED AND LOST MY TEMPER...
I SHOULD BE A PATIENT ELDER BROTHER, YET I SPARED HIM NOTHING...
PERHAPS IT IS NO WONDER, THEN, THAT LICHT WOULD EXPRESS HIS LOATHING FOR ME...
......
AH!
F-FORGIVE ME, MASTER, FOR MY RAMBLING...!

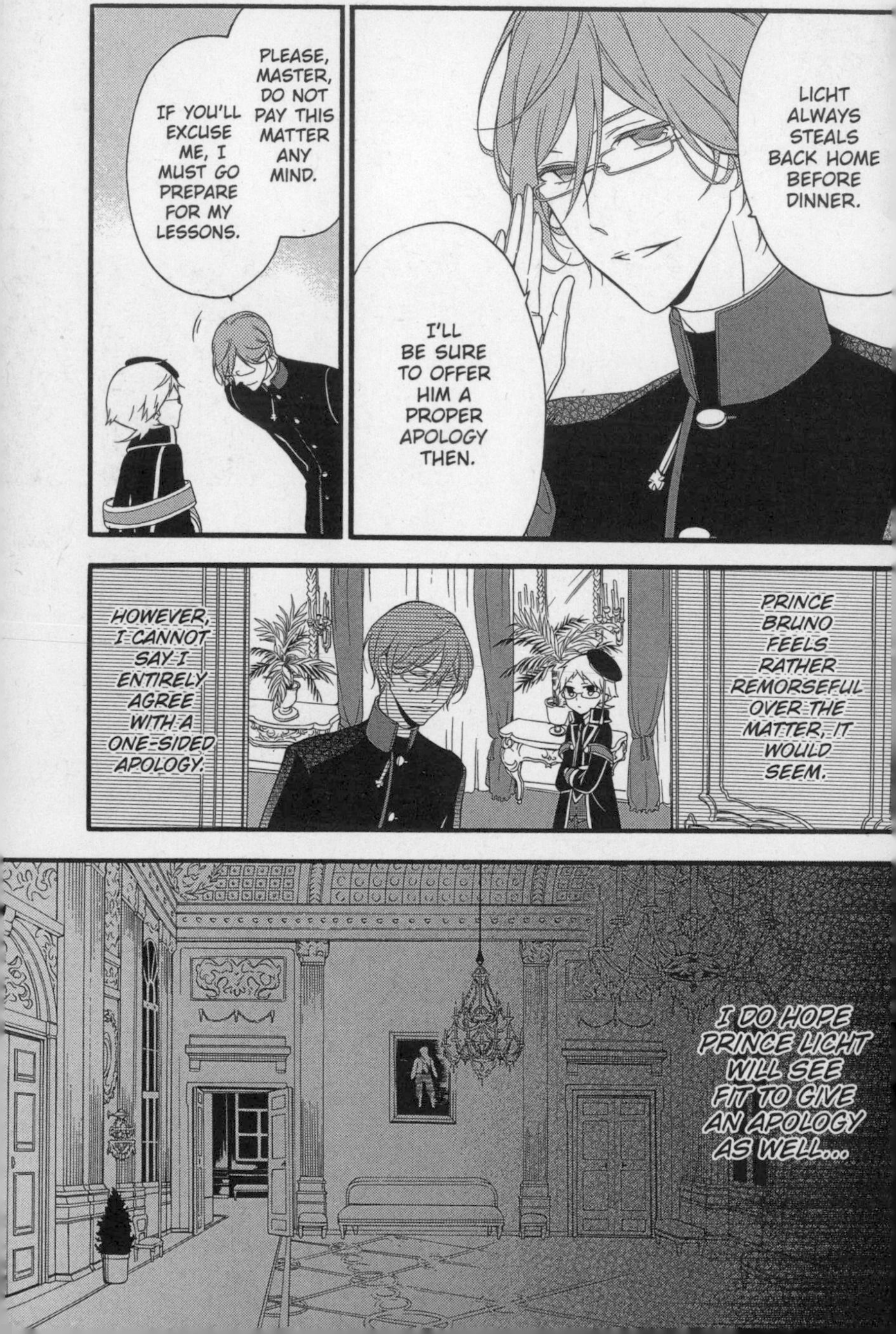
LICHT ALWAYS STEALS BACK HOME BEFORE DINNER.
I'LL BE SURE TO OFFER HIM A PROPER APOLOGY THEN.
PLEASE, MASTER, DO NOT PAY THIS MATTER ANY MIND.
IF YOU'LL EXCUSE ME, I MUST GO PREPARE FOR MY LESSONS.
PRINCE BRUNO FEELS RATHER REMORSEFUL OVER THE MATTER, IT WOULD SEEM.
HOWEVER, I CANNOT SAY I ENTIRELY AGREE WITH A ONE-SIDED APOLOGY.
I DO HOPE PRINCE LICHT WILL SEE FIT TO GIVE AN APOLOGY AS WELL...

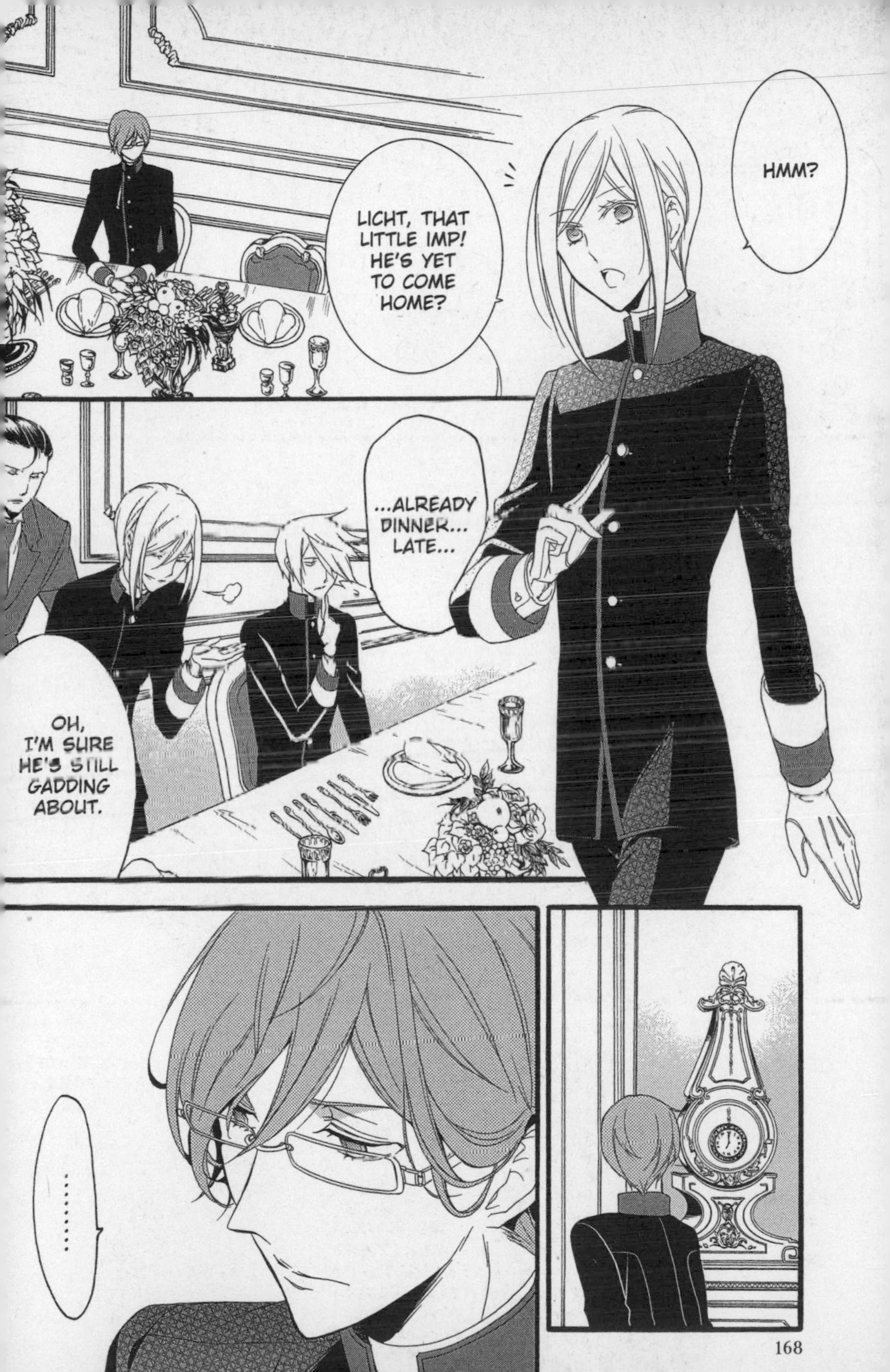
HMM?
LICHT, THAT LITTLE IMP! HE'S YET TO COME HOME?
...ALREADY DINNER... LATE...
OH, I'M SURE HE'S STILL GADDING ABOUT.
......

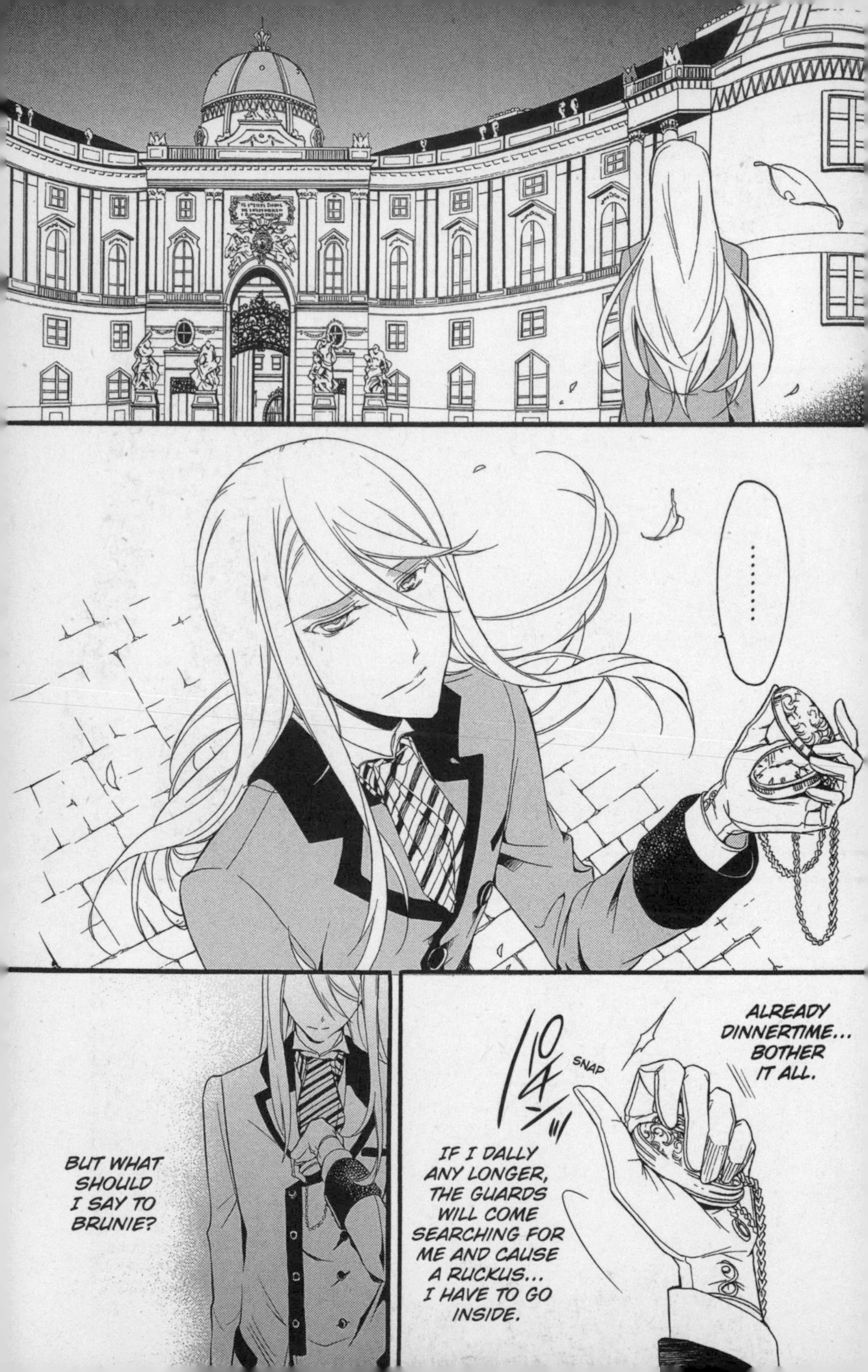
......
ALREADY DINNERTIME... BOTHER IT ALL.
SNAP
IF I DALLY ANY LONGER, THE GUARDS WILL COME SEARCHING FOR ME AND CAUSE A RUCKUS... I HAVE TO GO INSIDE.
BUT WHAT SHOULD I SAY TO BRUNIE?

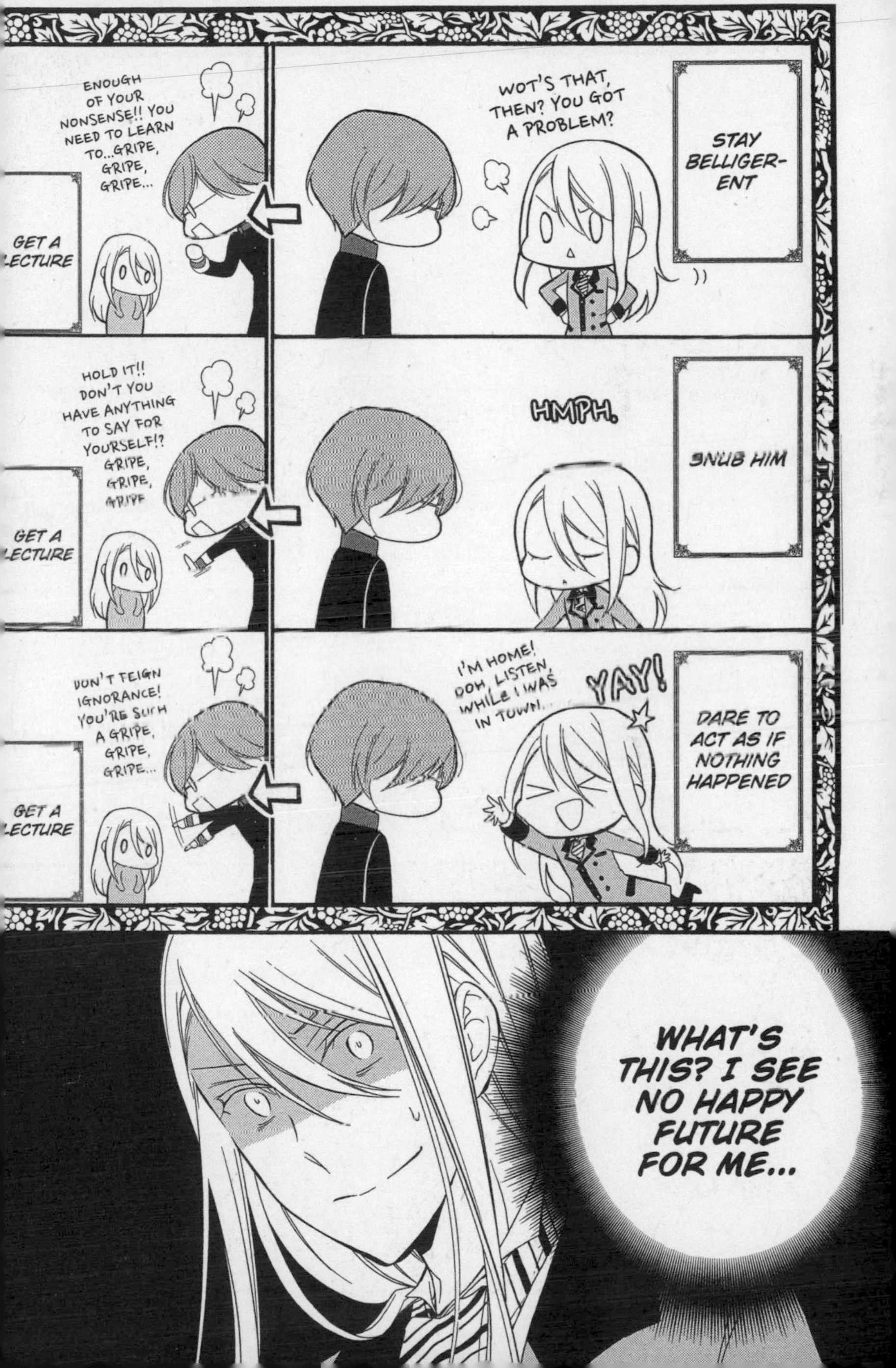

STAY BELLIGERENT
WOT'S THAT, THEN? YOU GOT A PROBLEM?
ENOUGH OF YOUR NONSENSE!! YOU NEED TO LEARN TO...GRIPE, GRIPE, GRIPE...
GET A LECTURE
SNUB HIM
HMPH.
HOLD IT!! DON'T YOU HAVE ANYTHING TO SAY FOR YOURSELF!? GRIPE, GRIPE, GRIPE
GET A LECTURE
DARE TO ACT AS IF NOTHING HAPPENED
YAY!
I'M HOME! OOH, LISTEN, WHILE I WAS IN TOWN...
DON'T FEIGN IGNORANCE! YOU'RE SUCH A GRIPE, GRIPE, GRIPE...
GET A LECTURE
WHAT'S THIS? I SEE NO HAPPY FUTURE FOR ME...

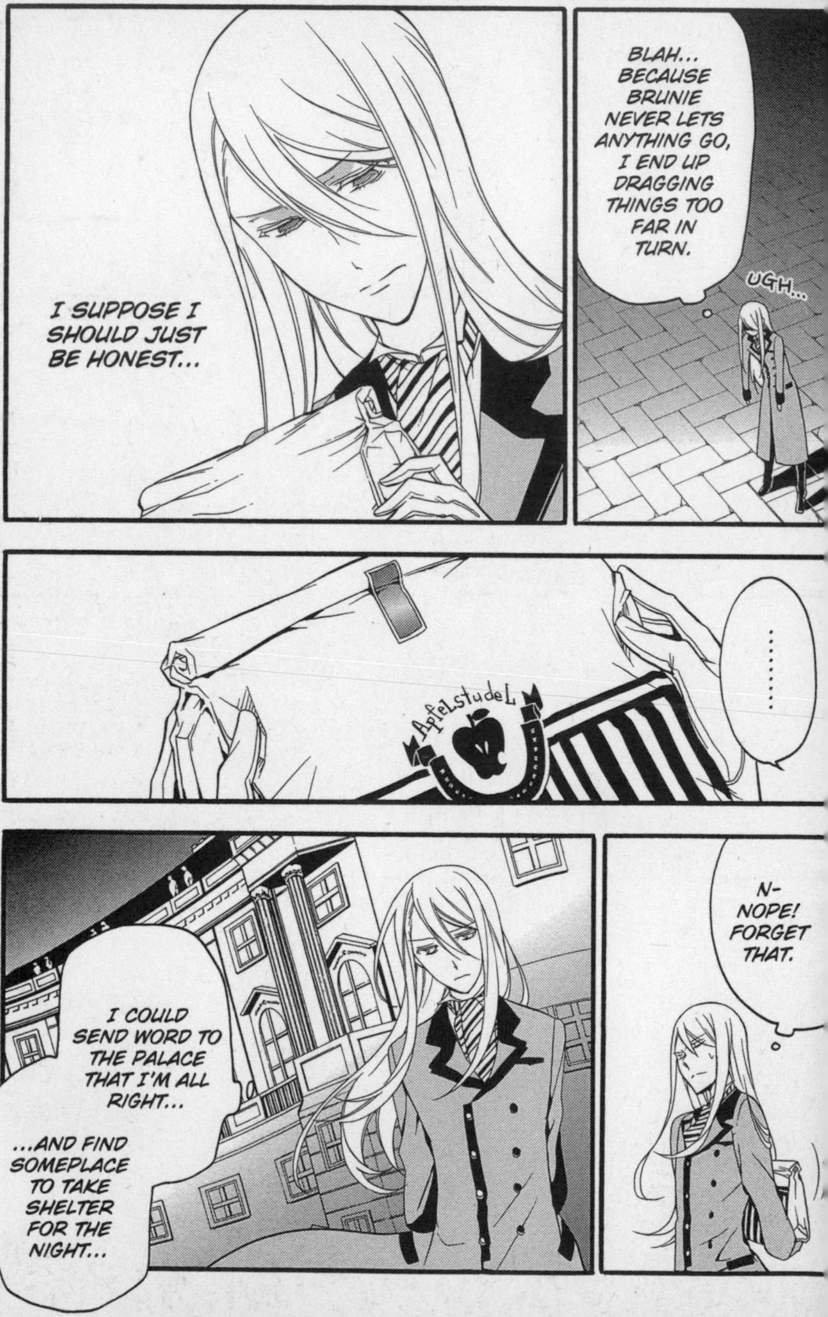
BLAH... BECAUSE BRUNIE NEVER LETS ANYTHING GO, I END UP DRAGGING THINGS TOO FAR IN TURN.
UGH...
I SUPPOSE I SHOULD JUST BE HONEST...
....
Apfelstudel
N- NOPE! FORGET THAT.
I COULD SEND WORD TO THE PALACE THAT I'M ALL RIGHT...
...AND FIND SOMEPLACE TO TAKE SHELTER FOR THE NIGHT...

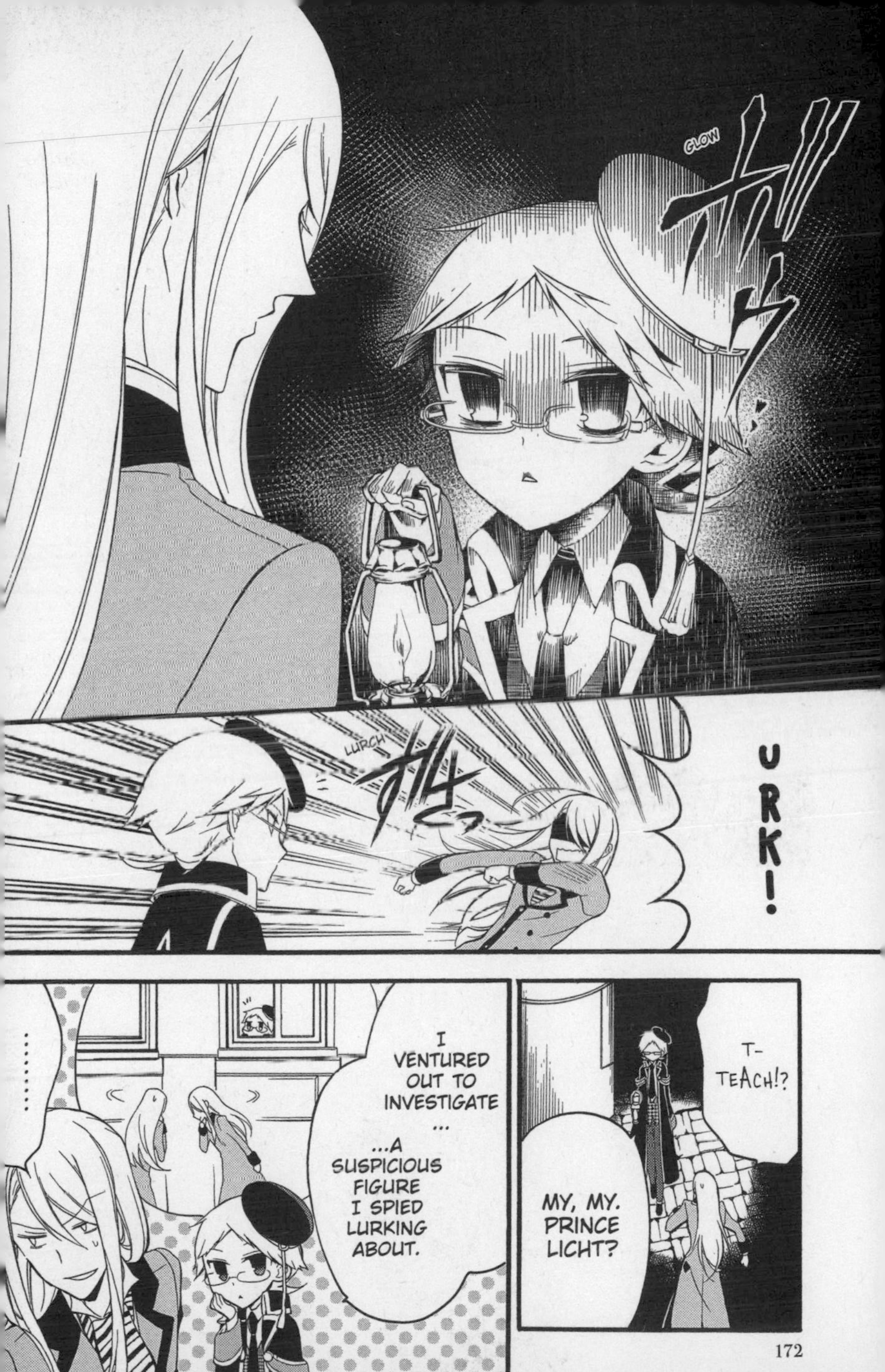
GLOW
URK!
LURCH
T-TEACH!?
MY, MY. PRINCE LICHT?
I VENTURED OUT TO INVESTIGATE ...
...A SUSPICIOUS FIGURE I SPIED LURKING ABOUT.
......

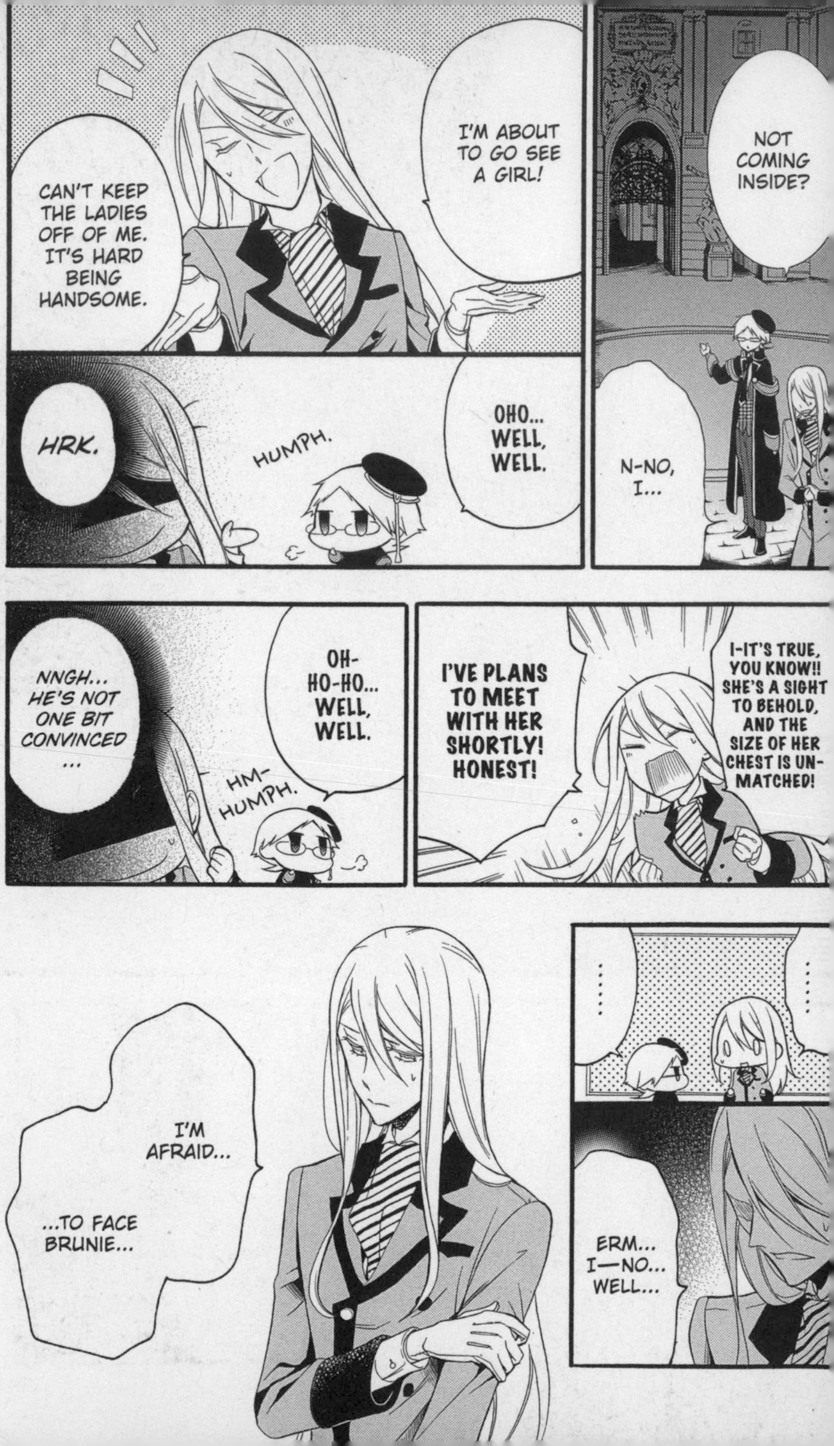
NOT COMING INSIDE?
N-NO, I...
I'M ABOUT TO GO SEE A GIRL!
CAN'T KEEP THE LADIES OFF OF ME. IT'S HARD BEING HANDSOME.
OHO... WELL, WELL.
HUMPH.
HRK.
I-IT'S TRUE, YOU KNOW!! SHE'S A SIGHT TO BEHOLD, AND THE SIZE OF HER CHEST IS UN-MATCHED!
I'VE PLANS TO MEET WITH HER SHORTLY! HONEST!
OH-HO-HO... WELL, WELL.
HM-HUMPH.
NNGH... HE'S NOT ONE BIT CONVINCED ...
......
......
ERM... I—NO... WELL...
I'M AFRAID...
...TO FACE BRUNIE...

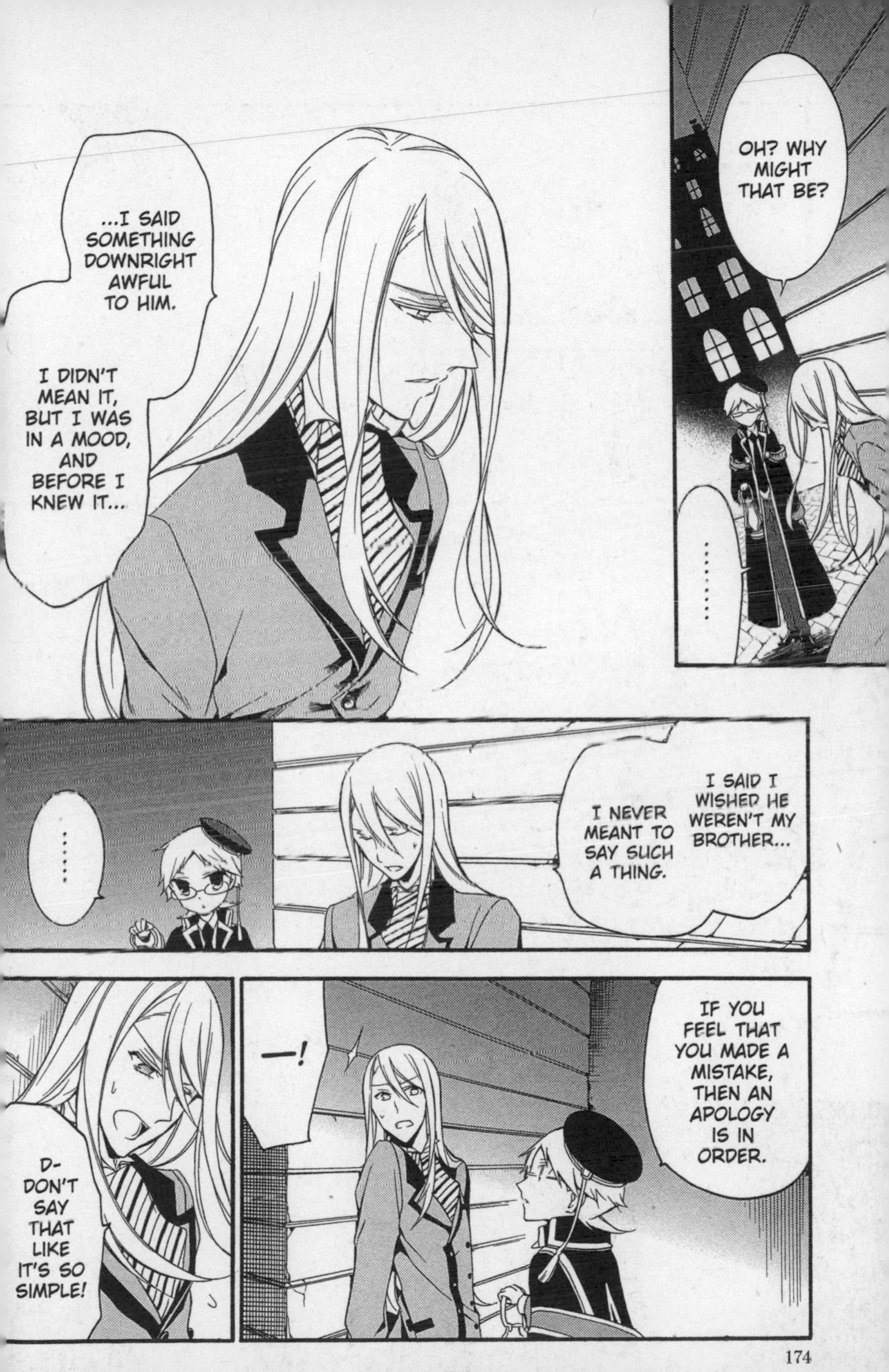
OH? WHY MIGHT THAT BE?
......
...I SAID SOMETHING DOWNRIGHT AWFUL TO HIM.
I DIDN'T MEAN IT, BUT I WAS IN A MOOD, AND BEFORE I KNEW IT...
I SAID I WISHED HE WEREN'T MY BROTHER...
I NEVER MEANT TO SAY SUCH A THING.
......
IF YOU FEEL THAT YOU MADE A MISTAKE, THEN AN APOLOGY IS IN ORDER.
—!
D-DON'T SAY THAT LIKE IT'S SO SIMPLE!

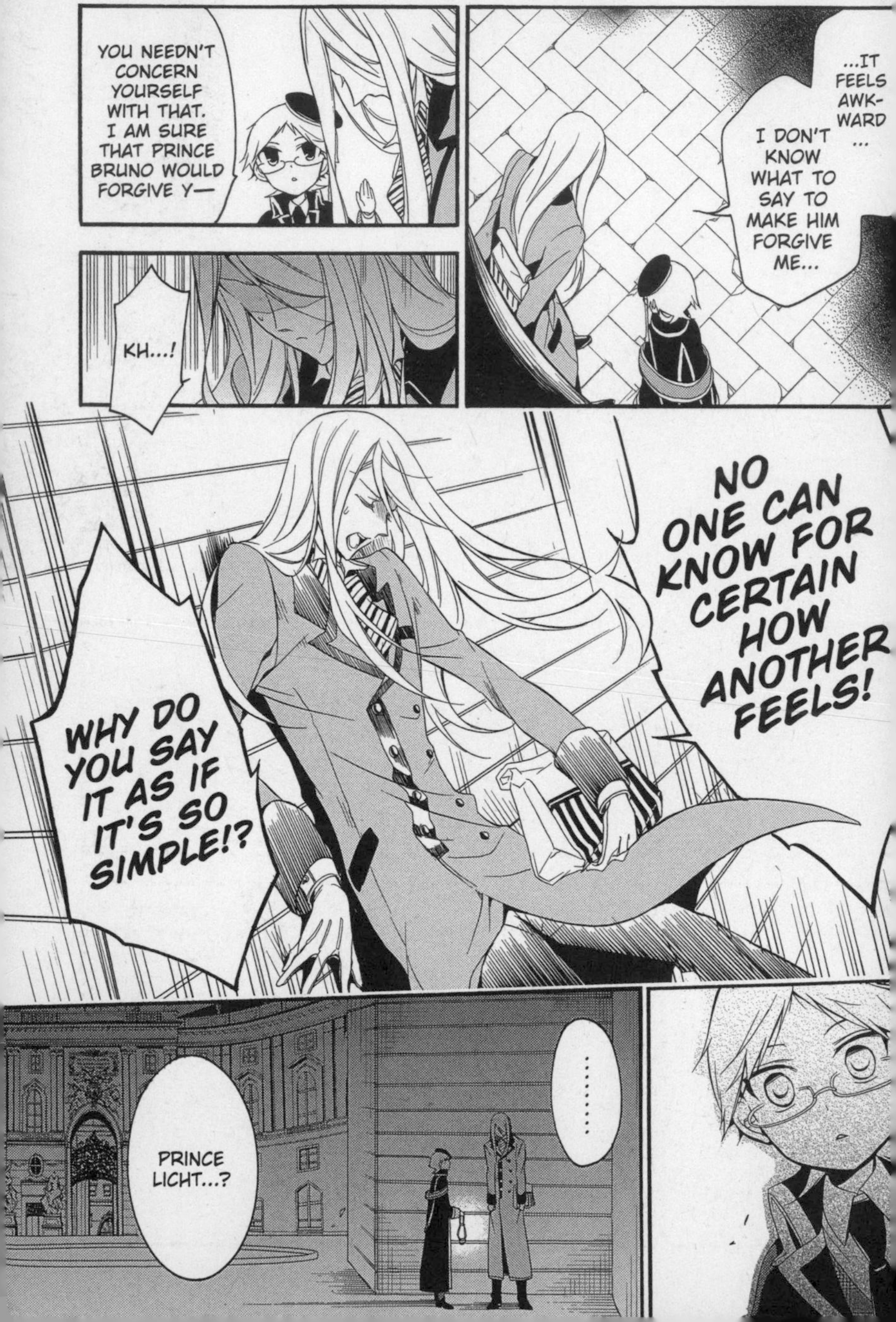
...IT FEELS AWKWARD...
I DON'T KNOW WHAT TO SAY TO MAKE HIM FORGIVE ME...
YOU NEEDN'T CONCERN YOURSELF WITH THAT. I AM SURE THAT PRINCE BRUNO WOULD FORGIVE Y—
KH...!
NO ONE CAN KNOW FOR CERTAIN HOW ANOTHER FEELS!
WHY DO YOU SAY IT AS IF IT'S SO SIMPLE!?
......
PRINCE LICHT...?

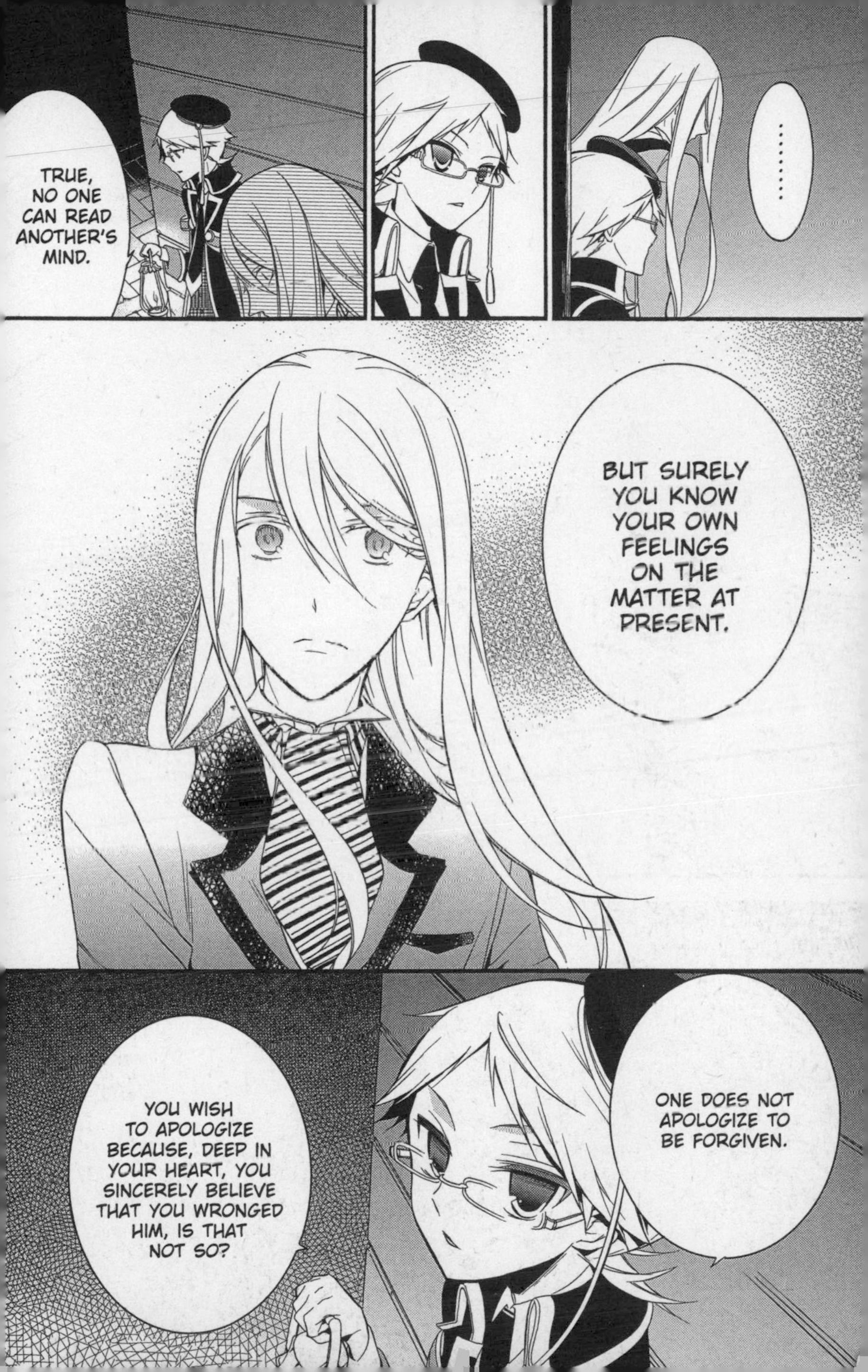
......
TRUE, NO ONE CAN READ ANOTHER'S MIND.
BUT SURELY YOU KNOW YOUR OWN FEELINGS ON THE MATTER AT PRESENT.
ONE DOES NOT APOLOGIZE TO BE FORGIVEN.
YOU WISH TO APOLOGIZE BECAUSE, DEEP IN YOUR HEART, YOU SINCERELY BELIEVE THAT YOU WRONGED HIM, IS THAT NOT SO?

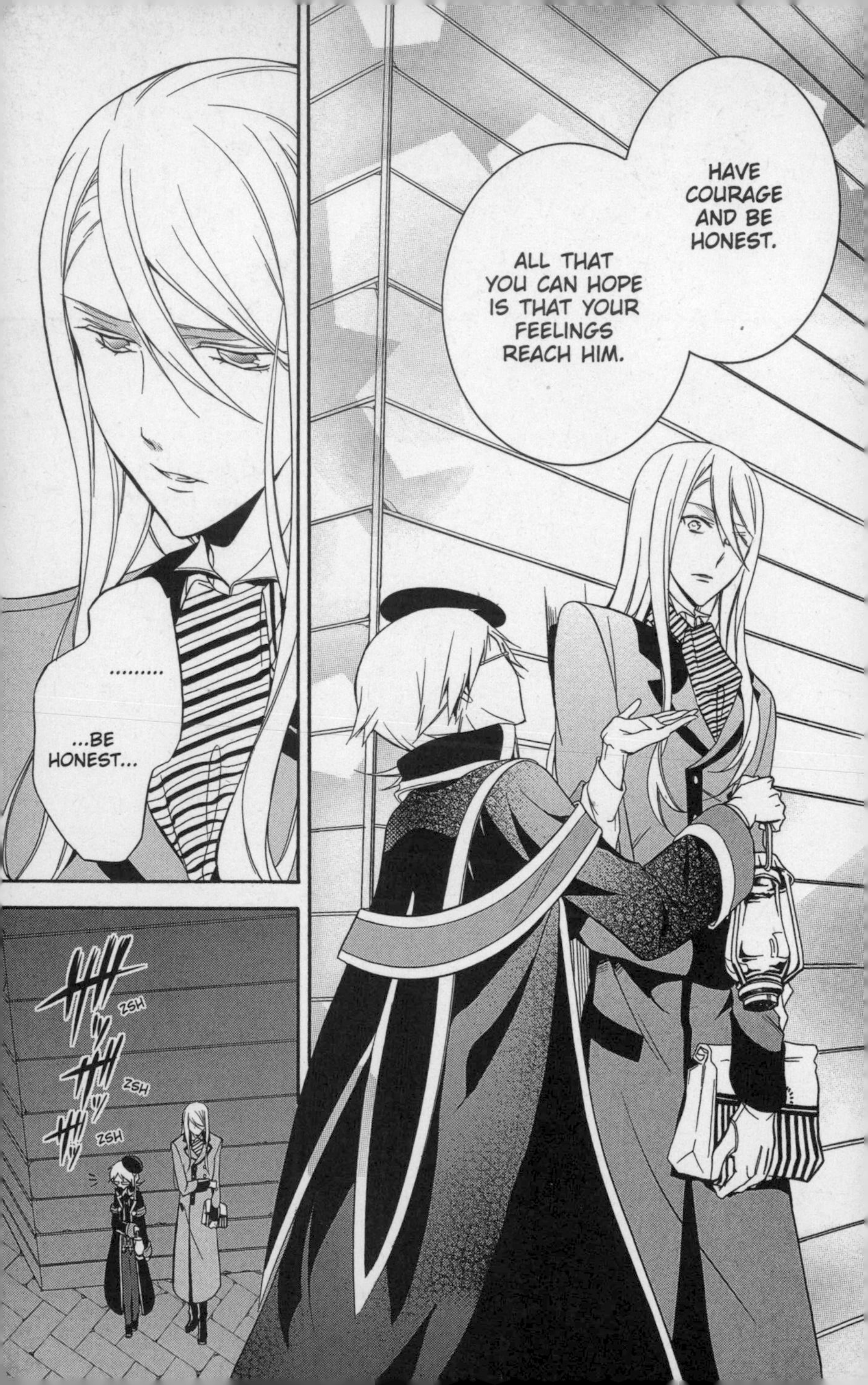
HAVE COURAGE AND BE HONEST.
ALL THAT YOU CAN HOPE IS THAT YOUR FEELINGS REACH HIM.
....
...BE HONEST...
ZSH
ZSH
ZSH

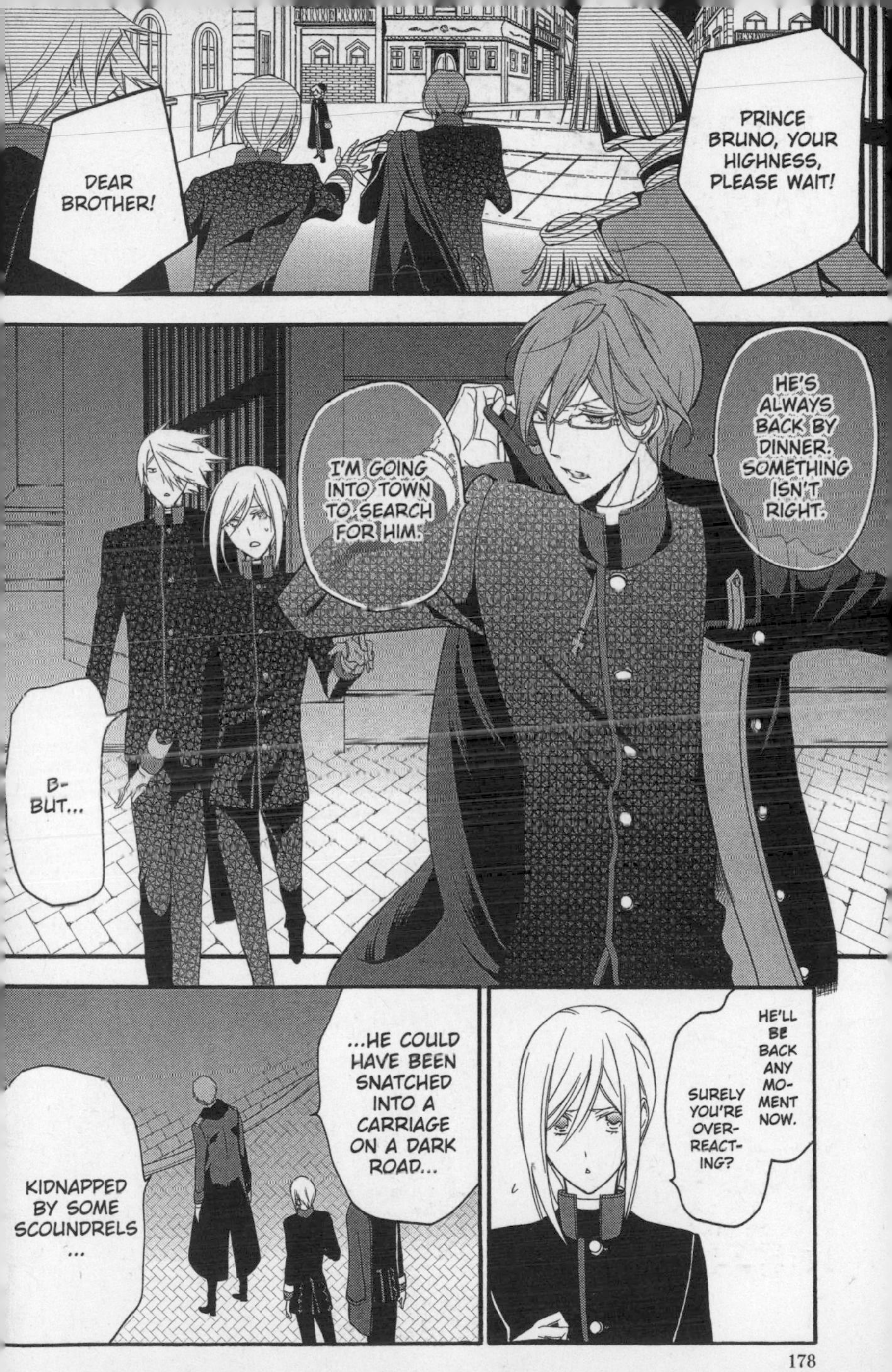
PRINCE BRUNO, YOUR HIGHNESS, PLEASE WAIT!
DEAR BROTHER!
HE'S ALWAYS BACK BY DINNER. SOMETHING ISN'T RIGHT.
I'M GOING INTO TOWN TO SEARCH FOR HIM.
B-BUT...
HE'LL BE BACK ANY MO-MENT NOW.
SURELY YOU'RE OVER-REACT-ING?
...HE COULD HAVE BEEN SNATCHED INTO A CARRIAGE ON A DARK ROAD...
KIDNAPPED BY SOME SCOUNDRELS ...

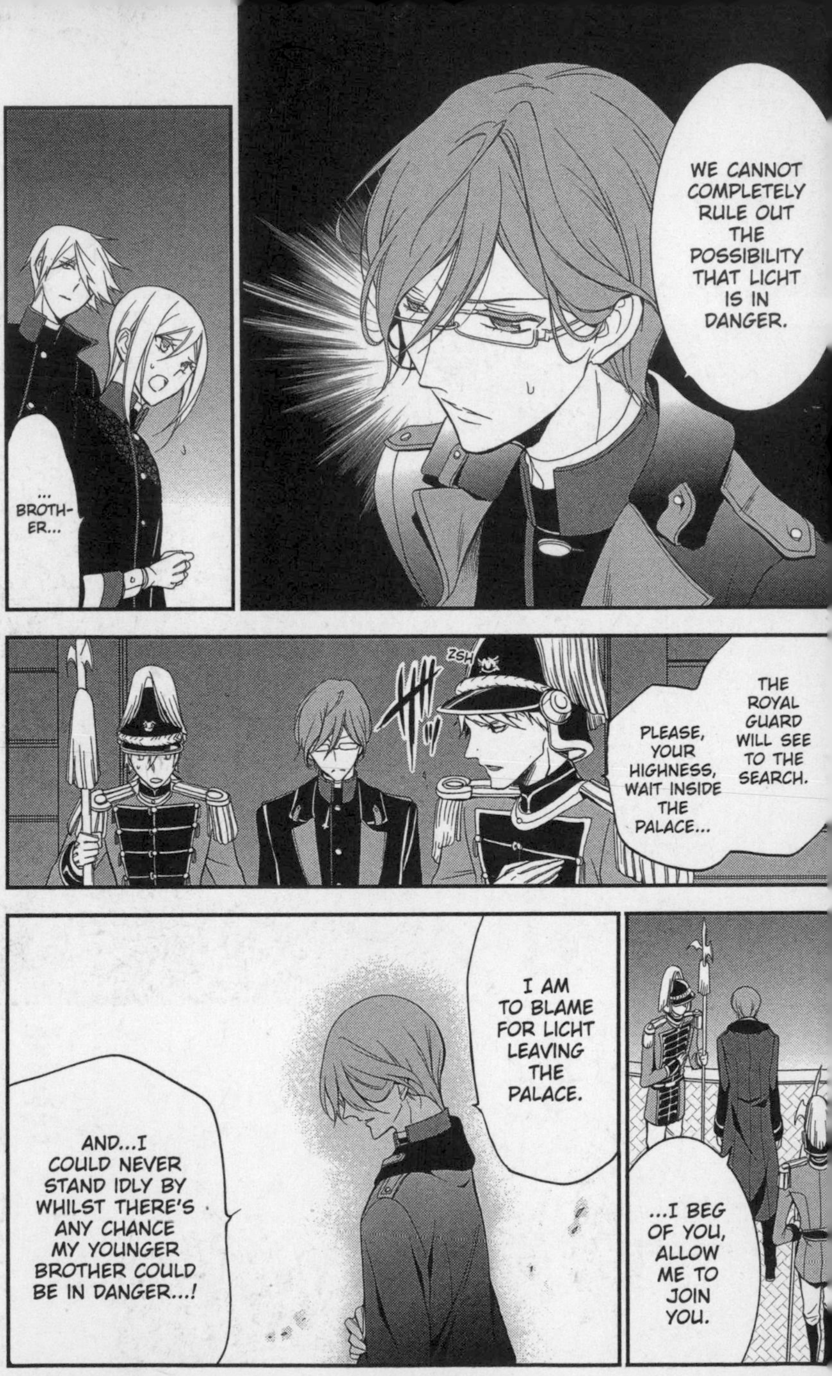
WE CANNOT COMPLETELY RULE OUT THE POSSIBILITY THAT LICHT IS IN DANGER.
...BROTHER...
THE ROYAL GUARD WILL SEE TO THE SEARCH.
PLEASE, YOUR HIGHNESS, WAIT INSIDE THE PALACE...
ZSH
...I BEG OF YOU, ALLOW ME TO JOIN YOU.
I AM TO BLAME FOR LICHT LEAVING THE PALACE.
AND...I COULD NEVER STAND IDLY BY WHILST THERE'S ANY CHANCE MY YOUNGER BROTHER COULD BE IN DANGER...!

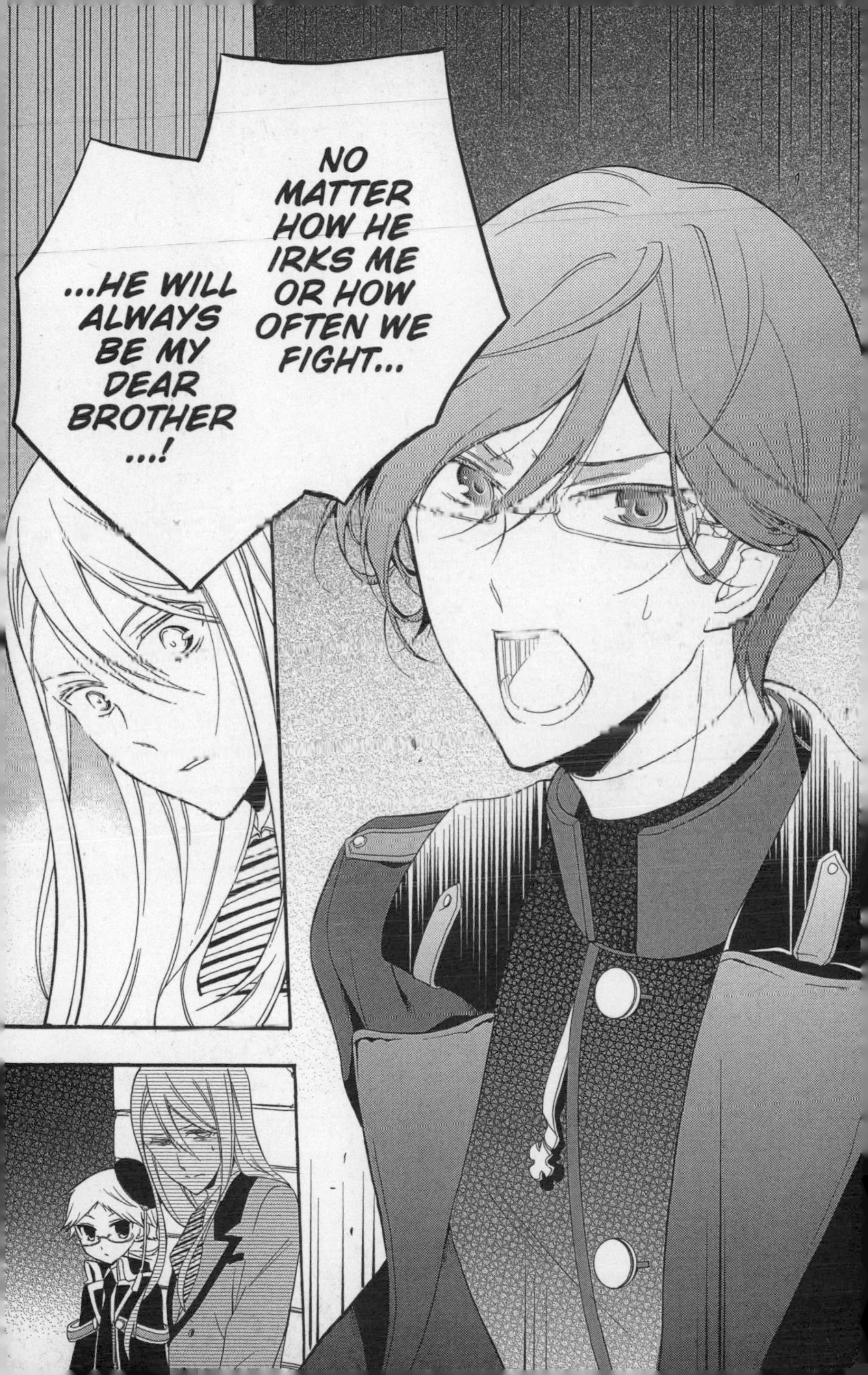
NO MATTER HOW HE IRKS ME OR HOW OFTEN WE FIGHT...
...HE WILL ALWAYS BE MY DEAR BROTHER ...!

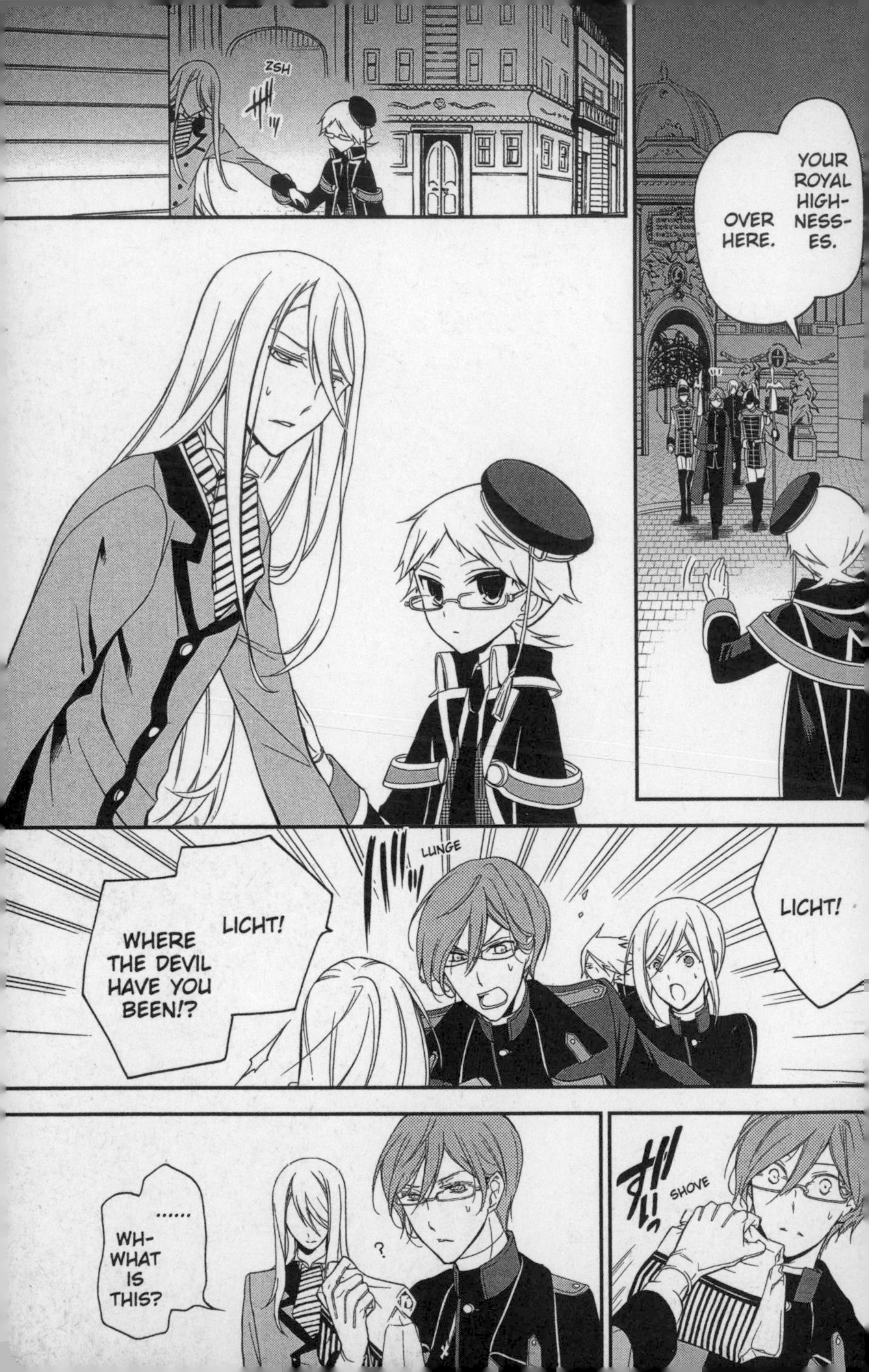
YOUR ROYAL HIGHNESSES.
OVER HERE.
ZSH
LICHT!
LUNGE
LICHT!
WHERE THE DEVIL HAVE YOU BEEN!?
SHOVE
......
WH-WHAT IS THIS?

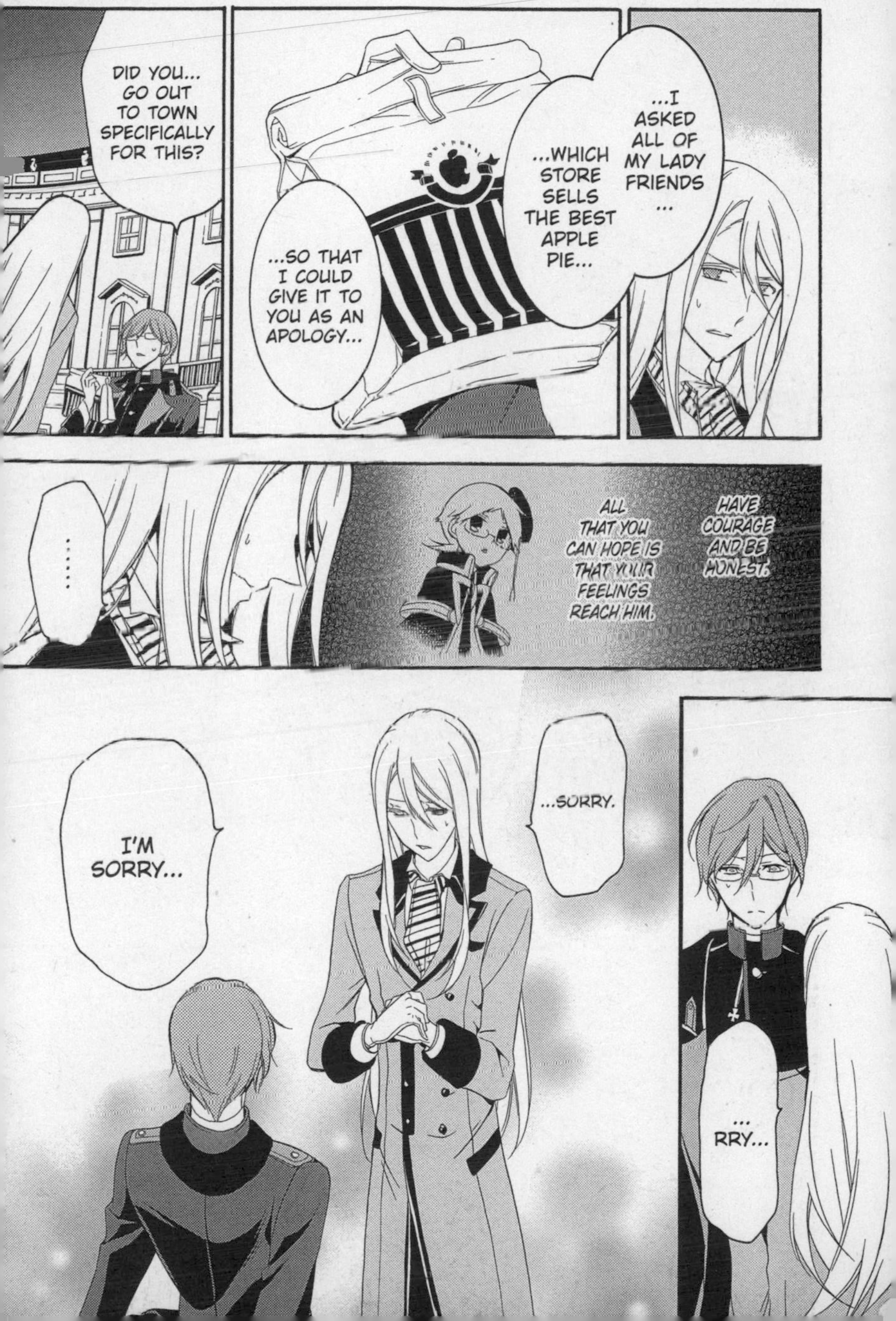
...I ASKED ALL OF MY LADY FRIENDS...
...WHICH STORE SELLS THE BEST APPLE PIE...
...SO THAT I COULD GIVE IT TO YOU AS AN APOLOGY...
DID YOU... GO OUT TO TOWN SPECIFICALLY FOR THIS?
HAVE COURAGE AND BE HONEST.
ALL THAT YOU CAN HOPE IS THAT YOUR FEELINGS REACH HIM.
......
...RRY...
...SORRY.
I'M SORRY...

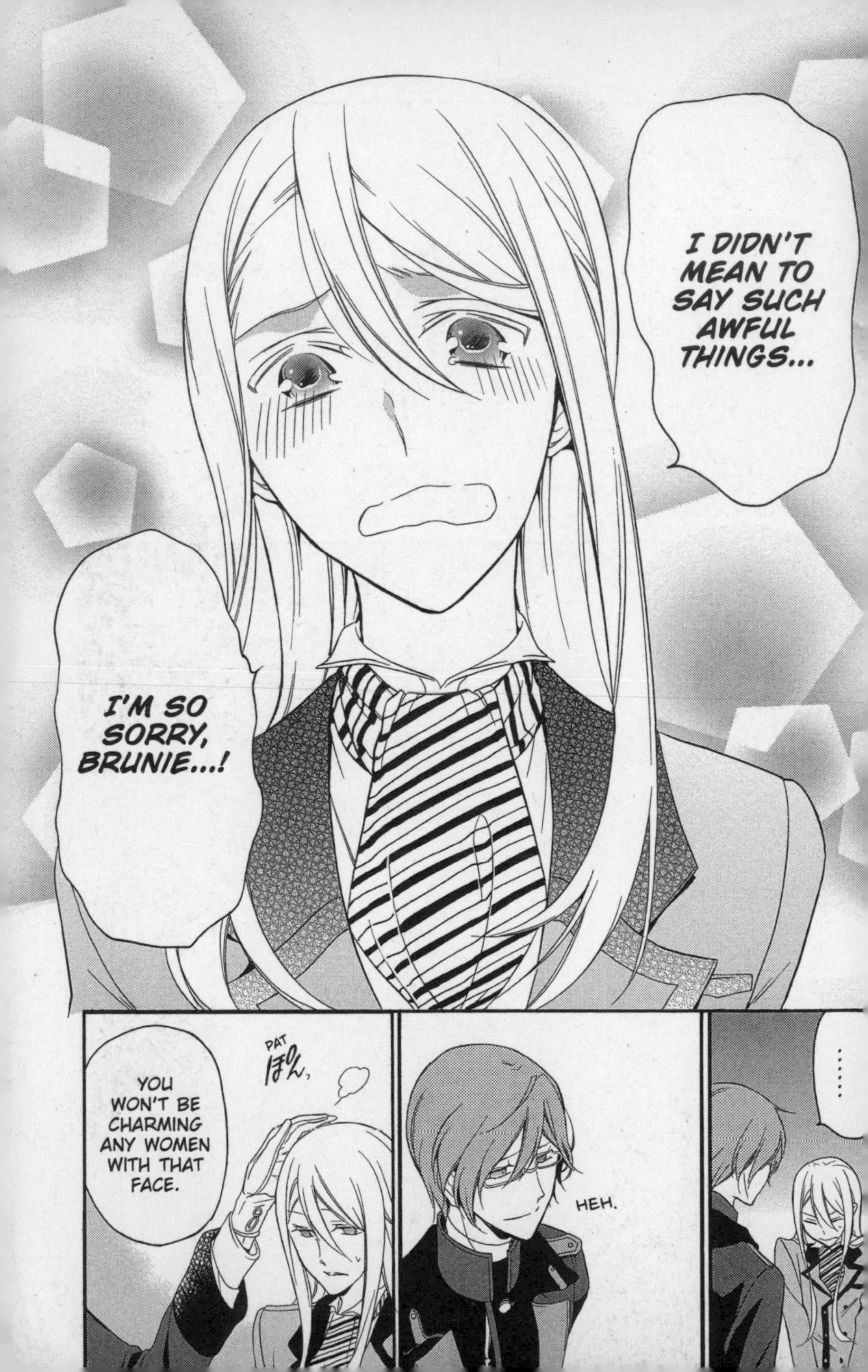
I DIDN'T MEAN TO SAY SUCH AWFUL THINGS...
I'M SO SORRY, BRUNIE...!
......
HEH.
PAT
ぽん
YOU WON'T BE CHARMING ANY WOMEN WITH THAT FACE.

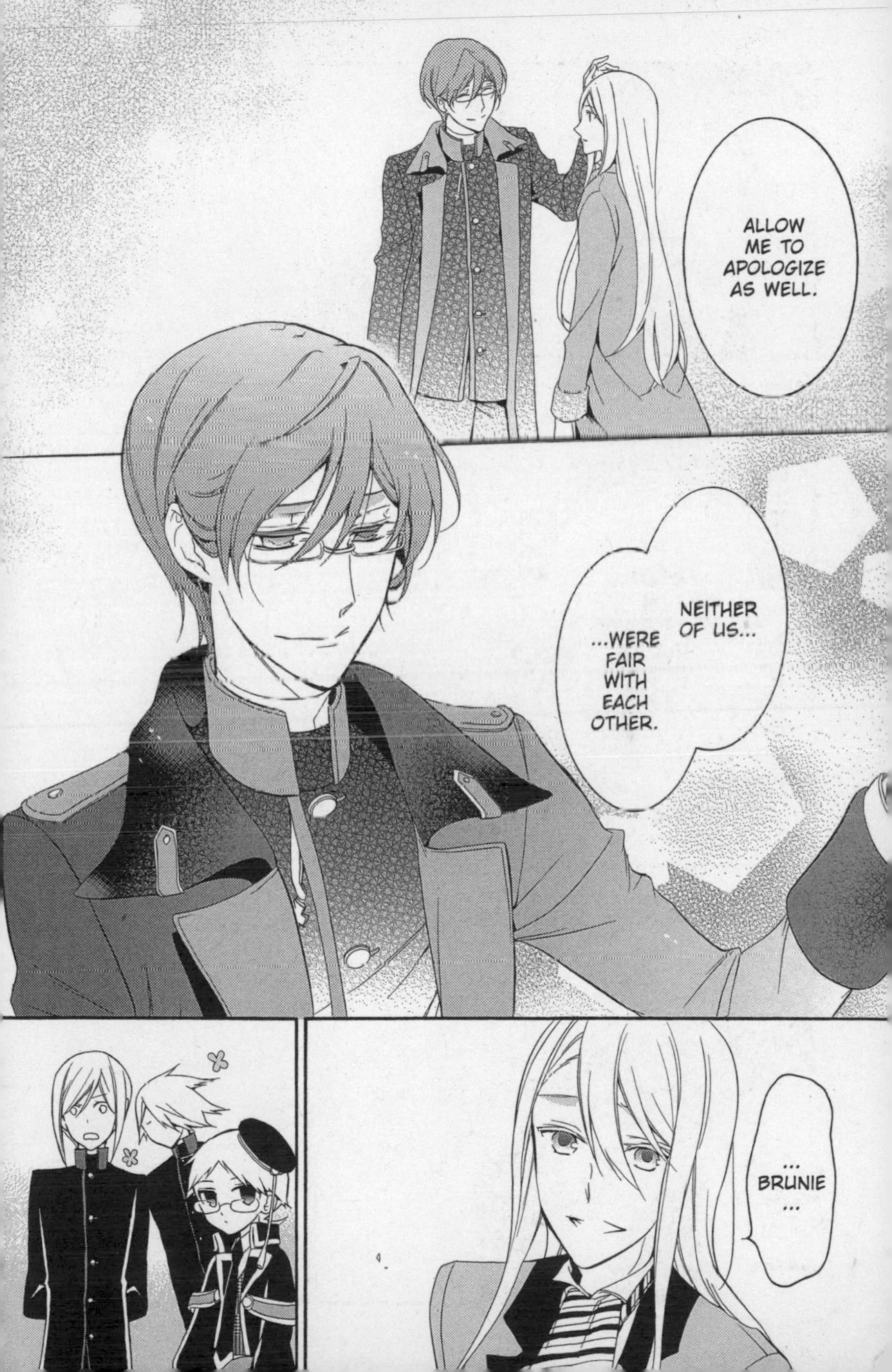
ALLOW ME TO APOLOGIZE AS WELL.
NEITHER OF US...
...WERE FAIR WITH EACH OTHER.
... BRUNIE ...

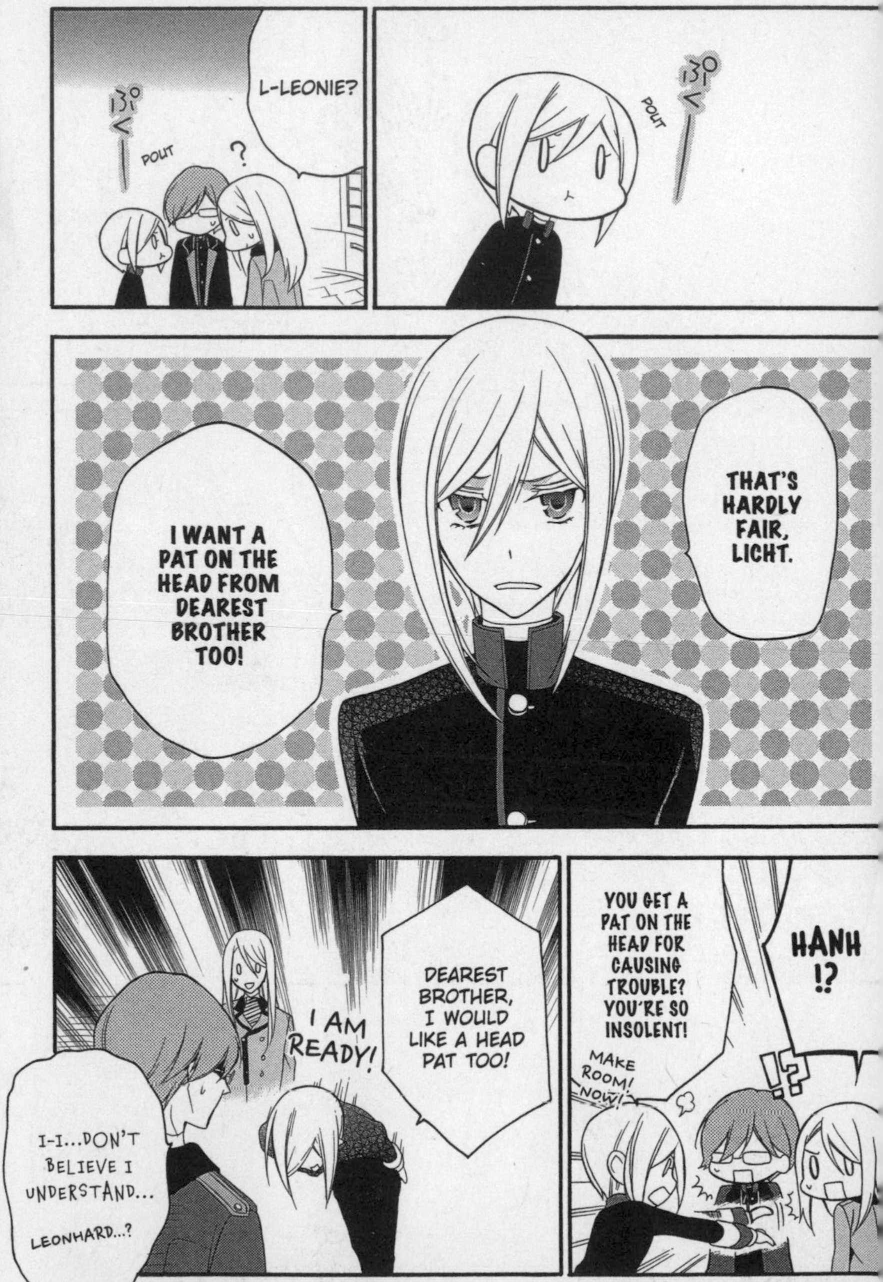
ぷくー
POUT
L-LEONIE?
?
ぷくー
POUT
THAT'S HARDLY FAIR, LICHT.
I WANT A PAT ON THE HEAD FROM DEAREST BROTHER TOO!
HANH!?
YOU GET A PAT ON THE HEAD FOR CAUSING TROUBLE? YOU'RE SO INSOLENT!
!?
MAKE ROOM! NOW!
DEAREST BROTHER, I WOULD LIKE A HEAD PAT TOO!
I AM READY!
I-I...DON'T BELIEVE I UNDERSTAND...
LEONHARD...?

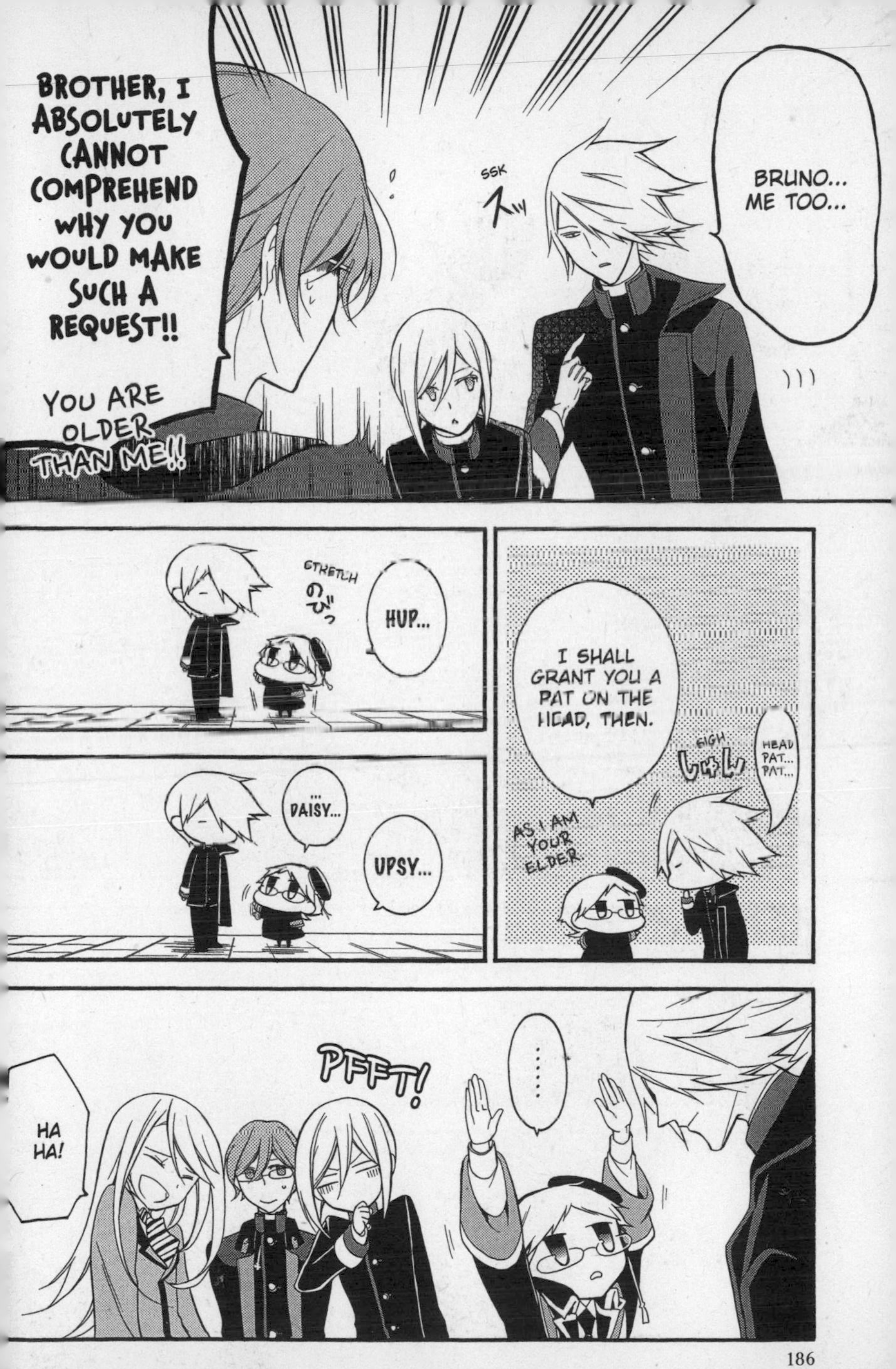
BRUNO... ME TOO...
SSK
BROTHER, I ABSOLUTELY CANNOT COMPREHEND WHY YOU WOULD MAKE SUCH A REQUEST!!
YOU ARE OLDER THAN ME!!
I SHALL GRANT YOU A PAT ON THE HEAD, THEN.
AS I AM YOUR ELDER
SIGH
HEAD PAT... PAT...
STRETCH
HUP...
...DAISY...
UPSY...
......
PFFT!
HA HA!

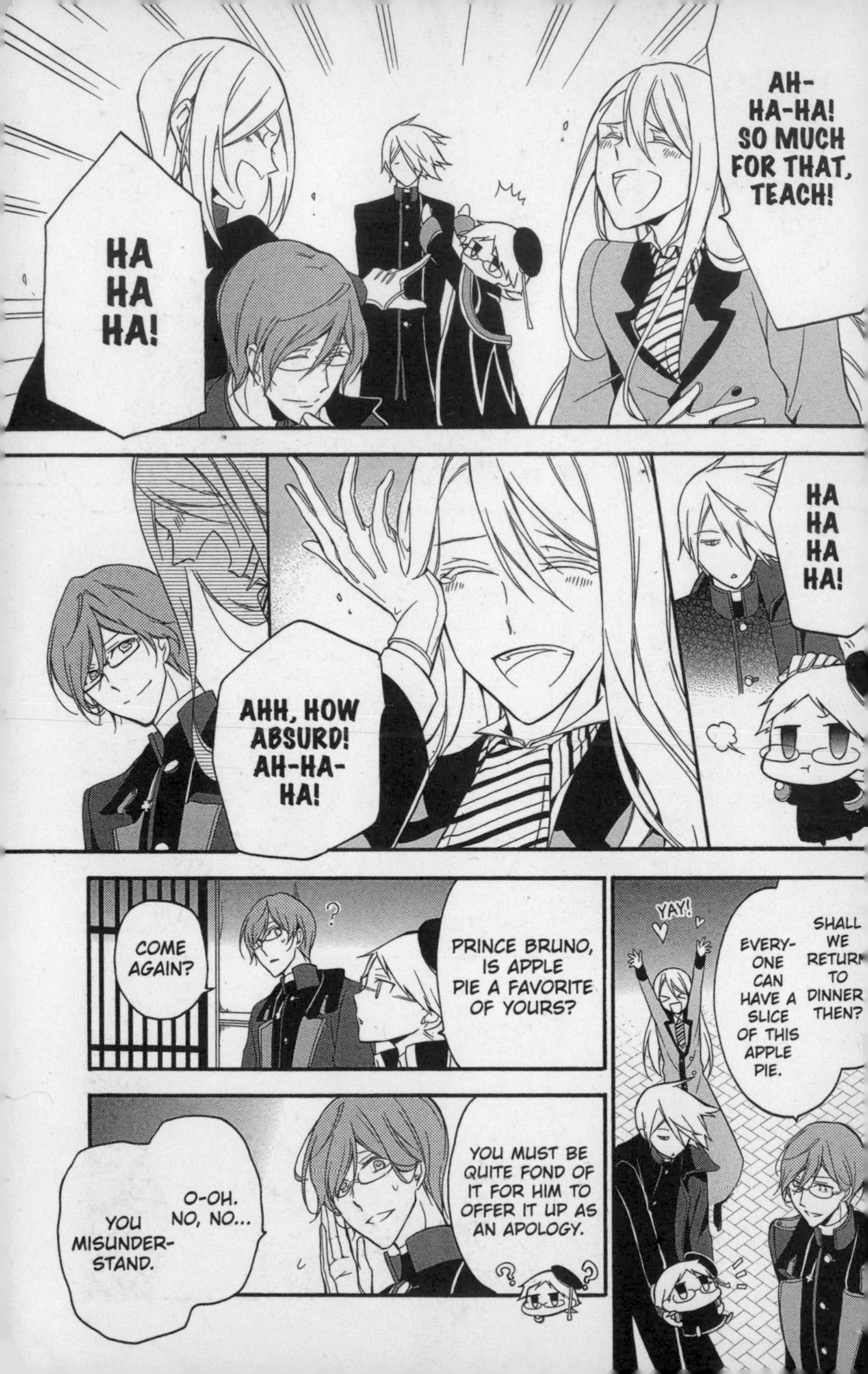
AH-HA-HA! SO MUCH FOR THAT, TEACH!
HA HA HA!
HA HA HA HA!
AHH, HOW ABSURD! AH-HA-HA!
SHALL WE RETURN TO DINNER THEN?
EVERYONE CAN HAVE A SLICE OF THIS APPLE PIE.
YAY!
PRINCE BRUNO, IS APPLE PIE A FAVORITE OF YOURS?
COME AGAIN?
YOU MUST BE QUITE FOND OF IT FOR HIM TO OFFER IT UP AS AN APOLOGY.
O-OH. NO, NO...
YOU MISUNDERSTAND.

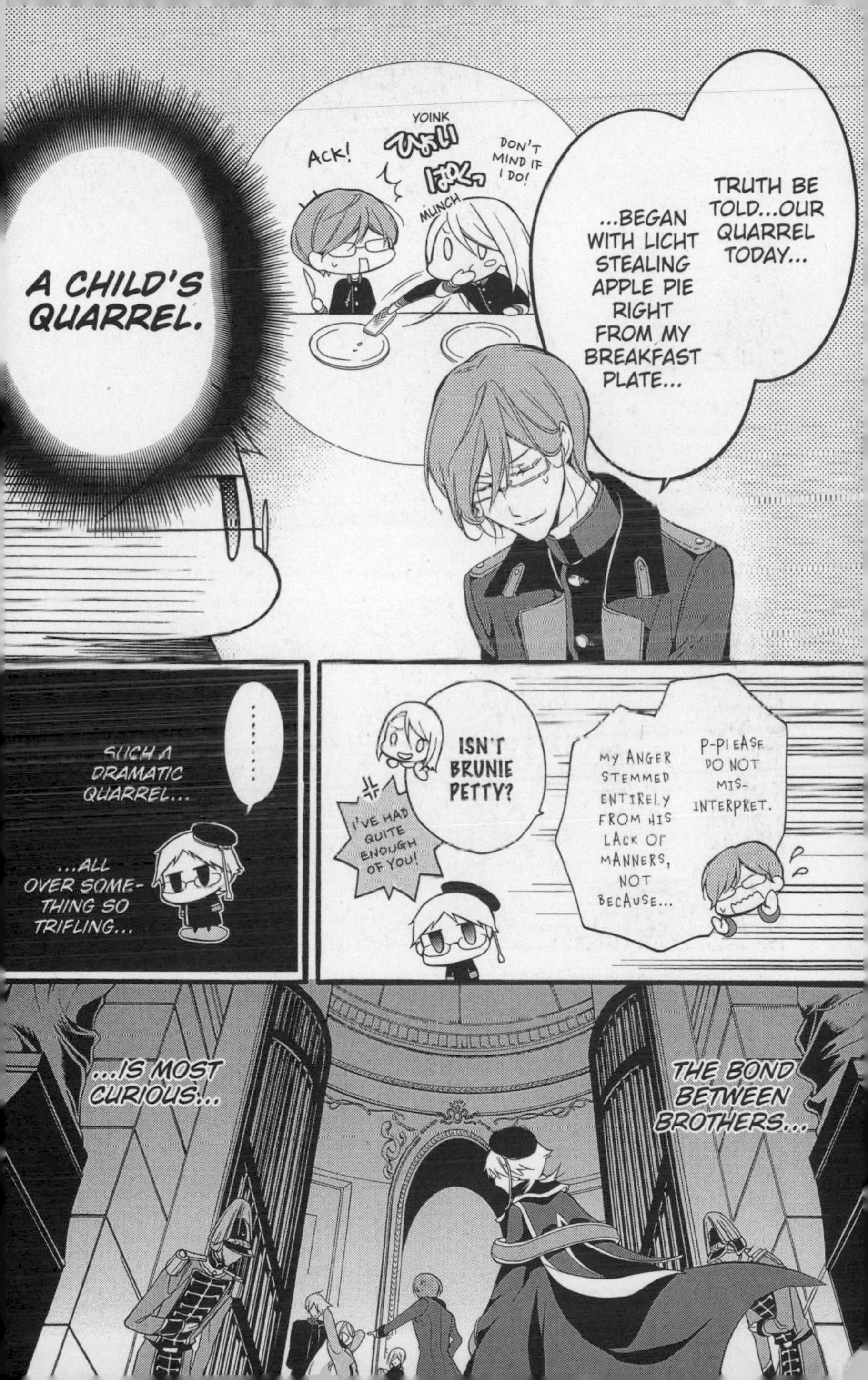
TRUTH BE TOLD...OUR QUARREL TODAY...
...BEGAN WITH LICHT STEALING APPLE PIE RIGHT FROM MY BREAKFAST PLATE...
DON'T MIND IF I DO!
ひょい
YOINK
ぱくっ
MUNCH
ACK!
A CHILD'S QUARREL.
P-PLEASE DO NOT MIS- INTERPRET.
MY ANGER STEMMED ENTIRELY FROM HIS LACK OF MANNERS, NOT BECAUSE...
ISN'T BRUNIE PETTY?
I'VE HAD QUITE ENOUGH OF YOU!
......
SUCH A DRAMATIC QUARREL...
...ALL OVER SOME- THING SO TRIFLING...
THE BOND BETWEEN BROTHERS...
...IS MOST CURIOUS...

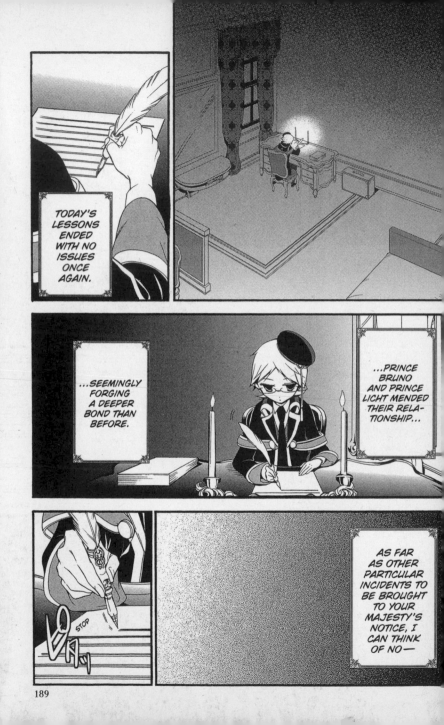

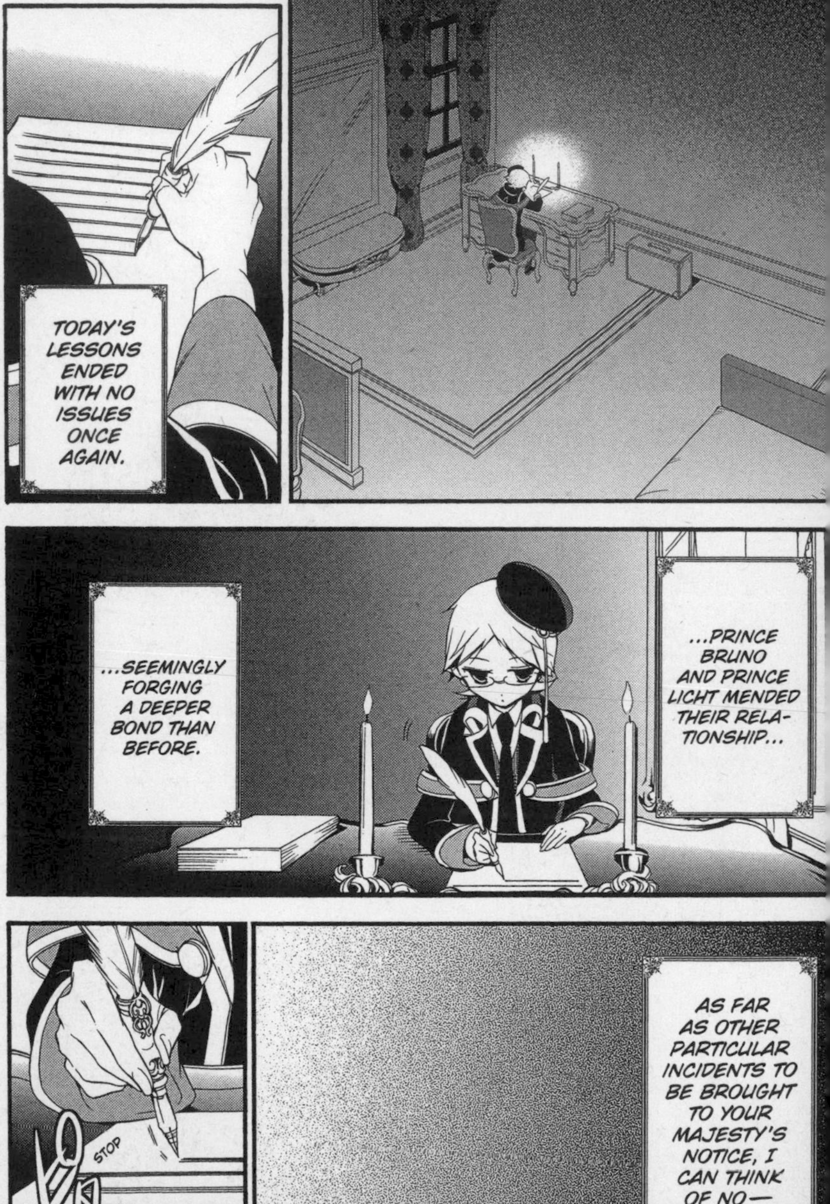
TODAY'S LESSONS ENDED WITH NO ISSUES ONCE AGAIN.
...PRINCE BRUNO AND PRINCE LICHT MENDED THEIR RELA-TIONSHIP...
...SEEMINGLY FORGING A DEEPER BOND THAN BEFORE.
AS FAR AS OTHER PARTICULAR INCIDENTS TO BE BROUGHT TO YOUR MAJESTY'S NOTICE, I CAN THINK OF NO—
STOP

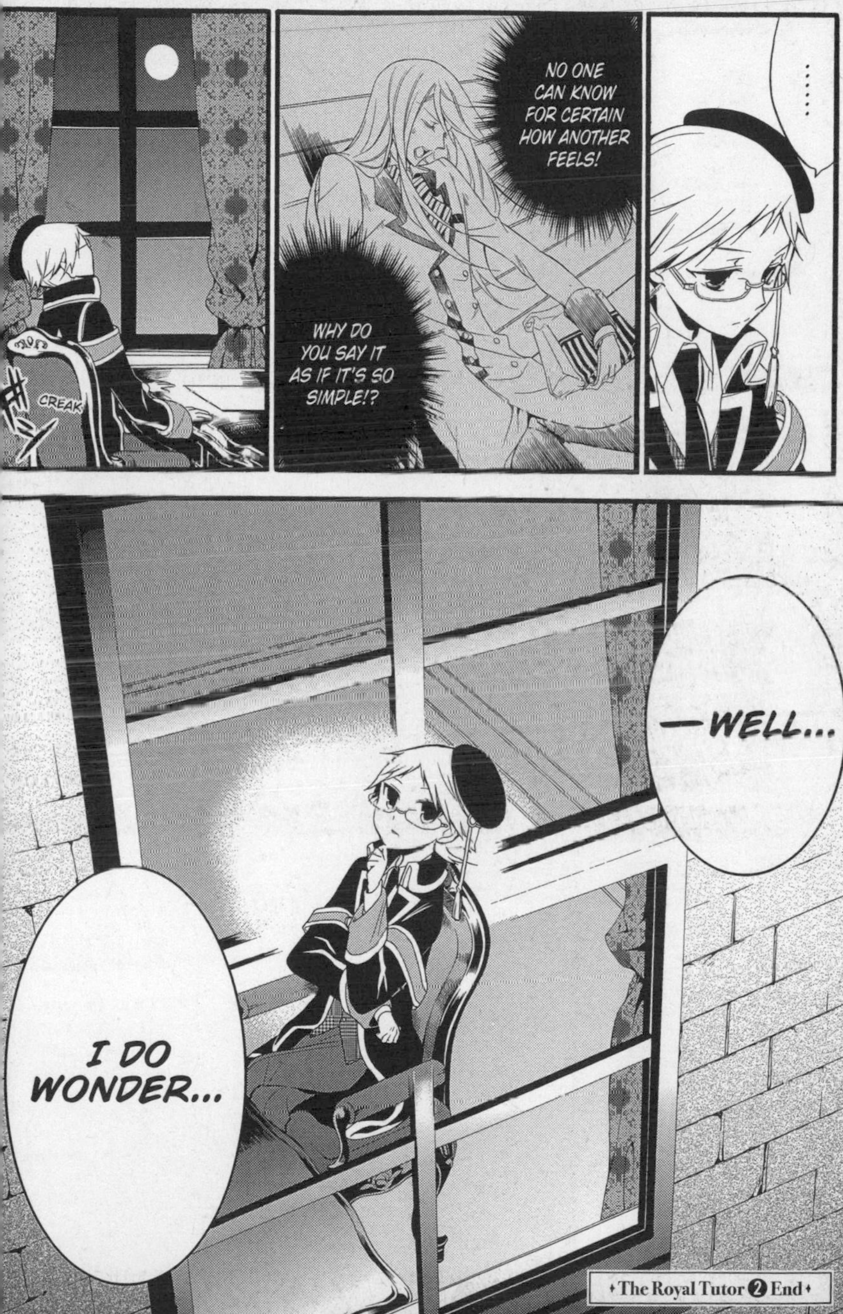
......
NO ONE CAN KNOW FOR CERTAIN HOW ANOTHER FEELS!
WHY DO YOU SAY IT AS IF IT'S SO SIMPLE!?
CREAK
—WELL...
I DO WONDER...
The Royal Tutor 2 End

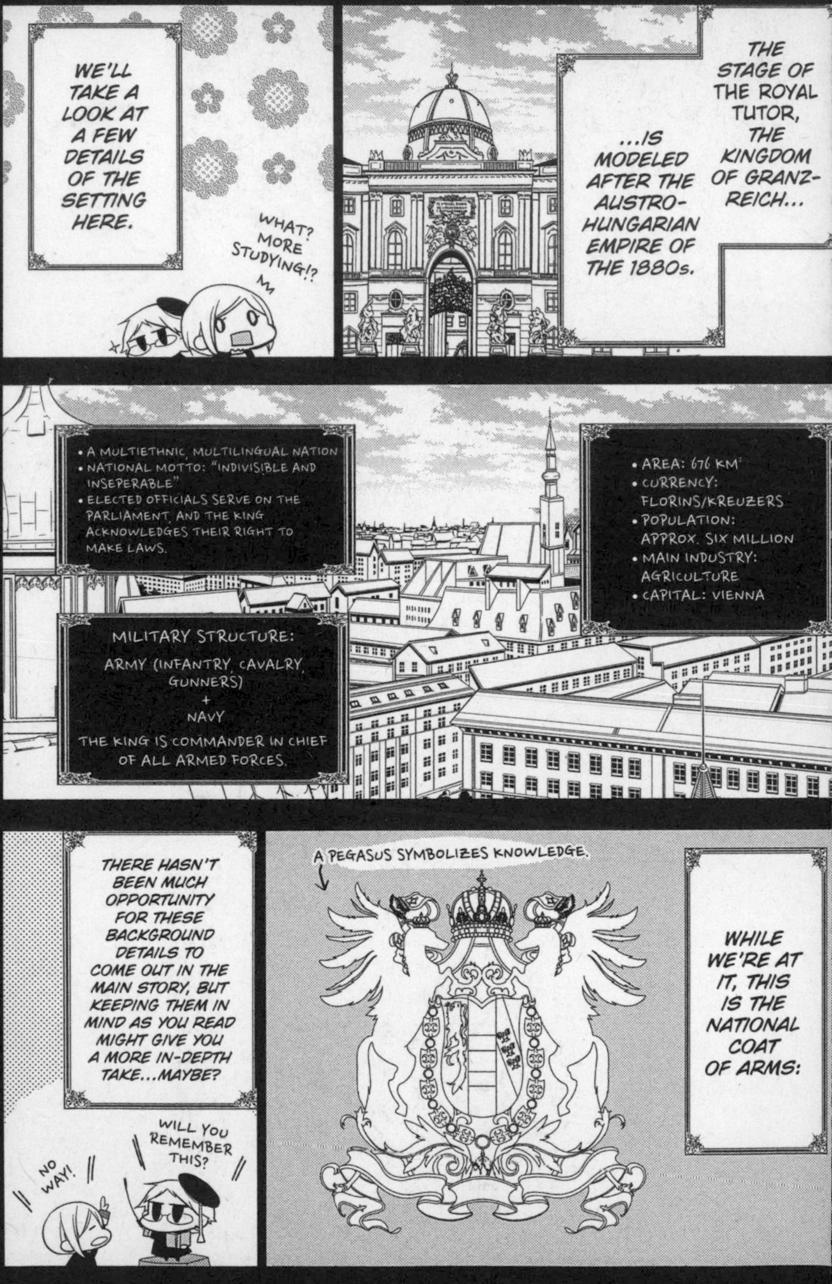
THE STAGE OF THE ROYAL TUTOR, THE KINGDOM OF GRANZ-REICH...
...IS MODELED AFTER THE AUSTRO-HUNGARIAN EMPIRE OF THE 1880s.
WE'LL TAKE A LOOK AT A FEW DETAILS OF THE SETTING HERE.
WHAT? MORE STUDYING!?
• AREA: 676 KM^2
• CURRENCY: FLORINS/KREUZERS
• POPULATION: APPROX. SIX MILLION
• MAIN INDUSTRY: AGRICULTURE
• CAPITAL: VIENNA
• A MULTIETHNIC, MULTILINGUAL NATION
• NATIONAL MOTTO: "INDIVISIBLE AND INSEPERABLE"
• ELECTED OFFICIALS SERVE ON THE PARLIAMENT, AND THE KING ACKNOWLEDGES THEIR RIGHT TO MAKE LAWS.
MILITARY STRUCTURE:
ARMY (INFANTRY, CAVALRY, GUNNERS)
+
NAVY
THE KING IS COMMANDER IN CHIEF OF ALL ARMED FORCES.
WHILE WE'RE AT IT, THIS IS THE NATIONAL COAT OF ARMS:
A PEGASUS SYMBOLIZES KNOWLEDGE.
THERE HASN'T BEEN MUCH OPPORTUNITY FOR THESE BACKGROUND DETAILS TO COME OUT IN THE MAIN STORY, BUT KEEPING THEM IN MIND AS YOU READ MIGHT GIVE YOU A MORE IN-DEPTH TAKE...MAYBE?
WILL YOU REMEMBER THIS?
NO WAY!

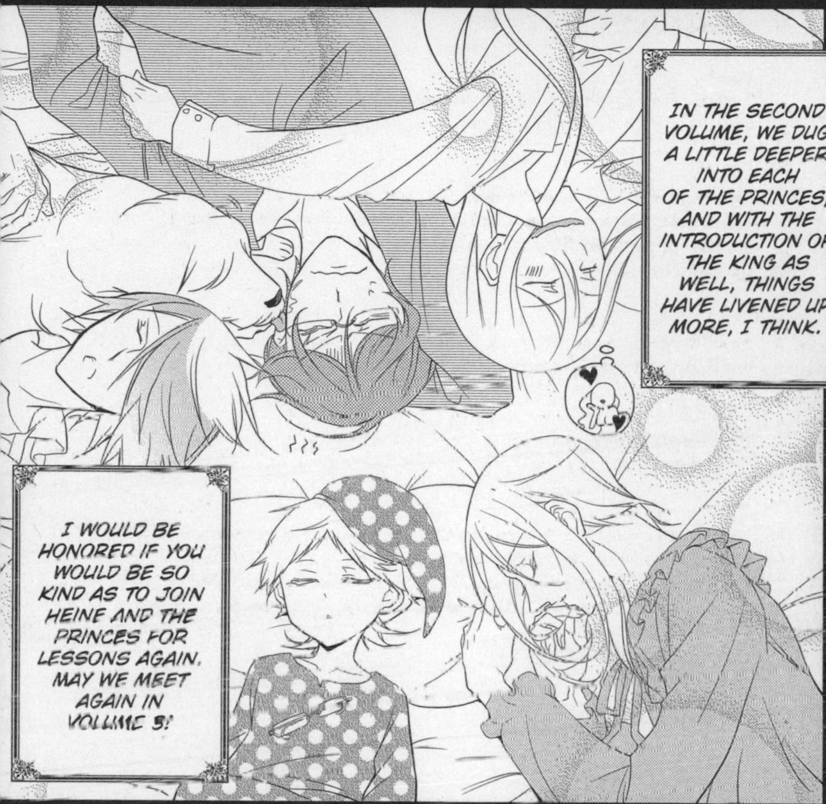
IN THE SECOND VOLUME, WE DUG A LITTLE DEEPER INTO EACH OF THE PRINCES, AND WITH THE INTRODUCTION OF THE KING AS WELL, THINGS HAVE LIVENED UP MORE, I THINK.
I WOULD BE HONORED IF YOU WOULD BE SO KIND AS TO JOIN HEINE AND THE PRINCES FOR LESSONS AGAIN. MAY WE MEET AGAIN IN VOLUME 3!

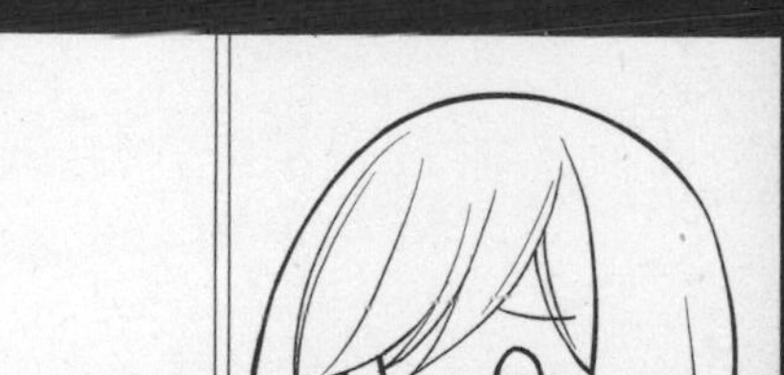

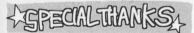

★SPECIAL THANKS★

TO THOSE WHO ARE CONSTANTLY HELPING ME:

YOSHI KOUJU-SAN SHOU YUDUKI-SAN

MY EDITOR, AKIYAMA-SAN

AND FOR MAKING TIME IN HER BUSY SCHEDULE TO CONTRIBUTE TO THE WRAPAROUND ON THIS VOLUME:

JUN MOCHIZUKI-SENSEI

THANK YOU VERY MUCH.

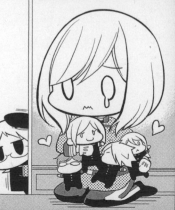

Translation Notes

Page 16

Ringstrasse: The Ringstrasse is a real road in Vienna, and Heine's explanation is accurate to the Ringstrasse in our world too.

Page 19

Currency: Kreuzer coins were used in Austria and the southern German states. In 1857, Austria-Hungary decimalized their money system so that one hundred kreuzer were equivalent to one florin. The name "florin" comes from Florence, the Italian city where the florin coins were first minted.

Page 27

Käsekrainer: A variety of Slovenian pork sausage with chunks of cheese stuffed inside. The "*Käse*" portion of the name means "cheese" in German.

Page 121

Niedergranzreich: *Nieder* means "low" in German, so Niedergranzreich refers to Lower Granzreich.

Page 192

The Japanese editions of manga often come with disposable paper wraparounds (*obi*) printed with ad copy, announcements, sales figures, etc. Jun Mochizuki, the artist of *PandoraHearts*, contributed to the *obi* for the Japanese release of *The Royal Tutor*, Volume 2. Also, Shou Yuduki is another manga artist working for Square Enix.

The Royal Tutor ❷

Higasa Akai

Translation: Amanda Haley • Lettering: Erin Hickman

THE ROYAL TUTOR Vol. 2 ©2014 Higasa Akai/SQUARE ENIX CO., LTD. First published in Japan in 2014 by SQUARE ENIX CO., LTD. English translation rights arranged with SQUARE ENIX CO., LTD. and Yen Press, LLC through Tuttle-Mori Agency, Inc., Tokyo.

English translation ©2015 by SQUARE ENIX CO., LTD.

Yen Press
1290 Avenue of the Americas
New York, NY 10104

Visit us at yenpress.com
facebook.com/yenpress
twitter.com/yenpress
yenpress.tumblr.com
instagram.com/yenpress

First Yen Press Print Edition: July 2017
Originally published as an eBook in August 2015 by Yen Press.

Yen Press is an imprint of Yen Press, LLC.
The Yen Press name and logo are trademarks of Yen Press, LLC.

Library of Congress Control Number: 2017938422

ISBN: 978-0-316-56284-3 (paperback)

10 9 8 7 6 5 4 3 2 1

BVG

Printed in the United States of America